Cambridge studies in medieval life and thought

Edited by WALTER ULLMANN, LITT.D., F.B.A.
*Professor of Medieval Ecclesiastical History
in the University of Cambridge*

Third series vol. 1

THE KING'S HALL WITHIN THE UNIVERSITY OF CAMBRIDGE IN THE LATER MIDDLE AGES

Letters Patent of Edward III, dated 7 October 1337, for the foundation of the royal College of the King's Hall, Cambridge. Great seal of Edward III. [*K.H. Cabinet*, no.8.]

THE KING'S HALL
WITHIN THE UNIVERSITY OF
CAMBRIDGE IN
THE LATER MIDDLE AGES

ALAN B. COBBAN

Lecturer in Medieval History
University of Liverpool

CAMBRIDGE
AT THE UNIVERSITY PRESS
1969

Published by the Syndics of the Cambridge University Press
Bentley House, 200 Euston Road, London N.W.1
American Branch: 32 East 57th Street, New York, N.Y.10022

Library of Congress Catalogue Card Number: 69–10193
Standard Book Number: 521 04678 5

Printed in Great Britain
at the University Printing House, Cambridge
(Brooke Crutchley, University Printer)

TO
THE MASTER AND FELLOWS
OF
TRINITY COLLEGE, CAMBRIDGE

72849

CONTENTS

Contents

GENERAL EDITOR'S PREFACE

This volume opens a new—the third—series of the *Cambridge studies in medieval life and thought*. Inaugurated by the late Dr G. G. Coulton, the *Studies* were, after a lapse of some years, resuscitated in the post-war period by Dom David Knowles, sometime Professor of Medieval History, and lately Regius Professor of Modern History, in the University of Cambridge. No change of plan, conception or scope is envisaged for the Third Series, except that both the Cambridge University Press and the editor have agreed on some minor but desirable typographical modifications. As hitherto, the contributions will be mainly from Cambridge authors, though works from other scholars will be welcomed.

The appearance of the first volume of the Third Series makes it incumbent upon the new editor to put on record the indebtedness which medieval scholarship owes to the outgoing editor for the energetic promotion of specifically Cambridge studies through the vehicle of the series. Perhaps nothing reveals his catholicity better and more convincingly than the wide range of subjects treated in the individual monographs. The initiative of Coulton and the dynamic policy of Knowles have firmly secured the international reputation of the *Studies*.

To follow these two editors imposes no small responsibility upon their successor. But I view it as auspicious that the first volume of the Third Series is intimately concerned with the early history of the university itself and with one of its medieval constituent parts which has just passed the 650th year of its original foundation. It is perhaps no more than a mere coincidence that both author and editor belong to the *familia* of the descendant of this medieval college. The skilful exploitation by Dr Cobban of the sources—still preserved in their pristine and virgin state—allows us a most welcome and unexpected insight not only into the relation between the college and the university, but above all into the highly interesting social stratification with its economic accompaniments which characterised this college. The growth of the university in the vital decades of the fourteenth century is here depicted against the academic, political, governmental and royal background of the period, so that through this integrative process we gain a new historical perspective of this ancient university. May this volume successfully inaugurate the Third Series of the *Studies*.

WALTER ULLMANN

AUTHOR'S PREFACE

This book is based largely on the hitherto virtually neglected accounts of the King's Hall, which was one of the constituent colleges amalgamated with Michaelhouse in 1546 to form Henry VIII's new royal foundation, Trinity College, Cambridge. These accounts constitute the longest single series of paper collegiate records in England and have been studied in conjunction with the sizable corpus of extant exchequer material relating to the King's Hall, Cambridge.

The fortuitous survival of no fewer than twenty-six volumes of these King's Hall accounts, spanning the entire life of the college, has encouraged me to attempt what I think has not been done before. For I believe that a substantial body of collegiate domestic documents has never been broken down, sifted and analysed in any comprehensive fashion. One of the objects of this volume is to provide such an analysis. Furthermore, my research has necessitated my ranging over the whole field of English collegiate history of the pre-Reformation era and has prompted a new assessment of the status of Cambridge University in the middle ages: it has also brought me to a realisation of the important contribution which the King's Hall had to make to its development. And it is perhaps a timely circumstance that the appearance of this book should so closely coincide with the six-hundred-and-fiftieth anniversary of the establishment of the King's Scholars in Cambridge.

Every historian appreciates that, owing to the intrinsic difficulties of reading and interpretation, data derived from a set of medieval accounts will not be accurate in all respects and that at the interpretative level some allowance has to be made for a margin of error. Fortunately, for so long and full a series of accounts as those of the King's Hall this will be minimal, especially where numerical data have been reduced to the form of averages. These averages form the basis upon which rest many of my conclusions about internal economic aspects of college life detailed in chapter 4. I wish to take the opportunity here to acknowledge the technical assistance of my science colleagues of the Cavendish Laboratory in reproducing fair copies of my handwritten figures.

Because of length considerations, it is regretted that it was not possible to include an edition of a typical annual account. As a compromise measure, I have supplied several photographs in the appendix illustrative of different sections of the King's Hall records.

There remains for me to express my deep gratitude to the Master and Fellows of Trinity College for electing me into a Prize Fellowship in 1963. This has endowed me with both the leisure and a congenial atmosphere for conducting my researches into medieval Cambridge. In addition, I have to thank the officials of the Public Record Office for their assistance in my searches through the exchequer sources and the Cambridge Microfilms Committee of the Faculty of History for a most generous grant towards the cost of having the bulk of this material microfilmed. My thanks are also due to the Governors of the John Rylands Library for permission to reprint from the *Bulletin* of the Library, volume XLVII (1964), material included in chapter 1. I should like to express my profound appreciation to Dr A. B. Emden for placing at my disposal, a year before publication, a proof copy of *A biographical register of the University of Cambridge to 1500* (Cambridge, 1963). The full extent of my debt to Dr Emden will become evident in the course of the book. Above all, my warmest thanks are due to my former research supervisor, Professor Walter Ullmann, for his unfailing encouragement, stimulus and wise counsel: I am indeed most grateful for his guidance over the years.

ALAN B. COBBAN

Trinity College, Cambridge
September 1966

NOTE TO PREFACE

I had also intended to include in the appendices items concerning the following points:

(*a*) List of long-tenured King's Hall fellowships. (For analysis of material see below, pp. 57–8.)

(*b*) Evidence for survey of probable geographical origins of King's Scholars. (See below, pp. 157–61.)

(*c*) List of Cambridge civil law graduates (late thirteenth to mid-fifteenth century). (See below, p. 256.)

(*d*) List of all known King's Hall commoners and semi-commoners. (See below, pp. 273–9.)

(*e*) List of King's Scholars who took the M.A. and/or degrees in the superior faculties between 1317 and 1450. (See below, pp. 54–5.)

(*f*) List of children and clerks of the chapel royal admitted to the King's Hall between 1382 and 1417. (See below, p. 56.)

(*g*) Evidence for numerical analysis of committees of King's Hall seneschals. (See below, pp. 177 ff.)

(*h*) Lists of King's Hall ex-fellow pensioners. (See below, pp. 262 ff.)

But as these are rather lengthy and may be of interest to only a handful of scholars I have, in order to save both space and cost, decided not to include them in the appendices. Instead, I have deposited these lists, with full details of names, dates, degrees and other appropriate matter, in Trinity College Library, Cambridge, where they may be freely consulted.

ABBREVIATIONS

B.A.	Bachelor of Arts
B.C.L.	Bachelor of Civil Law
B.Cn.L.	Bachelor of Canon Law
B.I.H.R.	*Bulletin of the Institute of Historical Research*
B.J.R.L.	*Bulletin of the John Rylands Library*
B.R.U.C.	A. B. Emden, *A biographical register of the University of Cambridge to 1500* (Cambridge, 1963)
B.R.U.O.	A. B. Emden, *A biographical register of the University of Oxford to A.D. 1500* (3 vols., Oxford, 1957–9)
B.Th.	Bachelor of Theology or Divinity
Cal. Close R.	*Calendar of Close Rolls*
Cal. Pat. R.	*Calendar of Patent Rolls*
Camb. Docs.	*Documents relating to the University and colleges of Cambridge* (3 vols., ed. by the Queen's Commissioners, London, 1852)
C.A.S.	*Cambridge Antiquarian Society*
D.C.L.	Doctor of Civil Law
D.Cn.L.	Doctor of Canon Law
D.Mus.	Doctor of Music
D.N.B.	*The Dictionary of National Biography*
D.Th.	Doctor of Theology or Divinity
Econ.Hist.Rev.	*Economic History Review*
E.H.R.	*English Historical Review*
Inc.A.	Inceptor of Arts
J.T.S.	*Journal of Theological Studies*
K.H. Accts.	*King's Hall Accounts*
K.H. Cabinet	*King's Hall Cabinet*
Lic.C.L.	Licentiate of Civil Law
Lic.Cn.L.	Licentiate of Canon Law
M.A.	Master of Arts
M.Th.	Master of Theology or Divinity
O.E.D.	*The Oxford English Dictionary*
Oxf. Hist. Soc.	Oxford Historical Society

Abbreviations

P.R.O.	Public Record Office
Sch.C.L.	Scholar of Civil Law
Sch.Cn.L.	Scholar of Canon Law
Statutes	Statutes of the Colleges of Oxford (3 vols., ed. by the Queen's Commissioners, Oxford and London, 1853)
T.R.H.S.	Transactions of the Royal Historical Society
V.C.H.	Victoria County History

All other abbreviations are considered self-explanatory.

INTRODUCTION

The King's Hall, Cambridge, has been one of the most neglected of English academic institutions. The older and still much quoted histories of Cambridge University, especially those by T. Fuller[1] and G. Dyer,[2] give it but scant and wholly inadequate attention; and even the more recent and scholarly works of Dean Rashdall,[3] C. H. Cooper[4] and J. B. Mullinger[5] have dismissed this royal Society in a peremptory fashion that is altogether disproportionate to the vital contribution made by the King's Hall to the evolution of the medieval University of Cambridge itself and to its important formative influence in shaping the course of English collegiate development in the pre-Reformation era. Moreover, academic historians have not drawn sufficient attention to what is indisputably the most striking feature of this Cambridge foundation: namely, that in origin, the Society of the King's Scholars was nothing less than an extension or arm of the chapel royal set in the University of Cambridge and that throughout the greater part of its history it remained a kind of physical adjunct or supplement to the royal household and to the court, with one of its chief aims apparently the provision of a reservoir of educated personnel from which the king could draw to meet his particular requirements. It is this, combined with the telling fact that eleven successive English kings from Edward II to Henry VIII considered it worth while to maintain this Cambridge foundation out of exchequer revenues for over two centuries, which not only colours the entire history of the college but also singles it out as

[1] See the references by T. Fuller, *The history of the University of Cambridge* (ed. M. Prickett and T. Wright, London and Cambridge, 1840), pp. 87–90, 134.

[2] G. Dyer, *The history of the university and colleges of Cambridge* (2 vols., London, 1814), II, 284–5, 287. Dyer does not even devote a separate section to the King's Hall: his few brief references are incorporated in the chapter on Trinity College.

[3] See the short notice on the King's Hall in H. Rashdall, *The universities of Europe in the middle ages* (3 vols., ed. F. M. Powicke and A. B. Emden, Oxford, 1936), III, 299–300.

[4] See the more lengthy outline by C. H. Cooper, *Memorials of Cambridge* (3 vols., Cambridge, 1861–6), II (1861), 193–212.

[5] See the discussion by J. B. Mullinger, *The University of Cambridge* (3 vols., Cambridge, 1873–1911), I (1873), 252–4, 258 n. 1, 288.

an institution *sui generis* among English academic societies of the middle ages. The relation of the two English universities to medieval household government is a subject which has been but little explored. Consequently, a study of the King's Hall is particularly valuable as we are here investigating a society which formed the first institutional link between the central government and the English universities. And so, if a proper historical perspective is to be attained, the King's Hall must not only be evaluated within the sphere of academic history but must also be considered in relation to royal household government of which it properly forms a part.

It is common knowledge that only a small corpus of medieval material relating to Cambridge University has survived by comparison with the very copious records which exist for medieval Oxford. Even so, until very recently,[1] Cambridge historians have not evinced a due interest in the history of their own university. As a result, much of the writing of Cambridge history has been left either to amateurs or else to Oxford scholars, such as Dean Rashdall, who have tended to allow their conclusions to be coloured, not so much, as is often alleged, by the veil of prejudice, but by an insufficient appraisal of the available evidence; the upshot of this being, for the period before 1400 at any rate, that Cambridge University has been generally accredited with a very low European reputation,[2] which would now appear to be historically undeserved.

Nowhere has Cambridge suffered more than in its collegiate history. It would be at least partially true to say that the main lines of English collegiate history have been blurred by that kind of

---

[1] For examples of the recent progress which has been made in the history of the medieval University of Cambridge see W. Ullmann, 'The University of Cambridge and the Great Schism', *J.T.S.* IX (1958), 53 ff.; also Ullmann, 'The decline of the chancellor's authority in medieval Cambridge: a rediscovered statute', *Historical Journal*, I (1958), 176 ff. For the first complete survey of the archives of the University of Cambridge see H. Peek and C. Hall, *The archives of the University of Cambridge* (Cambridge, 1962). An invaluable new source of information is provided by A. B. Emden, *A biographical register of the University of Cambridge to 1500* (Cambridge, 1963). See also my article, 'Edward II, Pope John XXII and the University of Cambridge', *B.J.R.L.* XLVII (1964), 49 ff., and V. Skånland, 'The earliest statutes of the University of Cambridge', *Symbolae Osloenses*, fasc. XL (1965), 83 ff.

[2] See e.g. Rashdall's disparaging remarks, *op. cit., ed. cit.* III, 284: 'Up to the end of the fourteenth century...Cambridge was a third-rate university...Not a single schoolman can be shown to have taught at Cambridge...' But cf. also A. B. Emden's qualification of Rashdall's harsh judgment, Rashdall, *loc. cit.* n. 2.

parochialism from which amateur productions are prone to suffer. This insular type of study, which fails to take full cognisance of important comparative material, has meant that English collegiate studies have taken on a somewhat patched appearance, forming a mosaic of separate pieces rather than a unified whole. In addition, it must be stressed that the Cambridge colleges have received far less attention from historians than their Oxford counterparts, a comparison which is equally valid for most other aspects of English academic history. Because there has been a tendency to attribute too much here to one particular institution and too little there to another, the result has been that the general picture of English collegiate development has been put out of focus in several important respects: whilst, overshadowing all, there has sometimes been a facile disregard of those impersonal forces of change, both social and economic, which underlay and largely determined the major upheavals and deflections in this field of study.

As far as the King's Hall is concerned, it is no exaggeration to assert that in so many discussions on English academic history this royal foundation has been taken only slightly into account or even overlooked altogether. It would therefore seem that this remarkable Cambridge society has not hitherto received an adequate historical evaluation: it is one of the objects of this book to attempt such an appraisal.

The fragmentary nature of the evidence available for English collegiate life in the middle ages, as it appeared to late nineteenth-century eyes, was summed up by John Venn, the Cambridge historian. Addressing an audience in Caius College Chapel in 1894, he referred to the existing state of knowledge on this subject for the period before 1500: 'Further back than that we cannot go with much confidence. In the existent state of our records, and of most other sources of personal information, the outlines then begin to crumble away. In place of the words and deeds of living men, we are left in possession of nothing beyond a few names and dates.'[1] This judgment was not based on an exhaustive survey of all the available sources. Since Venn wrote, a wealth of collegiate material has been made accessible. The Oxford Historical Society has published excellent editions of college records and the corresponding Cambridge

---

[1] J. Venn, *Early collegiate life* (Cambridge, 1913), p. 18.

Antiquarian Society has performed invaluable service in rescuing from oblivion much material relating to the university and its colleges and hostels. College muniment rooms have now been extensively searched and their contents systematically sifted. The result of these labours has been the appearance of several well-documented college histories,[1] which have had the effect of raising the subject from the antiquarian to a professional level. And yet the plentiful material that has been found in muniment rooms and university archives has not altogether nullified the force of Venn's conclusions. For, more often than not, the greater part of the contents of muniment rooms yields information about only one aspect of collegiate development. Royal or episcopal foundation charters, letters patent and close, papal bulls, title deeds, notarial instruments and the like have proved indispensable for filling out the external history of an institution. With material of this nature, the historian may particularise the stages in the acquisition and extension of the site, may trace the dealings of the college with neighbouring landowners, with institutions and, if he is especially fortunate, with the university authorities. Only incidentally, however, does this type of material contribute to a knowledge and understanding of the inner workings of a collegiate society. In these circumstances, authors of college histories have, of necessity, drawn heavily upon the early codes of statutes for the medieval centuries. For some of the later foundations, such as William of Wykeham's New College, Oxford, and King's College, Cambridge, where the statutes are sufficiently lengthy and detailed, a considerable body of information may be gleaned.[2] But in the majority of cases the yield is poor, providing only the barest of outlines of institutional organisation, and even this may not be entirely reliable. Early college statutes are notoriously misleading; in large measure, they remained statements of a founder's ideal rather than a blueprint for the present. This was so because lack of adequate endowments in the early years caused a marked divergence to develop between the statutory provisions and the actual everyday arrange-

---

[1] See e.g. A. H. Lloyd, *The early history of Christ's College* (Cambridge, 1934); also J. R. Magrath, *The Queen's College* (2 vols., Oxford, 1921).

[2] See the excellent use made of the long detailed statutes of King's College, Cambridge, by J. Saltmarsh, 'King's College', *V.C.H.* (Cambridge) (London 1959), III, 382–5; also the utilisation of the New College statutes by A. H. M. Jones, 'New College', *V.C.H.* (Oxford) (London, 1954), III, 154–8.

ments worked out in these small, financially embarrassed communities. As their wealth increased, these societies were better able to bring their organisation into closer conformity with the founder's original aims: but this was often a late medieval or even a post-Reformation development.

The question, then, may be posed: is there an adequate corpus of documents which will enable us to build up a picture of collegiate organisation and life in the centuries before the Reformation? Until fairly recently, the medieval account was one of the less popular historical sources. In the past, historians have tended to fight shy of the difficulties inherent in medieval accountancy and business terminology. Not so today. Accounts are in vogue: their value for social and economic history is obvious. Whether the accounts are those of medieval Italian merchant families,[1] of the households of English kings,[2] queens[3] and members of the nobility,[4] or of a humble English chantry,[5] they provide a valuable insight into the business habits and daily life of different classes of the medieval community.

As in the case of university records, a larger quantity of collegiate material has survived for Oxford than for Cambridge. These college records have been described in some detail by A. B. Emden in the introductions to his *Biographical Registers* of both universities[6] and therefore need not be here further itemised. Two general observations, however, must be made. Apart from the lengthy and valuable series of documents which survive for such colleges as Merton, Oriel,

---

[1] See e.g. R. de Roover, 'The development of accounting prior to Luca Pacioli according to the account-books of medieval merchants', and F. Edler, 'Partnership accounts in twelfth-century Genoa', *Studies in the history of accounting* (ed. A. C. Littleton and B. S. Yamey, London, 1956), pp. 114 ff. and pp. 86 ff.

[2] See e.g. A. R. Myers, *The household of Edward IV* (Manchester, 1959).

[3] See e.g. the account-book of Joan of Navarre (widow of Henry IV) at Leeds Castle, Kent, 1420–1, summarised with passages *in extenso* by A. R. Myers, 'The captivity of a royal witch', *B.J.R.L.* XXIV (1940), 263 ff.

[4] See e.g. M. S. Giuseppi, 'The wardrobe and household accounts of Bogo de Clare, 1284–6', *Archaeologia*, LXX (1920), 1 ff.; also E. M. Myatt-Price, 'Cromwell household accounts, 1417–1476', *Studies in the history of accounting, ed. cit.* pp. 99 ff.; see further J. Gage, 'Extracts from the household book of Edward Stafford, Duke of Buckingham', *Archaeologia*, XXV (1884), 311 ff.

[5] For example, the account-book of Munden's chantry, Bridport. See K. L. Wood-Legh (ed.), *A small household of the fifteenth century* (Manchester, 1956).

[6] A. B. Emden, *A biographical register of the University of Oxford to A.D. 1500* (3 vols., Oxford, 1957–9), I, xxi–xxix, and *B.R.U.C.* pp. xv–xxi.

Queen's, New College and the Benedictine institution, Canterbury College, Oxford, and for Peterhouse, Corpus Christi and King's College, Cambridge, many of the sets of early medieval college records are so fragmentary that it is difficult to extract much information of historical worth. Secondly, many sets of collegiate documents deal mainly with estate management and, self-evidently, it is not to be expected that these would provide data concerning the internal organisation, administration and economy of the academic societies to which they belong.

The especial value of the magnificent set of twenty-six volumes of the King's Hall accounts, preserved in the Muniment Room of Trinity College, Cambridge, lies in the fact that they are free from both of these limiting features, forming as they do the longest single series of paper collegiate records in England. In the introduction to his Cambridge Register, Dr Emden describes the King's Hall accounts in these terms: 'So long a sequence of domestic records written in book form on paper has no parallel in any other college in Oxford or Cambridge.'[1] As the King's Hall derived its revenues primarily from the exchequer and from a number of churches appropriated to the college, it did not have to rely for its income upon successful estate management. Consequently, in the accounts, external affairs are reduced to a minimum: like those of the contemporary institution, Canterbury College, Oxford, the King's Hall records are in the main concerned with details of internal affairs.[2]

In a recent assessment of the latest state of research on the English universities J. P. C. Roach has stressed that what is now required is an investigation into the economic structures of collegiate societies.[3] This emphasis is right since, for the medieval period at any rate, such a study has not before been attempted on any scale. But what is equally required is not only an examination of internal collegiate economy but also a full inquiry into the constitutional, administrative and business organisation of a medieval college.[4] In view of

---

[1] A. B. Emden, *B.R.U.C.* p. xvi.

[2] W. A. Pantin, ed., *Canterbury College Oxford* (3 vols., Oxf. Hist. Soc., new series, 1946–50).

[3] See the remarks of J. P. C. Roach, 'The Victoria County History of Cambridge', *C.A.S. Proceedings*, LIV (1961), 112 ff. at p. 124.

[4] See the remarks of W. A. Pantin, 'College muniments: a preliminary note', *Oxoniensia*, I (1936), 140 ff. at p. 140: 'A college therefore deserves at least some of

what has already been said concerning the copious and continuous nature of the King's Hall accounts, it will be clear that these records can form the basis of such an enterprise. And this constitutes the second object of this book.

The King's Hall accounts have previously been consulted by a number of historians for particular purposes. A very brief report on these records, with a series of single-line extracts from the first volume, was compiled by H. T. Riley for the first report of 1870 of the royal commission on historical MSS. (under Trinity College, p. 82). In the late nineteenth century, R. Willis and J. W. Clark extracted material relating to the buildings and to the site for the architectural survey they were preparing on the university and colleges of Cambridge:[1] and J. E. T. Rogers incorporated into his great pioneer work on English agriculture and prices a few random price quotations taken from the wealth of price data available in the King's Hall records.[2] At the beginning of the twentieth century, A. E. Stamp published a list of the names of the King's Scholars, with their dates of admission and vacation, in the first volume of *Admissions to Trinity College, Cambridge*.[3] For this list, he relied mainly on the broken series of accounts submitted annually at the exchequer by the wardens of the King's Hall and which are now preserved in the Public Record Office, using the college accounts only to check or to supplement the information obtained from the exchequer sources.[4] (In 1443-4 the external audit required annually at the exchequer came to an end and from that time the Society entered upon a new phase of greater sovereignty and independent development.) In 1917 the Cambridge mathematician, W. W. Rouse Ball, produced for private circulation a brief study entitled: *The King's Scholars and*

that exhaustive and sympathetic study which we have learnt to give to a medieval monastery or a Roman villa. In the past, college histories have generally tended to deal rather disjointedly with certain aspects, such as the biographies of college worthies, or architectural description.'

[1] For the section on the King's Hall see R. Willis and J. W. Clark, *The architectural history of the University of Cambridge and of the colleges of Cambridge and Eton* (4 vols., Cambridge, 1886), II, especially 430 ff.

[2] See the appropriate sections in J. E. T. Rogers, *A history of agriculture and prices in England* (7 vols., Oxford, 1866-1902).

[3] A. E. Stamp, *Admissions to Trinity College, Cambridge* (ed. W. W. Rouse Ball and J. A. Venn, London, 1916), I, 79-140.

[4] *Ibid.* I, 82.

King's Hall: Notes on the History of King's Hall published on the six-hundredth anniversary of the writ of Edward II establishing the King's Scholars in the University of Cambridge. Here, however, it must be stressed that Rouse Ball was but slightly acquainted with the contents of the King's Hall volumes and relied primarily on the available printed sources and, for his references to the Society's accounts, on incidental information received from A. E. Stamp which he had noted while engaged in the preparation of his list of King's Scholars.[1] The King's Hall records were also consulted by L. F. Salzman, who has drawn attention to one or two interesting entries in his study of building in England before 1540.[2] And, most recently, A. B. Emden examined these volumes in order to check Stamp's list of Scholars when collecting material for his Cambridge Register. It is therefore apparent that while the King's Hall accounts have been explored by several historians for their specific requirements, they have quite clearly never been adequately investigated or hitherto made the subject of any kind of comprehensive inquiry.

This book does not set out to present a 'straight' chronological history of the King's Hall, Cambridge. The approach is thematic throughout and because of the overwhelming bulk of the source material some measure of selection has been inevitable, a point which has a special relevance for chapter 4 and for the three sections of chapter 6.

[1] Rouse Ball, *The King's Scholars and King's Hall* (privately printed, Cambridge, 1917), p. 1: 'For information about these records—and in particular about the King's Hall Books—the writer of this sketch is greatly indebted to friends who have freely put at his disposal their knowledge of the subject.' The 'friends' refers to A. E. Stamp and to W. H. B. Bird, who drew up a catalogue of the medieval muniments (see chapter 4, p. 113, n. 1).

[2] See the references to the King's Hall by L. F. Salzman, *Building in England down to 1540* (Oxford, 1952). His footnotes concerning the King's Hall records are very inaccurate.

Chapter 1

ORIGINS

ACADEMIC AND ROYAL SIGNIFICANCE

On 7 July 1317 Edward II issued a writ[1] to the sheriff of Cambridgeshire ordering him to pay from the revenues of his bailiwick sums
necessary for the maintenance of John de Baggeshote, clerk, and
twelve children of the chapel royal whom the king had sent to be
educated in the schools at Cambridge.[2] As far as is known, this writ

[1] Printed in *Camb. Docs.* I, 66–7. The writ was sealed at Buckby, Northamptonshire,
where the king was then in residence. See C. H. Hartshorne, *The itinerary of King
Edward the Second* (presentation copy in Cambridge University Library, privately
printed, 1861), p. 19. Part of this chapter is reproduced in my article, 'Edward II,
Pope John XXII and the University of Cambridge', *B.J.R.L.* XLVII (1964), 49 ff.

[2] Both A. E. Stamp and W. W. Rouse Ball assumed that when this writ was issued
the Society had not yet come into existence. They considered it to be a preparatory
step taken by the king before sending his chapel children to Cambridge: consequently, the arrival of Baggeshote and ten of the children in Cambridge on 9 July
1317, journeying from the court at Buckby, was interpreted by each of these
writers as the first settlement of the King's Scholars in the university. See Stamp,
Admissions to Trinity College, Cambridge, ed. cit. I, 82–3, and Rouse Ball, *The King's
Scholars and King's Hall, cit.* pp. 2–3. This assumption is open to dispute on two
accounts. First, it disregards the tense of the verb 'envoyer' used in the writ: the
medieval French form 'nous eioms envoiez' almost certainly proves that the
establishment of the Society was anterior to the writ ('Come nous eioms envoiez
noz chers clercs Johan de Baggeshote et douze autres einfaunz de notre chapelle a
luniversite de Cantebr' a demorer ỹ en estodỹ a noz coustages pour profiter...').
Secondly, in the writ of 7 July the number of Scholars is given as twelve: only ten
accompanied Baggeshote to Cambridge two days later. The following explanation
is suggested. The first complement of Scholars, consisting of twelve chapel children
and their warden, John de Baggeshote, was settled in Cambridge at some date prior
to the issue of the writ. At a later date, the Society paid a brief visit to the court, then
at Buckby, and shortly afterwards returned to Cambridge. (For an example of such
a visit see Rouse Ball, *op. cit.* pp. 6–8, where interesting details are given of a
Christmas expedition to the court at York in 1319; part of this material is reproduced by F. M. Stenton, 'The road system of medieval England', *Econ. Hist. Rev.*
VII (1936), 1 ff. at p. 20, and by J. W. F. Hill, *Medieval Lincoln* (Cambridge, 1948),
p. 306.) If two of the original Scholars remained behind, this would account for the
discrepancy between the ten who arrived in Cambridge on 9 July and the 'twelve'
mentioned in the writ. (After the Christmas visit to York, three of the Scholars were
left behind in the city: Rouse Ball, *op. cit.* p. 8.) If this interpretation is correct, one

remains the earliest extant evidence for the existence of the Society of the King's Scholars. Unfortunately, the compressed nature of the document does not allow us to say with complete accuracy how long the Society had then been functioning although from the wording of the writ it is certain that it was of recent origin.

The King's Scholars were at first lodged in rented premises as a charge on the exchequer and remained so until Edward III purchased a house for them in 1336 from Robert de Croyland, rector of Oundle,[1] which he assigned to the Society as part of the endowment of the King's Hall, the royal college founded on the basis of the existing Society in October 1337.[2] The rented hostel inhabited by the King's Scholars before the grant of Robert de Croyland's house as their permanent home has not yet been identified but it is possible that it was the same building. Technically speaking, Edward III was the founder of the endowed College of the King's Hall but there is no doubt at all that in the medieval period Edward II alone was regarded by both the university and the Society as the one true founder. Under the provisions of the statute *De exequiis annuatim celebrandis* the regent masters of the university were enjoined to assemble in the church of Great St Mary on 5 May every year to celebrate the exequies of Edward of Carnarvon, designated the founder of the King's Hall:[3] and in the Society's accounts there are annual entries in connection with the purchase of wine and spices for

may assume that this writ exhorting the sheriff of Cambridgeshire to make payment of arrears in their allowances (the sums due to the Scholars necessarily become 'arrears' if the language of the writ is construed in a past sense) was issued to coincide exactly with the return of the Scholars to Cambridge.

[1] Willis and Clark, *Architectural history*, II, 420–1.

[2] See the letters patent of 7 October 1337 conferring upon the Society the manse of Robert de Croyland and the advowson of the church of St Peter, Northampton, *K.H. Cabinet*, no. 8; see also *Cal. Pat. R.*, 1334–1338, p. 541. The full designation of the King's Hall is *Aula scolarium Regis Cantebrigiae*, but the shortened form *Aula Regis* is more commonly found, and occasionally *Aula Regia* and *Aula Regalis* are used. According to medieval usage, the English translation is 'the King's Hall' and this is the form adopted consistently throughout this book. See e.g. *K.H. Cabinet*, no. 106: (Thomas St Just) 'maister or keper of the College called the kinges hall in the Universitie of Cantebrigge'; no. 139: (Geoffrey Blythe) 'maister off the kyngshalle in Cambryge'; also nos. 109, 124, 138, 149; see further, *K.H. Accts.* xv. fo. 123 (1478–9): 'Inventarium jocalium Collegii vulgariter nuncupatum le kyngshall...'

[3] See the university statute *De exequiis annuatim celebrandis* in *Camb. Docs.* I, 404 ff. at p. 405.

the fellows[1] on the occasion of the commemoration of the death of their founder, Edward II.[2]

There can be little doubt that Edward II's academic conception marks a new departure in the sphere of English university history. Sufficient evidence has been found to prove that in the twelfth and thirteenth centuries several kings had made a practice of maintaining individual clerks in the schools.[3] In general, the motive behind royal monetary assistance to clerks was no more than a desire to satisfy the requests of relatives or other members of the court circle who had petitioned the king to sponsor an advanced educational training for deserving protégés. There is, however, some evidence to suggest that, in the thirteenth century at any rate, expediency rather than charity or patronage was often an important consideration behind money grants made by the king; and that a large proportion of the awards made in the reign of Henry III were given with a view towards cementing military alliances across the Channel or were used as minor pawns in the diplomatic chessboard.[4] However this may be, it is evident that before the opening of the fourteenth century royal support for clerks at the English universities had at best been both desultory and confined to individuals. It will therefore be readily

[1] Scholar (*scolaris*) was the contemporary term for a member of the Society of the King's Scholars. But after the Society became the endowed College of the King's Hall in 1337, both scholar and fellow (*socius*) are used as wholly interchangeable terms for members of this royal foundation. Hence, King's Scholar and fellow are employed with equal regularity throughout this book. For a special instance of a meaningful distinction between scholar and fellow see below, pp. 184–6.

[2] See e.g. *K.H. Accts.* II, fos. 36, 53; IV, fo. 58; V, fo. 130v; VI, fo. 144; IX, fo. 37; X, fo. 58; XVII, fo. 41v; XIX, fo. 113v; XXI, fo. 80; XXII, fo. 19v; XXIII, fo. 6v; XXIV, fo. 48v; XXV, fo. 10; XXVI, fo. 7v. The exequies are variously designated as those of the founder (*fundatoris*), of the king (*regis*), of Edward II (*Edvardi secundi*) and of Edward of Carnarvon (*Edvardi de Carnarvan*). See also the fifteenth-century antiquary, John Rous, *Historia Regum Angliae* (2nd ed. by T. Hearne, Oxford, 1745), p. 203, where Edward II alone is named as the founder of the King's Hall.

[3] For examples, see H. G. Richardson, 'The schools of Northampton in the twelfth century', *E.H.R.* LXI (1941), 595 ff. at pp. 597, 603; and further F. Pegues, 'Royal support of students in the thirteenth century', *Speculum*, XXXI (1956), 454 ff.

[4] See the conclusions of Pegues, *art. cit.* p. 454: 'The most significant money grants made by Henry III (from whose reign comes the bulk of the evidence on royal support of students in thirteenth-century England) to students were used as minor diplomatic instruments or as accessories in the creation of military alliances.' It is similarly suggested below (pp. 18 ff.) that royal motives of expediency, though now of a purely insular and household character, lay behind the inception of the Society of the King's Scholars in Cambridge at the beginning of the fourteenth century.

appreciated that in this matter of royal financial aid to students the inception of the Society of the King's Scholars in Cambridge constitutes the first establishment of a royal 'colony' of clerks in an English university setting.[1] Why Edward II chose to send his household scholars to the smaller and less celebrated Cambridge *studium* and not to Oxford, which, by all accounts, was then at the peak of its prestige, is a natural and historically important question to raise and will be fully considered at a later stage.[2]

It has been far too easily assumed that Edward II's intentions regarding the institution of the King's Scholars were the same as those of Edward III when he endowed the Society twenty years later. More than one writer has claimed that in founding the college Edward III was merely carrying out the predetermined aims of his father who did not live to achieve this purpose;[3] but there appears to be no evidence in support of such a contention.[4] If this had in fact been so, the direct continuity of purpose would surely have been expressed in the letters patent of 7 October 1337 wherein Edward III's motives concerning the foundation of the college are explained. Here, however, the king's motives are presented as those of Edward III alone[5] and there is no indication in this document that they necessarily coincided with those of Edward II when he established the Society of the King's Scholars in Cambridge *c.* 1317. On the

[1] Until the foundation of King's College, Cambridge, in 1441, the Society of the King's Scholars, which became the endowed College of the King's Hall in 1337, remained the only true royal establishment at either of the English universities. Oriel (1324) and Queen's (1341) cannot be reckoned royal foundations in any technical sense. Oriel, founded by the chancery clerk, Adam de Brome, was later re-established with the king as nominal founder. (See H. Rashdall, *The universities of Europe in the middle ages*, ed. cit. III, 204–5.) Queen's was founded by Robert de Eglesfield, chaplain to Queen Philippa, consort of Edward III, and placed under the patronage of the queens of England (*ibid.* III, 207).

[2] See below, pp. 24 ff.

[3] See C. H. Cooper, *Memorials of Cambridge*, cit. II, 194, and Rouse Ball, *op. cit.* p. 9, who cites Cooper as his reference.

[4] Cooper does not give a reference but it seems clear that his source was Fuller, *History of the University of Cambridge*, pp. 87–8: 'King Edward the Third understanding it was his father's intention to erect a college in Cambridge in order whereunto he had for some years maintained 32 scholars in the University, laid the foundation of King's Hall, out of some remorse that he had consented to the death of so affectionate a father.' Fuller offers no evidence at all for this statement and I am inclined to disregard it as a complete fabrication.

[5] See below, p. 13 and n. 4.

contrary, there is only the briefest of all possible references, almost incidental in character, to Edward II's original scheme.[1]

The extant evidence does not permit us to say that Edward II had planned a collegiate status for the Society from the start. Indeed, for reasons which will be discussed below,[2] there is every likelihood that the Society of the King's Scholars was conceived on an experimental basis and that no final decision as to its future orientation was taken during the lifetime of Edward II. Edward III, however, was faced with the problem of how best to deal with a financially unstable institution inherited from his father's reign. Shortly after he came to the throne the financial deficiencies of the Society were so acute[3] that it would almost certainly have foundered if decisive action had not been taken to save it. Fortunately for Cambridge, Edward III recognised the potential value of the institution. In the preamble to the letters patent of 7 October 1337 the need to step up the output of university graduates is stressed so that a regular supply of young men capable of giving beneficial service in both the ecclesiastical and secular spheres may be ensured.[4] As this appears to have already

---

[1] 'Edwardi nuper Regis Anglorum patris nostri qui pia consideratione triginta duobus scolaribus illuc pro studio vacaturis fecit ad tempus sustentationis necessaria ministrari necnon pro nostri ac Philippe Regine Anglorum consortis nostre... animarum salute...': *K.H. Cabinet*, no. 8; *Cal. Pat. R.*, 1334–1338, p. 541.

[2] See below, pp. 22 ff.

[3] The financial instability of the Society may be gauged from the numerous writs issued by the king between 1317 and 1337 ordering the sheriff of Cambridgeshire to make payment of arrears of sums due to the King's Scholars from the exchequer grant: e.g. in 1335 no fewer than five such writs were necessary. See the many references to the King's Scholars in *Cal. Pat. R.* and *Cal. Close R.*

[4] *K.H. Cabinet*, no. 8 (preamble not given in *Cal. Pat. R.*): '...desiderantes ad multiplicacionem sapientium in Universitate Cantebr'...'; '...ut iuvenes ingenio perspicui fiant per studium eruditi et ad publica consilia magis apti'; [iuvenes] 'qui fidem possint dilitare catholicam et regale solium ac rem publicam consiliis providis roborare'. The contribution which endowed colleges were expected to make to the well-being of religious or civil life or both is emphasised to a greater or lesser degree in the preambles to numerous codes of English and French college statutes. See e.g. the letters of Edward I for Peterhouse, where the king expresses the hope that 'viri fiant pro utilitate rei publice sapientes quorum prudentia regimini regni et sacerdotii provide consulatur...' and that from this institution '...posse rei publice multa commoda pervenire...' (*Camb. Docs.* II, 1); see also the wishes of the founder of Clare, 'cupientes...ad augmentum cultus divini reique publice commodum...' (*ibid.* II, 121); see further the similar sentiments of the founder of the Parisian college of Boncour (1353), whose aim was to educate his scholars 'soient faits sages hommes par lesquels le pays là où ils demeurent, soit

become the primary function of the Society of the King's Scholars, it was to the king's obvious advantage to perpetuate it; accordingly, Edward III decided to stabilise its uncertain position by conferring upon it an endowed collegiate status.

Before taking this step, the king set up a royal commission on 2 April 1332 consisting of Ralph de Nevill, steward of the household, Richard de Bury, Walter de London and John de Langtoft, then warden of the King's Hall, to examine his Cambridge Scholars with a view to purging the Society of those of its members considered to be sufficiently beneficed and those who were deemed not to be making suitable progress in the schools of the university.[1] The findings of the commission are unknown and the extent of the purge cannot be gauged. What is of special interest in the terms of this commission, however, is the enunciation of two pre-conditions of continued membership of the Society which presumably were also to underlie the tenure of fellowships in the future College of the King's Hall. The first of these stated that Scholars who had become adequately beneficed were to be removed:[2] clearly, this was incorporated into the constitution of the later college in the form of the statutory provision enacting that the acquisition of a benefice equal to or above a stipulated value automatically necessitated forfeiture of a fellowship,[3] unless a special royal licence to the contrary had been obtained.[4] This fixed principle governing the retention of fellowships at the King's Hall was shared by the majority of English colleges and there is no reason to suppose that it was not observed. The second pre-condition implies that membership of the Society would cease if a minimum level of academic success could not be

enluminé, conseillé et conforté' (quoted from the Boncour statutes in A. L. Gabriel, *The college system in the fourteenth-century universities* (Baltimore, 1962)). But in the preambles to the statutes of Michaelhouse, Cambridge, and of Oriel, Queen's and Lincoln Colleges, Oxford, the objectives of the founders are framed exclusively in religious terms, it being stressed that these institutions had been erected '...ad honorem Dei et augmentum (augmentationem) cultus divini (cleri)...' (See A. E. Stamp, *Michaelhouse* (privately printed, Cambridge, 1924), p. 41; *Statutes*, 1, ch. (3), 5; ch. (4), 4; ch. (6), 4.)

[1] The letters appointing the commission are printed in Rymer, *Foedera* (ed. A. Clarke, London, 1818), II, pt. ii, 831; *Cal. Pat. R.*, 1330–1334, p. 291.
[2] '...volentes...illos qui sufficienter beneficiati...amoveri...'
[3] See below, pp. 145–6, 146, n. 1.
[4] For examples, see below, p. 143, n. 5.

attained.[1] This might seem to be an eminently sensible and obvious guiding rule for a collegiate institution to adopt but a study of the tenure of King's Hall fellowships will demonstrate that in a significant number of instances the principle was to remain inoperative.[2]

Though the new college of 1337 was in every way a physical continuation of the existing royal Society, Edward III's saving act of endowment effected a decisive alteration in the position of the King's Scholars within the university. Previously, this royal Society had held a somewhat anomalous status within the *studium*: it had been neither a college nor a hostel though it undoubtedly possessed some of the essential attributes of each. As its members lived in unendowed rented premises, it was in this respect similar to the societies of the numerous hostels with which Cambridge was then studded and which accounted for the bulk of the academic population in the early fourteenth century.[3] On the other hand, whereas the inhabitants of the hostels were required to pay for their board and lodging to the graduate principal who had leased the premises, the King's Scholars were supported throughout from exchequer revenues covering the costs of their basic food requirements, clothing and accommodation: clearly then, to this extent, the Society was endowed after the manner of a college before achieving collegiate status in 1337. Thus, hovering so to speak between the position of a hostel and a college, its finances in a parlous state and its future in the balance, the Society must have had a most uncertain and ill-defined standing. But with the endowment there inevitably followed a much needed measure of definition: henceforward, the Society of the King's Scholars, with its household origins and court connections, was firmly embodied in a collegiate form bringing it closely into line with contemporary English colleges and making of it a really integral and permanent part of the setting of the medieval University of Cambridge.[4]

[1] Scholars were to be removed who were found to be '...minus sufficientes ad proficiendum in scolis...'
[2] See below, pp. 56–7, 89–91.
[3] For the medieval hostels of Cambridge see H. P. Stokes, 'The mediaeval hostels of the University of Cambridge', *C.A.S.* (octavo publications), XLIX (1924); also Willis and Clark, *op. cit.* I, xix–xxviii, and J. B. Mullinger, *The University of Cambridge, cit.* I, 217–21.
[4] The special place occupied by the King's Hall within the Cambridge *studium* is discussed in chapter 3.

Though the evidence is not wholly conclusive, there is a strong probability that the 'Soler Halle' mentioned by Chaucer in *The Reeve's Tale* is to be identified with the King's Hall:

> And nameliche ther was a greet collegge
> Men clepen the Soler Halle at Cantebrigge.[1]

Several literary commentators and historians have been too un-critical in their unreserved acceptance of this identification;[2] but if, for the present, there must remain an element of doubt, the circum-stantial evidence does indeed indicate that the King's Hall served as the poet's historical model. Even if Chaucer did not actually visit the college (although he may very well have done), his close court con-nections and career as a royal civil servant[3] make it more than likely that some of the King's Scholars would have been numbered among his acquaintance. Moreover, his description of 'Soler Halle' as a 'greet collegge' would surely preclude the possibility that the institu-tion the poet had in mind was either Garret Hostel or University Hall (later Clare Hall), both of which have been put forward as contenders for the title.[4] The case in support of the former is particu-larly weak since this institution was not even a college:[5] and it is

[1] See *The works of Geoffrey Chaucer* (2nd ed. by F. N. Robinson, Boston, 1957), p. 56 (lines 3989–3990).

[2] See e.g. *ibid.* p. 687 (note on these lines) where *Soler Halle* is categorically identified with the King's Hall; E. P. Kuhl, 'Chaucer's "My Maistre Bukton"', *Publications of the Modern Language Association of America*, xxxviii (1923), 115 ff. at p. 123; F. P. Magoun, Jr., 'Chaucer's Great Britain', *Mediaeval Studies*, xvi (1954), 131 ff. at p. 148, who presents a more reliable state of the evidence in commenting that *Soler Halle* [is] 'conceivably but with no certainty to be identified with the former King's Hall, Cambridge': his discussion, however, is marred by a series of most misleading references to the early history of the college. The identification is accepted without qualification by H. Riley, *Royal commission on historical manuscripts* (1st report, 1870), appendix, p. 82, and by Gabriel, *op. cit.* p. 5.

[3] For a recent survey of Chaucer's life and career see Robinson, *Works of Geoffrey Chaucer*, xix–xxviii.

[4] See Cooper, *op. cit.* I, 32: 'An opinion has long prevailed that this [i.e. Clare College or its predecessor, University Hall] was the great college called Soler Hall...We think, however, that there is good reason for believing that the Soler Hall was in reality the hostel called Garret Hostel, a soler or sun-chamber being equivalent to a garret'; see also Stokes, *op. cit.* p. 98. Willis and Clark (*op. cit.* II, 403–4) reject Cooper's nomenclature and consider that Garret Hostel derived its name 'from "garyte" meaning a watchtower, lookout place or high window, which may have characterised its early form'.

[5] For the history of Garret Hostel see Willis and Clark, *op. cit.* II, 551 ff.; Stokes, *op. cit.* pp. 76–8.

rather difficult to believe that Chaucer would have used the adjective 'greet' with University (Clare) Hall in mind, an establishment which seems not to have had a complement of more than thirteen fellows present at any one time throughout the medieval period.[1] Indeed, as the King's Hall was by far the largest of the fourteenth-century Cambridge colleges,[2] having a complement of thirty-two or more fellows, it is hard to imagine that the poet would have used the phrase 'greet collegge' with reference to any other institution than this royal foundation.

The designation 'Soler Halle' is not found anywhere in the King's Hall records and, apart from *The Reeve's Tale*, I am unaware of its occurrence in any other contemporary source. 'Soler' is most certainly derived from *solarium* meaning an upper room or sun-chamber of a house.[3] It is beyond dispute that every upper chamber of the King's Hall was called a solar (*solarium*) and every first-floor room a celar (*celarium*).[4] But, as this contemporary terminology was a common one, it does not by itself afford conclusive proof of the identification with Chaucer's 'greet collegge'. Nevertheless, if the identification cannot be definitely proven from the existing evidence, it is assuredly the most probable hypothesis.

As the letters patent of 7 October 1337 do not fully explain the circumstances governing the inception of the Society of the King's Scholars *c.* 1317, it is now essential to turn to an examination of the objectives behind the original scheme.

'The object of the foundation was to provide a home for students who entered the University with the object of preparing themselves for future work in Church and State...'[5] If this view were entirely correct, one could assume that Edward II's motives were wholly identical with those of the English collegiate founders of the thirteenth and fourteenth centuries. There was undoubtedly, at this period, a pressing need to provide accommodation and financial support for secular scholars capable of study beyond a first degree. This need was partly met by the foundation of a number of endowed

---

[1] W. J. Harrison, 'Clare College', *V.C.H.* (Cambridge), III, 340.
[2] See below, pp. 45–6.
[3] OE *solor*, OF *soler*, *solair*, adapted from Latin *solarium*.
[4] See conveniently the fourteenth-century lists of rooms allocated to King's Hall fellows in Willis and Clark, *op. cit.* II, 431, 434, 435.
[5] Rouse Ball, *op. cit.* p. 3.

colleges.[1] Oxford led the way with Merton's foundation of 1264, which became the prototype of the English 'graduate' college of the pre-Reformation era.[2] It was followed by University College *c.* 1280 and by Balliol in 1282.[3] At Cambridge, the only thirteenth-century college, Peterhouse, was established by Hugh de Balsham, bishop of Ely, in 1284.[4] Walter de Stapledon's Oxford foundation, Exeter College,[5] was the last collegiate institution to be erected before the settlement of the King's Scholars at Cambridge.

Considerations of piety apart, these establishments were founded primarily to enable selected scholars with the bachelor's or master's degree to remain at university to take higher degrees in canon or civil law or in theology.[6] But to try to fit the royal 'colony' exclusively into this pattern of university development is to overlook a feature of crucial significance. As the background to the foundation

[1] For the general features of medieval English colleges see H. E. Salter, *Medieval Oxford* (Oxf. Hist. Soc., 1936), pp. 95–102.

[2] It is relevant to point out here that De Vaux College, founded at Salisbury by Bishop Bridport in 1262, has some claim to be regarded as 'the first university college in England': K. Edwards, 'College of de Vaux Salisbury', *V.C.H.* (Wiltshire) (Oxford, 1956), III, 369 ff. at p. 371; see further A. F. Leach, *A history of Winchester College* (London, 1899), p. 86. An award of 1279 between the chancellor and subdean of Salisbury cathedral 'shows that most of the essentials of a *studium generale* or university then existed at Salisbury': Edwards, 'The Cathedral of Salisbury', *op. cit.* III, 169, and *The English secular cathedrals in the middle ages* (Manchester, 1949), p. 194. This nascent university was evidently not sustained, but De Vaux College remained in existence until its dissolution in 1542 and throughout its history a fair proportion of its fellows are known to have taken degrees at Oxford and elsewhere. For a detailed examination of this college see Edwards, *op. cit.* III, 369–85.

[3] Although the scholars of John de Balliol were settled in Oxford before June 1266, the college dates as a legal corporation from the issue of the first statutes in 1282. On this point see Rashdall, *op. cit.*, *ed. cit.* III, 180–1, and H. W. C. Davis, *A history of Balliol College* (2nd ed. by R. H. C. Davis and R. Hunt, Oxford, 1963), pp. 8–9.

[4] The existence of a college is not, of course, conclusive proof of the presence of a university: that there was a well-established university at Cambridge long before Peterhouse was founded is proved by the survival of early statutes (see below, p. 34 and n. 3) and numerous royal writs and papal documents of the thirteenth century which mention a chancellor and a university of masters and scholars. Several of these writs are preserved in Cambridge University Archives. The earliest known recognition of Cambridge by the Holy See is contained in two papal indults of 1233: see *Register Gregory IX* (ed. L. Auvray, Paris, 1896), I, 779, nos. 1388, 1389; *Cal. of Papal Letters*, I (ed. W. H. Bliss, London, 1893), 135, 136; Rashdall, *op. cit.* III, 279.   [5] Founded *c.* 1314.

[6] The exact provisions varied in each case according to the interests or prejudices of the founder.

has not hitherto been adequately examined, the king's motives have consequently been considered only from an 'academic' point of view; whereas the available evidence strongly suggests that in origin the Society of the King's Scholars was, at least in part, a product of the political and household manœuvres of the reign of Edward II.

The key to the wider historical or 'national' significance of the royal foundation lies in the character of its personnel. Without exception, the first detachment of King's Scholars was composed of children from the chapel royal.[1] Throughout the fourteenth and early fifteenth centuries a varying percentage of Scholars was drawn directly from this source or from the court circle.[2] Even after direct recruitment from the chapel had apparently ceased,[3] the connection with the court continued and the college became to an ever increasing extent a base for graduate fellows, especially for civil lawyers,[4] who were frequently non-resident and were employed in various capacities in ecclesiastical and secular business.[5]

As far as can be determined, the functions of the English chapel royal, in contrast to those in continental Europe and particularly those in Germany and Sicily, were wholly ecclesiastical and liturgical in character.[6] Judging from the account of William Say, dean of the chapel in the reign of Henry VI, the institution was seemingly geared solely to serving the religious needs of the king, queen and their immediate entourage.[7] There would therefore appear to be very good grounds for asserting that in England the chapel royal did not constitute a special training area for clerks destined for office in the church or governmental service. But the intimate connection of the Society of the King's Scholars and the later College of the King's Hall with the chapel and royal household indicates that in

---

[1] Their names have not been recovered but most of them are probably identifiable with those which recur in later lists found among accounts for their maintenance enrolled on the Pipe Roll.

[2] See below, pp. 56, 62–3, 186–8.

[3] No Scholar admitted to the college after the first quarter of the fifteenth century is specifically designated a boy or clerk of the chapel royal. This information is derived from an examination of the numerous extant writs of privy seal for the appointment of new Scholars interspersed among the exchequer material relating to the King's Hall.

[4] See below, pp. 54–5, 255 ff.   [5] See chapter 7.

[6] W. Ullmann, ed., *Liber regie capelle* (Henry Bradshaw Society, XCII, Cambridge, 1959), pp. 7–8.   [7] *Ibid.* p. 8.

the early years of the fourteenth century an attempt was made to extend the scope of the functions of the chapel by developing them externally in an academic direction. Indeed, it is certain that, initially, the royal Society was nothing less than an extension or arm of the chapel royal set in the University of Cambridge and that throughout the greater part of its history it remained a kind of physical adjunct or supplement to the household and to the court. This being so, one can only conclude that the King's Scholars of Edward II and the subsequent college together formed the first institutional link between the household and the English universities. The value of such a connection from the monarchical standpoint may be gauged from the salient fact that eleven English kings, spanning the period 1317 to 1546, thought it a worthwhile enterprise to maintain the Society out of royal finances for over two centuries.[1] It is thus clear that when the household was first extended outwards to embrace university society, the Cambridge *studium* alone was selected for this new venture: as far as is known, Oxford was here completely by-passed and does not appear to have participated in this early institutional link-up between the central government and the English universities which stands out as one of the most important and exciting academic developments of the fourteenth century.

Evidence for the ties that resulted between the chapel royal and the English universities is to be found in the household ordinance known as the Black Book of the Household of Edward IV.[2] In the section concerning the children of the chapel, it is stated that if upon reaching the age of eighteen a youth cannot be given immediate preferment within the chapel or elsewhere within the court then, provided that he consents, he is to be sent 'to a college of Oxenford or Cambridge, of the kinges fundacion, there to be in finding and study sufficiauntly tyll the king otherwise list to avaunce hym'.[3] It is therefore apparent that by the third quarter of the fifteenth century the link established between the chapel and the English universities had been written into

---

[1] The King's Hall was dissolved on 17 December 1546, when its buildings, site and property were, along with those of Michaelhouse, incorporated in Henry VIII's new royal foundation, Trinity College.

[2] Concerning the date of the Black Book: 'We can only be sure that the Black Book was composed some time during the decade 1467-77; but during that period some date during 1471 and 1472 seems most likely' (A. R. Myers, *The household of Edward IV, cit.* p. 33).   [3] The Black Book, ch. 59, *ed. cit.* p. 137.

the ordinances of the household.[1] On the strength of this entry, it would seem that the ties initiated by the King's Scholars in the early fourteenth century had later widened out to become only part of a more comprehensive household policy embracing all 'royal' colleges at either of the two universities (i.e. at Cambridge, the King's Hall, King's College and Queens'; at Oxford, Oriel and Queen's, though these latter were not strictly speaking royal foundations *ab initio*). Here, however, it is essential to stress that the relationship between the King's Hall and the central government was substantially different from that of any other medieval college which may either technically or loosely be designated 'royal' and which would presumably come within the terms of reference of the clause cited from the Black Book of Edward IV. For, throughout its long history, the King's Hall remained the intensely personal and flexible instrument of the Crown: successive English kings retained the patronage entirely in their own hands, every fellow being individually appointed by writ of privy seal and every warden being a Crown appointee and responsible to the king alone.[2] It is this peculiar constitutional feature which decisively marks off the King's Hall from all other categories of English colleges with royal associations. Although King's College, Cambridge, for example, was in every sense a true royal foundation, its subsequent position in relation to that of the university's first royal establishment has not formerly been sufficiently considered. Whereas the Crown exercised a complete physical control over the personnel of the King's Hall, Henry VI, on the other hand, resigned all powers of patronage into the hands of the provost and fellows at the beginning.[3] And so this second Cambridge royal foundation, planned on a vast and magnificent scale, was from the start, like almost any other English college, a sovereign, self-perpetuating society, run on democratic lines and functioning under only a very remote royal supervision. As the links with the central

---

[1] There is no trace of this connection in the *Liber regie capelle*, which has been ascribed by its editor to some date before May 1449. See Ullmann, *op. cit.* pp. 10–11. Nor does it occur in any of the household ordinances hitherto published.

[2] See below, pp. 148 ff.

[3] For the 'democratic' arrangements for the election of the provost and fellows see the statutes of King's College in *Camb. Docs.* II, 504 ff. and 487 ff. For details of Henry VI's act of foundation and of the early organisation of the college see J. Saltmarsh, 'King's College', *V.C.H.* (Cambridge), III, 376 ff.

administration were so tenuous even in the case of a splendid royal foundation such as King's, one can well imagine that they would be much more so for those colleges such as Oriel and Queen's, Oxford, whose regality derived from the consideration that the Crown had intervened as second founder.[1] It would therefore seem to be no exaggeration to claim that, by virtue of its unique relationship to the royal household, the King's Hall must have remained the sheet anchor of the university–court nexus throughout the medieval period.

But in order to grasp its full significance, the Cambridge chapel settlement has to be seen in relation to the general curial policies of Edward II's reign, whose essence lay in the development of the potentialities latent in the royal household. The reforms of this period were either due to the efforts of the Ordainers to enforce the Ordinances or they resulted '...from the attempts of the *curiales* to entrench themselves more securely in the last strongholds of the household'.[2] At the core of the administrative system lay the king's household; Edward's strength derived from its adaptability. As the baronial opposition tried to 'capture' the main government departments such as the exchequer, chancery and the privy seal, the king withdrew further into the safety of his household. There, a number of expedients were devised to free the monarchy from the baronial restraints of the Ordinances.[3] For example, revenues due to the exchequer were diverted to the chamber, which was subsequently developed as a central organ of finance.[4] Another device was the emergence of the secret seal as a counterweight to the privy seal, which, for at least part of the reign, was under baronial control.[5] Considering the trend of curial policies in the second decade of the fourteenth century in relation to the household origins of the Society of the King's Scholars, it seems probable that the Cambridge chapel settlement was conceived as one of those several expedients of the

[1] See above, p. 12, n. 1.

[2] T. F. Tout, *The place of the reign of Edward II in English history* (2nd ed. by H. Johnstone, Manchester, 1936), p. 143.

[3] Of the general characteristics of the reforms of the period of the struggle for the Ordinances, Tout writes: '...these were...more largely efforts to buttress the court against baronial attacks than honest attempts to improve the machinery of government for its own sake' (Tout, *Place of Edward II*, p. 142).

[4] For the revival of the chamber under Edward II, see *ibid.* pp. 151–8.

[5] *Ibid.* pp. 153–5.

reign designed to bolster the resources of the household: more specifically, the scheme was almost certainly envisaged as a long-term 'investment' aimed at buttressing the waning power of the Crown by increasing the number of educated clerks at its disposal. It came into being at a time when there was an ever growing demand for English university graduates, especially those with degrees in law and theology, for the staffing of government departments[1] and for important ecclesiastical offices.[2] And it would seem very probable that this Cambridge foundation had as one of its chief aims the provision of a reservoir of educated personnel from which the king could draw to meet his particular requirements.

The timing of the royal foundation further supports the assumption that its origins are indeed closely linked with the policies of the *curiales*. As previously mentioned, the first detachment of Scholars from the chapel royal was settled in Cambridge at some date before 7 July 1317: and it is just then that a revival in the strength and fortunes of the household can be detected. For the restoration of household power began late in 1316. By this time, Edward had come to realise that the actual authority and influence of the earl of Lancaster in no wise corresponded to his exalted position as head of the council.[3] The growing independence of the king was positively asserted by the return to office of several of the *curiales* who had formerly been dismissed by the Ordainers.[4] Both Ingelard of Warley and John Ockham were made barons of the exchequer,[5] and in November 1316 the Ordinances were further flouted by the combination of the offices of keepership of the privy seal and controllership of the wardrobe under the curialist, Thomas Charlton; while on 20 May 1317 the king replaced Walter Norwich as treasurer by

---

[1] For this see Tout, 'The English civil service in the fourteenth century', *Collected Papers of T. F. Tout*, III (Manchester, 1934), 191 ff. at pp. 200, 201.

[2] Evidence for the increasing utilisation of university talents by the church at this time is seen from the character of Edward II's episcopate. Dr Edwards has supplied figures which reveal that the number of bishops under Edward who were university graduates was proportionally greater than the number who were 'magistri' under Henry III. Especially noticeable is the larger number of Edward's bishops who incepted in the higher faculties of theology and law. See K. Edwards, 'Bishops and learning in the reign of Edward II', *Church Quarterly Review*, CXXXVIII (1944), 57 ff., particularly pp. 58–61.

[3] Tout, *Place of Edward II*, p. 97.

[4] *Loc. cit.*   [5] *Ibid.*

appointing to that important position John Hotham, Gaveston's former confidant and now bishop of Ely.[1] Of this appointment, Tout has written: 'It is significant of the reviving power of Edward that while Norwich had been nominated treasurer "by the King and Council", Hotham's appointment was "by the King".'[2]

These facts establish beyond reasonable doubt that the settlement of the chapel children in Cambridge was made just at the time when the *curiales* were firmly re-entrenched in the principal offices of the household. As the chapel was one of the most intimate of all the household departments, there is a strong likelihood that this academic undertaking was in some measure a consequence of the revival in the power of the king and his most trusted advisers.

But why should the king send his Scholars to Cambridge University and not to Oxford, the more obvious choice? Was there at this juncture a positive pull or attraction towards Cambridge? Alternatively, had Edward II his reasons for avoiding or even slighting the Oxford *studium*? It is common knowledge that in the early fourteenth century Oxford's European reputation was far greater than that of Cambridge; and one would naturally assume that the king would send his household children to be educated at Oxford. From the point of view both of prestige and of scholastic achievement Oxford would appear to have had far more to recommend it than had Cambridge. For this very reason, it is all the more pertinent to ask ourselves why Edward II chose to single out and favour the Cambridge *studium* in 1317 by adorning it with England's first royal university foundation.

A consideration which might very well have influenced the king in his choice is associated with the career of the curialist, John Hotham. A Yorkshireman, Hotham had entered the king's service as a clerk, probably introduced by his uncle, William Hotham, a Dominican who became archbishop of Dublin.[3] He appears to have

---

[1] Tout, *Place of Edward II*, p. 97.

[2] *Ibid.*; also T. Madox, *The history and antiquities of the exchequer of England* (1st ed. London, 1711), p. 572.

[3] For details of Hotham's life and career see the article by W. Hunt, *D.N.B.* xxvii (London, 1891), 407–8; also J. Bentham, *The history and antiquities of the conventual and cathedral church of Ely* (2nd ed. Norwich, 1812), pp. 155–8; and further K. Edwards, 'The social origins and provenance of the English bishops during the reign of Edward II', *T.R.H.S.*, 5th series, ix (1959), 51 ff. at p. 58.

rapidly ingratiated himself both with the king and with his Gascon favourite and in 1310 was appointed Gaveston's deputy as keeper of the forest north of Trent as well as escheator north of Trent.[1] Consequently, it is not surprising that in the Articles of 1311 he was specifically named by the Ordainers as one of those royal officials who were to be immediately dismissed from the king's service.[2] Despite the injunctions of the Ordainers, the king continued to show him favour and employed him in a diplomatic capacity in which he undertook several delicate missions including two important ones to Ireland and to France.[3] In July 1316 he was elected bishop of Ely, and consecrated on 3 October of that year;[4] and finally, on 27 May 1317, after Hotham's return from Avignon, the king further disregarded the baronial opposition by appointing him to the office of treasurer.[5] As head of the exchequer by express command of the king at a time when the *curiales* had recaptured the main offices of the household, Hotham had clearly become the *de facto* chief minister of the Crown:[6] moreover, his twin positions as treasurer and bishop of Ely might well have had a significant bearing upon the king's choice of Cambridge for his academic foundation.

The evidence at our disposal suggests that the scheme for the establishment of the Cambridge Society came to fruition shortly after Hotham's appointment as treasurer.[7] Considering that the King's Scholars were, from the outset, maintained by means of exchequer funds, one may safely assume that by virtue of his office as head of the exchequer Hotham must have been closely associated with the project. Indeed, as the scheme was in all probability conceived as one of the curialist expedients of the reign, the treasurer

[1] Tout, *Place of Edward II*, pp. 320, 322.

[2] J. C. Davies, *The baronial opposition to Edward II, its character and policy* (Cambridge, 1918), pp. 383-4. Hotham surrendered his offices of escheator and deputy keeper on 2 February and 2 December 1311 respectively (Tout, *Place of Edward II*, pp. 320, 322). During Gaveston's exile, Hotham acted as his attorney (*ibid.* p. 86, n. 2).

[3] *D.N.B.* XXVII, 407; Bentham, *History of Ely*, p. 155.

[4] *D.N.B. loc. cit.*; Bentham, *loc. cit.*; see also F. M. Powicke and E. B. Fryde, *Handbook of British chronology* (2nd ed. London, 1961), p. 223.

[5] Tout, *Place of Edward II*, p. 298; Madox, *History of the exchequer*, p. 572.

[6] 'The head of the exchequer, the treasurer, was a great officer of state, generally second only to the chancellor, though, if endowed with greater capacity or more fully possessed of his sovereign's confidence, he might easily become the *de facto* chief minister...' (Tout, *Place of Edward II*, p. 42). This was undoubtedly the case with Hotham.   [7] See above, p. 9, n. 2.

might even have been one of its prime movers. However this may be, there can be little doubt that in Hotham's position as bishop of Ely there lay a powerful inducement for the king to establish the Society at that *studium generale* situated within the diocese of his chief minister.

It has often been asserted that one of the causes which prompted Henry VI to choose Cambridge for King's College was the alarming prevalence of Wyclifism at Oxford.[1] It is therefore all the more fascinating to consider that there may have been a parallel reaction against Oxford in the case of Cambridge's first royal foundation. In support of this contention, at least two reasons can be advanced as to why Edward II had cause to feel ill disposed towards the Oxford *studium* in 1317.

The first of these concerns the king's Gascon favourite, Piers Gaveston. After Gaveston's capture by Pembroke and Warenne, Pembroke signed an agreement on 19 May 1312 assuring the prisoner's safety and promising that his fate would be settled in parliament.[2] In an unguarded moment, however, Gaveston was seized by the earl of Warwick and imprisoned in Warwick castle.[3] According to the *Vita Edwardi*, Pembroke immediately sought the aid of the earl of Gloucester: meeting with a curt refusal, he then proceeded to Oxford and there laid the case before the clerks of the university and the burgesses of the town.[4] Pembroke appealed both for advice and help to recover the person of Gaveston, but his request failed to stir either the clerks or the burgesses to any action which might save the royal favourite from his fate. In the words of the monk of Malmesbury: 'Sed nec clerici nec burgenses rem ad se non pertinentem tractare vel attemptare curabant.'[5] As this episode was so closely bound up with the dramatic train of events culminating in Gaveston's murder, one can well imagine that the unrespon-

---

[1] See Rashdall, *op. cit.* III, 316; also the letters patent of Henry VI of 10 July 1443 (*Camb. Docs.* II, 471) where the king states that the college had been founded 'ad honorem Omnipotentis Dei...extirpacionem quoque heresum et errorum qui solemnium Regnorum ac Universitatum pacem perturbant regnumque nostrum Angliae...'

[2] M. McKisack, *The fourteenth century, 1307–1399* (Oxford, 1959), p. 25.

[3] *Ibid.* p. 26.

[4] *Ibid.* See *Vita Edwardi II monachi cujusdam Malmesberiensis* in *Chronicles of the reign of Edward I and Edward II* (R.S., ed. W. Stubbs, 1882), II, 178–9; also 2nd ed. (with translation) by N. Denholm-Young (Nelson's medieval texts, 1957), p. 26.

[5] Malmesb., *Vita Edwardi, ed. cit.* p. 179; Denholm-Young, *loc. cit.*

sively neutral or even hostile attitude adopted by the Oxford clerks and burgesses would leave a bitter and lasting imprint upon the mind of the king.

During Edward II's reign, relations between the king and the chancellor and masters of Oxford were severely strained over the controversial issue of the position the friars were entitled to occupy within the academic community. The king actively supported the Mendicants, several writs being addressed to the chancellor on their behalf.[1] In addition, Edward sent a number of letters to the papal curia in furtherance of their claims;[2] and in 1318, the king '...went so far as to order the chancellor to desist from exercising authority over the Friars Preachers since they were exempt from secular jurisdiction not only by reason of their Order, but by apostolic privilege'.[3] At Cambridge, too, serious conflicts arose between the university authorities and the friars. A quarrel broke out in 1303 and three statutes were passed harmful to the interests of the friars, who then appealed to the pope.[4] A compromise settlement was reached at Bordeaux in 1306, however, and though the differences remained the struggle did not revive in any serious form until the second half of the century.[5]

It would thus seem that, whereas the friar problem had reached a critical phase of development at Oxford during the reign of Edward II, at Cambridge in the same period the issues at dispute were temporarily shelved. Bearing in mind the king's deep attachment to the cause of the Mendicants, it is probable that this difference in the relative position of the friars at the English universities at this time provides us with a further clue as to why royal patronage was then attracted to the Cambridge *studium*.

Edward II might conceivably have been further influenced in his choice of university by considerations of prestige. In the early

[1] See Strickland Gibson, 'The University of Oxford', *V.C.H.* (Oxford), III, 7.

[2] *Ibid.* The friars presented the case against the university to the papal curia in 1311.

[3] *Ibid.* Edward's support for the friars was perhaps strengthened by feelings of gratitude towards the Oxford Dominicans who sheltered the headless corpse of Gaveston in their convent for more than three years. The embalmed body was subsequently removed by the king and buried at King's Langley. Malmesb., *Vita Edwardi*, pp. 180, 209; *Annales Londonienses* in *Chrons. Edw. I and II*, I, 207; see also McKisack, *op. cit.* pp. 26–7, 47.

[4] See J. P. C. Roach, 'The University of Cambridge', *V.C.H.* (Cambridge), III, 153.

[5] *Ibid.* III, 153, 154.

fourteenth century, there are signs of the emergence of what can best be described as a more insular attitude towards the English *studia*.[1] At this period, Oxford was a university of the first rank whose scholars were playing a leading part in the development of European thought and learning. Although Rashdall's stress upon the insignificance of medieval Cambridge is now seen to be in need of long-overdue revision,[2] the fact remains that Cambridge was by far the smaller[3] and less prominent of the English universities. In view of the efforts then being made by the king and his supporters to restore the waning fortunes of the monarchy, Edward may well have been intent upon boosting the reputation of the Cambridge *studium* in order to increase his own national prestige.[4] Obviously, the establishment of a royal 'colony' at Cambridge would be a decisive step in this direction.

INFLUENCE UPON CAMBRIDGE UNIVERSITY IN THE MIDDLE AGES

There is a substantial body of evidence to show that the establishment of the Society of the King's Scholars in Cambridge had a pronounced effect upon the way in which the *studium* developed in the first half of the fourteenth century; and the thesis is advanced that the university owes a greater debt to its earliest royal foundation as

[1] Dr Kathleen Edwards has drawn attention to the prevalence of this attitude among the bishops of Edward II's reign. In their registers she has detected indications of the growth of a 'spirit of nationalism' towards the English *studia* and especially towards Oxford. See Edwards, *Church Quarterly Review*, cxxxviii (1944), 75.

[2] Several eminent scholars including Thomas of York, Duns Scotus, John Bromyard, Robert Holcot and Thomas Cobham are now known to have studied or taught at Cambridge. See Rashdall, *op. cit.* iii, 284, n. 2.

[3] Although the figures cannot be compiled with any great degree of accuracy, it has been roughly computed that before the middle of the fifteenth century Cambridge University, numerically speaking, was only about a third of the size of the Oxford *studium*: see Emden, *B.R.U.O.* i, xvi.

[4] It was largely out of considerations of prestige that Edward II wrote to the pope on 26 December 1317 requesting that the *ius ubique docendi* recently granted to the University of Paris be formally conferred upon the University of Oxford. This letter is printed by H. Denifle and A. Chatelain, *Chartularium Universitatis Parisiensis*, ii (Paris, 1891), i, no. 756. The king's request was not granted. It has been suggested that one of the reasons for the pope's refusal may have been associated with the current dispute between Oxford University and the Dominicans. See G. L. Haskins, 'The University of Oxford and the "ius ubique docendi"', *E.H.R.* lvi (1941), 281 ff. at p. 287.

a more immediate and effective stimulus to collegiate expansion than to Peterhouse, the solitary, episcopal college of the thirteenth century.

One would naturally expect that Edward's chapel foundation would provide a royal lead or example; would set, so to speak, an academic fashion. And, indeed, this was apparently the case.[8] For there is good circumstantial evidence to support the inference that it was the introduction of this royal community into the university which was largely instrumental in attracting to Cambridge the interest and wealth of the more enlightened members of Edward's episcopate and official circle. This conclusion is based upon the eloquent fact that all the most important benefactions of the early years of the century followed in quick succession from the establishment of the King's Scholars in Cambridge; and, moreover, that the benefactors themselves, both statesmen and ecclesiastics, were among the most trusted of Edward II's ministers.

Of the members of Edward's circle who were drawn, apparently by the royal example, to give of their wealth to Cambridge there may be mentioned Hervey de Stanton, chancellor of the exchequer and founder of Michaelhouse;[1] John Salmon, bishop of Norwich[2] and formerly prior of the cathedral monastery of Ely, named in the Clare statutes of 1359 as an early benefactor of University Hall;[3] Thomas Cobham, the learned bishop of Worcester, also cited as a benefactor of University Hall;[4] and John Hotham, bishop of Ely, recorded as a benefactor of Peterhouse.[5] Mention must also be made of Roger de Northburgh, keeper of the privy seal from 1312 to 1316, treasurer of the wardrobe from 1316 to 1322, and bishop of Coventry and Lichfield between 1322 and 1359.[6] The traditional claim that Northburgh was chancellor of the university is now open to serious dispute,[7] but his undoubted interest in the *studium* is known from the

---

[1] With one short interval, Hervey de Stanton was chancellor of the exchequer from 22 June 1316 to 18 July 1326. See Stamp, *Michaelhouse*, pp. 8–9.

[2] Salmon was chancellor from 26 January 1320 to 5 June 1323 (Tout, *Place of Edward II*, p. 290).　　　[3] *Camb. Docs.* II, 142.　　　[4] *Loc. cit.*

[5] R. Parker, *The history and antiquities of the University of Cambridge* (London, 1721(?)), p. 37.　　　[6] Tout, *Place of Edward II*, pp. 316, 317.

[7] See Emden, *B.R.U.C.* p. 427, where reasons are given for doubting the validity of this claim first advanced by Fuller, *History of the University of Cambridge*, ed. cit. p. 36: this point, which was previously raised by Dr Kathleen Edwards, is further discussed by A. C. Chibnall, *Richard de Badew and the University of Cambridge 1315–1340* (Cambridge, 1963), pp. 8–10.

fact that in 1321 he moved the king to grant a licence to the chancellor and masters enabling them to acquire advowsons of churches to the annual value of forty pounds for the endowment of colleges to be founded for scholars in theology and logic.[1]

If a wider view is taken of this subject, it is indeed arguable that the Society of the King's Scholars provided a more actual impetus towards the university's early collegiate development than did Peterhouse, the first of its colleges. For in the thirty years following the foundation of Peterhouse in 1284 no other college was erected and no marked interest was seemingly taken in the *studium*; whereas at Oxford in the late thirteenth and early fourteenth centuries three colleges[2] were founded which, with Merton, brought the number up to four. It is plainly observable, however, that, after the settlement of the King's Scholars in Cambridge, the pattern of collegiate expansion at both universities radically altered. At Oxford only two colleges, Oriel in 1324 and Queen's in 1341, were founded in the remainder of the first half of the fourteenth century. At Cambridge, on the other hand, no fewer than seven colleges were established in the period 1317 to 1352.[3]

These facts would seem to point to the conclusion that the coming of royal patronage to Cambridge had caused a reorientation in the attitude towards the English universities of those sections of society which produced the college founders and benefactors of the medieval era. Whereas Oxford had hitherto drawn off much of the surplus wealth available for university learning, now affluent high-ranking members of the ministerial class such as Hervey de Stanton, ecclesiastics like Bishop Bateman,[4] and rich lay patrons, of whom Lady Clare and the countess of Pembroke are good examples, all these had clearly come to regard Cambridge as a sound 'investment' for the future, sealed with the stamp of royal approval. It would surely be reasonable to infer that one of the chief inspirations behind this new-found confidence in Cambridge University, expressed in the sudden

[1] It is probable that as archdeacon of Richmond he himself had contemplated such a foundation. See Rashdall, *op. cit.* III, 303, n. 3.

[2] University College (*c.* 1280); Balliol (1282); and Exeter (*c.* 1314).

[3] Michaelhouse (1324); University or Clare Hall (1326); the King's Hall (1337); Pembroke Hall (1347); Gonville Hall (1349); Trinity Hall (1350); and Corpus Christi College (for long more usually styled St Benet's College) (1352).

[4] Bishop of Norwich and founder of Trinity Hall.

flow of interest and material resources towards the *studium*, was the encouraging presence there of Edward's royal foundation.

Apart from being largely instrumental in sparking off Cambridge's first wave of collegiate expansion, it would appear that the royal establishment made another vital and hitherto unobserved contribution towards the evolution of the medieval *studium*.

It is widely assumed that Pope John XXII officially conferred the status of *studium generale* upon the University of Cambridge in 1318. It has been accepted as an established fact that before this date Cambridge had not yet acquired an equality of status with Oxford which, for over a century, had been recognised as a *studium generale ex consuetudine*. In the light of recent research, however, there would now appear to be an urgent need for a revision of this long-standing conclusion; and new evidence brought to bear on this subject indicates that there is a legitimate demand for a reassessment of the status of medieval Cambridge during the first hundred years of its existence.[1] It would, furthermore, seem profitable to examine the circumstances which prompted the papal letter of 1318, as there are sufficient grounds for believing that a causal relationship exists between the establishment of the Society of the King's Scholars in Cambridge *c.* 1317 and Edward II's petition to Pope John of which the apostolic award was the outcome. It is the likelihood of such a relationship that will now be considered in some detail.

Should Edward II's petition to Pope John XXII of 18 March 1317 be regarded as merely coincidental with the inception of the Cambridge Society or is there a causal connection between the two events? One of the king's motives, and perhaps the chief motive behind the petition, can be readily assessed. It is only natural that Edward should have been concerned about the status of the university to which he had sent his Scholars. To ensure that the standing of that university was consistent with the dignity of his royal foundation, one can well imagine that the king would be particularly anxious to have the status of Cambridge as a *studium generale* undisputedly confirmed in a formal papal document.[2] If, on

---

[1] See below, pp. 34 ff.

[2] In this connection, it should perhaps be pointed out that the settlement of the King's Scholars in Cambridge and Edward II's petition to Pope John XXII came just at the time when the earliest Oxford petitions for benefices submitted to the papal curia can be traced. These concern the numerous provisions for fellows of

the other hand, the king had sent his chapel boys to be educated at Oxford, it is equally likely that this would have prompted him to seek a similar mark of papal favour for that university as well. The probable connection between the royal settlement and the petition will be more apparent when a number of relevant factors are considered.

At the beginning of his reign, on 9 June 1309, Edward confirmed the existing privileges of the university.[1] In 1313, the old borough charters were likewise confirmed.[2] Before this date, there is no indication of any royal policy designed to raise the standing of the university either from a 'national' point of view or at the expense of the mayor and burgesses of Cambridge. In February 1317, however, the university's privileges were again confirmed and new ones granted which provoked strained relations between the burgesses and the university.[3] On 18 March 1317, the king addressed letters to Pope John XXII requesting him to strengthen and 'perpetuate' the university and to confirm and augment its privileges.[4] It will be recalled that the King's Scholars were settled in Cambridge at some date before 7 July 1317.[5] As it was necessary to find suitable rented

Merton in 1317. (See Rashdall, *op. cit.* I, 555 n.; Emden, *B.R.U.O.* I, xxxvi.) As far as can be determined, the earliest traceable list of Cambridge petitioners is one for 1331, though of course earlier ones may have existed. (See Emden, *B.R.U.C.* p. xxiv.) Although there is as yet no substantial evidence to corroborate the point, it is possible that an additional motive for seeking that the status of the Cambridge *studium* be formally confirmed by the pope was that such an act would impart greater weight to Cambridge University's *rotuli* of petitions for benefices to be sent to the curia shortly afterwards: in particular, it might help to ensure that petitions from Cambridge would receive an attention equal to that then given to those from Oxford. On this subject of rolls of petitions see, in addition to the references cited, E. F. Jacob, 'Petitions for benefices from English universities during the Great Schism', *T.R.H.S.*, 4th series, XXVII (1945), 41–59; 'English university clerks in the later middle ages: the problem of maintenance', *B.J.R.L.* XXIX (1946), 304–25; 'On the promotion of English university clerks during the later middle ages', *J. Eccles. Hist.* I (1950), 172–86; more recently D. E. R. Watt, 'University clerks and rolls of petitions for benefices', *Speculum*, XXXIV (1959), 213–29.

[1] *Cal. Charter Rolls*, III (London, 1908), 129, 226.   [2] *Ibid.* III, 226.

[3] The charter is preserved in Cambridge University Archives, *Cabinet*, no. 19. For the possible role of Robert de Baldock in the chain of events culminating in the issue of this charter of privileges see Chibnall, *op. cit.* pp. 3–4, 25–6.

[4] This petition is printed in Rymer, *Foedera*, ed. cit. II, pt. i, 357; see also *Camb. Docs.* I, 6. The document will be more extensively quoted below.

[5] See above, p. 9, n. 2.

accommodation and generally to prepare for their reception, the decision to send the chapel children to Cambridge must have been taken several weeks or even months before the first settlement. We can be reasonably assured, therefore, that the project concerning the King's Scholars and Edward's petition to Pope John were both conceived about the same point in time in the early part of 1317; and in view of what has been said with reference to the king's motives, the probability is that this chronological relationship was also causal.

It is, moreover, relevant to consider that Edward's petition was timed to coincide with a royal mission to Avignon. The envoys were the earl of Pembroke, Lord Badlesmere, Hotham, bishop of Ely, and Salmon, bishop of Norwich.[1] They set out for Avignon in December 1316 and started their return journey for England in April 1317.[2] Their general object was to win the support of the new pope for the English king; their particular aims were to gain for Edward permission to tax the English clergy and to enlist papal aid against the Scots.[3] It is known, however, that the ambassadors' brief extended to other matters of a more secret nature;[4] and it is almost certain that the mission would provide Hotham and perhaps Salmon with the opportunity to open discussions on the Cambridge *studium* preparatory to the arrival of the king's petition. The exact date in April on which the ambassadors left the curia to return home has not yet been ascertained: but as they assuredly did not depart until April and the king's letter is dated 18 March, it is very likely that they were still at Avignon when the petition actually arrived.

As a direct consequence of Edward II's petition of March 1317, Cambridge University received the apostolic award of John XXII in June 1318.[5] It has long since been evident that Denifle's interpretation of this document is wholly unacceptable. He regarded it as a

---

[1] Tout, *Place of Edward II*, p. 101.

[2] *Loc. cit.*

[3] *Loc. cit.*; also J. C. Davies, *op. cit.* p. 429.

[4] For example, Hotham and Salmon presented a letter to the pope concerning the king's request for permission to receive the miraculous oil alleged to have been given to Thomas Becket by the Virgin Mary. See the reply of John XXII to Edward II in *English coronation records* (ed. L. G. Wickham Legg, Westminster, 1901), pp. 69–76 (with translation); also W. Ullmann, 'Thomas Becket's miraculous oil', *J.T.S.* VIII (1957), 129 ff., especially at p. 129.

[5] I have published a critical edition of the text of this papal letter in *B.J.R.L.* XLVII (1964), 76–8.

foundation-bull which, in effect, created the *studium* at Cambridge.[1] But this is patently inaccurate. An examination of the *studium* in the thirteenth century reveals that it already possessed the main features which characterised the *studium generale* (i.e. students from distant regions, a plurality of masters, and teaching in at least one of the higher faculties, theology, law or medicine).[2] If more specific evidence is required, it can be pointed out that a very high degree of university organisation and advanced state of learning is presupposed in the statute of 17 March 1275.[3] But this topic need not be further examined as it has been widely recognised that long before 1318 Cambridge had attained the status of at least *studium generale respectu regni*.[4]

The most recent commentators upon the letter of Pope John XXII have considered it to be a formal papal recognition which officially conferred the status of *studium generale*, and consequently the *ius ubique docendi*, upon the University of Cambridge.[5] In the light of a critical reappraisal of this document, however, there would now seem to be a good case for regarding the papal letter as a confirmation which merely strengthened an already existing *studium generale* without in any way improving upon its status.

The letter of Pope John XXII was still in the possession of the university in 1420. In that year it was listed in the detailed inventory of the contents of the common chest compiled by a certain master William Rysley.[6] Unfortunately, its subsequent history is unknown

---

[1] See H. Denifle, *Die Entstehung der Universitäten des Mittelalters bis 1400* (Berlin, 1885), I, especially pp. 352–3, 375–6; Rashdall, *op. cit.* III, 283.

[2] For the general characteristics of European *studia generalia* see Rashdall, *op. cit.* I, 7: the earlier and divergent views of H. Denifle, C. Meiners, F. C. von Savigny, A. Pertile, F. Schupfer and G. Kaufmann on the essential features of *studia generalia* are conveniently summarised by G. Ermini, 'Concetto di "Studium Generale"', *Archivio Giuridico*, CXXVII (1942), 3 ff. at pp. 3–7.

[3] The significance of this statute for the early history of the university is discussed by W. Ullmann, *Historical Journal*, I (1958), 176 ff., especially at p. 180.

[4] Rashdall, *op. cit.* III, 284.

[5] See Roach, 'The University of Cambridge', *op. cit.* III, 154; also Chibnall, *Richard de Badew*, p. 4.

[6] *Registrum Librorum*, fo. 10v (preserved in Cambridge University Archives). A description of Rysley's inventory is given in Peek and Hall, *The archives of the University of Cambridge*, pp. 4–6, and a transcript of his catalogue has now been published in full by C. P. Hall, 'William Rysley's catalogue of the Cambridge University muniments, compiled in 1420', *Transactions of the Cambridge Bibliographical Society*, IV (1965), 85 ff. at pp. 91 ff.

and it has since disappeared.[1] The text of the letter which forms the basis of my critical edition was taken from a photostatic copy of the entry in the Vatican Register of John XXII, volume LXVIII, fo. 66, no. 1230. It was found that this corresponded almost exactly with the transcript of the letter contained in the document entitled 'Processus Barnwellensis ex mandato Martini Papae V, cum bullis Johannis XXII et Bonifacii IX'. This is a parchment document, dated 10 October 1430, and is preserved in Cambridge University Archives.[2] A number of printed editions of the text have hitherto appeared:[3] among these, there are several textual differences in points of detail but in one important and, as will be seen, misleading respect, they are all at variance with the copies of the letter in the Vatican Register and in the 'Processus Barnwellensis'.

Generally speaking, it may be said that papal letters or formal bulls for the erection of European *studia generalia* fall into one of at least four categories. They may erect a new *studium generale* where none has existed before;[4] they may found a *studium* on the basis of an older one which has since declined or even disappeared;[5] they may seem to erect a new *studium* without reference to a former one, though it is known that an existing *studium* was flourishing at the time of the papal letter;[6] or lastly, the existence of a *studium generale*

[1] The letter was reported missing in 1876 by H. R. Luard, the University Registrary. See Luard, 'A list of the documents in the University Registry, from the year 1266 to the year 1544', *C.A.S. Communications*, III (1864–76), no. xxxviii, 385 ff. at p. 389.

[2] Cambridge University Archives, *Cabinet*, no. 108.

[3] Printed editions of the text are given by Parker, *op. cit.* pp. 22–3; T. Hearne, ed., *Thomae Sprotti Chronica* (Oxford, 1719), pp. 256–8 (in the appended *Historiola de Antiquitate et Origine Universitatis Cantabrigiensis* by the Carmelite friar, Nicholas Cantelupe); Fuller, *op. cit.*, *ed. cit.* pp. 80–1; and by G. Dyer, *The privileges of the University of Cambridge; together with additional observations on its history, antiquities, literature, and biography*, I (London, 1824), 60–1. A translation based on Fuller's text is printed by J. Heywood, ed., *Collection of statutes for the University and the colleges of Cambridge* (London, 1840), p. 45.

[4] For example, see the foundation-bull for Prague (1347–8) printed in *Monumenta Historica Universitatis Praguensis*, II (ed. Dittrich and Spirk, Prague, 1834), 219–22; also Rashdall, *op. cit.* II, 215.

[5] See e.g. the foundation-bull for Perpignon (1379) printed by M. Fournier, *Les Statuts et Privilèges des Universités Françaises depuis leur fondation jusqu'en 1789*, II (Paris, 1891), no. 1438, in conjunction with the earlier history of the *studium* given by Rashdall, *op. cit.* II, 96–7.

[6] For example, see the bull of Nicholas IV for Montpellier (1289) in Fournier, *op. cit.* II, no. 903, together with the past history of the university outlined in Rashdall, *op. cit.* II, 119 ff., especially at p. 130.

is admitted in the preamble of the document which then, on request of the ruler to strengthen it, proceeds to confirm the institution.[1] And it is suggested that both structurally and in its signification the Cambridge award closely conforms to the fourth of these categories of papal documents.

Edward II's petition to Pope John XXII is most illuminating as it indicates what the substance of the award is expected to be. It begins by stressing the antiquity of the Cambridge *studium*; and it continues by asserting that such a great university deserves to be raised in the public estimation.[2] According to the king, therefore, the paramount need of the university is that it be strengthened and further 'propped up' by the Holy See: 'Cum igitur universitas predicta, cuius statum prosperari cupimus et firmari, sacrosancte sedis apostolice gratiosa munificentia muniri iam indigeat et fulciri...supplicamus...'[3] Towards this end, the pope is then petitioned to 'perpetuate' the existing university,[4] to confirm all its privileges and, if it pleases him, to grant new ones. The essence of this petition, minus the augmentation clause, is repeated in the papal letter of 1318.

It is beyond doubt that the whole tenor of Edward's supplication is directed towards obtaining a strengthening or confirmation, by a mark of papal favour, of an old-established *studium* with its own advanced organisation and code of privileges. There is every justification for saying that if the king had in fact petitioned that Cambridge be formally recognised by the pope as a *studium generale*, this would almost certainly have been specifically stated; but there is no reference to this, nor to the *ius ubique docendi*, in the king's letter. Also, at a later stage, it will be seen that the clause 'apud Cantebrigiam... desiderat vigere studium generale...', reported in the papal letter as part of Edward's petition (though it does not occur in this same form in the actual petition), cannot be interpreted as meaning a request that a *studium generale* be established but, on the contrary, must be taken to mean that Edward desired the existing one to flourish and prosper by virtue of an additional papal support.

[1] See e.g. the bull of Alexander IV for Salamanca (1255) in *Archiv für Literatur- und Kirchengeschichte*, v (ed. H. Denifle and F. Ehrle, Freiburg im Breisgau, 1889), 168–9; also the remarks of Rashdall, *op. cit.* II, 77.

[2] '...tanta universitas memorata majori mereretur attolli preconio...' (Rymer, *op. cit., ed. cit.* p. 357).

[3] *Ibid.*   [4] '...dictam universitatem perpetuare...' (*ibid.*).

The first essential feature of the fourth category of papal documents listed above is that at some point in the letter or bull before the enactment clause is reached, the institution is expressly admitted to have been a *studium generale*. For example, when Pope Alexander IV confirmed the *studium* at Salamanca in 1255,[1] it was recognised in the preamble of the bull that the institution had been a *studium generale* ever since its first foundation.[2] Similarly, in the case of Cambridge, it is clear that the address of the papal letter of 1318 contains an unequivocal admission on the part of the pope that the university had, by this date, already acquired the status of *studium generale*. But in this crucially important matter of the exact form of the address all the printed texts differ markedly from the original wording. Without exception, they give as the address of the letter: '...dilectis filiis Universitatis Cantebrigie Eliensis diocesis salutem...' According to the entry in the Vatican Register, however, as well as to the copy of John's letter in the 'Processus Barnwellensis', the correct wording is: '...dilectis filiis *Universitatis Magistrorum et Scolarium studii generalis Cantebrigie* Eliensis diocesis salutem...'[3]

There can be no legitimate doubt that this address is an explicit recognition of Cambridge as an already existing and properly constituted *studium generale*. As the term occurs in a fourteenth-century papal letter, it is evident that it is used in the technical and precise sense implying the *ius ubique docendi* which the concept of *studium generale* had then acquired.[4] There is, moreover, no reasonable justification for considering the address to be a slip on the part of the papal chancery. Thus, even if there were no further pieces of evidence to substantiate the conclusion, the occurrence of this address in such an important official document lends powerful support to the view that long before 1318 Cambridge had, in actual fact, been fully recognised as a *studium generale*.

After the address, the king's petition is next related. It is stated that as he desires the *studium generale* at Cambridge to flourish and be well frequented by masters and students, he has requested that the existing *studium* be strengthened by papal authority. At this juncture, it is

---

[1] See *Archiv für Literatur- und Kirchengeschichte, loc. cit.*
[2] '...apud Salamantinam...generale studium statuisti,...' (*ibid.*).
[3] See my edition in *B.J.R.L. art. cit.*
[4] Rashdall, *op. cit.* I, 10.

instructive to compare the wording of the Cambridge letter with the similar way in which the Salamancan petition is reported:

Salamanca	Cambridge
'...et ut generale studium [i.e. the *studium generale* already recognised] a doctoribus et docendis in posterum frequentetur, humiliter postulasti a nobis apostolico id munimine roborari.'[1]	'...apud Cantebrigiam desiderat vigere studium generale [i.e. the *studium generale* already expressly recognised in the address] et quod a doctoribus et docendis in posterum frequentetur humiliter postulavit a nobis ut studium ab olim ordinatum et privilegia... concessa, apostolico curaremus munimine roborari.'[2]

It will be observed that there is no essential difference in kind between these two petitions. In each case, the king has asked that the *studium* be merely strengthened by papal confirmation, without seeking that its status be in any way altered or improved: and it seems that this form of petition constitutes the second characteristic feature of our fourth category of papal documents.

Whereas in the Salamancan case the simple form 'confirmamus' is used to confirm the institution, the Cambridge letter carries the formal enactment: '...ut in predicto loco...sit de cetero studium generale...vigeat perpetuis futuris temporibus in qualibet facultate'. This, however, is a set formula common to several kinds of papal bulls of erection. Before it can be properly interpreted in any one case, the historical circumstances governing the issue of the bull or letter have to be carefully considered. Take just one example: this form of enactment occurs in the bull of Nicholas IV for the erection of a *studium generale* at Montpellier in 1289.[3] The erection is treated as a new foundation; there is no mention of an existing *studium* in the preamble of the document; and yet 'there can be no doubt that the *studium* had long been treated as "general" both by custom and by express apostolic recognition'.[4] What at first sight would seem to be an ordinary foundation-bull, on further inquiry turns out to be a formal papal recognition.

[1] *Archiv für Literatur- und Kirchengeschichte*, v, 169.
[2] See my edition in *B.J.R.L. art. cit.*
[3] Fournier, *op. cit.* II, no. 903.
[4] Rashdall, *op. cit.* II, 130.

When examining documents of this kind, therefore, it is necessary to bear in mind that in isolation the enactment clause is sometimes misleading as to their essential character. In several instances, it is only when the clause is considered in relation to the historical background of the bull, or to a petition, or to some other feature of the bull itself, that it can be accurately interpreted: and this is the case with the Cambridge letter. When the enactment clause is set in the context of all that is known of the development and organisation of the *studium* before 1318, and is seen in relation to the petition of Edward II, and to the form of address in the letter itself, there can be little dispute that the clause is merely confirmatory in character.

A further piece of evidence in support of our conclusion is the entry for this document contained in master William Rysley's detailed inventory of the contents of the university's common chest, which incidentally constitutes the earliest extant catalogue of the medieval muniments.[1] In the section devoted to the papal records then in the possession of the university the letter of John XXII is described in this manner: 'Item nova *confirmatio* universitatis per Johannem XXII aº ij.'[2] Although this inventory was compiled in 1420, a hundred years or so after the letter was issued, it nevertheless remains an illuminating and telling fragment of Cambridge University comment upon the real contemporary significance of the papal award of 1318. Rysley has not yet been identified, but as the responsibility for the contents of the common chest lay with the proctors, the guardians of the university's movable goods, it has been conjectured that he himself may have been one of the proctors in 1420.[3] However this may be, Rysley's catalogue of the early muniments was henceforth accepted as the authoritative list and was recognised as such, without fresh enumeration, in the surviving series of proctors' indentures concerning the chest which begins in 1431.[4] This is strong testimony indeed that Rysley's description of the letter of John XXII as a *confirmatio* went unquestioned in the medieval university. It was only because of the uncritical acceptance of inaccurate post-Reformation transcriptions that this sound fifteenth-

---

[1] Peek and Hall, *op. cit.* p. 4.
[2] *Registrum Librorum*, fo. 10v; C. P. Hall, *art. cit.* p. 94, line 30.
[3] Hall, p. 90; Emden, *B.R.U.C.* p. 482.
[4] Peek and Hall, *op. cit.* p. 5; Hall, *loc. cit.*

century classification was confounded and the subsequent errors of interpretation were transmitted over the centuries from commentator to commentator without any attempt being made to take cognisance of extant medieval copies of the text.

As it would now appear that the letter of John XXII was nothing more than a papal confirmation, it will be appreciated that this has very important implications for the history of the medieval university. For it clearly signifies that at no time did the pope presume to confer, even officially, the status of *studium generale* upon the University of Cambridge but intervened only to strengthen it by apostolic confirmation. From this, it logically follows that throughout at least part of the thirteenth and early fourteenth centuries Cambridge had already been recognised as a *studium generale* in the widest sense of the term and not merely *respectu regni*. As it had not been recognised as 'general' by papal authority, it must have been treated as 'general' by custom. Thus we may claim that even if Cambridge did not then possess a European reputation as great as that of her more prominent counterpart, she nevertheless in this period enjoyed a status in every way equal to that of Oxford.[1] Indeed, there is now justification for ranging the Cambridge *studium* with all those older *studia* such as Paris, Bologna, Oxford, Padua and Orléans which had attained positions as *studia generalia* by custom (*ex consuetudine*) and not by formal papal enactment.[2] As a supplement to this picture of

---

[1] It is perhaps well to point out that this conclusion concerning the equality of Cambridge with Oxford University is confined solely to the matter of the *status* of the *studium* before and in 1318. It is in no way suggested that Cambridge in the same period enjoyed an equality of *privilege* with Oxford. Indeed, it is undeniable that in terms of concrete privileges Cambridge lagged behind the Oxford *studium* until the latter part of the fourteenth century: in the case of the privilege of freedom from ecclesiastical authority, it was not until the Barnwell Process of 1430 that Cambridge finally and incontrovertibly obtained a complete papal exemption from the episcopal and archiepiscopal jurisdictions of Ely and Canterbury. (See chapter 3.)

[2] Although at a later stage of development all of these universities, except Oxford, received varying degrees of papal recognition for their positions as *studia generalia*. In 1291–2, two bulls were issued by Pope Nicholas IV which formally conferred the *ius ubique docendi* upon the old-established universities of Paris and Bologna. The bull for Paris is printed in C. E. Bulaeus, *Historia Universitatis Parisiensis*, III (Paris, 1666), 449–50, and for Bologna in M. Sarti, *De Claris Archigymnasii Bononiensis Professoribus a saeculo xi usque ad saeculum xiv* (Bologna, 1769–72), I, i. 59. In 1306, by a bull of Clement V, Orléans, which had been recognised as a *studium generale* before the mid-thirteenth century (i.e. *ex consuetudine*: Rashdall, II, 143), was granted all the privileges of the *studium generale* of Toulouse. (The bull is

the standing of medieval Cambridge, it should be stressed that by the beginning of the fifteenth century the university appears to have acquired a European renown in no wise inferior to that of Oxford. Adequate proof for this contention can be deduced from the revealing fact that at the conclusion of the Council of Constance in 1417 the cardinals took the trouble to send a special letter to the university to inform it of their choice of a new pontiff. As far as is known, there is no such corresponding announcement to the University of Oxford.[1]

The direction of recent research has been to revise and largely to reject the traditional image of Cambridge University prevalent for the thirteenth and fourteenth centuries. Just as the image has been at least partially corrected in the sphere of scholarly achievement, so there is need for a reassessment of the status of the university during the first century of its existence. In the light of a critical re-examination of the letter of Pope John XXII of 1318 there is persuasive evidence for asserting that this document is far less of a landmark in Cambridge history than has hitherto been supposed. Since it now appears that the letter is wholly confirmatory in character, there is every justification for contending that not even in an official sense did Cambridge owe its position as a *studium generale* to a formal act of papal foundation. In reviewing the history of the English universities before 1318, therefore, we are led to affirm that by right Cambridge ought now to be placed on a proper basis of equality of status with Oxford and with all those other European *studia* of similar rank.

In the course of this chapter it has also been submitted that the significance of the first attraction of royal patronage to Cambridge has not been sufficiently appreciated. The establishment of an arm of the chapel royal in Cambridge had the important effect of forging the initial institutional link between the court and the English universities, a connection which, inaugurating a new royal policy, was subsequently expanded and inserted into the written Ordinances of

printed by Fournier, I, no. 19.) In the case of Padua, the university acquired a confirmation of all its privileges as a *studium generale* by a bull of Clement VI in 1346. For this bull see Antonio Riccobonus, *De Gymnasio Patavino* (Padua, 1722), fos. 4, 5.

[1] For a detailed analysis of this whole subject see W. Ullmann, 'The University of Cambridge and the Great Schism', *J.T.S.* IX (1958), 53 ff. at pp. 65 ff.: an edition of the text of the cardinals' letter is given at pp. 75 ff.

the household. There are, moreover, substantial grounds for regarding the chapel settlement as being in some measure conceived as one of the several curial expedients of the reign designed to buttress the waning power of the monarchy: and when to the household origins of the royal foundation are added the probable motives for the king's choice of Cambridge for his protégés, it certainly seems that the fortunes of the university were more closely interwoven with the political tensions and personalities of the reign than has perhaps been formerly realised. In addition, an examination of the events culminating in the apostolic letter of John XXII indicates a causal connection between the inception of the royal Society and Edward II's petition to the pope of which the outcome was the award of 1318. Finally, there remains the consideration that in all probability the university derived greater benefit from the royal institution as a more real and immediate spur to its collegiate expansion than from Peterhouse, the lone foundation of the thirteenth century.

Chapter 2

THE KING'S HALL:
EDUCATIONAL SIGNIFICANCE

THE PLACE OF THE KING'S HALL IN
ENGLISH COLLEGIATE HISTORY

The dangers of overestimating the importance of the colleges in writing the history of the medieval English universities have been properly and sufficiently emphasised.[1] With one or two notable exceptions,[2] the colleges of the pre-Reformation era were small communities of limited financial means and provided, generally speaking, for only a few selected graduate scholars, enabling them to remain at university to acquire the master's degree in arts or degrees in the superior faculties of law, theology, and occasionally medicine.[3] The vast majority of the undergraduates[4] lived wherever they could find accommodation compatible with their resources either in halls or hostels,[5] in taverns, or in the rooms of private houses in the town.

---

[1] See H. E. Salter, *Medieval Oxford, cit.* pp. 95–102, and *idem*, 'The medieval University of Oxford', *History*, XIV (1929), 57 ff.

[2] Merton and New College, Oxford, the King's Hall and later King's College, Cambridge, were designed on an unusually large scale compared with the size of the average English collegiate institution, which commonly had an actual complement of less than a dozen fellows. A. L. Gabriel has estimated that the average number of bursars in a French college of the fourteenth century lay somewhere between six and sixteen, although here he is relying upon statutory figures which cannot always be taken as a reliable guide to the real numbers involved: Gabriel, *The college system*, p. 14. As was the case in England, however, several of the French foundations, among them the College of Navarre (with a statutory complement of 70 students), Du Plessis (with 40), Lisieux and Dormans-Beauvais (with 24 each), were of impressively large dimensions (Gabriel, *loc. cit.*).

[3] See Salter, *Medieval Oxford, loc. cit.*; A. B. Emden, 'Learning and education', in *Medieval England* (2nd ed. by A. L. Poole, 2 vols., Oxford, 1958), II, 528.

[4] Throughout this book the term 'undergraduate' is taken to mean a scholar who has not yet 'determined' as a bachelor.

[5] Academic terminology differed at the English universities. At Oxford, rented premises run by graduate principals for the reception of fee-paying students were designated halls: at Cambridge, they were called hostels. (Emden, *An Oxford hall in medieval times* (Oxford, 1927), pp. 43–5.) For a very useful summary of the main

The place of the medieval English college in relation to the great bulk of the academic populations of Cambridge and Oxford will be more readily apparent when a series of detailed figures is considered.

In the fourteenth century, the statutes of the eight Cambridge colleges provided for a total of 137 fellowships distributed as follows: Peterhouse 14;[1] Michaelhouse 6;[2] the King's Hall 32;[3] Clare 19;[4] Pembroke 24;[5] Gonville 20;[6] Trinity Hall 20;[7] and Corpus Christi 2.[8] Apart from the King's Hall, Michaelhouse, Corpus Christi and possibly Peterhouse, however, these statutory computations bear little resemblance to the actual numbers of fellows supported. The number of fellows at Clare probably never exceeded 13;[9] the usual number at Gonville appears to have been about 4,[10] and at Trinity Hall it was about the same or even occasionally less;[11] and in the mid-fourteenth century, Pembroke had only about 6 fellows, increasing to about 9 at the beginning of the fifteenth century.[12] These actual numbers, added to the fairly reliable statutory figures for the King's Hall, Michaelhouse, Corpus Christi and Peterhouse, produce the revised and far more accurate total of about 80 fellowships furnished by the Cambridge colleges in the fourteenth century. This is higher than the corresponding number of fellowships provided by the Oxford colleges in the period before 1379. It has been reckoned that before the number of fellowship places was doubled with the founding of New College in that year, the six secular colleges[13] together supplied a total of only 63 fellows.[14] Although the problem of res-

features of the halls see Salter, *art. cit.* p. 59; for the Cambridge hostels see H. P. Stokes, 'The mediaeval hostels of the University of Cambridge', *C.A.S.*, *art. cit.*

[1] *Camb. Docs.* II, 19–20.

[2] See the statutes of Michaelhouse printed by Stamp, *Michaelhouse, cit.* p. 41; also Mullinger, *The University of Cambridge*, I, 640–1.

[3] See the statutes of the King's Hall printed by Rouse Ball, *The King's Scholars and King's Hall*, p. 64.

[4] *Camb. Docs.* II, 129.   [5] *Ibid.* II, 193.

[6] P. Grierson, 'Gonville and Caius College', *V.C.H.* (Cambridge), III, 357.

[7] *Camb. Docs.* II, 417–18.

[8] J. P. T. Bury, 'Corpus Christi College', *V.C.H.* (Cambridge), III, 372.

[9] See the remarks of W. J. Harrison, 'Clare College', *ibid.* III, 342.

[10] Grierson, *V.C.H.* (Cambridge), III, 357.

[11] See the details given by C. W. Crawley, 'Trinity Hall', *ibid.* III, 363.

[12] A. Attwater, *Pembroke College, Cambridge* (ed. with an introduction and postscript by S. C. Roberts, Cambridge, 1931), p. 15.

[13] Merton, University College, Balliol, Exeter, Oriel and Queen's.

[14] Salter, *Medieval Oxford*, p. 97.

ident numbers at the medieval English universities is one to which no wholly satisfactory answer may ever be given, it is abundantly clear from these figures that college personnel must have comprised only a fractionally small proportion of the total academic population. Considering that Oxford was the larger university in the fourteenth century[1] and that the Cambridge colleges provided a superior number of endowed fellowships, it follows that the ratio of college fellows to the university population must have been greater at Cambridge than at Oxford. It would therefore seem valid to conclude that before 1379 the Cambridge colleges occupied a slightly more prominent place within the *studium* than did their Oxford counterparts.

On the basis of the statutory computations, it would appear that the King's Hall accounted for just over a fifth of the total number of fellowships supplied by the Cambridge colleges in the fourteenth century.[2] But the actual proportion as evidenced by the second set of figures is almost double that of this misleading statutory estimate. As these figures can be taken as being reasonably accurate, we may confidently affirm that the King's Hall provided about 40 per cent of all the Cambridge college fellowships of the fourteenth century.[3] This is a very high percentage output of fellows for a single college and is paralleled only by the performance of Merton College, Oxford. Since Merton made provision for 30 or more out of a total of about 63 fellowships before 1379,[4] it is apparent that both the King's Hall and Merton each supplied just under half of the fellowships of their respective universities. From this, it is evident that the King's Hall was by far the largest and most important of the Cambridge colleges for well over a hundred years until its position within the *studium* began to be challenged by King's College in the second half of the fifteenth century.[5] Indeed, it has not been generally appreciated that prior to the foundation of New College, Oxford, the King's Hall shared with Merton the distinction of being the largest

[1] See above, p. 28, n. 3.
[2] The King's Hall supplied the statutory number of 32 out of a total statutory number of 137 fellowships.
[3] This percentage is derived from the fact that the King's Hall supplied 32 or more out of an actual total of about 80 fellowships.
[4] Salter, *Medieval Oxford*, p. 97.
[5] Founded 1441.

and most celebrated of all the English colleges.[1] Whereas Merton's reputation derived originally from its antiquity and position as the prototype of the 'graduate' college of the pre-Reformation era and was sustained by a steady output of prominent schoolmen, the King's Hall was marked out by its household origins, its royal status and size and, above all, by its special relationship to the king and the court.[2]

It is generally assumed that the establishment of New College, Oxford, by William of Wykeham in 1379 was something of a landmark or decisive turning point in English collegiate history. It is frequently argued that in several respects this academic project was a striking innovation. This is undoubtedly true regarding the scale of the foundation, for, both in the number of its fellowships[3] and in the magnificence and layout of its buildings,[4] the college superseded all earlier foundations. But it is further claimed for this institution that 'in its educational programme it started a new era'.[5] Evidence which has come to light for the King's Hall, however, indicates that a revision of this firmly held claim is necessary and signifies that there is much need for a historical reappraisal of this whole subject of collegiate educational development at the English universities in the middle ages.

The claims which have been advanced for William of Wykeham's Oxford college embody several highly important educational features, each of which has to be considered in turn. The first of these

---

[1] The very high regard in which the King's Hall was held in university circles in the medieval period (and after) is well brought out in Richard Parker's *History and antiquities of the University of Cambridge*, completed in 1622. Here, it is recorded that in the King's Hall there were elderly fellows so noted for their gravity and wisdom that the college was looked upon as the *oracle* of the university: 'In hac Aula Socii aetate provectiores commorabantur, tanta gravitate, tantoque consilio pollentes, ut Collegium hoc, quasi Universitatis Oraculum, tunc temporis haberetur.' (See the Latin text first published by T. Hearne in his edition of J. Leland, *Collectanea*, v (Oxford, 1715), 185 ff. at p. 244; for translation see Parker, *History of the University of Cambridge, cit.* p. 139; reproduced by E. Carter, *The history of the University of Cambridge* (London, 1753), p. 307.) As Parker, himself a fellow of Caius, was writing less than eighty years after the dissolution of the college, one may reasonably assume that his comments would embody something of the contemporary reputation enjoyed by the King's Hall within the medieval university.

[2] See chapter 1.

[3] New College was designed for a warden and 70 scholars: *Statutes*, I, ch. (5), 2.

[4] A. H. Smith, *New College, Oxford and its buildings* (Oxford, 1952).

[5] A. H. M. Jones, 'New College', *V.C.H.* (Oxford), III, 154.

concerns the relationship forged between New College, Oxford, and Wykeham's complementary institution, Winchester College. Wykeham's idea was that Winchester should serve his college at Oxford as a 'feeder' school in which young boys would be given a sound grammar education before proceeding to New College to embark upon the arts course at the university.[1] It is upon such a nexus that Wykeham's reputation as an educational innovator primarily rests.[2] In this connection, it has been recognised that previous foundations such as Merton and Queen's College, Oxford, had made a very limited provision for the instruction of a handful of poor youths in the rudiments of grammar; but these boys had either lived in the college itself or been boarded out in the town and in no wise formed a separate educational establishment.[3] For this reason, it is frequently asserted that Wykeham's most important innovation was that he 'made his school a separate and distinct foundation independent of though connected with the Oxford College'.[4] On the strength of this, the conclusion is usually drawn that Wykeham was the first English college founder to make permanent provision for a sizable undergraduate element which was also to form a wholly integral part of the collegiate institution.[5]

If these assumptions were entirely correct, one might truly assert that New College, Oxford, and its separate though complementary grammar school together constituted a radical departure in the sphere of English collegiate history. For, so the argument runs, prior to Wykeham's twin foundations, the English colleges had developed along the lines formulated by Walter de Merton in the second half of the thirteenth century. It has been admitted that differences are to be found in points of detail and that some codes of college statutes,

---

[1] See e.g. Jones, *loc. cit.* 154–5.
[2] *Ibid.*; also H. Rashdall and R. S. Rait, *New College* (London, 1901), pp. 25–6; A. F. Leach, *A history of Winchester College*, pp. 89–90; G. R. Potter, 'Education in the fourteenth and fifteenth centuries', *Cambridge Medieval History*, VIII (ed. by C. W. Previté-Orton and Z. N. Brooke, 1936), 688 ff. at p. 693: 'The ideal relation of school and university in the fourteenth century was that planned by William of Wykeham'; C. P. McMahon, *Education in fifteenth century England* (reprinted from *The Johns Hopkins University Studies in Education*, no. 35, Baltimore, 1947), p. 28, and J. Simon, *Education and Society in Tudor England* (Cambridge, 1966), p. 42.
[3] On this topic see Leach, *The schools of medieval England* (London, 1915), especially pp. 171 ff.; also below, pp. 50–3.
[4] Leach, *op. cit.* p. 205.   [5] See e.g. A. H. Smith, *op. cit.* p. 16.

notably those of Queen's, Oxford, and of Peterhouse and Michael-house, Cambridge, evinced original features which owed nothing at all to the Merton pattern;[1] but it has nevertheless been widely accepted as an established fact that none of the collegiate institutions founded before 1379 was designed for the regular reception of undergraduates. Accordingly, they have been lumped together and classified as 'graduate' societies in the Mertonian sense.[2] This common interpretation has enabled recent commentators to assign to New College, Oxford, a central pivotal position in the evolution of the English medieval college.[3] It has been rightly stressed[4] that a university society organised solely on Mertonian lines led to a divorce between the senior graduate members domiciled in the colleges and the great sprawling mass of the student population, living a separate existence in hostels, inns or private lodgings. Consequently, it has been claimed that if the English university was moving in this direction 'it was powerfully and finally deflected by the design of William of Wykeham's foundation'.[5] In other words, New College, Oxford, has been regarded as the 'catalyst' by which the Mertonian collegiate tradition was 'deflected' into those channels which produced the 'mixed' or consciously balanced societies of the sixteenth century. To express it another way, New College has been singled out as the original pattern of the kind of academic collegiate society which has characterised the post-Reformation age: that is to say, a mixed society in which undergraduates studying for a first arts degree shared a life in common with the graduate members of the community, who were themselves preparing for higher degrees or who were already doctors in the different faculties.

The high claims which have been made for New College, Oxford, afford an example of the somewhat narrow kind of approach which has tended to pervade some branches of English academic history. An objective examination of the entire field of English collegiate development would, however, render these claims open to serious doubt. Apart from everything else, it would seem rather unrealistic

---

[1] See the corrective footnotes to Rashdall's commentary on the English colleges in Rashdall, *op. cit.* III, 169 ff.

[2] See the general arguments of Salter, Jones, Smith, Leach and Rashdall in the works cited.

[3] See e.g. Smith, *op. cit.*, especially pp. 16 ff.

[4] *Ibid.*   [5] *Ibid.*

to attribute to one institution alone what was effected over a long span of time and was, in any case, largely due to the operation of impersonal economic and social forces of change. Moreover, with the undoubted exception of Wykeham's salaried tutorial system, those essential educational features which have come to be associated with New College and generally recognised as innovatory would seem to have been fully anticipated at the King's Hall earlier in the fourteenth century.

The piecemeal transference of the undergraduate population of the halls and hostels to the 'graduate' colleges was a movement which, largely completed by the Reformation, would presumably have taken place even if New College had never been. This is not the place to enter into a full-scale investigation of this subject, but for the sake of perspective it will be necessary to give a general indication of how this academic migration came about.

The main disadvantage of the halls or hostels[1] was that they were unendowed societies with no security of tenure beyond the year for which the premises had been leased. Consequently, they were potentially unstable institutions, a situation worsened by an unedifying mercenary competition between their graduate principals for the custom of the fee-paying undergraduate population. From the university standpoint, therefore, the halls or hostels proved quite unequal to the task of solving the problem of the extension of university discipline over its younger and more unruly members. Moreover, lacking the resources with which the colleges were able to erect their increasingly imposing buildings in the later middle ages, these insecure institutions had, by the late fifteenth and sixteenth centuries, come to be eclipsed or dwarfed by comparison. When the colleges began to open their doors to fee-paying undergraduates, the position of the halls or hostels became acutely embarrassing and they began to disappear from the university scene. The pressures acting upon the colleges to admit undergraduates or commoners were mostly economic. Inflation in the late fifteenth and sixteenth centuries meant for the colleges, whose revenues derived in the main from fixed

---

[1] For this paragraph I am indebted to H. E. Salter and A. B. Emden, whose researches have thrown much light upon the reasons behind the gradual infiltration of undergraduates into the colleges. See, conveniently, Emden, *An Oxford hall in medieval times*, *cit*. introductory.

rents, finding alternative ways of augmenting their incomes. Obviously, one such method was to open up their exclusive societies to fee-paying undergraduates. An internal pressure, however, was the increasingly strong desire on the part of college fellows to supplement their incomes with tutoring fees: and when the necessary regency system fell into decay at the university schools, the colleges were able to attract a steady stream of undergraduates on the strength of the tutorial advantages which they could now offer.

It would therefore seem that the mixed type of collegiate society would have emerged and become a permanent feature of the English universities even without the important stimulus of Wykeham's foundations: New College appears to have been an excellent though inessential prototype, an early foretaste of a later natural development. The available evidence compels us to view the King's Hall, Cambridge, as the original pattern of English collegiate organisation as it was to evolve throughout the subsequent ages.

It has not yet been properly appreciated that the King's Hall was the first English college of either university to make regular provision for the admission of undergraduates.[1] Before investigating this point, however, it is necessary to examine the position of grammar education in the English colleges of the fourteenth century.[2] As already mentioned, several of the 'Oxbridge' colleges did indeed make a limited provision for the grammatical instruction of a handful of poor boys, who lived either within the college or were housed in the town. In this connection, there are a number of highly relevant features to consider. There was evidently a general idea current among college founders that some kind of arrangement ought to be made for grammar teaching in collegiate establishments. But this appears to have been a very subsidiary aim and if the various codes of college statutes are compared one is left in no doubt as to where the priorities lay. The overall impression derived is that the

[1] The claims of De Vaux College, Salisbury, in this direction cannot be disregarded. While the nascent University of Salisbury, which had almost emerged into a fully fledged *studium generale*, had disappeared by the early fourteenth century, the college remained and, perhaps from the start but certainly later, made continuous provision for the admission of undergraduate fellows studying in arts (K. Edwards, 'College of de Vaux Salisbury', *V.C.H.* (Wiltshire) III, especially pp. 372, 383).

[2] The following general conclusions are derived from a detailed study of all the fourteenth-century codes of English college statutes.

provisions concerning the instruction of poor youths were often tagged on as a sort of afterthought or as a conventional sop to charity: for it is always stressed that these 'grammar' clauses were to come into effect only if and when the funds of the particular college would permit. And so, generally speaking, this grammar element, as we may loosely call it, was firmly sacrificed to the needs of the graduate members of the college. For example, the Peterhouse statutes enact that, only if the finances of the institution will allow, provision is to be made for two or three indigent grammar scholars to live on the charity of the foundation. If they were to make good progress, they might be promoted to scholarships; if not, they were to be ejected from the college.[1] In much the same way, Walter de Merton made arrangements for the instruction of a number of *parvuli*, needy and orphan children of the founder's kin (*de parentela*); provided that the revenues of the college would suffice, they were to receive instruction in the elements of learning and the most promising of them were to be promoted to the status of scholar.[2] Similarly, the statutes of 1359 for Clare College, Cambridge, allow for the maintenance of ten poor boys from the parishes where the society held appropriated churches: they were to live apart from the other members of the college and were to be instructed in singing, grammar and dialectic until the age of twenty, after which they were to be either removed or advanced to scholarships.[3]

These representative examples reveal that, even at an optimistic statutory level, grammatical instruction for poor youths was to be supported only if the finances of the society were deemed adequate for this very secondary purpose; and, moreover, it is clear that these groups or 'colonies' of grammar boys did not constitute a really integral part of the college but remained outside the society after the manner of charitable appendages.[4] Since the majority of the English

---

[1] *Camb. Docs.* II, 24–6; see also the remarks of T. A. Walker, *Peterhouse* (College Histories Series, London, 1906), pp. 52–3.

[2] *Statutes*, I, ch. (2), 5 ff. at p. 6 (code of 1264). The provision is repeated in the code of 1270, where the maximum number of *parvuli* is given as both 13 and 15: *ibid.* p. 17. It is again inserted in the code of 1274, where the maximum is given as 13: *ibid.* p. 36. See also the remarks of H. W. Garrod, 'Merton College', *V.C.H.* (Oxford), III, 103.

[3] *Camb. Docs.* II, 140–1.

[4] H. W. Garrod has argued that in the case of Merton the 'pueri de genere Fundatoris' formed 'an integral part of the Domus' and that they were, 'in fact, under-

colleges could not find the resources to support even the full statutory complements of fellows, then, given the financial priorities, it is extremely likely that the size of these 'grammar schools' must have been exceedingly small and in some instances the provisions of the statutes largely inoperative.[1] There is just a possibility that before the foundation of the King's Hall two of the Oxford colleges had maintained a few undergraduate members as distinct from these charity grammar boys. Dervorguilla's statutes for Balliol of 1282 imply

graduates'. (See Garrod, *op. cit.* III, 103.) But this can hardly be so. Admittedly, there is ambiguity in the Merton statutes. The code of 1270 draws a distinction between scholars who had 'determined' as bachelors of arts and, by implication, those who had not. For the latter a lower rate of allowance is prescribed (40s per annum instead of the usual 50s): *Statutes*, I, ch. (2), 11. But the statutes of 1274 prescribe only one rate and nowhere is there mention of scholars who have not 'determined': *ibid.* I, ch. (2), 24. It would therefore seem that Walter de Merton had at one stage entertained the idea of the reception of a limited number of undergraduates but that this scheme was later shelved. For clearly, by 1274, no one below the status of bachelor was eligible for election to the college. Entering upon this controversy, H. E. Salter has expressed the view that 'from the beginning the interpretation of the statutes has been that none were eligible to the college except those who had attained the degree of Bachelor of Arts. On one occasion in our Register [Register of Merton College, 1483–1521] three were selected who were still undergraduates but they were not elected to the college until they had determined i.e. had become Bachelors': Salter, ed., *Registrum Annalium Collegii Mertonensis, 1483–1521* (Oxf. Hist. Soc., LXXVI, 1923), ix. The *pueri* or *parvuli* of the founder's kin were evidently young boys who were the special responsibility of the warden and lived in a separate hospice near the college where instruction was given in grammar (J. R. L. Highfield, *The early rolls of Merton College, Oxford* (Oxf. Hist. Soc., new series, XVIII (1964), 72)). Thus, they remained outside the college in the sense that they could not be elected scholars until they had 'determined' as bachelors and could not then be fairly described as forming an integral part of the collegiate society. The same considerations apply to Merton's *scolares in villa* and to Wylyot's portionists (Highfield, *op. cit.* pp. 72–4). These arguments are equally relevant for the *pueri* of Clare and for all such 'grammar colonies' to be found in English medieval colleges.

[1] The extreme case is that of Queen's, Oxford, where Eglesfield's statutes provided for the maintenance of poor boys up to the number of 70: *Statutes*, I, ch. (4), 30. In actual fact '...the poor boys rarely numbered more than one or two in the Middle Ages and three or four in the sixteenth century' (R. H. Hodgkin, 'The Queen's College', *V.C.H.* (Oxford), III, 132). The system of supporting poor students (*beneficiarii*) in separate accommodation outside the college appears to have been far more widespread in France than in England. No co-ordinated study of the *beneficiarii* has yet been made, but it seems probable that this charitable practice was initiated at the college of the Sorbonne and subsequently adopted by several of the fourteenth-century Paris collegiate foundations. For details, see A. L. Gabriel, *Student life in Ave Maria College, mediaeval Paris* (Publications in mediaeval studies, XIV, Indiana, 1955), pp. 110–11.

(though they do not state) that youths who had not yet taken a bachelor's degree in arts might be admitted to study for the master's degree.[1] Similarly, Walter de Stapledon's statutes for Exeter College made specific provision for the reception of sophists or undergraduates of two years' standing.[2] But as the total statutory complement was only thirteen and the sophist qualification for entry a minimum one, the number of undergraduates could not have been much more than one or two at any given time. Exeter was thus primarily a graduate society which might, on occasion, afford entrance to advanced undergraduates on the point of 'determining' as bachelors. An investigation of the changing composition of the Society of the King's Scholars, however, reveals that it made regular provision from the start for a steady intake of undergraduates in the strictest sense of the term:[3] consequently, the King's Hall appears to have been the first English college to possess a sizable undergraduate element which, at the same time, formed an integral part of the collegiate institution.

The period 1317 to 1450 is the most relevant one to consider for an examination of the constituent parts of this royal Society. This is so because it precedes that general migratory movement of undergraduate infiltration into the colleges set in motion in the latter half of the fifteenth century. Hence, the known presence of undergraduates in a college prior to this movement will have a peculiar significance for English academic history. It will here also be necessary to analyse the graduate composition of the college: this will enable us to establish that the King's Hall was a completely mixed type of collegiate society and will show that, as time went on, the undergraduate element came to be overshadowed by a steady increase in graduate members. Having presented this evidence of academic stratification, we may then revert to a more particular investigation of

---

[1] *Statutes*, I, v–vii; *Oxford Balliol Deeds* (ed. H. E. Salter, Oxf. Hist. Soc., LXIV, 1913), 277–9; see also the discussion by H. W. C. Davis, *A history of Balliol College*, cit. ch. I; see further Rashdall, III, 182, n. I.

[2] Concerning the election of the thirteen scholars: 'dum tamen eligendi sint sufficientes sophiste ad minus et de Dyocesi Exonie oriundi'. See Stapledon's statutes (1316) printed in *The Statutes of Exeter College, Oxford* (ed. by the Queen's Commissioners, London, 1855), p. 5.

[3] That is to say, youths who, upon admission to the college, had already attained the required proficiency in the rudiments of grammar and were deemed fit to embark upon the arts course.

the undergraduate constituent, an examination which will inevitably involve us in a discussion of the grammar school of the chapel royal.

Originally, the Society of the King's Scholars was wholly undergraduate in composition, being made up entirely of young boys sent from the chapel royal to be educated in the schools at Cambridge.[1] As the Society advanced towards greater maturity, however, its purely undergraduate character was broken down by the introduction of a number of graduate elements. Although information concerning the Scholars' degrees for the period 1317 to 1337 leaves much to be desired, there is sufficient to prove that by 1330 or later a handful of the Scholars had attained the status of at least M.A. either upon first entry or shortly afterwards; but in the same period there is evidence of only one Scholar having taken a law degree.[2]

The graduate element continued to increase steadily throughout the fourteenth century. Between 1337 and 1350, sixteen more Scholars are known to have acquired the status of *magister* either upon admission or in subsequent years and one of these was also a bachelor in civil law by 1350. But before the mid-fourteenth century, there was apparently only a sprinkling of law degrees and the general level of attainment appears to have been the M.A., although it is certainly conceivable that some degrees in the superior faculties are disguised among the *magistri*.[3] The undergraduate intake continued seemingly undiminished and it is abundantly clear that by 1350 the King's Hall had a thoroughly mixed type of society, with undergraduates sharing a life in common with senior graduate members of the college.

The most striking feature about the constituent proportions of the Society in the second half of the fourteenth century was the marked increase in the number of fellows who acquired degrees in civil or in canon law. Of the 172 King's Scholars who entered the Society between 1350 and 1400, 51 or about 30 per cent are known to have taken a second degree distributed as follows: M.A.: 22; D.C.L.: 1; Lic.C.L.: 3; B.C.L.: 18; Sch.C.L.: 1; Lic.Cn.L.: 1; B.Cn.L.: 3;

---

[1] See above, p. 9, n. 2.

[2] Richard de Wymundeswold, admitted 18 August 1329; D.C.L. in 1338.

[3] Where reliance has to be placed upon the term *magister* as evidence for a scholar's degree, it is fully realised that, in addition to M.A., this might well designate a doctoral or even a bachelor's degree in one of the superior faculties (Emden, *B.R.U.O.* I, xv).

Sch.Cn.L.: 2. These figures mean that about 58 per cent of all the second degrees taken in this period were law degrees and that the ratio of civil to canon law degrees was in the region of 4:1. From the mid-fourteenth century onwards, this emphasis upon civil law continues to grow and the whole shape and character of the Society undergo a transformation. Of the 127 fellows who entered the college between 1400 and 1450, 57 or about 45 per cent are now recorded as having taken a second degree. This breaks down as follows: M.A.: 25; D.C.L.: 3; B.C.L.: 22; B.Cn.L.: 4; D.Th.: 1; B.Th.: 2. From this, it can be calculated that about 51 per cent of all entrants in the first half of the fifteenth century known to have taken second degrees did so in civil or canon law and that now the ratio of civil to canon law degrees has increased to about 6:1. This growing concentration upon the attainment of degrees in the faculty of law, and especially in civil law,[1] provides a vital clue to the direction in which the Society was moving in the late fourteenth and fifteenth centuries.

An examination of the King's Hall accounts shows that a considerable proportion of the senior graduate members of the college were continually absent, making only brief returns at the festival periods of the ecclesiastical year. In the 1380s and 1390s this number did not exceed seven and is more usually in the region of three to five.[2] From 1400–1 to 1414–15, however, the average number of non-residents rose to between five and seven and from 1415–16 to 1443–4 it lay within the range of eight to thirteen, which, out of a complement of thirty-two, gives a proportion of between a quarter and just less than a half. It should perhaps here be stressed that in the medieval period legitimate non-residence was not normally regarded as a violation of the fellowship principle. Fellowships were looked upon rather in the nature of secular benefices having a dual function to perform within the community. First, they provided the means of financial support to enable the abler type of student to continue his academic career after the completion of the bachelor's degree; and, secondly, they furnished a kind of base for the senior members of the universities whose wider activities in the

---

[1] The significance of civil law studies at the King's Hall is discussed below, pp. 255 ff.

[2] For these and the subsequent figures see table 5 (pullout), column 4. The average number of non-resident fellows is calculated by subtracting the average number of fellows present per week in each year from the total statutory complement of 32.

ecclesiastical and secular spheres necessitated long absences for the greater part of the year. And it certainly seems that from the late fourteenth century onwards the King's Hall increasingly served the purpose of an academic launching-ground for graduates whose talents could be utilised in the service of the realm.[1]

The natural concomitant of this shift within the Society towards the graduate element was the reduction in the intake of undergraduate personnel. This development, however, must not be antedated. In the period between 1382 and 1417, for example, at least nineteen children and clerks of undergraduate status were freshly recruited from the chapel royal. Furthermore, it must be emphasised that there was always present a fair admixture of that older type of King's Scholar who, throughout the entirety of his residence in the Hall, appears never to have taken a degree at all. Admittedly, a proportion of Scholars of this category remained for only a short duration: some died soon after entry and others resigned their fellowships after the briefest of sojourns. But there are several recorded instances of King's Scholars who remained for periods of more than twenty, thirty, forty and even fifty years without attaining an academic distinction of any kind. For example, Robert (or Hugh) Lincoln resided in the college from 9 October 1382 till his death on 17 December 1440 without acquiring a degree;[2] and John Morley, a fellow from 7 November 1425 until 1450, was still without a degree in 1444.[3] Similarly, at least two of the Scholars recruited from the chapel royal, William Lake[4] and John Fissher,[5] resided in the Hall for twenty and fifteen years respectively and did not attain degrees. More examples of this type of Scholar could be cited, but enough have here been given to indicate that there was apparently no limitation at the King's Hall, as there was in some colleges,[6] to the number of years for which a fellowship might be retained. Nor does

[1] See chapter 7.
[2] Lincoln had not acquired even a bachelor's degree when his name and academic status appeared in the exchequer list for the distribution of gowns of 1439 (P.R.O. E101/409/6).
[3] Morley did not possess a bachelor's degree at the time of the compilation of the exchequer list for gowns of 12 January 1444 (P.R.O. E101/409/12).
[4] Admitted 26 April 1412; vacated 7 March 1432.
[5] Admitted 3 December 1417; vacated 7 July 1432.
[6] At Exeter College, for example, scholars were required to vacate their fellowships after 14 years (R. W. Southern, 'Exeter College', *V.C.H.* (Oxford), III, 108).

there seem to have been a minimum academic qualification required for the continuing tenure of a fellowship as had been clearly fore-shadowed in the terms of reference of the commission of inquiry set up by Edward III preparatory to the foundation of the King's Hall.[1] Why Scholars were permitted to remain for such lengthy periods without making even modest academic progress or participating in the administrative life of the college[2] is a question to which no ready answer can be found.

For the sake of completeness, it is convenient to point out at this juncture that in the first half of the fifteenth century there was a re-duction in the intake not only of undergraduate personnel but of Scholars of all types: in other words, the Society was visibly shrink-ing. This is borne out graphically by the salient fact that whereas 172 Scholars were admitted between 1350 and 1400, only 127 entered the college from 1400 to 1450. The explanation is at least to be partially sought in a general lengthening in the average period of tenure of fellowships, thereby causing a marked reduction in the number of vacancies. A few detailed figures will illustrate the point. Of the 472 Scholars admitted between 1317 and 1450, 53 are known to have held their fellowships for periods ranging from twenty to more than fifty years. These divide up as follows: 35 retained fellowships for periods extending from 20 to 29 years inclusive; 10 for periods ranging from 30 to 39 years; 3 for periods of from 40 to 49 years; and 5 for periods of from 50 to 58 years. When these long-tenured fellow-ships are arranged chronologically, the pattern which emerges re-veals a significant lengthening in tenure between 1350 and 1450: this stands out in sharp contrast to the relatively short tenures of the first half of the fourteenth century.

TABLE I

	Period	No. of Fellowships held for 20 years or more
(1)	1317–1337	8
(2)	1337–1350	?
(3)	1350–1400	22
(4)	1400–1450	23

[1] See above, pp. 14–15.
[2] None of the fellows cited gave service as a seneschal.

The retention of long-tenured fellowships continued to be an outstanding feature of the Society until its dissolution in the mid-sixteenth century. Of the 245 Scholars admitted between 1451 and 1543 (no accounts survive after this date), 36 retained fellowships for more than 20 years, 15 of them for periods of from 30 to 39 years. In order to keep the data within a manageable compass, details concerning long-tenured fellowships alone have here been submitted. But an analysis of all fellowships held by King's Scholars throughout the entire history of the Society shows a similar progressive lengthening in the case of the shorter tenures as well. From this investigation of fellowship tenures, it seems reasonable to conclude that the Society of the King's Scholars became progressively more constricted and static in form compared with its expanding and freer-moving nature characteristic of the earlier part of the fourteenth century.

The foregoing analysis of the shifting balance maintained between the constituent elements of the Society shows that we are here examining a thoroughly mixed type of collegiate institution. Though the 'mixture' was different at different times, the essential point is that the King's Hall brought together under one roof an association of university scholars sharing a life in common and all engaged in study at their own particular levels. Thus, the striking novelty of this foundation was that for the first time in English history a collegiate society had been established which made provision for a scholar to pass through the whole educational gamut within the walls of the same institution: that is to say, a student might enter this royal foundation at the age of fourteen,[1] trained only in the rudiments of grammar, and emerge about twenty years later as a doctor in one of the higher faculties. It will be recalled that these self-same features concerning the mixed society and the provision of a full educational coverage from undergraduate to doctoral level have been formerly classified as innovations exclusively associated with New College, Oxford: but clearly, they had in every essential respect been fully anticipated on an impressively large scale at the King's Hall, Cambridge.

The minimum age limit of fourteen mentioned above was written into the King's Hall statutes of 1380. These were not the original

[1] See below, p. 59.

statutes and most of the provisions are retrospective in character, merely embodying the practices which had grown up within the Society since its foundation.[1] The entry states that before a new Scholar may be admitted to the college, he must be at least fourteen years of age and sufficiently well versed in the rules of grammar to enable him to begin study in the arts course or in any other faculty to which the warden, after examination, may decide to assign him:

'Et quod admittendus de cetero...aetatis quatuordecim annorum vel ultra...quodque talis admittendus in regulis grammaticalibus ita sufficienter sit instructus quod congrue in arte dialectica studere poterit seu in aliqua alia facultate ad quam prefatus Custos post examinationem et admissionem eius duxerit illum deputandum.'[2]

This appears to be the earliest information available for a college limitation upon age anywhere in England. As this particular statutory limit was designed primarily with the reception of undergraduates in mind,[3] the King's Hall entrance age must have been about four or five years lower than the minimum age of entry at most collegiate establishments. Although the youngest boys came up to university at fourteen or fifteen,[4] a considerable proportion of them did not immediately begin study in the arts course proper but were at first engaged in mastering the rudiments of grammar; and some had come not to take a degree at all but merely to receive an elementary business training.[5] For these reasons, it has been convincingly argued that 'it is unlikely that any student would be able to take his B.A. before he was nineteen and a half: seventeen, or at the earliest sixteen and a half, must have been the age when many began their studies in the Faculty of Arts'.[6] It is therefore apparent

---

[1] The statutes are discussed below, pp. 174 ff.

[2] See the statutes of the King's Hall printed by Rouse Ball, *op. cit.* p. 67. The warden's supervision of the studies of the younger Scholars of the King's Hall was akin to the practice prevalent in the Paris colleges where the master assumed direct responsibility for the guidance of the academic careers of the youthful members of the community. (See e.g. Gabriel, *Student life in Ave Maria College, cit.* p. 100; also the statutes of the Ave Maria College, nos. 11, 101, *ibid.* pp. 325, 356–7.)

[3] See above, p. 43, n. 4. For exceptions to the general type of undergraduate recruits received at the King's Hall see below, pp. 186–7.   [4] Salter, *art. cit.* p. 59.

[5] See the cautionary discussion on the age of medieval university undergraduates by E. F. Jacob, 'English university clerks in the later middle ages: the problem of maintenance', *B.J.R.L.* XXIX (1946), 308–9.   [6] *Ibid.* p. 308.

that the usual minimum entrance age for the majority of the 'graduate' colleges would have been about nineteen or twenty. Even at New College, the youngest undergraduates were not admitted until they had completed their fifteenth year[1] and were consequently almost two years older than the youngest undergraduates received as fully incorporated fellows at the King's Hall.

The stress laid by Wykeham upon a sound grammar education as a necessary preliminary to entry at his Oxford college had received an equal emphasis in the statutes of the King's Hall. Although there are one or two instances of very young boys from the chapel royal being permitted to enter the Society without having full qualifications in the rudiments of grammar,[2] nevertheless, as in the case of the young Wykehamists, the general arrangement was that this part of their elementary education should be wholly completed before admission to the college: and this circumstance leads us into a consideration of the kind of educational nexus which existed between the chapel royal and Cambridge's first royal foundation.

It is not perhaps generally well known that the English chapel royal incorporated what can best be described as a sort of independent grammar school. The chapel children were first of all given a basic grounding in plainsong, the organ, and the principles governing correct social behaviour by a master of song who was a member of the chapel and appointed by the dean.[3] After they were deemed to

---

[1] See the statutes of New College in *Statutes*, I, ch. (5), 7: 'statuentes...quod nullus qui vicesimum aetatis sue annum excedit nec aliquis qui quintumdecimum aetatis sue annum non compleverit in dictum nostrum collegium Oxonie eligatur nec etiam assumatur...'

[2] E.g. Richard Lunteleye to be admitted 'non obstant que le dit Richard nest pas suffissantement enformez en gramer' (writ of privy seal of 10 July 1385: P.R.O. E101/348/16); see also writ of privy seal of 3 December 1417 whereby John Fissher, one of the chapel children, is to be admitted, 'ce quil nest nye uncore pleinement enformez en son gramer non obstant' (P.R.O. E101/348/30); see further writs for the admission of John Newman and Thomas Pynchebek of 18 November 1413 and 27 June 1416 (P.R.O. E101/348/28, 29).

[3] See the entry under the heading, *Children of Chapell, VIIJ*, in the Black Book of the household of Edward IV in Myers, *The household of Edward IV, cit.* p. 136: 'Wich maister (of song) is apoynted by the seyd dean and chosen one of the numbyr of the seyd felyshipp of chapell; and he to draw thees chyldren all as well in the scoole of facet [from the book *Facetus de Moribus* used in schools as a book of instruction in behaviour, Myers, p. 273] as in song, organes, or suche other vertuouse thinges'; see also Ullmann, ed., *Liber regie capelle, cit.* p. 57: 'Unus etiam magister cantus ad docendum et instruendum debite in cantu plano et organico pueros antedictos.'

be old enough and had acquired a proficiency in descant, the choristers were then qualified to graduate to the household school run by
a master of grammar who was himself a member of the chapel and,
if a priest, had a number of specified devotional duties to perform.[1]
Both the fifteenth-century *Liber regie capelle* and the Black Book of
Edward IV indicate a loosely organised household grammar school
of fluid and diversified composition which, though seemingly a constituent part of the chapel, was quite clearly open to all the boys of
noble birth brought up in the court, to the king's squires and pages
(*henxmen*), the clerks of the almonry and all other resident members of the household who had a mind to utilise these educational
facilities.[2] Since the master of grammar was immediately subject to
decanal jurisdiction, the school presumably functioned under the
general supervision of the dean of chapel: and as the school formed
a part of the chapel, it may on occasion have been transformed into
an itinerant body accompanying the person of the king in his numerous travels throughout England and abroad. In 1420, for example,
the composer John Pyamour, one of the chapel clerks, was commissioned to impress boy choristers and transport them across the
sea to the king's presence in Normandy, where the chapel had been
since 1417;[3] and in 1520 the composer William Cornysh took
charge of the choristers when the chapel accompanied Henry VIII to
the Field of the Cloth of Gold.[4] Nevertheless, it appears that from
1526 onwards the household school became permanently based at
Westminster, because an ordinance of that year stipulates that only
a small part of the chapel, comprising the master of the children, six
men and several officers of the vestry, should henceforth be required
to be in continual attendance upon the king on his progresses
throughout the country.[5]

[1] Ullmann, *op. cit.* p. 57; Myers, *op. cit.* p. 138.
[2] See Ullmann, *op. cit.* p. 57, under the heading, *Numerus Capelle*: 'Est etiam unus
magister grammatice ad docendum pueros nobiles nutritos in curia Regis et pueros
Capelle cum senuerint, scientiam grammatice,...'; also Myers, pp. 137–8, where a
master of grammar is hired to teach: 'scilicet, the kinges henxmen, the children of
chapell, after they can theyre descant, the clerks of the awmery, and othyr men,
and children of court disposed to lern in this science, if they be of ordinate maistyrs
within this court'.   [3] *Cal. Pat. R.*, 1416–1422, pp. 127, 272.
[4] 'The Eton Choirbook: I' (transcribed and ed. by F. Ll. Harrison), *Musica Britannica*,
x (1956), xviii.
[5] F. Ll. Harrison, *Music in medieval Britain* (London, 1958), pp. 171–2.

The first recorded household grammar master was John Bugby, a chaplain engaged by Henry IV to teach the boys of the chapel and who, incidentally, went without remuneration for his services for three years.[1] In the course of the fifteenth and early sixteenth centuries, a succession of composers were appointed masters of the king's choristers, and these would almost certainly have been masters of song in charge of musical instruction. The *Liber regie capelle* and the Black Book both clearly imply that the chapel offices of master of song and master of grammar were quite distinct and held by different persons. In the puzzling absence of evidence for royal appointments to the position of household master of grammar, it is just conceivable, though perhaps unlikely, that the offices were occasionally in actual practice combined.[2] However this may be, it seems probable that John Pyamour acted as master of the king's choristers during the latter part of the reign of Henry V.[3] This was certainly the case with the composer John Plummer, who, in 1444, 1445 and 1446, was paid a yearly stipend of forty marks for the maintenance and daily instruction of eight chapel boys under his care.[4] The next master of whom there is evidence was Henry Abyndon, the second known recipient of the doctoral degree in music at Cambridge,[5] who was appointed in March 1456 and may have held this post without interruption until September 1478.[6] During the remainder of the century, the position was held by Laurence Squyer,[7] probably an Oxford graduate,[8] and by the composers Gilbert Banaster[9] and William Newerk.[10] The latter was succeeded in 1509 by the celebrated composer, William Cornysh.[11]

There can be no doubt that a considerable proportion of the under-

---

[1] J. H. Wylie, *History of England under Henry the Fourth*, II, 487; Harrison, *op. cit.* p. 22.

[2] Professor Myers has kindly drawn my attention to the fact that since both masters of grammar and masters of song were employed in noble households of the fifteenth century there is a strong likelihood that they would also have been separate officials in the royal household.

[3] See above, p. 61, n. 3.

[4] *Cal. Pat. R.*, 1441–1446, pp. 311, 333, 455.

[5] The first appears to have been Thomas St Just, warden of the King's Hall, D.Mus., admitted 1461–2 (Emden, *B.R.U.C.* p. 503). Abyndon was granted a grace for inception as D.Mus. in 1464: *ibid.* p. 1.

[6] *Cal. Pat. R.*, 1452–1461, p. 279; 1461–1467, p. 457; 1467–1477, p. 243; 1468–1476, p. 154; 1476–1485, p. 133.　　[7] *Ibid.* 1485–1494, p. 138.

[8] Emden, *B.R.U.O.* III, 1748.　　[9] *Cal. Pat. R.*, 1476–1485, p. 133.

[10] *Ibid.* 1485–1494, p. 449.　　[11] Harrison, *op. cit.* p. 23.

graduates who entered the King's Hall in the fourteenth and early fifteenth centuries were the products of this royal grammar school. Apart from the boys and clerks of the chapel royal itself, who were recruited directly from this source, there was, in addition, a substantial intake of undergraduates who were the sons of household and court officials.[1] In view of what the Ordinances have to say on this matter, it is virtually certain that recruits of this latter kind would have acquired their elementary education by attending the grammar lessons in the chapel school. It is now plainly observable that there existed between the King's Hall and the court a type of complementary academic relationship similar in all its essential features to that which operated between Winchester and New College, Oxford: namely, the household grammar school served the King's Hall as a 'feeder' institution in which young boys of noble lineage or with high court connections were given a basic grammatical training before coming up to the college to embark upon the arts course at Cambridge University. Here we have displayed the essence of Wykeham's conception: for although the King's Hall–court nexus never embodied that measure of conscious balance which characterised the Oxford scheme and was never regulated by rigorous statutory control, it nevertheless stands out as the original pattern for the association between a university college and an independent grammar school, albeit of a very special kind. Henry VI may have acknowledged his debt to Wykeham when establishing his twin foundations of Eton and King's College,[2] but there is persuasive evidence for believing that Wykeham, in his turn, found one of his chief sources of inspiration in the King's Hall, Cambridge.

In all the many discussions upon the various institutions which might possibly have influenced Wykeham in the formulation of his academic project,[3] there has up to date been no reference to the

---

[1] For further details see below, pp. 151–2.

[2] Though there are original features, the King's College statutes are largely modelled on those of New College (Rashdall, III, 316–17).

[3] See e.g. A. F. Leach, *A History of Winchester College, cit.* ch. VII, pp. 77 ff. Leach's contention (pp. 86–7) that one of Wykeham's models may have been provided by De Vaux College, Salisbury, with its alleged but now wholly disproven institutional link with Oxford, is clearly without foundation. Of Leach's conclusions K. Edwards asserts that they 'seem to be almost entirely legends' (*V.C.H.* (Wiltshire), III, 372); see also the discussion of Wykeham's possible models by A. W. Parry, *Education in England in the middle ages* (London, 1920), pp. 191–3.

King's Hall. It has been rightly stressed that, in the compilation of his lengthy code of statutes, he borrowed heavily from sections in those of Merton and Queen's College, Oxford.[1] Furthermore, it has been suggested that Wykeham may have been influenced by the scale and magnificence of some of the Paris colleges, especially Navarre, founded by the queen of France in 1304.[2] Surprisingly, however, Wykeham's name has never been linked with Cambridge's fourteenth-century royal foundation.

Preparatory to the execution of his grand design, Wykeham, the enlightened educationalist, is known to have made a detailed study of the statutes and ordinances governing a wide range of collegiate establishments.[3] Even if there were no further evidence to substantiate the point, it is inconceivable that his investigation would not have embraced the King's Hall, one of the two largest colleges in England. There is, however, more concrete information to suggest that Wykeham had a really intimate knowledge of the innermost workings and organisation of this royal Society. As the king alone, as founder, remained the legal visitor to the college,[4] this meant that the visitatorial duty in actual practice devolved upon the office of chancellor.[5] Wykeham held that office between 1367 and 1371[6] and must have been in close contact with the Society in these years. Indeed, in 1368, Wykeham, acting for the king, presented five books on civil law to the college for the special use of Walter de Herford, one of the King's Scholars, an indenture to this effect being drawn up at Westminster between the chancellor and Nicholas Roos, then warden of the King's Hall.[7] Even before he became chancellor, there are entries in the King's Hall accounts which testify to the fact that as keeper of the privy seal Wykeham was sometimes in charge of

---

[1] See the discussion by Leach, *op. cit.* p. 205.   [2] *Loc. cit.*

[3] In the final rubric of his statutes for New College of 1400 he states that he has consulted the ordinances and statutes of numerous institutions and is perturbed that they are so little observed: *Statutes*, I, ch. (5), 112–13.   [4] See below, p. 102.

[5] On this point see R. Phillimore, *The ecclesiastical law of the Church of England* (2nd ed. London, 1895), II, 1452.

[6] Wykeham was keeper of the privy seal from 1363 to 1367 and chancellor from 1367 to 1371.

[7] The indenture is in French and half of it has been translated from the entry in the Close Rolls in the P.R.O. and printed by C. E. Sayle, 'King's Hall Library', *C.A.S. Proceedings*, XXIV, old series, no. lxxii (1921–2), p. 56: *Cal. Close R., 1364–1368*, pp. 408–9.

royal business relating to the college. In 1364, for example, there is an entry for expenses incurred by warden Roos in journeying to London and Windsor at the request of the queen and William of Wykeham to transact business concerning the church of Fakenham;[1] and, in the same year, there is a further entry recording a payment made to Wykeham for drawing up a legal document connected with the appointment of Roos to the wardenship.[2] Moreover, it must be stressed that as every King's Scholar was appointed directly by the Crown under writ of privy seal, Wykeham must have been closely involved with the personnel of the King's Hall when acting as keeper of the privy seal from 1363 to 1367. Thus, whether as educationalist with an obvious interest in one of the two largest colleges in England, or as head of a department through which passed all the writs of appointment to vacant King's Hall fellowships, or as chancellor and actual visitor to the college itself, William of Wykeham had excellent opportunities to make a detailed first-hand study of this royal Cambridge foundation.

There would therefore seem to be very good reasons for suggesting that the King's Hall was one of Wykeham's principal English models. With the exception of Wykeham's salaried tutorial system,[3] it is clear that the main points of his educational programme were already firmly embodied in this Cambridge college from the early part of the century. For this reason, it is only right that the central pivotal position which New College, Oxford, has hitherto occupied in the history of English collegiate development should be substantially modified: and if we are to look in the medieval period for the earliest prototype of that kind of collegiate society which characterised the post-Reformation era and was a close antecedent of the modern type of 'Oxbridge' college, we shall find that original pattern displayed in the King's Hall, Cambridge.

---

[1] *K.H. Accts.* II, fo. 122: 'Item in expensis factis per custodem apud London' et Wyndeshore ad presentand' literas comitive et presentationem quandam ecclesie de fakenham ad rogatum domini [*sic*] Regine et domini Wilhelmi de Wikham...'

[2] *Ibid.* II, fo. 72: 'Item pro factura unius bille porrecce domino Wilhelmo Wycham pro creatione nove [*sic*] custodis vid.' (i.e. Nicholas Roos, appointed 2 December 1364).

[3] See below, pp. 66–7.

GROWTH OF EARLY TUTORIAL AND LECTURE SYSTEMS

Despite the amount of research which has been carried out in this century on the history of the medieval universities, still comparatively little has been discovered about teaching organisation in the colleges. There are two interrelated problems confronting the academic historian. First, when did the collegiate tutorial system originate and, secondly, at what point in time did college teaching cease to be merely supplementary and begin to supersede the lectures of the regent masters in the university schools? Although the full answers to these problems may never be found, any information which serves to extend the present severely limited state of our knowledge is particularly valuable. In this respect, it is felt that the King's Hall accounts make a not unimportant contribution.

It is a natural arrangement that in any kind of academic society the senior members will aid and teach their younger colleagues: this was essentially the practice in the earliest of the English medieval colleges. For example, the Merton statutes of 1270 prescribe that teachers are to be selected from among the more advanced scholars to help the younger ones in their studies and to look after their moral welfare.[1] This was paralleled in the Peterhouse statutes with the provision that the senior members of the college were enjoined to share their rooms with junior scholars so that the young might be stirred to greater application to study and to higher standards of moral rectitude:[2] and, generally speaking, this obligation on the part of the older fellows to instruct and guide the younger and less experienced members of the society was one common to most early English colleges. Quite clearly, this was the simplest of all forms of tutorial organisation, wholly informal, unpaid and confined solely to members on the foundation. But a new and important advance came with the institution of Wykeham's salaried tutorial system: in practice, this meant that a sum of money was set aside from the college funds as payment for fellows or scholars who acted as tutors (*informatores*) to the younger element in the society.[3] There is here no positive indica-

---

[1] See Merton statutes of 1270 in *Statutes*, I, ch. (2), 12.
[2] *Camb. Docs.* II, 12.
[3] See the statutes of New College in *Statutes*, I, ch. (5), 54.

tion that these tutorial facilities were extended to pupils who were not members of the college: furthermore, at this stage in the late fourteenth century there is nothing to show that the finances of Wykeham's undergraduates were vested in the persons of the fellows or senior scholars who acted as their tutors. The point is raised as the management and control of undergraduate finances came to be one of the primary functions of the college tutor and therefore one of the essential features of the fully fledged tutorial system.

There is no evidence to prove that the King's Hall ever possessed a salaried tutorial system in the Wykehamite sense: there is, however, substantial evidence for the assertion that the college had evolved tutorial arrangements open to the reception of private pupils who were not themselves members of the foundation; moreover, it is equally clear that those fellows who served in the capacity of tutors to pupils of this kind were also responsible to the college for the expenses incurred by their private charges.

The evidence for these conclusions is contained in a series of entries in the King's Hall accounts extending from the 1430s to the opening of the sixteenth century in which seventeen different fellows settled with the seneschals, or administrative officers of the college, for sums due for commons and sizings[1] for themselves and for their pupils (*pupilli*). Typical examples are:

(1436–7): 'Memorandum quod magister Ricardus Cost satisfecit pro se et pupillis...pro anno preterito.'[2]
'Memorandum quod magister John Paston satisfecit collegio pro se et pupillis...'[3]

(1437–8) Pyghttesley [heading]
'Item pro pupillo per iiij dies x d.; item pro eodem pupillo per septimanam i s. iij d.; item pro eodem pupillo per iiij dies viij d.'[4]

(1438–9): 'Memorandum quod magister Ricardus Cost compoto plenarie facto undecimo die mensis septembris satisfecit pro se et pupillis suis...in repastis [sizings], communibus [commons]...'[5]

---

[1] 'Extra commons', i.e. food and drink ordered by a fellow in addition to his basic commons or meals.
[2] *K.H. Accts.* IX, fo. 29 v.
[3] *Loc. cit.*; this reference is cited by Willis and Clark, *Architectural history*, I, xci and n. 2, where it is suggested that the *pupilli* refer to young fellows: for reasons given below (p. 68), this view is no longer tenable.
[4] *K.H. Accts.* IX, fo. 44.   [5] *Ibid.* IX, fo. 92 v.

(1460–1) Morgan [heading]
'Item pro communibus Will' pupilli sui xij d.; item pro pupillo xij d. iiij d. ob. q. i d. i d. x d. q. ob. q.; item pro pupillo x d. iij d. ob. q. pro pupillo x d. ob. q.; item pro pupillo x d.; item pro pupillo x d. i d. . . .'[1]

(1478–9): 'pupillus fyncham x d. x d. x d. x d. x d. x d. x d. v d.
pupillus Browne x d. x d. x d. x d. x d. x d. x d. x d. x d. x d. x d. x d.
xij d. xij d. x d. x d. x d. x d. x d.'[2]

(1483–4): 'pupilli Ashman xx d. ij s. viij d. ij s. vi d. ij s. v d. . . .'[3]

(1494–5): 'pupillus Sokborn v d. pro anno elapso x d. x d. x d. x d. x d. x d. x d. x d. x d. iiij d.'[4]
'pupillus Both x d. x d. x d. x d. x d. x d. x d. x d. x d. iij d.'[5]

(1501–2): 'Item recepimus de magistro Jakson in partem solucionis pro duobus pupillis vi s. viij d.'[6]

From these extracts, it is evident that the fellows so named were financially responsible for their charges because they accounted on their behalf for commons and sizings directly to the college seneschals. This consideration quite definitely marks off the *pupilli* from all members on the foundation and from the ever growing number of *extranei*[7] then resident in the Hall. If these *pupilli* had been *extranei* in the ordinary sense, they would have been accounted for in that annually recurrent section of the records where all the *extranei* are listed so that each is made to account directly to the seneschals for his commons, for sizings and for the rent of his room. The positioning of the entries for pupils immediately after the yearly list of fellows confirms that these *pupilli* were neither self-supporting *extranei* nor younger fellows but private pupils, not on the foundation, and introduced into the college for a limited period to live presumably with the fellows to whom they had been assigned. As *pupilli* is obviously to be understood in an academic sense in this context, we have here set out an arrangement whereby several of the fellows stood in the relation of *in loco parentis* to a number of pupils for whose finances they had assumed responsibility. This tallies very well with what little is known of rudimentary tutorial organisation in the Oxford halls of the medieval period. Dr A. B. Emden has shown that, in at

[1] *K.H. Accts.* XIII, fo. 19.   [2] *Ibid.* XV, fo. 118.
[3] *Ibid.* XVI, fo. 115v.   [4] *Ibid.* XIX, fo. 17.
[5] *Ibid.* XIX, fo. 17v.   [6] *Ibid.* XX, fo. 15v.
[7] For the King's Hall *extranei* see below, pp. 259 ff.

least one academic hall of the early fifteenth century, the finances of those undergraduates who looked upon the principal as their tutor or creditor (as he styled himself) were entirely given over to his control and were accounted for term by term as money was expended on their behalf.[1] Both Dr Emden and H. E. Salter have remarked upon the striking similarity between these arrangements and those which are known to have prevailed in Oxford colleges of the seventeenth century.[2] And there can be little doubt that such tutorial provisions are essentially the same as those furnished by the King's Hall records between 1436 and 1502. Indeed, it may very well be that the King's Hall provides the earliest extant information available for a college[3] concerning that form of tutorial organisation in which the entire regulation of the pupil's finances is vested in the person of a fellow, in his capacity as tutor, and which became one of the chief characteristics of the English collegiate teaching system of the post-Reformation era.

Detailed analysis of the King's Hall data reveals that at least four of the seventeen fellows who acted as tutors took charge of two, or possibly even more, pupils at a time;[4] but clearly the retention of a single scholar was the more usual pattern. A small number of the fellow-tutors (as we may call them) are known to have supervised pupils for several years. For example, William Adam kept pupils over an unbroken four-year period from 1480 to 1484[5] and Thomas Swayn for three of the years between 1479 and 1484.[6] Mostly, however, individual fellows would be content with the retention of pupils

---

[1] See the significance of master John Arundel's logic notebook discussed by A. B. Emden, *An Oxford hall in medieval times*, p. 193. It is, however, probable that legists, who were of maturer years than the artists, would normally exercise a personal control over their expenditure. On this point see Salter, 'An Oxford hall in 1424', *Essays in history presented to R. L. Poole* (ed. by H. W. C. Davis, Oxford, 1927), pp. 421 ff. at p. 433; also Jacob, *B.J.R.L.* XXIX (1946), 310.

[2] Emden, *op. cit.* p. 193; Salter, *op. cit.* p. 421.

[3] Dr Emden has kindly informed me that he has not encountered references to *pupilli* in any of the many sets of English collegiate records he has had occasion to examine. He has, however, noted the appearance of *scolares* at Exeter College in the 1490s, which might well indicate the presence of undergraduate commoners. This terminology was not unknown at the King's Hall: in an entry of 1501–2 (XX, fo. 15v) *pupilli* and *skolares* are used seemingly as interchangeable terms to denote private pupils.

[4] *K.H. Accts.* IX, fos. 29v, 92v; XVI, fo. 115v; XX, fo. 15v.

[5] *Ibid.* XVI, fos. 40v, 59, 90v, 116v.   [6] *Ibid.* XVI, fos. 16v, 18v, 59, 116v.

for parts of one or two academic years. Although eleven of the seventeen tutors served at one time or another as college seneschals, only three of them assumed private teaching responsibilities in years of administrative office,[1] which perhaps suggests that tutoring activities made considerable inroads upon a fellow's time-table. As far as can be determined, the majority of the fellow-tutors held degrees in arts or in law[2] and this is reflective of the main academic concentrations within the college. The extremely wide range of expenditure on pupils[3] is explicable in terms of the sizable variation in the periods of pupil-retention: and it is clear that a private pupil might be maintained throughout the whole of the academic year or for only a small part of it.

The accumulative evidence does not permit us to conclude that the provision made for the reception of pupils for private tuition had as yet assumed the proportions of a regular collegiate system. For it cannot be said that the admission of these undergraduate semicommoners constituted an integral feature of college policy in the sense that automatic arrangements would be made for the accommodation and teaching of a limited number of pupils each year. Indeed, it is highly improbable that the college, as a collective body, was in any real sense the engineering force behind this important sporadic development. Although the college authorities obviously sanctioned the movement, the intermittent nature of the entries for pupils almost certainly indicates that the initiative in this direction lay with the individual fellow who desired to supplement his income with teaching fees. From later analogy, we may suppose that the fellow-tutor would enter into a private arrangement with a parent or guardian, who would then commit the pupil to his care, at the same time handing over a sufficient supply of money to be expended on the pupil's behalf over the agreed period.[4] As this would necessi-

---

[1] Alan Browne, Thomas Swayn and Sokeborne (Christian name unknown).

[2] Degrees were distributed among the fellow-tutors as follows: D.C.L.: 1; B.C.L.: 1; probably B.C.L.: 1; B.Cn.L.: 1; M.A.: 2; probably M.A.: 5; Inc.A.: 2; unknown: 4.

[3] E.g. in 1479–80 Alan Browne spent £1 14s 8d on behalf of his pupil (XVI, fo. 16); in 1482–3 John Totoft spent 10s (XVI, fo. 90v); and in 1494–5 Bothe spent 7s 9d (XIX, fo. 17v).

[4] For such arrangements in Oxford colleges of the seventeenth century see G. H. Wakeling, *Brasenose monographs*, II, pt. i (Oxf. Hist. Soc., LIII, 1909), xi, p. 14.

tate producing a private as opposed to a general college contract, it is not at all surprising that references to such documents do not occur in the King's Hall records.

The situation here described plainly denotes that every graduate fellow was a potential tutor and required only the ability or inclination to attract the necessary pupils. This presupposes that tutoring activities were geared to an open, competitive market—a system, so to speak, of academic free trade—and there was, as yet, no discoverable attempt made to limit tutoring functions to a few fellows specially earmarked by the college authorities for this purpose. Post-Reformation parallels are revealed to us briefly in the records of Gonville and Caius and of Trinity College, Cambridge, where it is evident that in the second half of the sixteenth century any fellow might become a tutor with often only one or two pupils under his charge.[1] In essence, this is patently the same system that was in operation at the King's Hall as early as the 1430s. There is no reason to suppose that the King's Hall evidence for tutorial organisation is anything but typical of the general medieval pattern; and judging from the records of Caius and Trinity, it seems that similar loose arrangements of this kind continued to linger on in Cambridge into the late sixteenth century until supplanted by that more centralised, collegiately controlled system of tutorial teaching which is still one of the prominent hallmarks of the 'Oxbridge' scene.

The admission of undergraduate commoners (strictly semi-commoners) at the King's Hall is a development of the first academic importance. It has already been shown that from the early fourteenth century the college made regular provision for the intake of undergraduates as fully incorporated fellows on the foundation. Clearly, from the 1430s onwards, this undergraduate element was augmented and diversified by the admission of an irregular succession of undergraduate commoners who were not on the foundation but lived in the college as private pupils paying half commons for their board. It is frequently stated that the admission of undergraduate commoners

[1] For tutorial arrangements at Gonville and Caius in the late sixteenth and seventeenth centuries see J. Venn, *Biographical history of Gonville and Caius College*, III (Cambridge, 1901), 251–2; for similar provisions at Trinity see Rouse Ball, *Cambridge papers* (London, 1918), ch. II, esp. pp. 31–6, and *Cambridge notes* (Cambridge, 1921), pp. 26–30; also G. M. Trevelyan, *Trinity College: an historical sketch* (Cambridge, 1943), p. 15.

is an innovation associated with Bishop Waynflete's Magdalen College, Oxford, founded in 1448. In the founder's statutes of 1479, provision was made for the reception of not more than twenty commoners who were to be the sons of noble or worthy persons and were to be permitted to live in college at their own expense under the direction of a tutor (*sub tutela et regimine creditorum vulgariter* creancers *nuncupatorum*).[1] On the strength of this, it has been asserted that 'from this new development Magdalen can claim to be not merely the last of the medieval colleges, but the first of the modern ones'.[2] While in no way wishing to detract from the undoubted importance of Waynflete's 'commoner' arrangements for the future orientation of the English universities, the evidence at our disposal would indicate that this development had already been introduced at the King's Hall, Cambridge, some considerable time before Waynflete's conception came to fruition.

The reception of private pupils by the King's Hall in the course of the fifteenth century furnishes a valuable insight into that migratory movement whereby the Cambridge undergraduate population came to desert the hostels and began to infiltrate into the colleges. In this connection, the King's Hall had peculiar advantages to offer. As it was one of the most spacious of the Cambridge colleges it could supposedly provide the roomy accommodation necessary for tutorial organisation on a fairly large scale. These facilities must have been considerably extended with the increase of non-residence among the senior fellows which reached sizable proportions in the first half of the fifteenth century.[3] As the *pupilli* made their *début* in the mid-1430s, it may well be that there is a connection between these two events.

From a philological point of view, there is much interest in the fact that the occurrence of this term *pupillus* in the King's Hall accounts appears to be the earliest known use of the word in an academic sense in any set of extant English collegiate records.[4] In its original legal sense, the term was used to designate a ward or

---

[1] *Statutes*, II, ch. (8), 60.

[2] N. Denholm-Young, 'Magdalen College', *V.C.H.* (Oxford), III, 195; see also Emden, 'Learning and education' in *Medieval England*, I, 536–7, for the admission of fee-paying commoners (*commensales*) at Magdalen.   [3] See above, p. 55.

[4] The *Oxford English Dictionary* quotes 'pupil' as first used in an academic sense as late as 1563 (*O.E.D.* VIII, 1607); the *Revised medieval Latin word-list* (prepared by R. E. Latham, London, 1965), p. 383, dates 'pupil' used in this same sense at *c.* 1550.

orphan assigned to the care and protection of a guardian who acted *in loco parentis* in relation to his charge: as such, the term was a technical one figuring prominently in Roman law.[1] It is not difficult to understand how this legal nexus between guardian and ward suggested to the medieval academic world an almost exact parallel with the relationship which arose between a college tutor and his pupils. For, during the time that an undergraduate resided in college, his tutor deputised for his legal parents or guardians, and thus, while *in statu pupillari*, the pupil remained in the position of an academic ward. Just when exactly this legal terminology was first borrowed and applied to tutorial organisation is a question which, at the moment, cannot be answered. But it can, however, now be asserted that it was in operation in at least one of the Cambridge colleges by the mid 1430s at the latest. It is perhaps relevant to add that the preponderance of civil lawyers at the King's Hall makes it certain that the fellows would have been thoroughly familiar with the Roman legal usage of the terms *pupillus* and *tutor*.

A study of the subsequent usage of this term *pupillus* reveals that in the fifteenth, sixteenth and early seventeenth centuries the word was particularly, one might say almost exclusively, associated with Cambridge University. There appears to be only one recorded instance of the use of the word in any code of Oxford statutes before 1600, namely, in the first body of statutes given to Cardinal College by Wolsey *c.* 1527.[2] Whereas in the Oxford statutes the word commonly used to denote a scholar in the charge of a tutor is *scholaris* or *discipulus*, at Cambridge, on the other hand, the usual term is *pupillus*. The term occurs in relation to the word *tutor* in the following sixteenth-century codes of Cambridge college statutes: in the statutes of 1551 for Clare;[3] in the first Trinity statutes given by Edward VI and dated 8 November 1552;[4] in those of Magdalene of 1553–4;[5] in the draft statutes for Gonville and Caius drawn up by Dr Caius in 1558;[6] and in the code for Emmanuel of 1585.[7] This leaves us in no

---

[1] From many examples, see *Inst.* I, 21; *Dig.* 26, 4; *Dig.* 26, 5; *Dig.* 26, 9; *Cod.* 5, 33.
[2] *Statutes*, II, ch. (II), 100.
[3] *Camb. Docs.* II, 179–80 (*De Tutorum et Pupillorum Officio*).
[4] See paper statutes of Edward VI, cap. II, pp. 15–16 (*Tutorum et Pupillorum Officium*) (Trinity College Library, O.6.7.).   [5] *Camb. Docs.* II, 355–6 (*De Tutoris Officio*).
[6] *Ibid.* II, 283 (*De Tutore et Fidejussore Pupillorum...*).
[7] *Ibid.* III, 509–10 (*De Tutorum Officio*).

doubt as to the prevalence of the term at Cambridge and its almost total absence at Oxford before the seventeenth century.[1] This conclusion is further borne out by the fact that in contemporary literature the word 'pupil' appears to be used mainly with reference to Cambridge;[2] and in the seventeenth and eighteenth centuries, 'pupil-monger' was a term in current vogue to describe a college tutor, especially one of Cambridge University.[3]

There would therefore seem to be good reason for believing that Cambridge University was largely instrumental in perpetuating the

[1] The term was clearly in use at Brasenose College, Oxford, during the seventeenth century, as is evident from the extant *Pupill Booke of Accounts* kept by Ralph Eaton, one of the college tutors of the Commonwealth period. This important source book is discussed by Wakeling, *Brasenose monographs, cit.* 14 ff.

[2] Upon investigation of the references cited for 'pupil' in *O.E.D.* it was found that in every case the term was used in connection with Cambridge University. E.g. during the visitation of Queen Mary's Commissioners in 1557, several members of the university were punished and '...some they forbade to have the charge of Pupils lest...' (quoted from J. Fox(e), *Acts and Monuments* (otherwise known as the Book of Martyrs) (9th ed. 3 vols., London, printed for the Company of Stationers, 1684), III, 648); see also J. Stow, *The Annales of England* (London, 1605), p. 1427: 'Among the mourners at the funeral of Archbishop Whitgift were the Earle of Worcester, and the Lord Zouche, which among other noble men had been his pupils when they were brought up in Cambridge...' The term also occurs fairly frequently in Samuel Clarke's *A collection of the lives of thirty-two English divines...* (3rd ed. London, 1677) where reference is made to the merits of particular Cambridge tutors of the early seventeenth century: e.g. Master John Cotton, tutor of Emmanuel, 'won the hearts of his Pupils both to himself, and to a desire of Learning ...His Pupils were honourers, and lovers of him...' (p. 218); Doctor Thomas Hill, tutor of Emmanuel, 'proved a diligent, painful, and successful Tutor of very many Pupils...' (p. 230); and Master Herbert Palmer, fellow of Queens' College, 'took many Pupils, of whom he was more than ordinarily carefull...' (p. 185). See further the seventeenth-century book of rules by James Duport, fellow of Trinity College, Cambridge, 'Rules to be Observed by Young Pupils and Schollers in the University', Trinity College MS. O.10A.33 (ed. by G. M. Trevelyan for *The Cambridge Review*, LXIV (1943), 328 ff.).

[3] See e.g. T. Fuller, *The history of the worthies of England* (London, 1662), II, 291: 'He (John Preston) was the greatest Pupil monger in England in man's memory...it was commonly said in the colledge [Queens', Cambridge] that every time Master Preston plucked off his hat to Doctor Davenant, the Colledge Master, he gained a chamber or study for one of his Pupils'; also G. Peacock, *Observations on the statutes of the University of Cambridge* (London, 1841), app. A. I: 'My ingenious and learned Friend Mr. Farmer, Fellow and Pupil-monger of Emmanuel College...' Quoted by Peacock from *Introductory Observations* by W. Cole from Cole's MSS., vol. XLIV, p. 353 (B.M.): *O.E.D.* (p. 1608) dates Cole's remarks 1773. For references to pupil-mongers at St John's College, Cambridge, in the eighteenth century see E. Miller, *Portrait of a college* (Cambridge, 1961), pp. 56, 57.

academic sense of the term *pupillus*: and it may very well be that, as far as England is concerned, the academic concept of 'pupil' originated in fifteenth-century Cambridge and that the King's Hall is particularly associated with its early currency. It seems relevant to add that the term is not discussed by J. F. Niermeyer in his recent lexicon of medieval Latin.[1] As this dictionary is the work of a Dutch scholar and is based upon an extremely wide range of European sources, the omission perhaps serves to indicate that the evolution of the term *pupillus* from a legal to an academic sense was largely an English transition finding little echo on the Continent.[2]

In addition to the tutorship of the *pupilli*, entries in the college's accounts suggest that, on occasion, the master and fellows may have undertaken the tutoring of one or two of the *extranei* (commoners or semi-commoners) resident within the Hall. For example, Thomas Aspilyon, fellow from 1437 to 1441, paid for the commons of one Alexander Marchal,[3] a semi-commoner accounted for during 1438–9 and 1439–40.[4] Similarly, among the personal expenses of the master, Richard Caudray,[5] are found payments for the commons and sizings of Henry, son and heir of the earl of Huntingdon, who, along with his two bastard brothers, John and William,[6] and a train of servants,

---

[1] J. F. Niermeyer, *Mediae Latinitatis Lexicon Minus* (Leiden, 1954–), fasciculus 10 (1963).

[2] I have found one reference to the use of this term in what seems to be an academic sense in the statutes of 1346 of the Ave Maria College in Paris where it is stipulated that young entrants in their eighth or ninth year are to be received 'in pupillari estate' (Gabriel, *Ave Maria College, cit.* p. 323). No further details are supplied but presumably these boys were given over into the charge of the master who had a direct statutory responsibility for the guidance of the studies of the younger members of the community. In one of his Cambridge letters of 8 July 1514, Erasmus has occasion to refer to one of his former pupils: here the term used is *discipulus* and this is doubtless representative of the normal continental usage (*Erasmi Epistolae* (ed. P. S. Allen, 12 vols., Oxford, 1906–58), I (1906), 569, lines 130–1).

[3] *K.H. Accts.* IX, fo. 92v: 'Memorandum quod recepimus de thoma aspleon per manus Johannis Halle (seneschal) pro coīs Alexandri Marchal' (sum not specified); IX, fo. 123v: similar entry for the receipt of £1 6s 8d from Aspilyon for the commons of Marchal.   [4] *Ibid.* IX, fos. 76v, 106v.

[5] Appointed 2 July 1431; vacated 29 September 1448. In medieval usage, master (*magister*) and warden (*custos*) are wholly interchangeable designations for the head of the King's Hall, a circumstance which applies throughout the entire history of the college. Indeed, the term *magister sive custos* is frequently found in the contemporary records. Accordingly, master and warden are used indiscriminately in this book.

[6] The brothers stayed for ten weeks in 1440–1 and for eleven weeks in 1441–2. They were charged identical rates for commons (an average of 1s 7d a week): no entry for sizings is recorded (*K.H. Accts.* IX, fo. 162; X, fo. 13v).

lived in the Hall as a commoner from 1439–40 to 1441–2.[1] Although the evidence is not conclusive, it seems likely that in each of these cases the relationship would be an academic one.

Concerning this subject of college teaching, a further important piece of evidence remains to be examined. This takes the form of an entry consisting of eleven lines written on a fragmentary leaf from which the rest of the folio has been cut away.[2] The dating is uncertain, but the entry most probably belongs to the year 1366–7.[3] This fragment is so interesting that it is given here in full: the dashes indicate the point in each line where the leaf has been cut.

[Heading] Thorneton.

In primis solut' magistro gramatice pro
coīs suis in xxxviij sept' xij d. —
sept' xiiij d. ob. It' in xxxvi sept'
pro coīs suis xiiij d. ob. It' in —
xxxvij s. —
xxxviij sept' xij d. ob. It' pro
coīs suis in xxxix sept' xij d. ob. It' —
Pincerne et coco xij d. It' lotrici iiij d.
It' pro pensione camere sue ix —
It' pro porrectis empt' xv —

This entry reveals that for a number of weeks in (?) 1366–7 a series of weekly payments for commons ranging from 1*s* to 1*s* 2½*d* were handed over to a master of grammar by or on behalf of one Thorneton, an *extraneus*, then residing in the college as a pensioner.[4] It may be that Thorneton was a young boy introduced into the Hall to gain

---

1 See Caudray's payment of Henry of Huntingdon's expenses, *ibid.* ix, fo. 123 v: 'Summa total' debit' per magistrum pro repastis suis annis xv xvi xvij xviij et pro domino henr' huntyngdon et famulis utriusque...' Henry was charged the same rates for commons as his brothers and, in addition, took regular sizings ranging from 7*d* to 1*s* 9*d* a week (*ibid.* ix, fos. 106 v, 162; x, fo. 13 v).
2 *Ibid.* ii, fo. 144. Several of the folios of the second volume of the King's Hall accounts have been cut in this way.
3 Following as they do upon the account for 1365–6 as well as from internal evidence, it is likely that the undated folios (133–45) are those for the year 1366–7.
4 As may be seen from the entry (line 10), the folio has been cut at the numeral 'ix' indicating the rent of the room: here, nine shillings is almost certainly to be understood, which, as an annual rent, accords well enough with the rates charged for pensioners recorded below, pp. 268 ff.

proficiency in the rudiments of grammar and that these payments for his board were furnished by a parent, guardian or patron. Indeed, there is just a possibility that this fragment is part of a record of expenses designed for the scrutiny of Thorneton's financial sponsors. The master of grammar cannot be further identified, nor can it be determined for how long he stayed in the college. An entry for his *repaste*,[1] however, in a list of expenses charged on the Society suggests that he lived in the Hall by invitation of the master and fellows. Although no more than an inference, it is possible that he was hired to coach some of the younger Scholars who had been admitted by special royal licence, notwithstanding the fact that they had not yet acquired the necessary skill in grammar for proceeding to the arts course.[2] However this may be, the entry reveals that as early as the second half of the fourteenth century there plainly existed opportunities for a youthful pensioner to receive grammatical instruction within the King's Hall.

In the closing years of the fifteenth century, a college lectureship was established in canon law. This was the practical outcome of a legacy of £70 bequeathed to the King's Hall by Robert Bellamy, D.Cn.L., a fellow of the college from 1464–5 until his death in 1492. By the provisions of his will, dated 8 October 1492, the money was to be invested for the establishment of an annual rent for the endowment of a perpetual lectureship in canon law.[3] The lectureship was evidently to be of a semi-public nature, because Bellamy stipulated that it was to be open and free to all the fellows of the college and to all other poor clerks studying in the university: but it was not to be open to those scholars deemed to hold sufficient exhibition at the university unless by special permission of the lecturer.[4] By 1494–5, the college had received £53 of the legacy from Bellamy's

---

[1] *K.H. Accts.* II, fo. 73.
[2] See above, p. 60 and n. 2.
[3] *Testamenta Eboracensia* (Surtees Society), IV (1869), 75: 'Item lego Aulae Regiae, in qua sum socius, lxx libras, ut magister et consocii eiusdem provideant et emant aliquem annum redditum: cum quo reddiyu provideatur pro una lectura in iure canonico in dicta aula imperpetuum continuanda...'
[4] *Ibid.* 75–6: 'Et volo quod dicta lectura sit generalis et libera omnibus et singulis consociis in dicta aula studentibus; necnon et aliis clericis pauperibus in Universitate studentibus; non tamen scolaribus qui sufficientem habent exhibitionem ad Universitatem, nisi ex speciali favore illius personae quae huiusmodi lecturae executionem in se susceperit.'

executors, who then held the balance of £17,[1] which was presumably paid over at a later date. In 1498–9, the money had been successfully invested in a number of Cambridge properties[2] and subsequent accounts contain the receipts from these quarters.[3] The properties were situated somewhere between the Great Bridge (now Magdalene Bridge) and the castle (*ultra pontem versus castrum*): they comprised four separate houses or tenements and brought in an annual gross income of £3 8s;[4] but because of the wide fluctuations in yearly expenditure on repairs, it is not possible to give a reliable figure for the average net income. The most valuable of these holdings was an inn called 'The Star' (*Sterr(e)*, *Stella*) which was purchased from a certain Master Thomas Worseley for £26 13s 4d[5] and which realised a rent of £2 a year. In 1519–20, the tenant of this inn (*apud signum stelle*) was named Gybson,[6] who apparently died shortly afterwards, as his widow continued to rent the property[7] until it passed, in 1523–4, to John Galaway;[8] and Galaway was still the tenant when the college ceased to draw receipts from its Bellamy investments *c.* 1528–9.[9] In the 1520s, the tenants of the other three holdings included Richard Colynson, a ropemaker, John Elyot and Elizabeth Broyke, who paid rents of 16s, 8s, and 4s respectively.

[1] *K.H. Accts.* XIX, fo. 1: 'Memorandum quod recepimus de executoribus Magistri belamy ad diversas vices ad perquisitandum certarum terrarum et tenementorum pro stipendio lectoris legentis lecturam in iure canonico liii libras et sic adhuc in manibus executorum xvii libras quia legavit lxx libras.'

[2] *Ibid.* XIX, fos. 139v, 140.

[3] *Ibid.* XX, fos. 51, 146v, 183v; XXI, fos. 7, 97, 130v, 178v; XXII, fos. 6v, 43, 72v, 103; XXIII, fos. 5v, 39v, 77v, 109v, 141v, 176; XXIV, fos. 6v, 164; XXVI, fo. 166v.

[4] The gross income became stabilised at £3 8s from 1518–19 onwards.

[5] *K.H. Accts.* XIX, fo. 139v. Thomas Worseley, clerk, appears on the Cambridge borough Hagable Rolls for 1483 and 1491 as having paid an annual rent of 1d for the tenement called 'le Sterre' (*Cambridge borough documents*, I (ed. W. M. Palmer, Cambridge, 1931), 57, 62). In the college account of 1498–9, the inn is first referred to as 'lee Sterne' but thereafter occurs in English variants of 'Star' or in its Latinised form, *Stella*. 'The Star' was included in a list of inns which a Cambridge vintner supplied *c.* 1511 (E. H. Minns, 'A Cambridge vintner's accounts, *c.* 1511', *C.A.S. Communications*, XXXIV (1934), 50 ff. at pp. 52, 56). The inn later passed into the hands of Trinity College and thence by way of Thomas Howard, earl of Suffolk, to Magdalene College in the early seventeenth century (Willis and Clark, *Architectural history*, II, 355).

[6] *K.H. Accts.* XXII, fo. 72v.

[7] *Ibid.* XXIII, fo. 5v.

[8] *Ibid.* XXIII, fo. 77v.

[9] The headings for the Bellamy properties continue for a few years longer but there are no entries for receipts or expenditure.

The first known appointee to the lectureship was Master Collett, a fellow of the college, who was given a salary of 20s in 1502–3 for his lecture course in the term of the Annunciation of the Blessed Virgin Mary:[1] and in the same year an identical remuneration was made to another fellow, Ralph Cantrell, for his lectures in the term ending at the feast of St John Baptist.[2] There is no further record of the names of the Bellamy lecturers, but the rents for their stipends kept flowing in until all receipts came to an abrupt end after 1528–9. It seems probable that the lectureship was discontinued from this year but, if not, it would certainly have been quashed under the terms of the royal injunctions of 1535 which abolished the study of canon law at the English universities.[3]

The evidence concerning the Bellamy lectureship in canon law is of particular interest because it ranks among the earliest known references to college lectureships in England. Lectureships of a very special kind made their first appearance at the Cambridge college of Godshouse (1439), which possessed its own lecturer or reader (*lector*) probably from its foundation.[4] In this connection, however, it has to be remembered that Godshouse was an exceptional type of collegiate institution, founded for the express purpose of training undergraduate scholars for the degree of master of grammar, preparatory to their acceptance of teaching posts at England's languishing grammar schools.[5] The instruction of these scholars was entrusted to a reader or lecturer elected to his position by the college.[6] A valuable record of an indentured form of agreement made in 1451 between the proctor and scholars of Godshouse and one Ralph Barton, hired

---

[1] *K.H. Accts.* xx, fo. 36v: 'Item Magistro Collett pro labore suo circa lecturam pro termino annunciacionis beate Marie Virginis xxs.'

[2] *Ibid.* xx, fo. 60v: 'Item solut' Cantrell pro lectura pro termino finito in festo nativitatis sancti Johanis Baptiste annis presentis xxs.'

[3] See below, p. 84.

[4] A. H. Lloyd, *The early history of Christ's College, Cambridge,* cit. pp. 131 ff.

[5] *Ibid.* pp. 12, 38, 40: see also H. Rackham, ed., *Early statutes of Christ's College, Cambridge with the statutes of the prior foundation of God's House* (privately printed, Cambridge, 1927), introduction, i. Newly elected undergraduate fellows were to apply themselves to sophistry and logic for two or three years, at the end of which time they were to turn to an intensive study of the subtler and deeper parts of grammar with a view to acquiring the degree of master of grammar. After this they were bound to accept suitable positions in grammar schools built within the last forty years. (See statutes in Rackham, *op. cit.* pp. 24, 26.)

[6] Rackham, *op. cit.* pp. 22, 24.

as a salaried lecturer,[1] proves that the office of *lector* was already in operation by that date: and it has been convincingly argued that the lectureship was most probably instituted from the beginning in 1439.[2] On the basis of this evidence, it is claimed that Godshouse was the first English college to have its own lecturer 'and so initiated a system which was adopted ultimately by all colleges, largely replacing the teaching given by university lecturers, and which remained the principal means of instruction until the position was reversed by the university statutes of 1926'.[3] There does, however, seem to be some confusion here. For surely the Godshouse *lector* cannot be placed in exactly the same category as the endowed lectureships of a later date, established in disciplines such as philosophy, theology and law, and which were instituted largely in competition with the lectures given by the regent masters in the university schools. It is evident that the needs of a college such as Godshouse, which called for a highly specialised concentration upon grammatical teaching, could only be met through the office of an internal *lector*. There was here no desire to emulate the public system of university instruction. On the good authority of the founder, William Byngham, the *raison d'être* for the college had been the alarming dearth of grammar masters both in the country at large and in the English universities.[4] Clearly, if the aims of the founder were to be realised, if his scholars were to receive grammatical instruction at this specialised level, then sheer necessity dictated that a private *lector* be installed from the start. It was the only way: the Godshouse *lector* was a *sine qua non* for the implementation of the founder's basic conception. The office was a logical outgrowth of the prevailing circumstances and was in no wise intended to compete with or supplant the teaching given in the university. For these reasons, we ought to regard the Godshouse reader as a case standing somewhat apart from the main evolution of the college lectureship at the English universities: consequently, it would be excessive to categorise it as that innovation which set in motion those events culminating in the transference of the greater part of university lecturing to the colleges.

The more characteristic and historically influential type of endowed lectureship appears to have been first established at Magdalen

---

[1] Printed by Lloyd, *op. cit.* pp. 375–7; also pp. 134 ff.
[2] Lloyd, *op. cit.* p. 131.   [3] *Ibid.* p. 133.   [4] *Ibid.* p. 40.

College, Oxford, where, by the statutes of 1479, provision was made for the foundation of three lectureships, two in philosophy and one in theology, open and free to all comers in the university.[1] College lectureships of this kind, which were mostly, though not always, of a public nature,[2] became a permanent feature on the English collegiate scene. Subsequently, with the exception of St Catharine's College, Cambridge, the statutes of every new foundation made provision for the establishment of lecturers[3] and, at the same time, most of the older colleges took steps to keep apace with this academic development. Indeed, by the beginning of the reign of Elizabeth, the colleges had become, to a lesser or greater extent, self-contained teaching units, increasingly less reliant upon the largely moribund system of public instruction offered by the universities. At this juncture, when the colleges were gradually taking over the entire burden of undergraduate teaching, a belated attempt was made to regenerate university lecturing by the institution of a body of salaried lecturers and professors. This movement,[4] which led ultimately to the replacement of the lecturing duties of the regent masters by those of a paid professoriate, was initiated by the foundation of the Lady Margaret Beaufort chairs of Divinity, permanently established at Oxford and Cambridge by 1503, although, as readerships, they had probably been in existence from 1497. Her initiative at Cambridge was followed by Sir Robert Rede, chief justice of common pleas, who, in his will of *c.* 1519, left money for three readerships in philosophy, logic and rhetoric. The climax of the movement came with the establishment at both universities of Henry VIII's regius

---

[1] *Statutes*, II, ch. (8), 47–9; N. Denholm-Young, 'Magdalen College', *V.C.H.* (Oxford), III, 194; Emden, 'Learning and education' in *Medieval England*, II, 536.

[2] E.g. the statutes of Brasenose of 1521 imply that college lecturers were to confine their lectures to undergraduate members of the college: *Statutes*, II, ch. (9), 15–16.

[3] See the statutes of Corpus Christi, Oxford, of 1517 and of Cardinal College of *c.* 1527, *Statutes*, II, ch. (10), 48–54, ch. (11), 71–2; the statutes of Christ's College, Cambridge, of 1506 and of Magdalene of 1553–4, *Camb. Docs.* III, 201–2, 351–2, and the Edward VI statutes for Trinity of 1552, p. 41 (Trinity College Library, O.6.7.); also the discussion of the Nicholas West statutes for Jesus College, Cambridge, of *c.* 1516–17 with reference to lectureships by J. G. Sikes and F. Jones, *V.C.H.* (Cambridge), III, 422; and for lecturers at St John's, Cambridge, E. Miller, *Portrait of a college, cit.* pp. 12–13.

[4] For a detailed survey of this movement see M. H. Curtis, *Oxford and Cambridge in transition 1558–1642* (Oxford, 1959), p. 101 with notes.

professorships of Divinity, Civil Law, Physic, Hebrew and Greek. But despite these efforts made to prop up the system of public university instruction, the course of events had gone too far in favour of the colleges to be reversed and by the third quarter of the sixteenth century these independent institutions had recognisably become the central teaching organs within the *studia*.

It is against this background of the emergence of the college lectureship as a permanent and vitally important fixture at the English universities that the Bellamy lectureship in canon law has to be assessed. If the Godshouse *lector* is disregarded as an exceptional case, it then follows that the King's Hall was the second[1] of the English colleges to possess a lectureship of a public (or at least semi-public) nature and certainly the first to provide one in the discipline of canon law. The foundation of this lectureship at the end of the fifteenth century, taken in conjunction with the development of rudimentary forms of tutorial organisation dating from the 1430s, is a measure of the important and hitherto quite unremarked contribution made by the King's Hall towards the expansion of both tutorial and lecturing facilities in the medieval University of Cambridge. In this matter of endowed college lectureships, as in so many other respects, the King's Hall stood in the forefront of bold institutional experimentation, revealing itself to be finely attuned and adaptable to the changing academic needs of the age.

But the Bellamy lectureship in canon law was by no means the sole contribution of the King's Hall towards the expansion of lecturing facilities at Cambridge. In addition to this extension within the framework of the traditional curriculum, the college assumed some active part in the promotion of humanist studies in the university. The evidence is too fragmentary to allow us to estimate the extent of that participation, but it does enable us to claim that in the early sixteenth century lectures were being provided for what appears to be elementary instruction in Greek. The relevant entry is for 1517–18: 'Item in regardis pro lectura litterarum grecarum xxd.'[2] From this tantalisingly laconic reference, it is not possible to determine if

---

[1] Although Jesus College, Cambridge, was founded in 1496, the provisions for lecturers appear only in the second code of statutes issued probably in 1516–17 (*V.C.H.* III, 422).

[2] *K.H. Accts.* XXII, fo. 18.

the instruction was of a public or semi-public nature or if it was
wholly confined to members of the college: nor is there any clue
to the name of the lecturer. But there may well be some significance in the fact that Cuthbert Tunstall, ex-fellow of the King's Hall
and one of the foremost Greek scholars in England,[1] was present in
the college for a brief period in 1518–19.[2] It is tempting to think that
Tunstall may have been in some way connected with the staging of
these lectures by his former college in the previous year; but, beyond
this, it would be idle to speculate. Moreover, too much emphasis
must not be placed upon a single reference. It may point to only an
isolated incursion into the realm of Greek studies, or it may be
representative of a more continuous pattern. Whatever the case, the
entry has its importance within the context of the determined efforts
of a small but dedicated group of early sixteenth-century Greek
scholars to have Greek learning established on a sure and lasting basis
in the universities.[3] The King's Hall evidence for Greek instruction
occurs in the year following the foundation of Foxe's Corpus
Christi College, Oxford, and six years after that of Fisher's St John's
College, Cambridge, both of which were destined to become the
first real academic centres of humanist studies in England. Furthermore, it appears only five years after the first known course of Greek
lectures to be sponsored officially at Oxford[4] and a year or so before
a regular course was set in motion at Cambridge.[5] Thus, however
brief and impermanent it may have been, the King's Hall venture, on
present knowledge, constitutes one of the earliest attempts made by
an English college to further interest in Greek studies through the
medium of a lecture or course of lectures.[6]

Evidence for the involvement of the King's Hall in the new learning is next found some eighteen years later. In 1535 the king
appointed Thomas Cromwell, the recently created chancellor of

---

[1] On Tunstall see Emden, *B.R.U.C.* pp. 597–8; also A. Tilley, 'Greek studies in
England in the early sixteenth century', *E.H.R.* LIII (1938), 221 ff. at pp. 224–5.

[2] *K.H. Accts.* XXII, fo. 55 v: 'Item in regardis Magistro Tunstall pro duobus caponibus
et vino ijs. viijd.'

[3] On this subject see Tilley, *art. cit.*

[4] J. K. McConica, *English humanists and Reformation politics* (Oxford, 1965), p. 83.

[5] Regular, as distinct from occasional, public lectures in the humanities seem to have
been provided from *c.* 1518 onwards (McConica, p. 80).

[6] *Lectura* is often used to denote a course of lectures and does not necessarily indicate
a single lecture.

Cambridge, visitor of the university with plenary powers to act 'according to his discretion, judgment and experience'.[1] At the same time, a series of royal injunctions were promulgated aimed at enforcing the university to swear to the king's succession and designed to effect the abolition of scholastic theology and canon law and to augment the scope of humanist studies at Cambridge.[2] Among the provisions was one which enjoined each college to support, at its own expense, two daily public lectures in Greek and Latin.[3] This directive was repeated in the visitatorial injunctions of Dr Thomas Leigh,[4] one of Cromwell's commissioners, who visited the university in October 1535, utilising the King's Hall as a base during the course of his investigations.[5] In addition to the injunction laid upon the colleges, he also ordered the university to institute and maintain a public lecture in either Greek or Hebrew.[6] The directive relating to the colleges is known to have been carried out at least in some instances: Gonville Hall, for example, which had already been maintaining a Latin lecture, now established one in Greek.[7] The King's Hall, however, followed the terms of the command given to the university and not that specifically issued to the colleges. In other words, it instituted

---

[1] Mullinger, *University of Cambridge*, II, 8; C. H. Cooper, *Annals of Cambridge* (4 vols., Cambridge, 1842–53), I (1842), 374.

[2] Mullinger, *op. cit.* I, 630; Cooper, *op. cit.* I, 375.

[3] *Ibid.*

[4] Leigh re-enforced the provisions of the royal injunctions on the head of each college and hostel, thereby confirming the directive imposed upon the colleges regarding public lectures in Greek and Latin (Cooper, *op. cit.* I, 376; Mullinger, *op. cit.* II, 10; J. Simon, *Education and society in Tudor England, cit.* p. 201).

[5] Dr Leigh resided in the King's Hall for nine days in October 1535 (*K.H. Accts.* XXV, fo. 43 v). His total bill for food, drink and fuel came to £4 17s 11½d (*ibid.* fo. 44) made up of £3 5s 10½d for items specially bought for the visitor and £1 12s 1d for commodities drawn from existing stock. During his stay, the royal commissioner ate and drank his way through beef, mutton and veal, capons, conies, mallards, chickens, larks and pigeons, pike, oysters, ling, salt salmon, plaice, whiting, tench, eels, perch and roach, warden pears and apples, eggs, butter and cream, various spices, bread, wine, three barrels of ale and more drawn from store, and *ypocras*, a cordial drink made of wine and flavoured with spices (for these individual expenses, see *K.H. Accts.* fos. 43 v, 44). Leigh's costs were charged on the King's Hall and several other Cambridge colleges whose names are not supplied. Of the total bill of £4 17s 11½d, the King's Hall paid £1 13s 7½d and the other colleges involved in this arrangement jointly contributed £3 4s 4d (*ibid.* fo. 44). The colleges were doubtless relieved when the commissioner's visit was over.

[6] Cooper, *op. cit.* I, 376; Mullinger, *op. cit.* II, 9.

[7] Quoted in J. Simon, *op. cit.* p. 201, n. 2.

public lectures in Greek and Hebrew (instead of Latin) and these were delivered in the university schools at the college's expense. The explanation is perhaps that the college was already supporting Latin lectures, as in the case of Gonville, and because of its superior wealth was required to institute the full quota of two fresh courses in the university. The lectures appear to have come into being immediately after Leigh's visitation in 1535[1] and were still functioning at the time of the last extant account of 1543–4.[2] In 1536–7 and 1537–8, the charge on the college was the modest sum of 4s 2d a term,[3] or 12s 6d for a year of three terms. But in 1539–40, lecture costs increased to 5s 8d a term;[4] and in 1543–4, the cost throughout the year was 4s 4d a term, an extra fourth term of lectures being put on during the summer.[5] This year, the lectures were given by master John Yong(e),[6] who is presumably to be identified with the John Yong(e) who became a King's Hall fellow in 1542–3 and remained as one of the foundation fellows of Trinity College in 1546.[7]

Taken together, the King's Hall evidence concerning early tutorial arrangements for undergraduate commoners and the institution of college lecturing facilities represent a substantial contribution to that revolutionary movement, which gained impetus in the latter half of the fifteenth and sixteenth centuries, whereby the greater part of university teaching came to be decentralised in the colleges, with the result that for the first time the several parts of the *studium* now became more important than the whole. It was this balance which persisted until the early twentieth century when once again the tide seemingly turned in the university's favour.

[1] *K.H. Accts.* xxv, fo. 45 v (1535–6): 'Item pro lectura ex iniuncto commissarii regis xiijs. iiijd.; item pro lecturis hebraica et greca in scolis publicis viijs. iiijd.'

[2] *Ibid.* xxvi, fo. 124 v.

[3] *K.H. Accts.* xxv, fo. 81 v (1536–7): 'Item pro lecturis hebraica et greca (in) scolis publicis pro uno termino finito in natale domini iiijs. ijd.; item pro lecturis hebraica et greca scolis publicis pro termino finito in festo Pasche iiijs. ijd.; item pro lecturis hebraica et greca scolis publicis pro termino finito in festo sancti Johanis baptiste iiijs. ijd.' See also *ibid.* xxv, fo. 119 v (1537–8).

[4] *Ibid.* xxvi, fo. 1 v.

[5] *Ibid.* xxvi, fo. 124 v.

[6] *Loc. cit.*

[7] Stamp, *Admissions to Trinity College, Cambridge,* i, 134.

Chapter 3

RELATIONS WITH THE UNIVERSITY
AND THE
ECCLESIASTICAL AUTHORITIES

It is common knowledge that the surviving muniments of Cambridge University of the fourteenth and fifteenth centuries are unfortunately far less numerous than those which exist for the Oxford *studium*. Consequently, any attempt to view the King's Hall and the King's Scholars in their essential context in relation to the university and to the ecclesiastical authorities of Ely and Canterbury must, of necessity, be based on a smaller corpus of documentary evidence than would otherwise be desired. The conclusions presented in this chapter have been derived from a study of college and university statutes, episcopal charters, episcopal and archiepiscopal registers, and a series of miscellaneous records preserved in the Muniment Room of Trinity College, Cambridge, and in Cambridge University Archives.

As might be expected from the peculiar circumstances governing the origin of the Society, the King's Hall and the King's Scholars occupied a specially privileged position within the medieval University of Cambridge. Although the college–university relationship does not appear to have embodied any unusual features, there is some body of evidence to support the contention that the King's Hall formed a kind of quasi-immunity or enclave set apart from the visitatorial powers of Ely and Canterbury, being in this respect subject only to the immediate jurisdiction of the king. In the related sphere of the university's own position vis-à-vis external ecclesiastical authority there are cogent reasons for challenging the deeply rooted assumption that by the papal award of John XXII of June 1318 the Cambridge *studium* acquired a complete theoretical exemption from episcopal and archiepiscopal jurisdiction.

Before presenting the evidence for these conclusions, it is necessary to make a few observations on the general attitude adopted by the Cambridge colleges towards external authority as represented in the

86

persons of the chancellor of the university and the bishop of Ely. There can be no doubt that right from the very start these small, self-governing collegiate societies were fiercely jealous of their independent status. A comparative study of their statutes reveals that in the ordinary way the jurisdiction of the chancellor and the bishop over purely secular college affairs was reduced to an absolute minimum. It is true that founders often stipulate that the election of the master requires to be confirmed by the chancellor;[1] where this is so, however, the proviso is always added that the approbation is to be of a nominal character and the chancellor is to have no power whatsoever even to question, let alone to quash, the election.[2] This apart, it was only in very special circumstances that the authority of either the chancellor or the bishop was to be invoked: and it is obvious that the attitude consistently maintained by the Cambridge colleges towards the university and the ecclesiastical authorities was essentially one of pragmatism. From the collegiate standpoint, chancellor and bishop signified two impartial personages who might occasionally be called upon to help resolve a problem of unusual constitutional difficulty.[3] Generally speaking, fourteenth-century college founders were keenly alive to the frustrating perplexities that would inevitably arise if, for example, the statutory procedure for the election of a new master ground to an electoral impasse. To obviate this, most codes of statutes grudgingly authorise, as a last-resort measure, that the chancellor or bishop be invited to appoint a master either from within the ranks of the college or, failing this, from elsewhere within the university.[4] Again, an embarrassing difficulty

---

[1] See e.g. the statutes of Michaelhouse printed by Stamp, *Michaelhouse*, p. 46, and Mullinger, *University of Cambridge*, I, 644; also the statutes of Clare and Gonville Hall in *Camb. Docs.* II, 123, 231.

[2] See e.g. the statutes of Michaelhouse in Stamp, *loc. cit.* and Mullinger, *loc. cit.*: '...et huiusmodi electio cancellario universitatis Cantebrig' notificetur simpliciter approbanda sed non examinanda. Nec per hoc habeat cancellarius dicte universitatis potestatem sive jurisdictionem dictam electionem quassandi...'; also the statutes of Trinity Hall in *Camb. Docs.* II, 421: 'Nullam autem potestatem habeat cancellarius predictus electionem predictam discutere vel eam reprobare nec aliam jurisdictionem preter hoc in electum nec eligentes exercere sed solum electum sibi per maiorem partem sociorum collegii presentatum illico extrajudicialiter approbare.'

[3] See the pertinent remarks on the services of the visitor by E. F. Jacob, 'Founders and foundations in the later middle ages', *B.I.H.R.* xxxv (1962), 29 ff. at p. 44.

[4] See e.g. the statutes of Clare, Gonville Hall and Trinity Hall in *Camb. Docs.* II, 124, 232, 421.

would present itself if the fellows found themselves saddled with a refractory or criminally negligent master who, despite their repeated protestations, refused to retire gracefully from office. For such exigencies, it was essential that the fellows be given some means of redress, and most founders accorded them statutory powers to invoke the assistance of the chancellor or bishop[1] so that the appropriate steps might be taken to effect the removal of the intransigent occupant. Finally, provision was sometimes made for consultation with the chancellor or bishop in the event of there being a serious internal dispute which could not be satisfactorily settled by the master and senior fellows.[2]

But even this severely limited area of statutory intervention accorded to the external authorities found no expression whatsoever in the statutes of the King's Hall. It was not required. For the unique position of the warden as a Crown appointee[3] ensured that constitutional difficulties of the kind mentioned above did not arise. As the warden was appointed by the king, there was no possibility of an electoral deadlock; if his subsequent conduct merited his removal, this was exclusively a matter for the Crown;[4] and if an internal dissension materialised which proved incapable of amicable settlement, this was likewise a concern for the king as visitor. In the light of these considerations, it is legitimate to differentiate the King's Hall from all other fourteenth- and fifteenth-century Cambridge colleges by virtue of the fact that it remained wholly uninvolved in that type of pragmatic relationship which existed between the latter and the university and ecclesiastical authorities.

As members of the academic community, the King's Scholars were subject in the normal way to the chancellor's jurisdiction. It is certain that within the university they had the status of clerks. Although most of the ecclesiastical and royal documents concerning the King's Hall refer to it as *collegium scolarium*[5] and describe the

---

[1] See e.g. the statutes of Clare and Trinity Hall, *ibid.* II, 128–9, 426.

[2] See e.g. the statutes of Michaelhouse in Stamp, *op. cit.* p. 44, and Mullinger, *op. cit.* I, 643; also the statutes of Clare in *Camb. Docs.* II, 137–8.

[3] See below, pp. 148–9.

[4] See the case of the removal of warden Simon Neylond discussed below, pp. 171 ff.

[5] See e.g. the letters patent of 7 October 1337 and the letters patent of 25 July 1342, *K.H. Cabinet*, nos. 8, 25; see further the charter of 23 October 1343 of the prior and chapter of the cathedral church of Ely, reinforcing the confirmation of the founda-

Scholars variously as *scolares aule regis, scolares aule nostre Cantebr'* or *scolares collegii nostri*,[1] the episcopal letters of confirmation of 18 October 1343[2] designate the college as *collegium clericorum*. Moreover, the technical status of clerk is clearly presupposed in the King's Hall statutes of 1380, where it is enjoined that every Scholar is to possess a gown tailored to fit the requirements of his clerical degree[3] and that none is to be permitted to carry a dagger, knife or any other dangerous weapon unbecoming to his standing as a clerk.[4] Having clerical status, the King's Scholars were, *ipso facto*, fully subject to the teaching and disciplinary regulations of the university. They were bound to hear the ordinary lectures in the schools, and if they attained the M.A. were required to deliver the usual statutory quota of lectures under the provisions of the necessary regency system;[5] and the bachelors among them were to be present at the repetitions and public disputations of the doctors and masters in their own particular faculties.[6] As already indicated, the King's Scholars were bound to observe the university rules concerning propriety and simplicity of dress as well as the disciplinary code against the breaking of the peace and the carrying of offensive weapons.[7] The college statutes also prescribe the attendance of the Scholars at three annual university processions suitably robed according to their degrees.[8]

There is here one enigmatic point which demands further investigation. The clause in the King's Hall statutes which enjoins attendance at the schools either to hear or to deliver ordinary lectures bears the startling proviso that Scholars may be excused not only on the grounds of infirmity but also of old age.[9] No other English code of

---

tion of the King's Hall by Simon Montacute, bishop of Ely, in October 1343, *K.H. Cabinet*, no. 27.

[1] Numerous examples of this terminology may be found among the documents in *K.H. Cabinet*.   [2] *Ibid.* no. 27.

[3] See the King's Hall statutes in Rouse Ball, *The King's Scholars and King's Hall*, p. 68: 'Item quod quilibet Scolarium predictorum de Liberatura sua sibi fieri faciat Robam Talarem decentem et honestam pro Statu Clericali...'

[4] *Ibid.*: 'Item quod nullus dictorum scolarium...basilardum portet seu aliquem alium cultellum statui Clericorum Indecentem...'

[5] Rouse Ball, *op. cit.* p. 66.   [6] *Ibid.*

[7] Rouse Ball, *op. cit.* p. 68; the corresponding university statutes are *Contra ferentes arcus aut balistas infra municipium* and *De pacis perturbatoribus* (*Camb. Docs.* I, 320–2).

[8] Rouse Ball, *op. cit.* p. 69.

[9] *Ibid.* p. 66: 'Nisi infirmitas aut senectus eos excusaverit scolas frequentent lectiones ordinarias audiant vel legant prout statuta exigunt Universitatis.'

college statutes embodies senility as an excuse for exemption from academic duties: nor is it to be found in the statutes of Cambridge University.[1] The following explanation is offered. Attention has been drawn above to the significant number of King's Scholars who succeeded in remaining at the college for periods of over twenty, thirty, forty or even fifty years without apparently obtaining a degree.[2] In order to qualify as a scholar of the university, however, and to enjoy the immunities inherent in the status of clerk, it was obligatory to have one's name inscribed on a regent master's roll (*matricula*), to be entered upon a definite academic course, and to attend at least three weekly lectures in the schools.[3] Because of this, it would have been essential for the older type of King's Scholar who had not yet advanced beyond the undergraduate stage to be enrolled annually for the B.A. course. But after spending twenty, thirty or more years striving to attain a first degree normally taken in three or four, he would, by medieval notions, have grown old in the course of the unequal struggle; and one may conjecture that in such cases the enrolment would serve as a mere technical device to enable him to perpetuate himself at the university. It was doubtless to cover 'mature' students of this kind that the senility clause was inserted in the King's Hall statutes, providing an interesting and amusing in-

---

[1] The relevant university statutes are *De Immunitate scolarium* and *De Falsis scolaribus et aliis pacis perturbatoribus* in *Camb. Docs.* I, 332–3 (i.e. nos. 42, 43, *Statuta Antiqua*; nos. 43 and 144 in the Old Proctor's Book). The wording and concentrated nature of the clause in the King's Hall code suggest that it was based on both of these university statutes. Father B. Hackett (whose study of an early text of Cambridge statutes is to be published by the Cambridge University Press as *The original Statutes of Cambridge University*) has kindly informed me that no. 42 is definitely to be dated before 1380 and the same probably holds for no. 43 although the most that can be said with confidence is that it is not later than 1401. It is surprising that the clause in the King's Hall statutes does not state, as the university statutes enjoin, that scholars may not absent themselves from lectures without the sanction of the regent master in charge of the course. It is most unlikely that this provision would not apply to the King's Scholars and it is presumably to be understood by correlating the abbreviated college statute with the fully extended university statutes itemised above. It is perhaps useful to note that the statutes of Cambridge University of the thirteenth (*ex inform.* Father Hackett) and fourteenth centuries do not have any special regulations for the colleges, only for the hostels or hospices.

[2] See above, p. 56.

[3] See the provisions of the university statute, *De Immunitate scolarium* in *Camb. Docs.* I, 332–3.

sight into a medieval academic practice which had perhaps a greater currency than is often realised.

There is no reason to suppose that the King's Scholars enjoyed a specially privileged legal position with respect to the juridical rights of the Cambridge chancellor. It is a lamentable circumstance for the history of the medieval university that most of the records of cases heard in the chancellor's court before the sixteenth century have either been destroyed or otherwise lost to view. It is therefore all the more providential that a record of one such case involving the King's Scholars has survived.

The evidence for this case is contained in an entry in the book known as the Register of Thomas Markaunt,[1] who was one of the proctors in 1417, and is concerned with a dispute between the King's Scholars and the master and scholars of Clare in 1373.[2] Markaunt's entry takes the form of a copy of royal letters of Edward III addressed to the chancellor, proctors and masters of the university which refer to a mandate previously issued by the king for the removal of the case from the chancellor's court to the king's council at Westminster.[3] It is unfortunate that the nature of the dispute cannot now be discovered, but it was evidently of such grave import that the king felt obliged on this one occasion to interrupt the normal course of university judicial procedure. But the fact that the king transferred this particular case from the chancellor's court to his own at Westminster does not signify that a dispute involving the King's Scholars did not ordinarily fall within the cognisance of the Cambridge chancellor. Quite the reverse, for the copy of the royal letters in Markaunt's book makes it very plain that prior to the king's decision to take the case into his own hands it did in fact go as a matter of course to be heard in the chancellor's court:[4] moreover,

---

[1] For doubts raised as to whether this paper volume of 81 folios should in fact be ascribed to Thomas Markaunt see W. Ullmann, 'The decline of the chancellor's authority in medieval Cambridge: a rediscovered statute', *Historical Journal*, 1 (1958), p. 179, n. 12.

[2] See *Registrum Magistri Thome Markaunt*, B. fo. 7v (preserved in Cambridge University Archives).

[3] The case was heard at Westminster before the bishops of London and Ely, the chancellor, and other members of the council, and a settlement agreeable to both parties was reached.

[4] '...ceperimus in manum nostram causas et inquisitiones super eisdem [i.e. dissensions arising out of the dispute between the King's Scholars and the scholars of

the central point of the royal letters of 1373 was to assure the university that no infringement of its liberties, privileges, rights, statutes or customs was intended[1] and that this single instance of removal would not in any way constitute a precedent for the future: '[It is not our intent]...quod dictum mandatum nostrum quovismodo tendat in preiudicium vestrum seu trahat in consequentia in futurum.'[2] The evidence of this isolated case seems to confirm the assumption that, as clerks, the King's Scholars were immediately subject to the chancellor's jurisdiction. One may readily suppose that the king would not normally attempt to remove a university case to a royal court, because intervention of this kind, unless hedged around with very special circumstances, would almost certainly be quickly construed as a violation of the chancellor's jurisdictional sovereignty. That the king felt impelled on at least one occasion to transfer a case involving the King's Scholars would seem to bear out the conclusion that, though the latter were unendowed with any exceptional rights or privileges with respect to the chancellor's authority, they were, nevertheless, the object of a somewhat greater measure of royal care and protection than their clerical counterparts elsewhere within the university.

It will be recalled that the Society of the King's Scholars was transformed into the endowed College of the King's Hall by letters patent of 7 October 1337.[3] On 16 October of that year Edward III addressed letters to Pope Benedict XII for the twofold purpose of obtaining papal confirmation for his foundation and the pope's consent to endow the Society with the advowson of the church of St Peter, Northampton, with leave to appropriate the same.[4] In furtherance of this second aim, the king sent off identical letters to three cardinals urging them to use their influence with the pope to expedite

---

Clare] coram vobis pendentes...' [for the sake of clarity the order of the wording has been reversed]. (See *Reg. T. Markaunt*, B. fo. 7v.)

1 'Nolentes libertatibus, privilegiis, iuribus, statutis seu consuetudinibus vestris in aliquo derogare' (*loc. cit.*).

2 *Loc. cit.*   3 See above, pp. 10 ff.

4 Rymer, *Foedera*, II, pt. ii, 1003–4: '...supplicamus quatinus...dignetur vestra benignitas illud [i.e. collegium] ex certa scientia confirmare...et praefatam ecclesiam dictis custodi et scolaribus...concedere...in usus suos proprios perpetuo possidendam...'; extracts from this letter are given by R. Parker, *The history and antiquities of the University of Cambridge*, *cit.* pp. 138–9, and by Archbishop Parker, *De Antiquitate Britannicae Ecclesiae* (ed. S. Drake, London, 1729), xxvii.

matters relating to the ecclesiastical endowment.[1] No papal reply to the king has yet been discovered but both of his requests were presumably granted. Although Edward may have acquired a papal confirmation for the King's Hall shortly after its foundation, it was not until 18 October 1343 that the college was confirmed by Simon Montacute, bishop of Ely, a surprising fact which calls for further elucidation.

Only from a narrow technical point of view ought October 1337 to be regarded as the foundation date of the King's Hall. It has been argued above that Edward III was finally moved to the act of endowment of that year by a desire to stabilise the ambiguous position of a potentially valuable royal institution whose finances had fallen into a parlous state and whose future hung in a precarious balance:[2] in the event, however, he provided only the minimum financial requirements necessary for the immediate purpose and these proved wholly inadequate to meet the permanent needs of the college. This original endowment comprised the house of Robert de Croyland, the advowson of the church of St Peter, Northampton, with its chapels and licence for its appropriation, and the continuance of the exchequer maintenance allowance calculated at the rate of twopence per Scholar per day.[3] That these arrangements constituted only an interim or stopgap endowment is evident from the various expedients resorted to in the years immediately succeeding as well as from information contained in the surviving records of the period.

On 24 February 1338 the king reinforced the obligation of the sheriff of the counties of Cambridge and Huntingdon to pay sums in arrears to the King's Hall out of the issues of his bailiwick (for which he rendered account at the exchequer);[4] on 10 March of the same year the king revoked the grant of the advowson of the church of St Peter, Northampton, on the grounds that he had forgotten that he had previously granted it to the Hospital of St Katherine near the Tower of London;[5] and in its place he bestowed the advowson of the church of Fakenham in the diocese of Norwich, then held for life by Queen Isabella, but with the promise of a later appropriation.[6]

---

[1] One of these letters is printed in full by Rymer, II, pt. ii, 1004.
[2] See above, pp. 13–15.
[3] See the letters patent of 7 October 1337, *K.H. Cabinet*, no. 8.
[4] *Cal. Pat. R.*, 1338–1340, pp. 20–1.
[5] *Ibid.* pp. 28, 29.   [6] *Ibid.* p. 28.

By 1340 it was obvious that the sheriff of Cambridge and Huntingdon could not meet his financial obligation with respect to the King's Hall. On 1 May of that year, therefore, part of this burden was transferred to the abbot of Waltham, who contracted to pay to the college the £55 due to the exchequer for the farm of the town of Waltham, the residue of a cash endowment of £103 8s 4d being supplied by the sheriff.[1] The college accounts of this period tend to corroborate the conclusion that these piecemeal and ephemeral arrangements did not add up to any very satisfactory endowment. While a balance on the credit side was registered for each year, except one, between 1337–8 and 1343–4, the sums recorded are exceedingly low.[2] Considering that at this early stage the college did not possess much in the way of capital reserves in the form of plate, property or valuable interior fittings, there seems to be little doubt that in the six years immediately following the foundation in 1337 the King's Scholars were tied to a restrictively tight budget.

TABLE 2

Harvest year	Credit			Debit		
	£	s	d	£	s	d
1337–8	9	16	9			
1338–9	13	2	7½			
1340–1	21	0	7			
1341–2	16	15	0½			
1342–3	12	3	4			
1343–4				14	1	

Moreover, the extant documents for this period afford adequate proof of the fact that neither the king, the bishop of Ely nor warden Thomas Powys reckoned that the college had been founded in anything more than a technical sense. For example, in the Muniment Room of Trinity College there survives a parchment compotus roll of Thomas Powys in which the warden accounts for expenses incurred in journeying to London, Lincoln, Norwich, Ely and elsewhere in connection with ecclesiastical and other business relating

---

[1] *Cal. Pat. R.*, p. 511.
[2] These figures have been derived from a series of financial statements given at the end of the annual accounts for several successive years in the first volume of the King's Hall records. For further details see below, pp. 118–19.

to the 'foundation' (*fundacio*) of the college in 1342–3.[1] And the matter would seem to be put beyond dispute by the letters patent of 24 May 1342 whereby the king set up a commission consisting of the chancellor, treasurer, keeper of the privy seal, the steward of the chamber, the master of the rolls of chancery, the king's confessor and the king's almoner to do all things necessary for the final completion of the foundation of the college and to evolve a rule of life for the Scholars.[2] As a result of the findings of this royal commission, letters patent were issued on 25 July 1342 assigning the advowsons of four churches of the king's patronage to the college with leave to appropriate the same.[3] Clearly, it was only then that the King's Hall was considered to have been well and truly founded in the sense that for the first time it was adequately and permanently endowed: and when the arrangements for this second foundation had been completed, six years after the original endowment of 1337, the bishop of Ely was moved to confirm the institution.

It is perhaps most convenient to note here just how closely the early financial history of the King's Hall appears to have been determined by the opening events of the Hundred Years War. Edward III had planned his first invasion of France in the autumn of the year in which the college had been technically founded.[4] As the king had to abandon his scheme for a French landing through lack of money,[5] it seems highly probable that Edward's urgent need for all available finances at this time accounts for the meagre and temporary character of the original collegiate endowment. Furthermore, the long delay of between four and five years before any steps were taken towards the ordering of the completion of the foundation of the college must surely, to some extent, have been occasioned by the absence of the king abroad during the greater part of this period. Edward left England for the Continent on 16 July 1338 and did not return for any length of time until the latter part of 1340.[6] This would accord very well with the fact that the royal commission of

---

[1] See the parchment roll in two membranes (defective) beginning 'Particule compoti Thome Powys Custodis Aule Scolarium...' in *K.H. Cabinet*, no. 30.

[2] *Cal. Pat. R.*, 1340–1343, p. 466.

[3] *Ibid.* pp. 495–6; *K.H. Cabinet*, no. 25.

[4] On this point see E. Perroy, *The Hundred Years War* (English ed. trans. by W. B. Wells, London, 1951), p. 97.

[5] *Loc. cit.*   [6] Perroy, *Hundred Years War*, pp. 101–6.

inquiry into the financial state of the King's Hall was not instituted until May 1342, that is to say, in the period following the king's return and before his subsequent departure for France in October 1342.[1]

Although the crucial documents themselves have not survived, there is a convincing body of related evidence which almost certainly proves that in 1342 the King's Hall succeeded in acquiring a lengthy and valuable royal charter of privileges and immunities closely modelled upon a similar grant made to a college of chantry priests founded at Stratford-on-Avon eleven years previously. Among the terms of reference of the royal commission of 1342 is one authorising the commissioners to confer upon the King's Hall warden and fellows, by letters patent under the great seal, such liberties as the king had lately awarded to the college of chantry priests founded at Stratford-on-Avon in 1331 by John de Stratford, then bishop of Winchester.[2] The commission resulted in the transference to the Hall of the advowsons of the aforenamed churches of the king's patronage, but no reference was made on this occasion to the Stratford privileges: nor is any to be found in the subsequent extant governmental records relating to the college. But for the fortunate survival of the immensely detailed parchment account roll of Thomas Powys,[3] one would be forced to conclude that the grant had not been implemented. As already indicated, this lengthy document accounts for the expenses incurred by warden Powys in the course of his protractedly tedious negotiations concerning the appropriation of the four churches and other business affecting the 'foundation' of the college. From the evidence of this compotus roll it is beyond doubt that Powys pressed hard to put the King's Hall in possession of the privileges accorded to the contemporary Stratford college. A detailed reconstruction of his movements is possible.

On 12 August 1342 Powys set out for London with the firm intention of acquiring the Stratford liberties. His first step was to remind the king of his promise (contained in the letters patent to the

---

[1] *Ibid.* p. 115.

[2] For details of this foundation see W. Dugdale, *Monasticon Anglicanum* (6 vols., ed. J. Caley, H. Ellis and B. Bandinel, London, 1817–30), VI, pt. iii, 1471; also Dugdale, *The antiquities of Warwickshire* (London, 1656), p. 521; see further, G. H. Cook, *Mediaeval chantries and chantry chapels* (2nd ed. London, 1963), p. 69.

[3] See above, pp. 94–5 and 95 n. 1.

commissioners of 24 May 1342) by sending him a document setting forth the tenor of the privileges in question:

...ad mittend' eidem domino Regi tenorem libertatum quas idem dominus Rex nuper concessit collegio capellanorum apud Stratforde super Avene per Archiepiscopum Cantuar' fundato...

The next stage was to obtain letters from the king to the chancellor authorising the issue of letters patent conferring the Stratford charter of privileges on the King's Hall:

...ad impetrand' alias literas domini Regis eidem cancellario quod habere faceret predictis custodi et scolaribus literas patentes de magno sigillo Regis ad habend' tot et tales libertates quot et quales idem dominus Rex predicto collegio capellanorum concessit et ulterius ad prosequend' facturam literarum predictarum pro libertatibus antedictis.

The letters referred to here have not been discovered and it might still be thought that the king had quashed the award at the last moment. But two entries in the compotus roll make it clear that Powys' mission was successfully completed. The first records a payment to a clerk for making a copy of the Stratford privileges:

Et ulterius hoc soluit uno clerico ad scribend' copiam dictarum libertatum de rotulis cancellar' xij d.

This is evidently the document containing the 'tenorem libertatum' required by Powys to 'jog' the king's memory. The second and critical entry is for a fee given to one, William Whythurte by name, for the writing of the letters patent conferring the Stratford privileges on the warden and fellows of the King's Hall:

Et domino Wilhelmo Whythurte ad scribend' literas patentes de eisdem libertationibus habend' iij s.

Thus the foregoing evidence, which it has been thought necessary to present in some detail, would seem to prove that the privileges and immunities itemised in the extant Stratford charter were acquired by the King's Hall in August 1342.

What then was the value of these liberties for the King's Hall and why were they so eagerly sought? The Stratford charter of privileges dated 26 March 1337,[1] which must of necessity be our sole guide in

---

[1] P.R.O. C 53/124; *Cal. Charter Rolls*, 1327–1341, pp. 422–3. Reference to this charter is made by Dugdale, *Antiquities of Warwickshire, loc. cit.*

this matter, is an exceedingly copious document, and little more than a bald summary can here be attempted. The central and perhaps most important section of the charter was designed to safeguard the moveable property and monetary resources of the 'men and tenants' of the college against possible future alienation in the law courts. The charter granted to the Stratford warden and chaplains all the chattels of their 'men and tenants' in their lands and fees with the added stipulation that if any of the latter was required to forfeit his chattels by due process of law for any offence whatever, judged in any court of the realm, then these same chattels would automatically revert to the warden and chaplains. It was further conceded that the warden and chaplains would have all fines, amercements, ransoms and forfeited issues of their 'men and tenants' in whatsoever of the king's courts such exactions might be imposed. Moreover, it was decreed that the warden, chaplains and all of their 'men' were to be quit of all tolls, aids and tallages to which they might be liable by reason of their lands, tenements, goods, chattels and rents. Exemption was also granted from all ecclesiastical tithes, both those imposed by Canterbury or York and by the papacy: it was further extended to embrace all temporal tithes on moveables, lands, tenements and rents. In addition, it was enacted that no magnate of the realm, or any of the king's officials, might lodge or quarter himself on the college without the full consent of the warden and chaplains. Nor was it to be lawful for pensions or corrodies to be thrust upon the society against its will. The charter ends with a general affirmation of royal protection whereby the chapel, its warden and chaplains with all their lands, possessions and chattels were taken into the king's special safe keeping: '. . . in nostram protectionem suscepimus specialem.'

Such, in essence, was the charter of privileges and immunities which we must now suppose was acquired by the King's Hall in 1342. The advantages are obvious: the charter ensured a specially privileged and protected status for the college under the Crown, granted valuable exemptions from lay and ecclesiastical tithes and other forms of levy, and guarded against the draining of collegiate revenues through unwelcome quartering by king's officers and members of the nobility. There is, however, a difficulty in explaining the relevance of the 'men and tenants' section of the charter when applied to the King's Hall. Who were the 'men and tenants' of this royal foundation? In the course of the fifteenth century, the college did in fact acquire numerous tenants by virtue of its property holdings in Cambridge.[1] Although the King's Hall remained propertyless in the fourteenth century, it seems likely that the eventual acquisition of property would have been envisaged from the start. Given this assumption, this part of the charter would have been regarded as a desirable insurance policy for the future. There is the further possibility that when construed in an academic sense the 'men' of the phrase 'men and tenants' was taken to embrace the college's domestic staff: this, however, is pure speculation for which there is no supporting evidence. Whatever the case, it is legitimate to conclude that this royal charter made the King's Hall into the most highly privileged and protected of the Cambridge colleges in the era before the foundation of King's in the mid-fifteenth century.

The episcopal letters of confirmation of 18 October 1343 would appear to highlight the equivocal status of the King's Hall as an institution *sui generis* finely balanced between the claims of royal jurisdiction and the juridical rights of the bishop of Ely. The usual procedure adopted for the foundation of a medieval academic college falls into five distinct stages. First, it was necessary for the patron or founder to obtain a royal licence from the chancery.[2] Having gained the king's consent, erected the buildings and compiled the statutes, he had to submit the entire project to the bishop of the diocese for confirmation. After due examination, the bishop would normally approve and confirm the institution. This confirmation might be further reinforced by that of the prior and chapter of the cathedral church, though this was not obligatory. Finally, the foundation had to receive the approbation of the chancellor and masters of the university. Where the records survive, it is apparent that, in this chain of events, it was the bishop's *confirmatio* following upon the *licentia regis*[3] that conferred legality on a collegiate institution lying within the diocese. For example, the episcopal charters for Pembroke, Gonville Hall and Trinity Hall, Cambridge, signify that

---

[1] See below, pp. 240 ff.

[2] For a discussion of the various types of documents connected with the foundation of a medieval college see Jacob, *B.I.H.R.* xxxv (1962), 29, 30.

[3] See e.g. the royal licence for the foundation of Corpus Christi, Cambridge, reported in the register of Thomas de l'Isle, bishop of Ely, 1345–61, fo. 44 v. (The Ely Registers are now deposited in Cambridge University Library.)

legality took effect immediately from the act of the bishop's confirmation. In the case of both Gonville and Trinity Hall, the wording is the same and thus can be conveniently quoted: '...auctoritate diocesana...approbamus, ratificamus et confirmamus dictum collegium *ex nunc* imperpetuum licitum et canonicum decernentes...'.[1] In marked contrast, the episcopal confirmation of the King's Hall was retrospective in character. The document did not *ex nunc* confer legality upon the college: on the contrary, it merely confirmed that in 1343 the King's Hall already was, and had been since the royal foundation of 1337, a legally constituted society: '...ipsumque collegium fuisse et esse legitimum...diffinimus, statuimus, decernimus...'.[2] Admittedly, the meaning is here capable of ambiguous interpretation: nevertheless, when the wording of this *confirmatio* is set against the usual *ex nunc* form, there are certainly grounds for believing that the episcopal confirmation of the King's Hall was of a purely nominal character affixed to an institution possessed of a prior legality derived from Edward III's act of foundation.

The consideration that perhaps the bishop of Ely did not presume to confer a legal status upon the royal college but merely confirmed its legality retrospectively leads naturally to the suspicion that the relationship between the King's Hall and the external ecclesiastical authorities was substantially different from that involving the other colleges of the medieval University of Cambridge.

Relations between the university and the external ecclesiastical authorities have to be assessed from two different points of view. As institutions lying within Ely diocese and Canterbury province, the university and its colleges were subject in the normal way to the ordinary jurisdiction of Ely and the metropolitan jurisdiction of Canterbury in all ecclesiastical and spiritual matters. In this respect, the position of the King's Hall was exactly the same as that of any other collegiate institution. For example, the copious documents relating to the ecclesiastical business of the college, such as those for the appropriation of the churches of St Mary's, Cambridge; Felmers-

---

[1] See the charter of episcopal confirmation of 20 January 1350 for Trinity Hall in *Warren's Book* (ed. A. W. W. Dale, Cambridge, 1911), p. 29; *Camb. Docs.* II, 416–17. For the bishop's confirmation of Gonville Hall of 15 January 1351 see the register of Thomas de l'Isle, fo. 45v; for the confirmation of 23 November 1349 for Pembroke see *ibid.* fo. 30v.

[2] See the charter of Simon Montacute of 18 October 1343 in *K.H. Cabinet*, no. 27.

ham, Bedfordshire; Hintlesham, Suffolk; and Grendon, North-amptonshire, reveal that affairs were conducted in every detail according to usual diocesan procedure.[1] Similarly, as members of the diocese, individual King's Scholars were subject to ordinary jurisdiction in purely spiritual matters. The registers of the bishops of Ely contain numerous entries to the effect that fellows of Cambridge colleges were licensed to choose their own confessors, or to say mass within the college, or to erect private oratories.[2] And in the register of Thomas Arundel, bishop of Ely, 1374–8, there is an entry recording the grant of such a licence to Thomas de London, King's Scholar, authorising him to choose his own confessor.[3] It is therefore apparent that in wholly ecclesiastical and spiritual affairs both the King's Hall as an institution and individual King's Scholars were subject to ordinary diocesan control.

The second and more momentous connection between the university and the bishop of Ely was that which resulted from the bishop's peculiar relationship to the *studium* through the office of chancellor. For, originally, the chancellor was merely an officer of the bishop, wielding delegated episcopal powers.[4] This remained the ultimate legal standpoint of the bishops of Ely until the university was granted a complete exemption from ecclesiastical authority by decision of the Barnwell Process of 1430. Before this date and irrespective of the actuality of the situation, the bishops consistently laid theoretical claim to the university, regarding it almost as a kind of physical possession in which both chancellor and masters exercised their functions only by episcopal licence and authority.[5] In more realistic terms, this meant that the university and its several colleges were required to submit to the visitation of the bishop of the diocese and of the archbishop of the province. The King's Hall and its Scholars, however, appear to have been exempt from the visitatorial powers of Ely and Canterbury.

---

[1] All of these documents and many more relating to the ecclesiastical business of the college are preserved in the Muniment Room, Trinity College. From many examples, see *K.H. Cabinet*, nos. 28, 40, 41, 42.

[2] See e.g. the register of Thomas de l'Isle, fos. 9v, 38v, 42v.

[3] See the register of Thomas Arundel, fo. 5v.

[4] On this point see the excellent discussion by G. Peacock, *Observations on the statutes of the University of Cambridge*, *cit.* pp. 17–18, and 18, n. 4.

[5] See conveniently *ibid.* p. 18. This point is emphatically made in the episcopal registers, where the possessive form *universitatis nostre Cantebr'* is repeatedly used.

As founder, the king served as sole visitor to the college, a duty which, it has already been remarked, devolved in actual practice upon the office of the royal chancellor:[1] and in matters of a non-spiritual nature the king jealously guarded his rights against possible encroachment by the ecclesiastical authorities. This is splendidly illustrated by the letters patent of 14 July 1383[2] whereby the king commissioned Thomas Arundel, bishop of Ely, to visit the Hall to investigate the alleged abuses which had arisen during the unhappy wardenship of Simon Neylond.[3] But the document makes it unequivocally plain that Arundel was to act, not in his capacity as bishop, but as king's commissioner wielding delegated royal powers. In the terms of the commission, Arundel is to visit:

...custodem, scolares et ministros eiusdem collegii in propria persona vestra nomine nostro ac iure regio...[4]

The sole jurisdictional rights of the Crown in relation to the King's Hall and the King's Scholars are further protected in a later passage where it is stipulated that Arundel is not to presume to exercise any ordinary jurisdiction over the college, its warden, scholars or 'ministers'; nor is the present visitation to be treated in any way as a precedent:

Intentionis tamen nostre non existit quod vos, prefate Episcope, in visitatione predicta aliquam iurisdiccionem ordinariam nisi solummodo auctoritate nostra in dicto collegio seu custode, scolaribus aut ministris eiusdem exerceatis, seu exercere presumatis, seu quod presens visitatio per vos auctoritate dicte commissionis nostre ista vice faciend' cedat al' in exemplum seu trahatur in consequentiam aliqualiter in futurum.[5]

In conjunction with the fact that there is no other recorded instance of a visitation by a bishop of Ely, this evidence points to the conclusion that throughout its entire history the King's Hall remained the exclusively private and intimate concern of the Crown, over which the bishop's jurisdiction in secular affairs did not extend.[6]

---

[1] See above, p. 64.

[2] See the register of Thomas Arundel, fo. 106 v.

[3] Warden of the King's Hall from 6 October 1377 until his removal on 19 May 1385.

[4] See the register of Arundel, fo. 106 v.   [5] *Ibid.*

[6] The fact that a detailed reference to Arundel's commission concerning the King's Hall is to be found in his register seems in itself to emphasise the point that this was

The document further reveals that the power to remove King's Scholars was one wholly reserved to the Crown. In the letters of commission Arundel is expressly forbidden to exercise any authority in this matter. On the contrary, it is stated that the removal (*amotio*) of Scholars who merit deprivation of their fellowships (*privandorum*) and the substitution (*subrogatio*) of others is an affair specially reserved to the king (*nobis specialiter reservat'*) to be decided in chancery.[1] As all King's Scholars were appointed directly by the Crown under writ of privy seal, it is only to be expected that the king would insist upon this exclusive right of removal: for otherwise he would not have a complete physical control over the movement of the personnel of his collegiate foundation. Thus, in this essential respect, the King's Scholars of the pre-Barnwell-Process period are to be distinguished from all other members of the Cambridge academic community, who, at least in theory, were subject to the disciplinary powers inherent in ecclesiastical visitation.[2]

Moreover, the available evidence strongly suggests that the King's Hall and its Scholars were exempt from the metropolitan visitation of the archbishop of Canterbury. This is negatively demonstrated by an entry in Arundel's Canterbury register concerning the archiepiscopal visitation of the university in 1401.[3] On this occasion, Arundel first visited the chancellor and the university in person and then the several colleges by commissaries.[4] Of the eight Cambridge colleges only two, Corpus Christi and the King's Hall, were not visited. C. H. Cooper has acutely drawn attention to the fact that this year the master of Corpus, Richard Billingford, was also chancellor of the university.[5] Consequently, it may very well be that the

---

no ordinary episcopal visitation: for the scant occurrence of visitation material in the Ely Registers most probably indicates that, 'as in other dioceses, separate visitation records were kept and have not survived' (D. M. Owen, 'Ely diocesan records', *Studies in Church History*, I (1964), 176 ff. at p. 177). If this were the case, then clearly the proper place for the recording of this exceptional royal commission was the register and not the separate visitation lists.

[1] See the register of Arundel, fo. 106v.
[2] By the fourteenth century, it is unlikely that in actual practice either the bishop or archbishop would take disciplinary action against a clerk without the closest cooperation and consent of the chancellor.
[3] The entry is printed by I. J. Churchill, *Canterbury administration* (2 vols., 1933), II, 152. [4] *Ibid.*
[5] Cooper, *Annals of Cambridge*, I, 147, n. 1.

archbishop considered that the college had been vicariously visited because of his personal visitation and questioning of its master. In the case of the King's Hall, however, the explanation would appear to be that the college was not visited simply because it was exempt from archiepiscopal jurisdiction.

Although Henry VI put his Cambridge foundation, King's College, under the visitatorial powers of the bishop of Lincoln, he nevertheless obtained for it a bull from Eugenius IV in 1445 granting exemption from the ecclesiastical jurisdictions of Ely and Canterbury.[1] As far as can be determined, the King's Hall never acquired a formal bull of exemption. But perhaps the key to an understanding of its status is to be sought once more in its household origins. As the Society evolved from a detachment of the chapel royal set in the University of Cambridge, it is reasonable to suppose that the privileges and immunities of that body would be transmitted to its academic offshoot. From the *Liber regie capelle* and the Black Book of Edward IV, it is known that members of the chapel and the household were exempt from episcopal and archiepiscopal jurisdiction, being directly subject to the jurisdiction of the dean of chapel.[2] When Edward II established his chapel 'colony' in Cambridge it was most probably endowed *a priori* with the same exemptions vis-à-vis ecclesiastical authority as those belonging to the chapel as a whole: these would automatically be transferred to the college founded by Edward III.

Remarkably few references to other Cambridge colleges occur in the King's Hall records. There are a few chance documentary survivals but the evidence is really insufficient to allow us to estimate the full extent of the relationships forged between the King's Hall and neighbouring institutions. Evidently, however, a close association developed between the college and St Catharine's, founded in 1473 by Robert Woodlark, provost of King's. For on at least two occa-

---

[1] See J. Saltmarsh, 'King's College', *V.C.H.* (Cambridge), III, 377.

[2] See W. Ullmann, ed., *Liber regie capelle*, p. 15: 'His jurisdictional power comes into play in all cases which would otherwise fall within the competency of the archidiaconal and episcopal courts'; also A. R. Myers, *The household of Edward IV, cit.* p. 134: '...Verum tamen in domo ista regia nullus episcopus quicquam habet juris nisi sibi committatur; rex enim patronus est et regimen sue capelle eciam hospitalis et spiritualis cure cuiuscunque presbitero ydoneo immediate potest committere.'

sions, the King's Hall was called upon to act as a guarantor of agreements involving St Catharine's. By an indenture of 14 October 1504,[1] the King's Hall and the Merchant Tailors of London were appointed joint guarantors of a composition whereby the executors of Hugh Pemberton, late alderman of the city of London, made a gift of two hundred marks to St Catharine's in consideration of the performance of certain specified duties. In the event of default or omissions on the part of the college in carrying out the full terms of the agreement, the guarantors were empowered to exact fines and other penalties itemised in the composition. Again, by an indenture of 20 August 1506,[2] the King's Hall agreed to act as principal guarantor of an agreement concerning the foundation of a fellowship at St Catharine's with plenary powers to exact penalties for non-performance of the conditions of the bond. As an additional safeguard, Jesus College and Peterhouse were designated subsidiary guarantors bound to step into the breach if the King's Hall failed to fulfil its duties in the case of default by St Catharine's. In the same year, the King's Hall also became a guarantor for Peterhouse: on 16 October 1506, Henry Hornbye, master of Peterhouse, drew up a bond for £20 with Geoffrey Blythe, master of the King's Hall, whereby the master and fellows of Peterhouse bound themselves to accept the decision of certain arbitrators in matters relating to tithes and to an enclosed croft in Trumpington Street then occupied by John Bedford, one of the bedels of the university.[3] That the King's Hall was invited to act as chief guarantor in compositions of this kind is yet another indication of its standing within the Cambridge *studium* and the high regard in which it was held by contemporary collegiate institutions. While these particular records show that intercollegiate relationships could be friendly and intimate, very much more material is required before we can say that this is representative of the general medieval pattern in Cambridge.

---

[1] *K.H. Cabinet*, nos. 119, 120; for translation see H. Philpott, ed., *Documents relating to St Catharine's College in the University of Cambridge* (Cambridge, 1861), pp. 42–9; see also W. H. S. Jones, *A history of St Catharine's College* (Cambridge, 1936), p. 212.

[2] *K.H. Cabinet*, no. 121; Philpott, *op. cit.* pp. 52–9, and Jones, *op. cit.* p. 208, where King's College is erroneously given for the King's Hall—a not uncommon error among authors who have made no great study of the medieval academic scene.

[3] *K.H. Cabinet*, no. 135.

Although the royal College of the King's Hall appears to have formed a quasi-immunity within the medieval University of Cambridge, a further re-examination of the papal award of John XXII of June 1318 necessitates a revision of the long-accepted view that, by the terms of this letter, the whole of the Cambridge *studium* acquired a full theoretical exemption from the episcopal and archiepiscopal authority of Ely and Canterbury. And our revised conclusion signifies that the Cambridge doctors were guilty of considerably more legal chicanery at the time of the Barnwell Process than has hitherto been supposed.

Commenting upon the letter of Pope John XXII, the Cambridge historian, J. Lamb, wrote:

The University acquired a full exemption from the ecclesiastical and spiritual power of the bishop of the diocese, and of the archbishop of the province; and these powers as far as members of the University were concerned, were vested in the Chancellor or Rector of that body. This privilege was, however, constantly disputed.[1]

Dr Lamb's commentary has been printed by C. H. Cooper;[2] J. B. Mullinger has paraphrased his remarks;[3] and the same view is expressed in the recent article on the University of Cambridge in the *Victoria County History*.[4] The section in Rashdall where the letter is discussed does not draw attention to the point of ecclesiastical exemption.[5] It is patently beyond dispute that Lamb's evaluation of this document with respect to ecclesiastical exemption has been generally accepted and perpetuated. Although the practical issue of exemption was not finally settled until the Barnwell Process, the claim is that the Cambridge *studium* was granted a theoretical exemption from all ecclesiastical and spiritual authority in 1318. And yet when one examines this document one finds that there is nothing in the text which could possibly be construed as supporting evidence for this contention.

[1] See J. Lamb, ed., *A collection of letters, statutes and other documents from the manuscript library of Corpus Christi College illustrative of the history of the University of Cambridge* (London, 1838), introductory remarks, xviii.
[2] Cooper, *Annals of Cambridge*, I, 77.
[3] Mullinger, *University of Cambridge*, I, 145–6.
[4] J. P. C. Roach, 'The University of Cambridge', *V.C.H.* (Cambridge), III, 154.
[5] Rashdall, *op. cit.* III, 283–4.

It will be recalled that the apostolic letter of 1318 confirmed all the rights and privileges inherent in the status of *studium generale* as then understood. In the language of the document, the *studium* is to enjoy all the rights of a *universitas legitime ordinata*.[1] These are not further defined: but one may suppose that definition was inessential as contemporaries would fully comprehend the nature and extent of rights in common pertaining to every legally constituted *studium generale*. Apart from the *ius ubique docendi*, a theoretical academic concept frequently violated in practice, the most important of these rights was the privilege of dispensation from residence for beneficed teachers and students attending *studia generalia*. For the present purpose, however, this subject need not be further explored except to emphasise that rights common to *studia generalia* cannot by definition embrace their particular relationships with external authorities. The relationships of European *studia* with external bodies, whether episcopal, archiepiscopal, civic, regal or imperial, were obviously so diverse that they could not be reduced to a simple formula, and could not possibly be deduced from the general phrase, *universitas legitime ordinata*.

Empirical proof that ecclesiastical exemption was a particular, not a common, privilege is not very hard to discover. For example, in April 1255, Salamanca was papally confirmed as a *studium generale*.[2] In the same year, a number of separate awards were issued conferring privileges additional to those then understood from the status of *studium generale*.[3] Among these was the particular privilege of ecclesiastical exemption,[4] which could therefore not have been assumed from the award of 1255. Further proof is afforded by the example of the French universities. Rashdall comments:

In almost every case the bishop has a much more important and powerful position in the University than he enjoyed at either Bologna or at Paris...

---

[1] See my edition of the text in *B.J.R.L. art. cit.*

[2] See *Archiv für Literatur- und Kirchengeschichte, cit.* v, 168–9.

[3] See Rashdall, *op. cit.* II, 77–8.

[4] *Archiv...*, v, 169. The pope granted the privilege of exemption from corporate excommunication without the special mandate of the Holy See. It was this same claim that was made in the forged bulls of Honorius I and Sergius I allegedly exempting Cambridge from ecclesiastical authority: *Early Cambridge University and college statutes in the English language* (ed. J. Heywood, London, 1855), pp. 184–5.

In many cases, statutes are issued by his authority. Later, his prerogatives were gradually diminished...But to the last the bishop retained considerable authority in nearly all the French Universities.[1]

In other words, the unequivocal status of *studium generale* did not, *ipso facto*, nullify episcopal control. A particular case will present the point more cogently.

In 1303 Avignon was erected into a *studium generale* by a bull of Boniface VIII. Notwithstanding this development, the bishop continued, as before, to exercise supreme authority over the *studium*. He issued a code of statutes (with the co-operation of the doctors), reserved to himself the right to confer the licence, and appointed the doctors.[2] Clearly, freedom from episcopal or archiepiscopal authority was not a right inherent in the fourteenth-century concept of a *studium generale*: for this, a university required an express papal award. Similarly, in the case of Cambridge, ecclesiastical exemption cannot be inferred from the grant of rights common to every fully constituted *studium generale*.

Nor is it in any way possible to extract a meaning of ecclesiastical exemption from that clause in the letter of John XXII which serves to confirm all previous papal or royal privileges and indults. There is no papal award to the university of the thirteenth or fourteenth century from which exemption could be inferred. The likelihood is that the 'papal privileges' of the award refer to those granted to the *studium* by Gregory IX in 1233[3] which comprise the earliest known papal recognition of the university. Likewise, an examination of all royal grants made to the university before 1318 leads to the same conclusion.

By the end of the thirteenth century, the chancellor had emerged as the *de facto* head of the *studium* with jurisdiction over all university clerks and with limited cognisance in cases where clerks and laymen were involved.[4] As at Oxford and Montpellier,[5] an important factor in the practical emancipation of the university from episcopal control

---

[1] Rashdall, *op. cit.* II, 208.   [2] *Ibid.* II, 175.

[3] See above, p. 18, n. 4; Rashdall, *op. cit.* III, 279.

[4] In 1305 the chancellor was given power to cite burgesses and other laymen to answer scholars in personal actions (Cooper, *Annals of Cambridge*, I, 71). These were particularised and further extended by Edward II's charter of 1317 (Cambridge University Archives, *Cabinet*, no. 19; Cooper, *op. cit.* I, 76).

[5] See Rashdall, *op. cit.* III, 114.

was the remoteness of the see of Ely from Cambridge. The bishop rarely intervened in the daily administration of the *studium*. But this did not nullify his legal right to do so. As mentioned above, the chancellor was originally merely the officer of the bishop wielding delegated episcopal powers.[1] This meant that at any time of his own choosing the bishop was within his legal rights to supersede the chancellor's authority. During the thirteenth century there are several instances of intervention by the bishop's official to settle internal university disputes or to hear appeals from the chancellor's court.[2] Even as late as the third quarter of the fourteenth century, the bishop claimed (unsuccessfully) to remove to his court cases pending before the chancellor.[3] It is therefore abundantly clear that in 1318 the University of Cambridge could offer not the shadow of a case for theoretical exemption from ecclesiastical authority on the basis of existing royal or papal privileges and immunities.

It is probable that Dr Lamb and his followers found corroboration for the alleged ecclesiastical exemption in the undoubted association of the apostolic letter with the celebrated Barnwell Process.

The award of Pope John XXII was solemnly produced by the university in 1430 during the legal proceedings in the chapter-house at Barnwell. It was presented as documentary evidence of apostolic confirmation of the alleged papal bulls of Honorius I and Sergius I.[4] By this association, it became an important exhibit in the university's claim to ecclesiastical exemption.[5] This rested upon the dual base of custom and the papal forgeries. In its petition to Pope Martin V[6] the university claimed that the chancellor '...has usually exercised ecclesiastical and spiritual jurisdiction in taking cognisance of and

---

[1] See above, p. 101.   [2] See Rashdall, *op. cit.* III, 280.

[3] *Ibid.* III, 281.

[4] The alleged bulls of Honorius I of 7 February 624 and of Sergius I of 3 May 699 are preserved in Cambridge University Archives, *Cabinet*, no. 115 (2 copies).

[5] It was presented as part of a public instrument on 9 October 1430 in the chapter-house at Barnwell along with the apostolical letters of Boniface IX (dispensing with episcopal confirmation of the chancellor elect), the forged bulls, and other muniments and statutes. This written evidence was furnished as documentary proof of the claims made by Wraby in his articles propounded three days earlier before the prior of Barnwell. (See *Processus Barnwellensis* (henceforth *Proc. Barn.*) in Cambridge University Archives, *Cabinet*, no. 108; for translation see Heywood, *Early Cambridge statutes*, *cit.* pp. 181 ff., especially pp. 196–205.)

[6] This petition is reported in *Proc. Barn.*; see also Heywood, *op. cit.* pp. 184–6.

deciding causes and matters which relate [to such persons and] to members of the University'.[1] This claim was incorporated in the third article delivered by William Wraby, proctor, representing the university before the prior of Barnwell as papal delegate.[2] It was further reinforced by the venerable testimony of John Dynne, the first and oldest of the seven witnesses furnished by the university.[3]

Important as long-established custom was to the university's case, it also derived or rather fabricated a documentary claim to ecclesiastical exemption from the supposed papal awards of the seventh century. It was alleged that the original bulls had been lost but that the university fortunately possessed accurate copies.[4] These forgeries purport to confer a full exemption from the ecclesiastical powers of any archbishop, bishop, archdeacon or their officials. The tenor of these documents was embodied in the petition to Pope Martin V[5] and, as propounded in Wraby's articles, they form the core of the university's case. On the twin bases of these bulls and the chancellor's customary exercise of ecclesiastical and spiritual jurisdiction, the prior upheld the university's claim to independence,[6] a decision confirmed by the bull of Eugenius IV on 18 September 1433.[7]

Thus, more than a century after it was issued, the general and therefore loose phraseology of the letter of John XXII was skilfully utilised to fit the university's claim to freedom from episcopal and archiepiscopal authority. It is incontrovertible that if it had been possible to extract ecclesiastical exemption from the document itself it would have been given a far greater prominence at the Barnwell Process: it would have been the prize exhibit, the only one necessary. Indeed, the papal forgeries would then have been entirely superfluous; the legal basis of the bishop's persistent claim to confirm the

---

1 Translation, Heywood, *op. cit.* p. 185.
2 The other proctors were Ralph Dukworth, M.A., John Athill (atte Hille) and William Gull (Heywood, p. 182, gives Tull); the chancellor was John Holbroke.
3 The witness, aged seventy-nine, claimed that when archbishops or bishops of Ely came to Cambridge they 'totally superseded and omitted the use and exercise of ecclesiastical jurisdiction at the request of the chancellor of the University for the time being, as far as regarded the persons who were subject to the said chancellor' (*Proc. Barn.*; Heywood, p. 193).
4 Information contained in the university's petition to Martin V (*Proc. Barn.*; Heywood, p. 186).
5 *Proc. Barn.*; Heywood, pp. 184-6.   6 *Proc. Barn.*; Heywood, pp. 206-8.
7 This papal confirmation is preserved in Cambridge University Archives, *Cabinet*, no. 114.

chancellor elect, which was officially abrogated by Boniface IX in 1401, would, already in the fourteenth century, have been completely undermined; and there would have been far less need for a papal investigation on anything like the scale of the Barnwell Process. Wraby's articles, however, do not even refer to the letter, and the prior's sentence in the university's favour was based wholly upon the customary powers of the chancellor and the evidence of the papal forgeries: there is no mention of John's letter in the university's petition to Martin V or in the confirmation of Eugenius IV.

It would therefore seem that, from the point of view of ecclesiastical exemption, the apostolic letter of 1318 has acquired significance only by deliberate and false historical association. For it is apparent that the Cambridge doctors could link the phrase in the letter confirming all former papal awards specifically with the alleged bulls of Honorius and Sergius. It has not been discovered when these forgeries were perpetrated but a reasonable guess would be the first quarter of the fifteenth century or at the very earliest the closing years of the fourteenth (i.e. when the issue of ecclesiastical exemption had reached a critical stage of development). Whatever the case, it is certain that the later interpretation placed upon the letter by the Cambridge doctors linking it with the alleged papal bulls at the time of the Barnwell Process could not possibly have been conceived by Edward II, Pope John XXII or the corporation of masters and scholars in June 1318. John's letter has been rightly associated with the university's fight for independence but this consideration has quite clearly tended to distort its original import. And the view that in 1318 the Cambridge *studium* was accorded a theoretical exemption from the 'ecclesiastical and spiritual power of the bishop of the diocese, and of the archbishop of the province'[1] appears to be in need of modification.

In the course of this chapter it has been argued that the College of the King's Hall was exempt from the visitatorial powers of Ely and Canterbury. Since there are no legitimate grounds for believing that the Cambridge *studium* acquired a similar exemption in 1318, the unique position occupied by the King's Hall as an institution *sui generis* within the medieval university is thrown into very sharp relief.

---

[1] See J. Lamb, *Letters from the manuscript library of Corpus Christi College*, introductory remarks, xviii.

Chapter 4

THE KING'S HALL ACCOUNTS:
INTERNAL ECONOMY

GENERAL

The King's Hall accounts form a remarkable and unparalleled sequence of paper collegiate records[1] covering a period of over two centuries and extending from the first foundation of the college in 1337 to 1544, two years before the dissolution of the Society and its subsequent incorporation in Henry VIII's royal establishment, Trinity College, Cambridge. Originally, the accounts were made up in separate quires year by year and remained so until these were bound up together, probably in the latter part of the seventeenth century, to form the impressive series of twenty-six volumes now preserved in the Muniment Room of Trinity College. It is true that there are gaps in the records, notably for the reigns of Edward III and Richard II: several accounts are missing for the 1350s and there are none at all for the period 1370–1 to 1381–2.[2] From 1382–3 onwards, however, the accounts are very full indeed and almost unbroken, punctuated only by occasional omissions and defects. With the early accounts chronology has been something of a problem; for in the binding process a number of the outer sheets or title pages of the individual quires became detached and were either bound up with the wrong account or have disappeared altogether.[3] But where dating is unspecified an approximate date may be assigned in one of two ways. Internal evidence, such as the presence of Scholars whose

[1] See the remarks of A. B. Emden on the King's Hall accounts in *B.R.U.C.* p. xvi (quoted above in introduction, p. 6).
[2] Full details concerning the chronology and the folio length of each volume are given in the bibliography.
[3] As several of the accounts have been bound up in the wrong chronological order, this has occasionally meant that in some of the series of footnotes references from 'later' volumes precede references from 'earlier' books (e.g. v, fo. 64 may precede IV, fo. 82). But where, in the citation of references, strict chronological order has not been important, these have been arranged in accordance with the present order of volumes.

dates of entry and vacation are known from exchequer material, will often narrow the margin of error considerably; and, occasionally, undated and misplaced folios may be correctly assigned by correlating their watermarks with those of quires whose chronology is beyond dispute.[1] This device is especially valuable for sorting out the leaves of 'mixed' accounts where the folios of one have been wrongly bound up with those of another. Fortunately, these chronological difficulties are in the main confined to accounts of the period before 1382–3; and between this date and 1443–4, the years selected for a detailed economic investigation, there are no uncertainties of this kind.

The King's Hall accounts are written on paper sheets measuring approximately 11¾ inches long by 8½ inches wide. The leaves of each volume have been paginated as well as foliated, but the eighteenth-century pagination is confused in several places and only folio references are given in this book. A few of the leaves of the first two volumes have been partially or almost entirely destroyed by the effects of dampness: in the succeeding volumes, however, this ceases to be any serious obstacle to interpretation although here and there part of a page has been cut away (perhaps during binding operations) or has been otherwise obscured through the natural processes of decay.

The language of the King's Hall accounts is medieval Latin of a particularly abbreviated character.[2] Difficulties of reading and translation are further augmented by the fact that diverse abbreviated forms of the same word may be used within the space of a few pages or even within the same page.[3] In the fifteenth and sixteenth centuries the Latin of the accounts is frequently interlarded with English and Anglo-French words or terms. This is a fairly common feature of business records of the late medieval period and is reflective both of the increasing popular currency of the vernacular in contemporary

[1] W. H. B. Bird, a former scholar of Trinity and editor of the *Cal. Close R.* from 1906, was, for several years, employed by the college to catalogue the muniment materials. He made a study of the watermarks contained in the King's Hall accounts and his notes and catalogues are available in the Muniment Room.

[2] See the photographs of extracts from the King's Hall accounts in the appendix.

[3] From many examples, see the account for 1393–4 where three differently abbreviated forms of the term 'commons' are used within the space of two and a half lines: *K.H. Accts.* IV, fo. 35.

society and of the growing inadequacy of Latin as a vehicle of expression for the ever widening range of terms and technicalities of a more complex business world. Roman numerals are used throughout for accounting purposes although at one or two points arabic characters are briefly introduced.[1] Where this occurs, the clerk is obviously ill at ease, the figures being the product of much effort, and roman numerals are reverted to after the completion of only a few lines of account. Nevertheless, the fact that arabic characters make a first tentative appearance in the late fourteenth century is worthy of remark because they do not seem to have been used to any significant extent in English archives until about a hundred years later.[2] Judging from the many references to the purchase of counters or jettons,[3] and in one instance to the purchase of a counting table itself,[4] it is evident that the exchequer method of accounting based on the abacus was employed: in 1432–3 a separate counting-house is mentioned.[5]

Generally speaking, for so long a series of medieval accounts, standards of accuracy are high and very few mistakes have been detected in the accounting processes. Errors do occur but are usually of an easily rectifiable kind. For example, in the numbering of the weeks in the annual account for the fellows' weekly commons it sometimes happens that one of the 'tens' has been omitted with the result that perhaps weeks twenty to thirty are 'repeated' in place of weeks thirty to forty. Or again, there are several instances of the same week being entered twice and, less commonly, of the failure to record a particular week at all. Where an error has been made, it is, in some cases, rectified at a later stage; but more often mistakes are passed over unnoticed.

---

[1] From several examples, see the account for 1383–4, weeks 20, 21, 22 and 23: *ibid.* III, fos. 94, 94 v; also XIX, fo. 54 v (1496–7).

[2] See H. Jenkinson, 'The use of arabic and roman numerals in English archives', *The Antiquaries' Journal*, VI (1926), 263 ff., especially pp. 263–4; also G. G. Neill Wright, *The writing of arabic numerals* (London, 1952), pp. 128–9. Arabic numerals occur in one or two places in the Merton bursars' rolls of the late thirteenth century (Highfield, *The early rolls of Merton College, Oxford, cit.* p. 3).

[3] See *K.H. Accts.* I, fos. 59, 147; IV, fo. 28; VI, fos. 19, 84 v, 108 v; VII, fo. 37. In 1393–4, 40 counters 'cum bursa' were purchased for 4½*d* (IV, fo. 28): in the first half of the fifteenth century counters cost 2*d*, 2½*d* or 3*d* a dozen.

[4] See *ibid.* III, fo. 58 v: 'Item pro i tabula cum ii tripedibus ad computand' is. viijd.'

[5] *Ibid.* VIII, fo. 45 v: 'Item pro una tabula in domo compoti is.'

It was an axiom of college life that whosoever incurred expenditure from the common funds rendered account for the same to the financial officers of the establishment. It is evident that the King's Hall accounts are a series of continuous entries made in a book or quire and compiled from the personal memoranda of the seneschals or administrative officers of the college, from the financial reports of individual fellows engaged on the Society's business, from the records of the various domestic departments and from the numerous indentures and business material stored in the common chest. A small fraction of this original material has survived including several indentures recording contracts made between the college and farmers and merchants of Cambridgeshire and neighbouring counties.[1] There have also survived a few fragmentary pieces of the accounts of the *prosecutor ad forinseca*, the fellow who managed the external finances of the college and who most closely approximated to the modern notion of a Cambridge senior bursar.[2] These scraps of paper itemise the personal expenditure of the *prosecutor* while engaged on college business in London and elsewhere relating to the collection of the exchequer maintenance grant, to the acquisition of the cloth for the fellows' gowns, and to the revenues due from the churches appropriated to the Hall.[3] Their chance preservation appears to have been due to the fact that in binding operations miscellaneous papers of this kind were sometimes used for strengthening purposes, being wedged between consecutive quires when bound up together to form the present King's Hall volumes.

The book or quire to which all the expenses of these individual personal accounts were transferred was designated the *Liber Expensarum* and was housed in the common chest.[4] The King's Hall statutes specify that the business of entry was to be undertaken at intervals of a week or a fortnight and was to be carried out under the supervision of the seneschals of the college.[5] From the evidence of the accounts

---

[1] For a detailed discussion of these contracts see below, pp. 212 ff.

[2] For the duties of this officer see below, pp. 194 ff.

[3] These were: Great St Mary's, Cambridge; Hintlesham, Suffolk; Felmersham, Beds.; and Grendon, Northants. For the net income derived from these churches see below, pp. 204–6.

[4] See the King's Hall statutes in Rouse Ball, *King's Hall*, p. 65: 'In qua vero Cista Sigillum Commune et Liber Expensarum dicte domus reponantur.'

[5] *Ibid.*: 'Singulisque septimanis vel quindenis (nisi ulterius differatur) prefate expense in dicto Libro inscribantur.'

themselves it seems that a clerk was specially hired to perform this task.[1]

If the mind of a society is expressed in its records, an examination of the King's Hall accounts is in itself a study in institutional growth. The accounts are written in primary entry form, all the Society's transactions being set down in a continuous record and subdivided into paragraph sections under separate headings: and at no time was this style of accounting superseded by that of more advanced bilateral forms.[2] In the early accounts, the entries are arranged under the most general of headings with a considerable measure of overlap between the different sections. With the advance of time, however, the accounts assume a more sophisticated format and it becomes easier for the historian to enter into the rhythms of medieval collegiate life. The most striking feature of this development in accounting methods is that the margin of overlap is progressively narrowed until it is excluded altogether, a process accompanied by a systematic breakdown of the general sections into their component parts. For example, food expenses are soon clearly differentiated from all other items of expenditure and separate sections appear for wheat (*frumentum*), for malt barley (*brasium*) and for general stores or provisions (*staurum*) comprising such items as fish, meat, vegetables, fruit, spices and seasonings: fuel purchases likewise came to be subdivided into peat or turf (*terricidium*), sedge (*segg'*), wood (*fagett'* or *lignum*), and occasionally coal (*carbon'*). Similarly, instead of arranging all expenses for the purchase of domestic articles such as crockery, utensils, furniture and napery under the general heading of *expense intrinsecarum*, these items came to be assigned to sections specifically devoted to the particular domestic departments for which they had been bought. As a result, there evolved separate and detailed accounts for the kitchen (*coquina*), the bakehouse (*pistrinum*), the butler's depart-

---

[1] See *K.H. Accts.* IV, fo. 98 (1397–8): 'Item Hesyl pro labore circa compotum vij annorum xiijs. ivd.'; 'Item clerico Hesyl iijs. iiijd.'

[2] For early forms of medieval accounting before the development of double-entry book-keeping see R. de Roover, 'The development of accounting prior to Luca Pacioli according to the account-books of medieval merchants' in *Studies in the history of accounting, cit.* pp. 114 ff.; a discussion of double-entry book-keeping copiously illustrated with extracts from the Medici accounts is provided by F. Edler, *Glossary of mediaeval terms of business* (Mediaeval Academy of America, Cambridge, Massachusetts, 1934), appendix II, 348 ff.

ment (*promtuarium*), the hall (*aula*) and, from the fifteenth century onwards, the library (*libraria*) and the dovecot (*columbarium*).[1] This process of subdivision and specialisation was subsequently applied to every portion of the annual account so that by the latter part of the fourteenth century the general and predominantly haphazard pattern of the earlier accounts had been strikingly transformed into a regular sequence of short, particularised sections under clearly marked, self-explanatory headings. Furthermore, it is evident that this greater efficiency and uniformity of method was accompanied by the practice of engrossing the sectional headings in advance. That this was done can be deduced from the fact that both the handwriting and the colour of the ink used for the headings are obviously different from those of the entries below. Miscalculations were sometimes made as to the size of the anticipated entry, and the occurrence of blank or semi-blank folios is not uncommon.

The final evolutionary stage in the layout of the account was the provision of an index. This never became a regular feature and indexes were incorporated at the end of only four of the accounts, those for 1492–3,[2] 1493–4,[3] 1498–9[4] and 1503–4.[5] In the indexes to the first three, the matter of the account is arranged to form logical groupings such as receipts, expenditure on the various domestic departments, wages, liveries and external business, expenditure on food and fuel, contracts and miscellaneous items: but no attempt at division was made in the index for 1503–4, which merely records the contents of the account according to strict folio order. Roman numerals are employed for folio references in the index for 1492–3 but arabic characters alone are used in the other three cases. Folio references are entirely accurate throughout despite the fact that only the account for 1503–4 bears contemporary arabic foliation.[6]

One of the most tantalising features of so long a series of medieval accounts as that of the King's Hall is that information of a certain kind may be revealed to us for a limited period of time, only to be

[1] A detailed discussion of the dovecot and the library is given below, pp. 244–5, 246 ff.
[2] *K.H. Accts.* XVIII, fo. 179 v.   [3] *Ibid.* XVII, fo. 26.
[4] *Ibid.* XIX, fo. 145.   [5] *Ibid.* XX, fo. 90 v: heading: *tabula libri.*
[6] There are only two other accounts with contemporary foliation: that for 1467–8 has roman numerals on the bottom right hand corner of each folio (*K.H. Accts.* XIII, fos. 107–122 v) and that for 1520–1 is numbered by means of letters of the alphabet until all the letters are used up, whereupon foliation comes to an abrupt end (*ibid.* XXII, fos. 99–134 v).

withdrawn from our view at an interesting point and superseded by data of a different category. It is generally true to say that the accounts of the late fourteenth, fifteenth and sixteenth centuries are more informative than those of the earlier period: there is, however, at least one important exception to this generalisation. For between 1342–3 and 1351–2 the King's Hall records furnish examples of six detailed profit-and-loss accounts in which annual college income is set against expenditure and the subsequent balance recorded. It seems likely that these financial statements constitute one of the earliest attempts on the part of a medieval English college to express a balance between expenditure and total receipt. Furthermore, profit-and-loss sheets of this kind show that the system of accounting in at least one fourteenth-century Cambridge college was noticeably more advanced than that currently employed in contemporary monastic establishments.[1] For these reasons and because they illustrate so well the accounting techniques in operation at the King's Hall, it is felt desirable that one of the six specimens should be given here in full (table 3). In the interests of clarity, the items of the original account are divided up and separately numbered.

It is apparent that this annual financial statement deals only with cash income and expenditure. No attempt is here made to evaluate cash, gold or silver reserves, or assets, such as plate or stores of food and fuel in stock, or to take cognisance of the value of the fabric and interior fittings of the college or of anticipated revenues, including outstanding debts, with the result that the cash balance cannot be taken as representing anything like the total wealth of the Society in this year. This failure to provide a total financial view in reckoning annual profit or loss was also a prevalent deficiency of monastic accounting of the later medieval period.[2] At the King's Hall, however, this omission had to some extent been remedied by the end of the fourteenth century when an attempt was made at the beginning of each account to furnish what was meant to be an overall assessment of the wealth available for the coming year. But this was very much a

[1] See M. D. Knowles, *The religious Orders in England*, II (Cambridge, 1955), 319–20: 'Two great differences between medieval and modern practice at once strike the reader of early fourteenth-century accounts. The first is the absence of any attempt to express a balance between expenditure and total receipt—in other words, to show a profit or loss; this (as we shall see) was remedied as the century wore on.'

[2] *Ibid.* II, 320.

TABLE 3. *Account of 16 Edward III (1342–3), K.H. Accts. 1, fo. 64v*

1. Summa vadiorum a primo die octobr' anno xvj usque ad ultimum diem septembr' sequent' pro custode et xxxv scolarium cix li. xs.
2. Item pro vad' Warde venent' primo die martii usque ultimum diem septembr' xxxvs. vid.
3. Summa omnium repastorum sociorum et extraneorum xviij li. iijs. iiijd.
4. Summa tot' recepta vi li. ix li. viijs. xd.
5. Summa omnium expn̄ fact' in cōi per custodem et comitiam et in pane et stipendiis famulorum iiij li. xix li. vis. ob.
6. Summa vadiorum absent' xvij li. ijs. ixd.
7. Pro vad' absent' Warde xvjs. viijd.
8. Summa tot' expn̄ cxvij li. vs. vd. ob.
9. Et sic sm̄' recept' exced' sm̄' expn̄ in xij li. iijs. iiijd. ob. que summa debet distribuari inter socios ut patet inferius in papiro.

These items appear in modern parlance in the following manner:

	Income	Expenditure
1. Exchequer maintenance allowance for the warden and 35 Scholars for the year	£109 10 0	
2. Maintenance allowance for Warde who came on 1 March till end of academic year	1 15 6	
3. Income accruing from sizings (i.e. items of food ordered over and above basic commons) of fellows and *extranei* living in the King's Hall	18 3 4	
4. Total income for year	£129 8 10	
5. Expenditure for all expenses incurred in common by the warden and the Society on food and on servants' wages		£99 6 0½
6. Maintenance allowance paid to absent fellows		17 2 9
7. Maintenance paid to Warde during absence		16 8
8. Total expenditure		£117 5 5½

9. So total income exceeds total expenditure by £12 3s 4½d and this sum is to be divided among the fellows.

partial assessment because no consideration whatsoever was given to the college's domestic furnishings or collection of plate which, in the later fifteenth century at any rate, was very considerable.[1]

This new form of statement, which was, in effect, a detailed exposition of the contents of the common chest, begins by itemising the

[1] See e.g. the plate inventories of 1478–9 printed by Rouse Ball, *op. cit.* pp. 50 ff.

revenues due for the year from the churches appropriated to the college and from the various bodies upon which the exchequer maintenance grant had been partially unloaded.[1] It continues by detailing what can only be the residue of sums of money set aside in the previous year for the purchase of fuel or grain or other items of food. Also recorded are the actual quantities of food and fuel remaining from the preceding year as well as quantities still due from traders and farmers under contract to the college. Arrears due for commons and rent from ex-fellows and other *extranei* who resided in the Hall as pensioners[2] are next set down, followed by the debts

TABLE 4. *Partial financial assessment at opening of academic year 1423–4*

	£	s	d
Gold, silver and cash reserves at opening of academic year 1423–4			
Gold (in 3 leather bags)	362	15	0
Silver	1	14	0
Cash (including 104 nobles)	42	9	0
Current value of plate fund[3]	30	0	0
'Fuel money' remaining from previous year	5	9	0
	£442	7	0
Anticipated revenues and arrears for year 1423–4			
Annual exchequer grant	103	8	4
Estimated annual net income from appropriated churches	70	0	0
Arrears due from *extranei* for commons and rent and for commons from chapel royal entrants[4]	21	10	9¼
Arrears due from appropriated churches and farmed exchequer sources	79	4	0
Monetary equivalent on amounts of grain and fuel outstanding and on quantities in stock[5]	11	5	0
	285	8	1¼
	442	7	0
Total gold, silver and cash reserves, anticipated revenues and arrears	£727	15	1¼

[1] For details see below, pp. 203–4.   [2] See below, pp. 272–3.
[3] For the contribution of new fellows to the plate fund see below, p. 138.
[4] For the accumulated debts of the chapel recruits see below, pp. 187–8.
[5] The quantities of grain outstanding are given and the monetary equivalent has been assessed on the basis of the average prices of quarters of wheat and malt barley this year, i.e. 5s 4d and 4s 4d respectively (see table 9, p. 144): likewise, from the entries in the accounts, it is known that turves for fuel were selling at the average price of 2s 3d per 1,000.

of the fellows for their commons and sizings. Miscellaneous entries, such as legacies left to the college by fellows and other benefactors, are sometimes recorded at this stage.[1] The section is rounded off with a statement of the cash, gold and silver reserves contained in a motley assemblage of bags (*bursae*) kept in the chest.

Examples of this form of statement are to be found in the King's Hall accounts between 1398-9 and 1423-4.[2] For illustrative purposes we may select the final account in this series (table 4) because the information is then obligingly full.[3] The order of the items has been altered to provide logical sequence, and an average sum for the estimated annual net income derived from the appropriated churches has been substituted for the gross figures of the original account.[4]

By comparison with the standards of accountancy employed in contemporary English collegiate and monastic establishments, the King's Hall system appears to have been reasonably comprehensive and efficient.

INTERNAL ECONOMY

From the point of view of internal economy, the most important section of the King's Hall records is undoubtedly the annual account for weekly commons. This may be generally described as a form of kitchen account wherein is set out all the essential information required by the college for the reckoning of the weekly amount to be charged to each fellow for his commons or basic food requirements. From this very copious series of records, it is possible to extract a wealth of economic data relating to the domestic expenditure of a collegiate society of the middle ages. In particular, it is hoped that this chapter may break new ground by presenting a first analysis of the expenditure rates and financial situation of the fellows of an English medieval college over a selected period, in this case extending from the late fourteenth to the mid-fifteenth century. Although much has been written on student life in the medieval universities

[1] For example, John Salle (King's Scholar, admitted 1 August 1396; vacated 23 June 1405) left 20s to the Hall (*K.H. Accts.* v, fos. 126, 145) and the bishop of Rochester made a handsome bequest of £20 (*loc. cit.*).
[2] See *ibid.* IV, fos. 122, 107; V, fos. 88, 126, 145, 166; VI, fos. 1, 15, 36, 57; VII, fo. 17.
[3] The following information is derived from the opening folio of the account for 1423-4, *ibid.* VII, fo. 17.
[4] See below, pp. 204-6.

from letters, poetry, sermons and so on,[1] still comparatively little is known of the internal economic arrangements of the colleges which, in England, were the principal hives of secular post-graduate activity. And certainly a substantial corpus of collegiate domestic documents has never before been broken down, sifted and analysed: for it is only then that the economic heart of a society is revealed and that well-substantiated conclusions based upon an awesome mass of distilled evidence can be drawn. From what I have seen of the lengthy series of accounts of Merton, New College and Canterbury College, Oxford, these do not appear to be amenable to this kind of investigation on a comparable scale.

Like every other section of the King's Hall records, the annual accounts for weekly commons were subject to a measure of evolutionary change. The earliest of these, dating from 1337–8, are still in a formative stage of development and are less fully itemised than the later accounts. That for 1382–3 has been selected as the first of the fifty-four analysed for the present study because in that year the commons account realised a maturity of form and expression which it retained until the mid-sixteenth century.[2] Before proceeding with this analysis, however, it is necessary to provide a full description and explanation of the several component parts of this important and little-utilised form of medieval account, specimens of which are given in the appendix.

In the King's Hall volumes the commons account assumes the complexion of weekly entries arranged horizontally and separately spaced under the general heading of *communes sociorum*. For the purposes of the current investigation, the figures contained in the entries for the year have been extracted and grouped in the form of tables with vertical columns, such that each line of the table, reading from left to right, gives at a glance all the figures of a particular weekly entry. As was usual in medieval colleges, the year of account is the

---

[1] See e.g. C. H. Haskins, *Studies in mediaeval culture* (Oxford, 1929), especially the first three chapters; also R. S. Rait, *Life in the medieval university* (Cambridge, 1912) and Rashdall, *Universities in the middle ages*, III, ch. XIV. For the *goliardi* see H. Waddell, *The wandering scholars* (7th ed., London, 1934). Goliardic poetry is discussed by F. J. E. Raby, *A history of secular Latin poetry in the middle ages* (2 vols., Oxford, 1934), II, 171 ff.

[2] The account for weekly commons of 1382–3 is given as the second of the five specimen examples in the appendix, pp. 310–11.

harvest year extending from Michaelmas to Michaelmas and the first column of the table represents the number of weeks distant from the Michaelmas festival.[1] With one or two exceptions,[2] the accounts for the period under consideration (1382–3 to 1443–4) extend for the full fifty-two (or three) weeks, whereas those of the earlier part of the fourteenth century sometimes break off about week forty, that is to say, at the beginning of the long vacation.[3] Where this is so, separate and telescoped accounting arrangements are usually employed over the vacation period. The only other noteworthy feature about numbering is that sometimes festivals, such as Christmas, Easter and Pentecost, are specifically designated; but the practice was by no means uniform and more often than not one is left to deduce the festival weeks from evidence of particularly heavy expenditure.

The second column of the table represents the actual number of fellows present in each week of the Michaelmas account.[4] It is relevant to emphasise here that these numbers do not indicate, or do so only occasionally, the total number of fellows on the boards of the college. And it is evident that the extent of non-residence in any given week of any given year is easily calculated by subtracting the actual numbers present from the total complement of thirty-two or more Scholars.[5] The incidence of non-residence over the period 1382–3 to 1443–4 has already been discussed and this subject need not be further pursued.[6]

The third column represents the total expenses incurred by the college for the provision of bread for the meals of all the fellows present in a particular week: likewise, the figures of column 4 are those of the college's expenditure on ale for the fellows' commons in the same week.[7] Normally, the bread and ale for this purpose were

[1] See the specimen accounts in the appendix.

[2] The account for 1387–8 is fragmentary and runs for only 17 weeks, while those for 1397–8 and 1401–2 extend for 27 weeks. The accounts for 1400–1, 1405–6, 1407–8, 1413–14 and 1433–4 run for 39, 40, 44, 41 and 45 weeks respectively.

[3] See e.g. the accounts for 1350–1, 1359–60, 1363–4, 1364–5 and 1365–6: *K.H. Accts.* I, fos. 142v–144v; II, fos. 15–16v, 66–67, 91–93, 114–115v.

[4] See the appendix.

[5] The exchequer accounts confirm that the complement of Scholars was fixed at about 32 from the late fourteenth century onwards. In the earlier part of the century it was sometimes more, rising to as high as 35 or 36. (See e.g. the specimen profit and loss account, p. 119.)

[6] See above, p. 55.   [7] See appendix.

baked and brewed on the premises from quantities of wheat and malt barley purchased from Cambridgeshire farmers at intervals throughout the year. Occasionally, when the bakehouse ovens were out of commission, all bread for that period was bought in directly from the town of Cambridge.[1] Similarly, baking operations were sometimes suspended during the long vacation, doubtless because of the unprofitability of keeping baking facilities in running order when numbers were especially low.[2] The accounts further reveal that between 1432–3 and 1443–4 supplementary supplies of bread and ale were purchased from the town for most weeks of the year.[3]

Columns 5 and 6 require careful consideration. The former quite clearly details week by week the total expenditure incurred by the kitchen department for the provision of the fellows' meals. But it is equally plain that these costs did not cover the expenses for the buying of the ingredients of the same meals. For column 6[4] gives the amount spent each week by the college for the purchase of all the provisions, such as fish, meat, vegetables, fruit, salt, honey, almonds, pepper, rice, garlic, mustard, saffron, verjuice and other seasonings used in the preparation of the meals as well as for peat and sedge used as cooking fuel. One must therefore conclude that the rather high kitchen expenses comprise such items as running costs, maintenance, the replenishment of utensils and the wages of the kitchen staff consisting of a cook, sub-cook and boys employed on a casual basis.[5] In the earlier accounts, of which that for 1360–1 appended below is a typical example,[6] separate figures for kitchen expenditure and for stores or provisions are specified: so that if we add together the weekly entries for expenditure on bread (column 3), on ale (column 4), on kitchen costs (column 5) and on stores and fuel (column 6), the total will be that given in column 7, which consequently represents the overall expenditure incurred in the provision of all the fellows' meals for the space of a week. But in the accounts for the years

---

[1] See e.g. the accounts for 1426–7 and 1427–8 (*K.H. Accts.* VII, fos. 74–76v; VIII, fos. 94–96v).

[2] See e.g. the accounts for 1419–20 and 1425–6 (*ibid.* VI, fos. 105–107v; VII, fos. 55–57v).

[3] See *ibid.* VIII, fos. 41–43v, 62–65v, 88–91v, 113–116v; IX, fos. 2–6, 32–36v, 61–65, 94–97v, 149–152; X, fos. 2–5v, 29–32v, 52–56.

[4] See the table for 1360–1, column 6, pp. 308–9.

[5] For the domestic staff see below, pp. 231 ff.   [6] See below, pp. 308–9.

following 1382–3 the procedure is slightly different and at first sight somewhat confusing. The difference, which concerns column 6 of the earlier accounts, is that, although the stores and fuel are itemised in the original entries as before, no figures (or very few) are now supplied, the result being, of course, that if we add up columns 3, 4 and 5 the total comes to just less than the recorded total expenditure for the week (i.e. column 7 in the accounts before 1382–3; column 6 in the accounts of the later period).[1] And so, in the fifty-four extant accounts for the years between 1382–3 and 1443–4, expenditure on stores and fuel is represented by the difference between the overall expenditure and the total resulting from the addition of the weekly expenditure on bread, ale and kitchen costs. It has been thought unnecessary to work this out week by week and to arrange the results as a separate column, but for averaging purposes the differences over the whole year have been taken.[2]

On the basis of all these expenses was calculated the amount due to the college by every fellow for his commons each week: these varying sums constitute column 7 (in the account for 1382–3 and those following) and form the real end-product of the account. The contents of column 8 are extraneous to the main body of the account; they do not in any way contribute towards the final reckoning of the weekly commons rate but comprise the total weekly amounts spent by all the fellows on their sizings (*repaste*),[3] the additional items of food and drink privately ordered over and above basic allowable requirements: in other words, 'extra commons'. The figures for sizings occur at the end of the original entries after those for total expenditure (column 6) and for commons (column 7) and were doubtless inserted at this point for the sake of completeness. For, in another section of the King's Hall accounts under the heading *Repaste Sociorum*, each fellow settles individually with the seneschals for his sizings.

This completes the description of the constituent parts of the account for weekly commons and it remains only to add that in the original entries none of the yearly totals is given, with the result that

[1] See the specimen accounts for 1382–3, 1408–9, 1424–5 and 1430–1, in the appendix.
[2] See table 5 (pullout), column 12.
[3] *Repaste* is the term most commonly used for sizings but occasionally *sy(i)sacio* is found: *K.H. Accts.* x, fo. 112. For a qualification see below, p. 131, n. 2.

TABLE 5

(1) Harvest year	(2) No. of weeks accounted	(3) Total no. of fellows present for given no. of weeks	(4) Average no. of fellows present per week	(5) Total college expenditure on bread for fellows' commons	(6) Average expenditure on bread per week	(7) Total college expenditure on ale for fellows' commons	(8) Average expenditure on ale per week	(9) Total college expenditure on kitchen (running costs, etc.)	(10) Average expenditure on kitchen per week	(11) Total college expenditure on stores and fuel	(12) Average expenditure on stores and fuel per week	(13) Total college expenditure for fellows' commons	(14) Average expenditure for fellows' commons per week	(15) Total sum charged to each fellow for commons	(16) Average sum charged to each fellow for commons per week	(17) Total amount spent by fellows on sizings	(18) Average amount spent on sizings by fellows per week
				£ s d	s d	£ s d	s d	£ s d	£ s d	£ s d	s d	£ s d	£ s d	£ s d	s d	£ s d	s d
1382–3	52	1,477	30	17 17 2	6 10½	29 15 5	11 5½	60 7 3½	1 3 2½	4 1 1½	1 6¾	112 1 0	2 1 6½	3 15 1½	1 5¼	14 15 11¼	5 8¼
1383–4	53	1,290	25	14 12 5	5 6¼	31 0 10	11 8½	56 4 11	1 1 2¾	2 1 0¼	9¼	103 19 2¼	1 19 2¾	4 0 3½	1 6¼	16 8 11½	6 2½
1384–5	52	1,279	27	11 15 1	4 6¼	26 16 11	10 4	63 2 10½	1 4 3½	2 11 9	1 0	104 6 7½	2 0 1½	3 5 4½	1 3	16 16 8½	6 5¾
1385–6	52	1,391	27	12 6 5	4 9	23 14 1	9 1½	60 13 8	1 3 4	8 11 1¾	3 3½	105 5 3¾	2 0 6	3 7 3½	1 3½	14 3 0	5 5¼
1386–7	52	1,387	28	10 1 10	3 10½	20 2 6	7 9	64 11 6½	1 4 10	7 2 5¾	2 9	101 18 4¼	1 19 2½	3 4 1	1 2¾	15 0 5¼	5 9¼
1387–8	17	496	29	3 13 0	4 3½	6 2 0	7 2	22 1 1½	1 5 11¼	2 4 11	2 7¾	34 1 0½	2 0 0¾	1 0 5½	1 2½	4 9 11¼	5 3½
1388–9	52	1,591	33	12 1 2	4 7¾	23 7 8	9 0	78 8 7	1 10 2	15 3 4	5 10	129 0 9	2 9 7½	3 7 6½	1 3½	27 2 1½	10 5
1389–90	53	1,501	29	21 17 6	8 3	31 9 2	11 10½	82 0 6	1 10 11½	17 8 9	6 7	152 15 7	2 17 7¾	4 0 3½	1 6¼	38 14 8½	14 7½
1393–4	53	1,372	27	9 16 6	3 8¼	22 7 5	8 5¼	76 19 3½	1 9 0½	10 2 4	3 9¾	119 5 6½	2 5 0	4 11 10½	1 8¾	8 1 11¼	3 0¾
1394–5	52	1,377	28	16 9 11	6 4	26 10 7	10 2½	76 3 3½	1 9 3½	13 10 7	5 2½	132 13 6½	2 11 0¼	4 11 4	1 9	10 8 4¾	4 0
1397–8	27	637	28	9 2 0	6 9	20 19 3	15 6¼	37 13 11½	1 7 11	5 5 2½	3 10¾	73 0 5	2 14 1	2 15 11	2 1	6 5 8¼	4 8
1398–9	53	1,376	27	17 5 2	6 6	29 17 2	11 3¼	77 10 11¼	1 9 3¼	13 4 6¾	5 0	137 17 10	2 12 0½	4 18 0½	1 10¼	9 19 7	3 9¼
1399–1400	52	1,325	27	19 18 1	7 8	30 2 4	11 7	68 16 6	1 6 5¾	13 1 9¼	5 0½	131 17 8¼	2 10 8¾	4 11 1	1 9	14 16 7	5 8½
1400–1	39	954	26	18 5 10	9 4½	21 6 10	10 10¼	45 8 8	1 3 3½	10 1 7½	5 2	95 2 11½	2 8 9½	3 10 8½	1 9¾	8 14 1¾	4 6½
1401–2	27	714	27	18 6 5	13 7	24 13 4	18 3¼	36 5 7	1 6 10½	5 8 8	4 0¼	84 14 2	3 2 9	2 17 4	2 1½	8 2 5¾	6 0¼
1403–4	52	1,310	26	15 16 6	6 1	36 10 11	14 0¾	83 4 11¼	1 12 0¼	12 0 2¼	4 7½	147 12 6½	2 16 9¼	5 0 1	1 11	20 0 3¼	7 8¼
1404–5	52	1,276	25	13 7 9	5 2¼	30 4 6	11 7½	78 14 5¾	1 10 3¼	12 3 4¼	4 8	134 10 3	2 11 9	5 0 3	1 11¼	10 4 6¼	3 11¼
1405–6	40	980	25	9 17 7	4 11¼	21 11 7½	10 9½	55 9 10½	1 7 9	8 3 0	4 1	95 2 1	2 7 6½	3 12 9	1 9¾	5 18 7	2 11½
1406–7	53	1,363	27	16 10 10	6 3	25 1 1	9 5½	71 6 7	1 6 11	13 14 4	5 2	126 12 10	2 7 9½	4 13 2¼	1 9	5 10 7¼	2 1
1407–8	44	1,083	25	13 7 8	6 1	18 7 10	8 4¼	51 13 3½	1 3 6¼	12 0 11½	5 5¾	95 9 9	2 3 5	3 10 11	1 7¼	6 11 8	3 0
1408–9	52	1,381	27	29 10 10	11 4¼	40 14 9	15 8	60 1 11	1 3 1¼	14 14 9	5 8	145 2 3	2 15 9¾	5 2 9	1 11¾	8 8 0	3 2¾
1410–11	52	1,366	26	12 19 5	5 0	30 10 6	11 9	62 11 5	1 4 0¾	11 7 7½	4 4½	117 8 11½	2 5 2	4 3 9	1 7¼	7 18 6	3 0½
1411–12	53	1,218	26	11 6 10	4 3	25 4 10	9 6¼	64 0 8	1 4 2	10 9 6¾	3 11½	111 1 10¾	2 1 11	3 12 2½	1 4¼	16 1 8½	6 1
1412–13	52	1,335	27	15 4 10	5 10	22 1 10	8 6	60 16 8½	1 3 4¾	10 4 6¼	3 11¼	108 7 10¾	2 1 8¼	3 14 9	1 5¼	12 2 11½	4 8
1413–14	41	1,066	26	13 19 6	6 9¾	23 0 7	11 2¾	49 2 1	1 3 11½	10 1 6½	4 11	94 3 8½	2 5 11¼	3 19 2	1 11¼	9 14 0½	4 8¾
1414–15	52	1,315	26	13 3 3	5 1¼	35 1 7	13 6	60 11 0	1 3 3½	12 6 6½	4 9	121 2 4½	2 6 7	3 19 10½	1 6½	18 19 10	7 3¾
1415–16	52	1,228	24	14 19 5	5 9	35 17 5	13 9½	62 5 6	1 3 11½	9 7 4½	3 7¼	122 9 8½	2 7 1¼	4 9 11½	1 8¾	17 15 8½	6 10
1416–17	52	1,270	25	26 8 1	10 2	39 19 7	15 4½	68 5 5½	1 6 3	12 12 3½	4 10¼	147 5 5	2 16 8¼	5 1 9½	1 11½	21 12 4½	8 3¾
1417–18	52	1,194	24	15 0 5	5 9¼	29 7 9	11 3½	64 12 10	1 4 10¼	11 8 4½	4 4¾	120 9 4½	2 6 4	4 8 6½	1 8½	18 11 6¾	7 1¾
1418–19	52	1,069	22	16 11 8	6 4½	21 0 6	8 1	58 13 8	1 2 6¾	12 3 9	4 8¼	108 9 7	2 1 8¾	4 3 0	1 7¼	22 6 0½	8 7
1419–20	52	841	17	10 9 1	4 0¼	17 17 6	6 10½	55 0 7½	1 1 2	11 9 0	4 4¾	94 16 2½	1 16 5½	4 6 2½	1 8	25 11 10¾	9 10
1421–2	53	547	10	8 17 0½	3 4	14 0 10½	5 3½	28 10 5½	10 9	5 9 8½	2 0¾	56 18 3	1 1 5¾	4 11 8½	1 8¾	8 14 4¾	3 3½
1422–3	52	793	15	10 1 4	3 10½	20 4 0	7 9¼	39 13 1½	15 3	6 3 6	2 4½	76 1 11½	1 9 3¼	4 8 5½	1 8½	7 5 9½	2 9¾
1423–4	53	976	19	11 13 3	4 4¾	24 9 0	9 2¾	51 8 0	19 4¾	9 11 7½	3 7½	97 1 10½	1 16 7¾	4 12 8	1 9	10 14 3¼	4 0½
1424–5	52	1,079	22	14 8 11	5 6¾	25 7 3	9 9	69 18 2½	1 6 10¾	8 16 4	3 4¾	118 10 8½	2 5 7	4 14 6	1 9¾	21 5 3	8 2
1425–6	51	934	20	9 15 8½	3 10	19 4 8	7 6½	54 8 7½	1 0 11½	5 12 7	2 2½	89 1 7	1 14 6½	4 4 8	1 8	12 18 11¾	5 1
1426–7	52	887	17	9 3 11½	3 6½	16 8 0½	6 4¼	51 2 1½	19 8	9 17 9½	3 9¾	86 12 1	1 13 3¾	4 10 10½	1 9	7 2 10½	2 9
1427–8	52	1,103	21	13 3 0½	5 0¾	25 14 2	9 10¾	69 7 4½	1 6 8	11 2 10½	4 3½	119 7 5½	2 5 11	4 12 5½	1 9¼	19 11 3	7 6¼
1428–9	52	1,086	21	18 1 2	6 11	26 9 3	10 2	65 10 5½	1 5 2½	8 14 11	3 4¼	118 15 10½	2 5 8¼	4 14 3½	1 9¾	19 2 8½	7 4
1429–30	53	1,141	22	24 9 9½	9 3	37 16 5	14 3¼	65 7 9½	1 4 8	10 6 0½	3 10¾	138 0 0½	2 12 1	5 1 11½	1 11	26 19 7½	10 2
1430–1	52	1,079	22	19 19 8	7 8¼	33 14 5	12 11¾	69 1 5¾	1 6 6¾	6 18 1¼	2 8	129 13 8	2 9 0½	5 0 0½	1 11	26 4 8	10 1
1431–2	52	1,025	20	9 12 1½	3 8¼	33 4 0	12 9¼	75 19 2½	1 9 2½	10 4 1	3 11	128 19 5	2 9 7¼	5 1 0	1 11	27 4 11	10 5¾
1432–3	52	999	20	20 6 4½	7 9¾	36 4 1	13 11	60 8 4½	1 3 3	7 2 7	2 9	124 1 5	2 7 8¾	5 4 7½	2 0	23 15 7	9 2¼
1433–4	45	936	21	16 14 3½	7 5	29 18 7½	13 3½	54 15 8	1 4 4¼	9 1 2	4 0¼	110 9 9	2 9 1¼	4 0 1½	1 9¼	27 1 11	12 0½
1434–5	53	1,193	23	18 19 6½	7 2	29 14 10	11 2¾	66 13 8½	1 5 2	8 4 0	3 1	123 12 1	2 6 7¾	4 2 0½	1 6½	30 15 1½	11 7¼
1435–6	52	1,187	24	19 18 6	7 8	26 4 1	10 1	70 6 9½	1 7 0¾	9 4 2½	3 6½	125 13 7	2 8 4	4 5 8	1 7¾	27 19 9¼	10 9¼
1436–7	52	1,198	24	19 12 2½	7 6½	22 3 3½	8 6¼	74 4 2	1 8 6½	9 15 3	3 9	125 14 11	2 8 4¼	3 19 5½	1 6¼	32 15 7½	12 7¼
1437–8	52	1,242	25	33 13 4½	12 11½	32 12 8	12 6¾	73 11 9	1 8 3¾	8 12 2	3 3¾	148 9 11½	2 17 1½	4 17 2½	1 10½	31 5 10	12 0½
1438–9	52	1,173	23	49 14 8½	19 1¼	48 3 1	18 6¼	65 9 10½	1 5 2½	10 1 4¼	3 10¼	173 9 1¼	3 6 8¼	5 19 2	2 3¼	37 17 0¼	14 6¾
1439–40	52	1,252	24	39 5 4½	15 1¼	39 12 11	15 3	65 12 2	1 5 3	9 11 8	3 8¼	154 2 1¼	2 19 3¼	4 19 11¼	1 11	34 12 5	13 3¾
1440–1	52	1,243	24	13 5 0	5 1	21 14 7	8 4¼	65 1 1¾	1 5 0¼	8 14 3¾	3 4¼	108 15 2½	2 1 10	3 16 10¼	1 5¾	17 18 8	6 10¾
1441–2	52	1,341	27	12 10 10¼	4 10	16 19 10	6 6¼	81 16 7¾	1 11 5¾	8 1 8¼	3 1¼	119 9 2½	2 5 11¼	3 17 11½	1 6	13 19 0	7 4
1442–3	52	1,295	26	11 5 3½	4 4	24 5 9	9 4	70 2 0	1 6 11½	8 19 10¼	3 5½	114 12 11	2 4 1	3 10 9	1 4¼	19 15 11	7 7¼
1443–4	52	988	20	9 10 0½	3 8	16 12 3	6 4¾	56 9 8½	1 1 8¼	9 2 8½	3 6	91 14 8½	1 15 3½	4 5 6¼	1 7¾	7 12 9¼	2 11¼

the totals of all the columns of the accounts under consideration
have had to be supplied in order that annual averages might be
worked out. It now seems desirable to include at this stage in the
text a comprehensive table (table 5 (pullout)) of eighteen columns,
under self-explanatory headings, which provides a complete numerical
summary in the form of totals and averages of all the essential
economic data contained in the fifty-four extant accounts between
1382–3 and 1443–4. It is on the basis of these figures that the investigation can now proceed.

In the light of what has already been said concerning the process
by which the commons rate was calculated week by week, it is clear
that the term 'commons' was one covering not only all the ingredients of the meal from the largest items of food right down to
the smallest of the seasonings but also the running costs of the
kitchen and the fuel used for cooking,[1] and probably included an
allowance for the payment of the servants. This places a rather wider
interpretation upon the concept of academic commons than is perhaps usually realised. For clearly it must not be supposed that
commons expenditure referred only to the items of food and drink
which went to make up a fellow's daily meals. In the case of the
King's Hall, at any rate, the weekly commons charge was finally
reckoned on the basis of the whole process involved in the production of the fellows' meals; and there is no reason to suppose that this
method of calculation was substantially different from that employed
in other contemporary English colleges.

Moreover, an analysis of the constituent proportions of 'commons' at the King's Hall reveals that bread and ale did not make up
as high a proportion as might otherwise be supposed. It is certainly
true that bread and ale together constituted the largest single food
item. Indeed, it appears that the commons rate was to a considerable extent determined by the initial expenditure on bread and ale,
which, in turn, was dependent upon current wheat and malt barley
prices. This is illustrated in figure 1 (p. 127), where the estimated
charge for weekly commons for each fellow averaged over each year
in the period 1382–3 to 1443–4 (a)[2] is compared with the estimated

---

1 Apart from cooking, fuelling costs may also embrace the heating of the dining hall
during meals. Fuel costs are specified in the accounts between 1385–6 and 1443–4
and ranged from 1s 6d to 4s a year.   2 See table 5 (pullout), column 16.

college expenditure on bread and ale for each fellow averaged over the same period (*b*).[1]

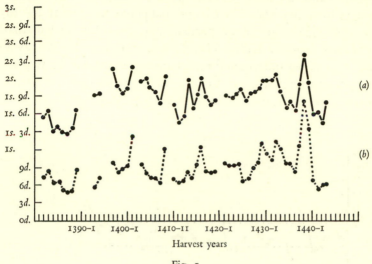

Harvest years

Fig. 1

The graph indicates quite a close relationship between the size of the commons rate and current expenditure on bread and ale. The variation in the differences between the curves, that is to say between the bread and ale constituent of the commons rate and the total commons levy, is to be explained by fluctuations in the prices of the other food items, fuel and so on which went to make up the full commons charge.

From the average figures derived and recorded in table 5 (pullout), it is possible to determine with some degree of accuracy the size of the proportion of 'commons' constituted by bread and ale. This is obtainable from figure 2 (p. 128), where the average estimated college expenditure on bread and ale for each fellow (averaged over each year in our period) is expressed as a percentage of the average estimated charge for weekly commons for each fellow over the same period.

[1] These figures are arrived at by adding those for the average expenditure on bread for all the fellows present per week per year (table 5, column 6) to the corresponding figures for ale (column 8) and dividing the sum each year by the average number of fellows present over the year (column 4).

If two lines are drawn through the points on the graph so that an equal number of 'high' and 'low' points remain outside the resultant band, we are left with an average range of values extending from 34 to 50 per cent. The exceptional percentages of 26 in 1393–4 and 72 in 1438–9 are to be partially explained by the fact that in the former year the King's Hall bought wheat at the low average price of 3s 6d per quarter and malt barley at the equally low price of 3s 8d per quarter;[1] while in 1438–9 the price of wheat had soared to 13s 10d per quarter, the maximum level for the period under review,

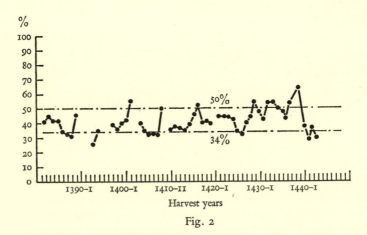

Fig. 2

and the price of malt barley had risen to 7s 1d per quarter.[2] But in average 'grain' years it would appear that expenditure on bread and ale was somewhere in the region of between a third and a half of the weekly commons rate. Consequently, the remaining half to two-thirds of the commons charge is to be accounted for by expenditure on all other items of food, fuel and kitchen expenses. One must therefore not overstress the importance of bread and ale as basic constituent parts of the weekly commons of the fellows of the King's Hall. Perhaps this caveat has a general application for the English medieval scene, although it may well be that items such as bread and ale would tend to assume greater proportions in collegiate establish-

[1] Averages based on entries for wheat and malt barley in *K.H. Accts.* IV, fo. 20. See table 9, p. 144.
[2] Averages based on entries *ibid.* IX, fo. 77. See table 9, p. 145.

ments where the commons rates were not so high and the food less diversified than in this royal foundation.

In order to give a reliable estimate of a fellow's basic maintenance costs in the King's Hall it is essential to discover just how much it cost the average King's Scholar to maintain himself in the college throughout the year. As a first step towards this end, the make-up of the commons rate must be further investigated.

The problem may be posed as follows: how much of the weekly commons charge levied by the college on every fellow for his meals had to be found from his own pocket? Whereas, in the case of every other English college, maintenance allowances for commons were administered from the revenues of the institution itself, in marked contrast the King's Scholars received a flat rate of 1s 2d per week by annual direct grant from the exchequer. Each Scholar was then credited with this sum for his weekly commons. As already indicated, this was a flat rate and the exchequer material relating to the King's Hall proves conclusively that this endowment never varied and was certainly not geared to a sliding scale dependent upon current grain prices. Here, it is apposite to ask if there was, in addition to the main exchequer subsidy, a grant made towards commons from the funds of the college. The possibility of such a second subsidy is indicated by a clause in the King's Hall statutes which makes provision for a small increment in the commons allowance at festival periods or in times of scarcity to be implemented at the warden's discretion.[1] This plainly implies that if there were to be a subsidy additional to the basic exchequer rate of 1s 2d, such a subsidy would be doled out to each Scholar from the revenues of the Society. And the possibility of a subsidy of this kind has been taken into account in reckoning a fellow's average expenditure on his commons. It will be recalled that in the accounts for 1382–3 and those following, column 6 represents the total expenditure incurred in providing all the fellows' meals for a week. Now, as the commons rate appears to have varied directly with this sum, it is clear that if this total is divided by the number of fellows present for the week, then, if

---

[1] See King's Hall statutes in Rouse Ball, *op. cit.* p. 69. The commons allowance was to be 1s 2d per week, 'Illis Septimanis exceptis in quibus Festa Principalia... contingerit evenire; necnon illis exceptis...ratione parcitatis et caristie victualium Custos predictus aut eius Vices gerens ipso absente aliter duxerit fore statuendum.'

there were no subsidy, the quotient ought to be equal to the commons rate fixed for that particular week. With this postulation in mind, a series of sample readings were taken from accounts distributed at random over the whole period. The object of the investigation may be put succinctly thus:

sample readings were taken of:

(Total cost incurred by the college for the provision of
commons for a week for a given number of fellows present)
_____
(Number of fellows present for the same week)

and compared with:

(Sum charged to each fellow for his commons for the same week.)

It was found that in every case the quotient was slightly larger than the stipulated commons rate. The results of a dozen years are arranged in table 6 and show at a glance the lower and upper limits of these differences between the quotient and the commons levy:

TABLE 6

Harvest year	Range of 'differences'
	(*pence*)
1382–3	$1\frac{1}{2}$–3
1383–4	$1\frac{1}{2}$–$4\frac{1}{2}$
1384–5	$1\frac{1}{2}$–4
1393–4	$\frac{3}{4}$–$2\frac{1}{2}$
1394–5	$\frac{3}{4}$–$3\frac{1}{2}$
1399–1400	1–$3\frac{1}{2}$
1403–4	$1\frac{3}{4}$–5
1410–11	$\frac{1}{4}$–4
1421–2	$\frac{3}{4}$–6
1426–7	$\frac{3}{4}$–$6\frac{1}{4}$
1434–5	$3\frac{3}{4}$–7
1443–4	$1\frac{1}{4}$–$4\frac{1}{4}$

The question naturally arises as to whether these 'differences' represent a subsidy on the fellows' weekly commons or whether they can be accounted for in any other way. In this connection, some small allowance has to be made for the commons expenses of private guests and relatives of individual fellows who would share the fellows' meals, dining in hall at the same table as their hosts. It is evident that the cost of providing meals for guests will be included in the total cost incurred by the college for the fellows' commons. But as it was customary for each fellow to account separately to the seneschals for any meals given to private guests introduced into the college, it follows that this item of expenditure would not form any part of the weekly sums paid over by each fellow for his commons. It would therefore seem that some small proportion of the difference between the total cost to the college for the provision of the fellows' weekly commons and the actual amount paid by the fellows for their meals must have been utilised to defray the expenses of meals for private guests;[1] and the residue, if there was a residue, can be accounted for by a small college subsidy.

But whether or not a college subsidy was given each year to the fellows for their commons, it is clear that any such sum had already been deducted from the amounts charged to each fellow for his commons before these rates were entered in the Society's records. And so, the figures quoted above (table 5, column 16) as the yearly average charge for weekly commons in the King's Hall are in actual fact sums made up of the basic exchequer allowance of 1s 2d per Scholar per week and an excess amount from which a college subsidy, if any, had already been deducted and which a fellow had to find from his own pocket.[2] It is now apparent that the amount actually spent by a fellow on his commons in any given year can be reckoned by subtracting the product of the exchequer subsidy of 1s 2d times the number of weeks accounted for in that year from the total amount due for commons from each fellow for the same year

[1] No account need here be taken of the large number of commoners and semi-commoners present in the Hall (see below, pp. 259 ff.) because these accounted separately to the college for commons and sizings and consequently the 'commoner' arrangements were wholly distinct from those for the fellows.

[2] In each annual account, under the heading *Repaste Sociorum*, is to be found a list of the names of the fellows resident throughout the year, against each of which are set down sums of money due to the college, usually for commons and sizings. These jottings, which were scored through when the debts had been paid, are, for this reason, very difficult to follow. Taken together, these rough entries appear to constitute the fellows' bills over the year. Although *Repaste* is the term used specifically for sizings throughout the King's Hall accounts (see above, p. 125, n. 3), it is clear that when used in the sectional heading *Repaste Sociorum*, it embraced commons as well as sizings and indeed any other item for which a fellow stood indebted to the college.

(table 5, column 15). The difference represents the amount of money due to the college which had to be drawn from a fellow's private source of income. For example, in 1382-3,[1] the average King's Scholar would be required to pay to the college from his own pocket $(£3 \ 15s \ 1\frac{1}{2}d) - (1s \ 2d \times 52) = (£3 \ 15s \ 1\frac{1}{2}d) - (£3 \ 0s \ 8d) = 14s \ 5\frac{1}{2}d$. Similar calculations have been carried out for all of the fifty-four accounts between 1382-3 and 1443-4[2] and the resulting set of figures is given below in table 7, column 2 (p. 133).

But figures for actual expenditure on commons alone do not provide us with the full information required for an assessment of the average amount spent by a King's Scholar on his maintenance throughout a given year. For clearly we must take cognisance of the money spent by the fellows on their sizings or 'extra commons'. Sizings were more often than not regular daily expenses and have consequently to be added to those for basic food necessities if we are to arrive at a reliable estimate of the amount of money which the average King's Scholar had to possess in order to live in the college from year to year. The average amounts spent on sizings or luxuries per fellow for each year of the period 1382-3 to 1443-4[3] have been worked out and the averages are shown in table 7, column 3 (p. 133). It is, of course, fully realised that different fellows will tend to spend differing amounts on their luxury requirements; but because the accounts provide only the gross expenditure by all fellows on sizings over the year, it is possible to evaluate only the average expenditure on sizings per fellow per annum. Assuming that there are no major discrepancies in 'luxury consumption' among the fellows, this approach would seem to be reasonably valid. Adding the second set of averages (table 7, column 3) to the first (table 7, column 2), a third is now obtained (table 7, column 4) which represents a fellow's combined average estimated expenditure on commons and sizings

---

[1] See the appendix, pp. 310–11, column 7.

[2] In cases where the account fails to provide information for all of the weeks of the year, the total amount due for commons per fellow per annum has been calculated on the basis of an average figure derived from the available data for the given number of weeks.

[3] This calculation is made by dividing the total amount spent by the fellows on their sizings over the year (table 5, column 17) by the total number of fellows present over all the weeks of the year (i.e. 'fellow weeks', column 3) and multiplying the quotient by 52 to give the average amount spent by one fellow over the year.

TABLE 7

	Average estimated expenditure											
(1) Harvest year	(2) Commons per fellow per year[1]			(3) Sizings per fellow per year			(4) Commons and sizings per fellow per year			(5) Commons and sizings per fellow per week		
	£	s	d	£	s	d	£	s	d	£	s	d
1382–3		14	5½		10	5	1	4	10½			5¾
1383–4		18	4		13	0	1	11	4			7¼
1384–5		4	8½		13	7¾		18	4¼			4¼
1385–6		6	7½		10	6¾		17	2¼			4
1386–7		3	5		11	3		14	8			3½
1387–8		2	2		9	5		11	7			2¾
1388–9		6	10½		17	8	1	4	6½			5¾
1389–90		17	6½	1	6	11	2	4	3½			10¼
1393–4	1	9	5½		6	1	1	15	6½			8¼
1394–5	1	10	8		7	10	1	18	6			9
1397–8	2	7	8		10	2¾	2	17	10¾		1	1¼
1398–9	1	15	5		7	5½	2	2	10½			10
1399–1400	1	10	5		11	7¼	2	2	0¼			9¾
1400–1	1	13	7		9	6	2	3	1			10
1401–2	2	9	10		11	10	3	1	8		1	2¼
1403–4	1	19	5		15	10¼	2	15	3¼		1	0¾
1404–5	1	19	7		8	4	2	7	11			11
1405–6	1	13	7		6	3½	1	19	10½			9¼
1406–7	1	10	8¼		4	2	1	14	10¼			8
1407–8	1	2	9		6	3½	1	9	0½			6¾
1408–9	2	2	1		6	4	2	8	5			11¼
1410–11	1	3	1		6	1	1	9	2			6¾
1411–12		10	2½		13	8¼	1	3	10¾			5½
1412–13		14	1		9	5¼	1	3	6¼			5½
1413–14	2	0	1		9	5¼	2	9	6¼			11½
1414–15		19	2½		15	0	1	14	2½			8
1415–16	1	9	3½		15	0½	2	4	4			10¼
1416–17	2	1	1½		17	8	2	18	9½		1	1½
1417–18	1	7	10½		16	2	2	4	0½			10¼
1418–19	1	2	4	1	1	8	2	4	0			10¼
1419–20	1	5	6½	1	11	7½	2	17	2		1	1¼
1421–2	1	9	5½		16	7¾	2	6	1¼			10¾
1422–3	1	7	9½		9	6½	1	17	4			8¾
1423–4	1	10	3½		11	4¼	2	1	7¾			9½
1424–5	1	13	10	1	0	5½	2	14	3½		1	0½
1425–6	1	6	0		13	4¾	1	19	4¾			9
1426–7	1	10	2½		8	4	1	18	6½			9
1427–8	1	11	9½		17	10¾	2	9	8¼			11½
1428–9	1	13	7½		18	3½	2	11	11		1	0
1429–30	1	19	4	1	4	7	3	3	11		1	2¾
1430–1	1	19	4½	1	5	3	3	4	7½		1	3
1431–2	2	0	4	1	7	7¼	3	7	11¼		1	3¾
1432–3	2	3	11½	1	4	9	3	8	8½		1	3¾
1433–4	1	11	5	1	10	0	3	1	5		1	2¼
1434–5		19	9½	1	6	9¼	2	6	6¾			10¾
1435–6	1	5	0	1	4	6	2	9	6			11½
1436–7		18	9½	1	8	5	2	7	2½			11
1437–8	1	16	6½	1	6	3	3	2	9½		1	2½
1438–9	2	18	6	1	13	6½	4	12	0½		1	9¼
1439–40	1	19	3½	1	8	4¾	3	7	8¼		1	3½
1440–1		16	2½		15	0	1	11	2½			7¼
1441–2		17	3½		14	10¾	1	12	2¼			7½
1442–3		10	1		15	10¼	1	5	11¼			6
1443–4	1	4	10½		8	2	1	13	0½			7½

[1] I.e. actual amount spent by fellow when exchequer and college subsidies have been deducted.

for each year in the period under review: column 5 of this table gives these figures in the form of weekly averages.

It may be seen from table 7, column 5, that between 1382–3 and 1443–4 the average King's Scholar was required to spend from his own private income sums ranging from as little as 2¾*d* per week in 1387–8 (when grain prices were unusually low) to as much as 1*s* 9¼*d* per week in 1438–9 (when grain prices were exceptionally high). When these figures are graphed (see figure 3, below), it is apparent that in average 'grain' years it was necessary for the King's Scholar to find from his own pocket sums ranging from about 6*d* to about 1*s* 2½*d* per week, i.e. from £1 6*s* to £3 2*s* 10*d* per annum to cover maintenance costs in the college.

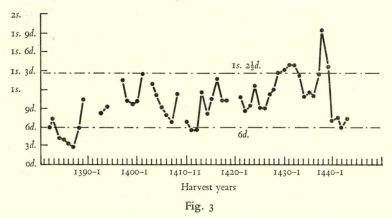

Fig. 3

Because of price fluctuations over this period, it is necessary to try to adjust these sums to allow for variations in the purchasing power of money. Consequently, an attempt has been made to 'correct' these figures by means of a price index. It is realised that to arrive at such an index one ought to take into consideration all the commodities embraced by commons expenditure. With the limited amount of data available, this is clearly impossible. However, an index has been constructed based solely on food consumption. Moreover, trial samples indicated that because of the major importance of wheat and malt barley in the composition of the diet only the price variations of these commodities need to be taken into account and that the effect of price fluctuations in items such as almonds, salt, pepper, honey and rice is negligible. It must be stressed, however, that these considerations apply only to basic commons; in the case of sizings (or luxury items) price fluctuations in these other commodities would doubtless assume greater significance. But since the composition of sizings remains unknown, it is not possible to compile an index incorporating these items in order to 'correct' the figures for 'luxury' consumption.

A study of the quantities of wheat and malt barley purchased annually leads to the conclusion that these commodities should be weighted in the ratio of one part wheat to two parts barley. Using the yearly average prices for wheat and malt barley (given below, pp. 144–5), the cost of purchasing one quarter of wheat and two quarters of barley was evaluated for each year in the period under investigation and an index constructed by referring all of these costs to that of a given reference year.[1] As this index has been based on grain prices alone it can therefore provide only a partial corrective to the sums representing the average expenditure on commons per fellow per annum; for reasons already stated, no attempt has been made to 'correct' the corresponding figures for sizings. The revised list for commons expenditure is as shown in table 8. The blanks in the 'corrected' column for 1421-2, 1422-3, 1426-7, 1440-1 and 1441-2 are because reliable wheat and malt barley average prices are not available for these years. Although these 'corrections' are far from complete, at least fluctuations due to price variations in wheat and malt barley have been 'ironed out'.

The 'uncorrected' figures for commons expenditure indicated that the average King's Scholar would spend on his commons and sizings sums ranging from £1 6s to £3 2s 10d over the whole period.[2] But if the 'corrected' commons expenditure figures are now combined with the 'uncorrected' figures for sizings[3] the range of expenditure is reduced to £1 14s to £3.[4] Expressed in weekly

[1] E.g. taking the reference year as 1382–3 where the cost came to 14s 10d, then the index for 1386–7 is 0·69 since the cost for that year was only 10s 3d: similarly, the index for 1401–2 is 1·49 because the cost in that year was £1 2s 2d.

[2] See above, p. 134.   [3] See table 7, column 3.

[4] The 'corrected' figures for commons were graphed and the revised range of expenditure of the average King's Scholar on his basic food requirements was seen to lie in the region of about £1 2s to £1 16s. A plot of the 'uncorrected' figures for sizings gave a range of about 12s to £1 4s. Consequently, we may say very approximately that the range of expenditure indicated by the 'partially corrected' combined commons and sizings figures is about £1 14s to £3.

TABLE 8. *Average estimated expenditure on commons per fellow per annum, i.e. actual amount spent by fellow when exchequer and possible college subsidies have been deducted*

Harvest year	'Uncorrected' sums			Index numbers	'Corrected' sums		
	£	s	d		£	s	d
1382–3		14	5½	1·000		14	5½
(*reference year*)							
1383–4		18	4	1·08		17	0
1384–5		4	8½	0·819		5	9
1385–6		6	7½	0·792		8	4
1386–7		3	5	0·69		4	11½
1387–8		2	2	0·651		3	4
1388–9		6	10½	0·623		11	0
1389–90		17	6½	0·825	1	1	3
1393–4	1	9	5½	0·73	2	0	0
1394–5	1	10	8	0·91	1	13	8½
1397–8	2	7	8	1·248	1	19	2
1398–9	1	15	5	0·88	2	0	3
1399–1400	1	10	5	0·927	1	12	11
1400–1	1	13	7	1·01	1	13	2
1401–2	2	9	10	1·49	1	13	6
1403–4	1	19	5	0·865	2	5	7
1404–5	1	19	7	0·711	2	15	7
1405–6	1	13	7	0·646	2	11	9
1406–7	1	10	8¼	0·724	2	2	3
1407–8	1	2	9	0·741	1	10	8
1408–9	2	2	1	1·248	1	13	10
1410–11	1	3	1	0·825	1	8	0
1411–12		10	2½	0·623		16	4
1412–13		14	1	0·629	1	2	4
1413–14	2	0	1	0·933	2	3	0
1414–15		19	2½	0·825	1	3	3
1415–16	1	9	3½	1·028	1	8	6
1416–17	2	1	1½	1·202	1	14	2
1417–18	1	7	10½	0·872	1	12	0
1418–19	1	2	4	0·78	1	8	7
1419–20	1	5	6½	0·635	2	0	3
1421–2	1	9	5½	—		—	
1422–3	1	7	9½	—		—	
1423–4	1	10	3½	0·944	1	12	1
1424–5	1	13	10	0·866	1	19	1
1425–6	1	6	0	0·765	1	14	0
1426–7	1	10	2½	—		—	
1427–8	1	11	9½	0·629	2	10	6
1428–9	1	13	7½	0·906	1	17	0

TABLE 8 *cont.*

Harvest year	'Uncorrected' sums			Index numbers	'Corrected' sums		
	£	s	d		£	s	d
1429–30	1	19	4	1·248	1	11	7
1430–1	1	19	4½	0·915	2	3	0
1431–2	2	0	4	0·758	2	13	1
1432–3	2	3	11½	1·01	2	3	3
1433–4	1	11	5	1·007	1	11	2
1434–5		19	9½	0·669	1	9	7
1435–6	1	5	0	0·731	1	14	3
1436–7		18	9½	0·731	1	5	8½
1437–8	1	16	6½	1·112	1	12	10
1438–9	2	18	6	1·89	1	11	0
1439–40	1	19	3½	1·55	1	5	4
1440–1		16	2½	—			—
1441–2		17	3½	—			—
1442–3		10	1	0·719		14	1
1443–4	1	4	10½	0·65	1	18	4

terms, the revised range is from 7¾*d* to 1*s* 1¾*d* compared with the 'uncorrected' range of 6*d* to 1*s* 2½*d* shown in figure 3.

From these data it is justifiable to conclude that before a Scholar could enter the King's Hall it was necessary for him to possess a source or sources of substantial private income to enable him to pay even his basic bills and certainly if he were to participate to the full in the communal life of the Society. The exclusive nature of this royal foundation is all the more apparent when it is considered that in addition to these high maintenance costs every Scholar, upon first entry, was required to pay burdensome admission charges. There is no mention of these entrance dues in the statutes of 1380[1] but from

[1] From the English statutory evidence it would appear that the custom of exacting entrance charges from a fellow, such as the requirement to present to the society items of plate or napery or to pay over sums of money to be appropriated for specified college purposes, was a practice which, though not widespread, was particularly associated with Cambridge. An examination of English college statutes from the thirteenth to the seventeenth century surprisingly reveals that in only two codes, those of the Cambridge colleges of Peterhouse and Michaelhouse, are entrance dues of this kind stipulated. (See the statutes for Peterhouse in *Camb. Docs.* II, 6, where it is enacted that, upon admission, a fellow must provide himself with a surplice (within three months) and must present a mazer cup (*ciphum murreum*) and a silver spoon to the society without delay. Similarly, at Michaelhouse, a new

the annual accounts it is abundantly clear that, upon admission, each new fellow was bound to make three separate payments to the Society. First, a King's Scholar had to provide a breakfast or feast for all the members of the college, rated at a monetary equivalent of twenty shillings:[1] next, he was required to make a contribution of twenty shillings towards a plate fund[2] from which the college could draw for the purchase of new items of plate and for repairs to the existing stock: and finally, each Scholar paid fourpence towards the fitting out, maintenance and running costs of the college boat.[3] In all, therefore, admission charges amounted to the very sizable sum of £2 0s 4d. When it is considered that the annual wage of the King's Hall butler was in most years only £1 6s 8d,[4] or that the wages of most categories of skilled medieval tradesmen of the late fourteenth and fifteenth centuries ranged from about threepence to sixpence a day, then, by comparison, the very high nature of these entrance dues can be appreciated. As only those scholars possessed of substantial sources of income or those supported by generous patrons could afford to meet these otherwise prohibitive financial demands,

fellow was required to have a white surplice and to give the college a silver spoon, a cup of *murra* and a napkin and cloth for the fellows' table: Stamp, *Michaelhouse*, p. 29.) Generally speaking, the thirteenth- and fourteenth-century English colleges were small communities whose finances were, in several instances, so deficient that some of even the most important of the founder's statutory provisions could not at first be given practical effect. One would therefore have thought that the levy of admission charges would have been something of an economic necessity, a convenient method of maintaining and adding to the material possessions of the college and of augmenting its revenues. Consequently, it is puzzling to find no trace of admission dues in any Oxford code before the seventeenth century. As in the case of the King's Hall, however, it may well be that the exaction of entrance charges belonged to the body of customary arrangements which had grown up after the founder's death and were never embodied in the statutory provisions. The practice of levying admission dues was fairly common among the fourteenth-century Paris colleges. For example, the founder of the Ave Maria College enacted that the boys newly admitted to the institution should bring with them their own linen, towels and items necessary for their beds: Gabriel, *Ave Maria College*, p. 94 and statute no. 88, pp. 349–50. At the colleges of Boncour (1357) and Dainville (1380) new entrants had to provide their own bed furnishings: *ibid.* p. 94, n. 6.

[1] See e.g. *K.H. Accts.* v, fos. 163, 183; vi, fos. 104v, 140; vii, fos. 1v, 111v; viii, fos. 1v, 18v, 40; ix, fos. 1v, 148v; x, fo. 82v.

[2] See e.g. *ibid.* iv, fo. 137; v, fos. 113, 130; vi, fos. 15, 99, 140; vii, fos. 69v, 111v; viii, fos. 18v, 40, 61v, 87v; ix, fos. 93v, 148v; x, fos. 1v, 28v.

[3] See e.g. *ibid.* v, fo. 130; vi, fos. 15v, 140; vii, fo. 1v; viii, fos. 18v, 87v; ix, fos. 93v, 148v; xi, fos. 1v, 61v.   [4] See below, p. 236.

it is arguable that the King's Hall entrance dues are a visible expression of that intimate connection between this royal foundation and the upper and wealthy strata of society for whom it appears to have been primarily designed.

It is almost certainly true to affirm that the cost of a fellow's maintenance in the King's Hall was well above the average level of other English colleges of the period. Even if there were no further evidence to support this claim, the basic rates for commons levied on King's Hall fellows would alone seem to substantiate the point. Between 1382–3 and 1443–4, the King's Scholars were charged for their commons average sums ranging from 1s 2½d per week in 1387–8 to 2s 3½d in 1438–9, which gives an average charge of 1s 8¼d per week over the whole period.[1] When these average figures are set against the statutory allowances made for commons in contemporary colleges, there can be little doubt that even the basic cost of maintenance in the King's Hall would have been equivalent to a fairly high luxury standard elsewhere.

It is here fully realised that two sets of figures are being compared which are not, on the face of it, strictly comparable: that is to say, the actual rates charged for commons in the King's Hall are compared with examples of statutory allowances for commons made to fellows in other collegiate societies. But in the absence of evidence for the actual rates levied in these colleges week by week over the same number of years, there is no alternative to the figures provided by the statutes. Whereas the King's Hall statutes prescribe a flat rate of 1s 2d per fellow per week, those of most medieval English colleges gear the allowance system to a sliding scale with stipulated minimum and maximum limits and governed by fluctuations in current grain prices. This would appear to signify that in the majority of English colleges, though not in the King's Hall, the system of allowances was so designed as to be sufficiently flexible to cover most of the costs of a fellow's basic food requirements even in years when grain prices were unusually high.[2] In view of this, it is reasonable to

[1] See table 5 (pullout), column 16.
[2] This would also appear to have been the standard practice in the Paris colleges. See e.g. the arrangements at the Ave Maria College where the founder, John of Hubant, stipulated that, during times of scarcity, the master and chaplain, with the consent of the governors, were to defray the additional expenses incurred for commons out of the funds of the society: Gabriel, *op. cit.* p. 223. It was only when these common

assume that these statutory sliding scales are a fairly reliable guide to the actual sums allowed for commons.

A few representative examples of such statutory allowances will bring out by comparison the very high cost of maintenance in the King's Hall. The standard maintenance allowance for commons in most fourteenth-century English colleges, including New College, Oxford, was 1s per fellow per week.[1] As already indicated, provision was normally made for this rate to increase proportional to the rising price of grain. The uppermost limits of these sliding scales varied from college to college. At Oriel College, for example, the maximum stipulated limit of 1s 3d was to come into force when the quarter of wheat was selling at 10s or more in Oxford or the surrounding district.[2] Wykeham, on the other hand, prescribed that the commons rate for his scholars might be increased to 1s 4d in times of scarcity; and in the event of the bushel of wheat fetching more than 2s in Oxford or neighbouring markets, the commons limit was to be advanced to 1s 6d.[3] Similar arrangements were made for King's College, Cambridge, in the mid-fifteenth century. There the commons allowance was to rise from the basic rate of 1s 4d a week to 1s 5d and 1s 6d in bad harvest years with an ultimate ceiling of 1s 8d when the bushel of wheat was selling at 2s or more in the Cambridge area.[4] To complete this short survey, it is perhaps especially illuminating to add that as late as 1489 John Alcock, bishop of Ely, inserted an ordinance in the statutes of Peterhouse to the effect that the master and scholars were to have no more than 1s 2d per week for their commons, although this might be slightly increased in lean harvest years.[5]

One can therefore assert that the sliding-scale system in operation in most English medieval colleges was designed to maintain a constant relationship between a fellow's commons allowance and current trends in food prices, thus relieving him of the necessity of

funds were deemed insufficient to meet the costs of the extra charge that, as a last resort, the students themselves were enjoined to find the necessary revenue from their private sources of income: see the statutes in Gabriel, *op. cit.* pp. 361–2.

[1] See e.g. the statutes of 1359 for Clare College in *Camb. Docs.* II, 135; the statutes of Michaelhouse in Stamp, *op. cit.* p. 43; and the statutes of Oriel and New College in *Statutes*, I, ch. (3), 7, ch. (5), 38–9.

[2] *Statutes*, I, ch. (3), 15.　　　　　[3] *Ibid.* I, ch. (5), 38–9.

[4] *Camb. Docs.* II, 527–8.　　　　　[5] *Ibid.* II, 48–9.

drawing upon his private financial resources to any great extent in order to meet the costs of his basic food requirements.[1] The system of maintenance in the King's Hall, however, was strikingly different. As the exchequer flat rate of 1s 2d was not geared to a sliding scale and as the small college subsidy, if there was one, had already been deducted from the commons rate before these charges were entered in the accounts, it is evident that these King's Hall levies for weekly commons—the sum of 1s 8¼d being the average charge over the entire period—in every instance exceeded the uppermost statutory limits of even the highest of the contemporary collegiate sliding scales. Moreover, when it is considered that in thirty-one out of the fifty-four years for which figures were obtained the average charge levied on the King's Scholars ranged between 1s 8¼d and 2s 3½d, there is added justification for the assertion that the basic cost of maintenance in this royal foundation must have been tantamount to a high luxury collegiate level elsewhere.[2] But given the household origins of the Society and the fact that the college always retained something of the atmosphere or flavour of the court from which it derived,[3] a conclusion of this kind is not unexpected. As in so many other respects, so here, the King's Hall stands apart from the generality of English colleges as an institution *sui generis* offering a level of material comfort midway between that of the average type of collegiate society of the fourteenth and fifteenth centuries and the more luxurious standards of the rich aristocratic households of the period towards which it undoubtedly gravitated.

[1] It is assumed that a fellow will almost certainly have some small source of private income.

[2] Dr Emden has produced evidence to show that in 1424 the average charge for commons per week in an Oxford hall was *c.* 6¼d, i.e. just under a penny a day (Emden, *An Oxford hall in medieval times*, p. 194). In the same year, the average sum charged to each King's Hall fellow was 1s 9¾d (table 5, column 16), i.e. just under threepence a day. This year is fairly representative since over the whole period the average charge for commons was 1s 8¼d per week (see p. 139). If the figures furnished for one Oxford hall in 1424 are typical of similar institutions, we may conclude that the average commons rate in the King's Hall was approximately three times that normally levied in the halls or hostels of the period. This conclusion would doubtless have to be amended in the case of the halls of the legists, where boarding rates were presumably significantly higher than in the establishments designed for the majority of less mature students.

[3] In this connection see e.g. the discussion of minstrel entertainments in the King's Hall, pp. 222 ff.

One further question arising out of this inquiry remains to be posed: did the average King's Scholar tend to live just within his annual private income or did he still retain a comfortable margin of cash after settling his bills and other necessary expenses? In view of the scarcity of evidence only very tentative conclusions may be drawn about this matter.

The sources from which the King's Scholars derived their private incomes must remain largely conjectural. As several of the Scholars were appointed by the king on the advice of members of the nobility and high-ranking ecclesiastics,[1] there is a strong likelihood that patrons of this kind would settle some small annuity upon their nominees. In addition, a proportion of the senior fellows would supplement their incomes with fees (*collectae*) received for lectures delivered in the university schools. Moreover, in the reign of Edward IV, the college evidently decided to re-introduce a practice whereby all its resident fellows would henceforth be endowed with what could fairly be described as a fixed dividend. More than a century earlier, the dividend principle had been adopted but seems to have been operative in only a handful of years.[2] From the early 1470s, however, dividend payments became a regular feature of the financial organisation of the college. In normal circumstances, dividends took the form of the annual allocation to each fellow in residence of one mark payable in two equal instalments at Christmas and towards the end of the academic year during Stourbridge Fair.[3] But these arrangements were clearly subject to modification when financial retrenchment was deemed necessary and this applied especially in periods of costly building concerns. The King's Hall

---

[1] See below, pp. 151–2.

[2] E.g. in 1342–3 dividends of 6s 8d were given to all resident fellows and in 1344–5 £9 5s 1¼d was distributed (*K.H. Accts.* I, fos. 64v, 88).

[3] See e.g. *ibid.* xiv, fos. 66v, 142v; xv, fos. 26v, 86; xvi, fos. 43, 46v; xvii, fos. 100v, 126v; xviii, fos. 40, 45v, 66v; xix, fos. 24, 25; xx, fos. 84, 85; xxi, fos. 61v, 62v. Occasionally, the dividends were paid in early December and mid August on the feasts of the Conception and Assumption of the Blessed Virgin Mary (xvii, fo. 48v; xxi, fos. 86v, 87v; xxvi, fos. 70v, 71). Bad nobles (a noble was worth 6s 8d or half a mark) were sometimes inadvertently given and these the college was always willing to exchange. In 1483–4, Sylvester received 6s 8d for such a coin: 'Item in uno nobile malo vis. viijd.' (xvii, fo. 126v); and in 1521–2 the unfortunate Master Belt had acquired two malformed nobles: 'M. Belt habet ij nobilia viciosa quae collegium debet mutare si M. Belt peterit' (xxiii, fo. 33v).

usually relied upon exchequer grants and private subscriptions to supplement the revenues which it could afford to apportion for construction work. As was right and fitting, the fellows themselves set an encouraging example in this matter of voluntary contribution:[1] and in 1489–90, the element of personal sacrifice was extended to embrace dividends. At a college meeting held that year it was enacted that, in view of the exigencies of the current building programme, all beneficed fellows would forgo their dividends entirely for the space of two years and their non-beneficed colleagues would receive only one instead of two nobles a year.[2] The decision was carried into effect and the account for 1490–1 reveals that only the non-beneficed fellows were in receipt of dividend, now halved to 6s 8d a year.[3] But what is perhaps of greater moment, and indeed a matter for some surprise, is that the list of fellows eligible for dividend shows beyond all reasonable doubt that in 1490–1 there were only nine fellows then without benefices;[4] in other words, about two-thirds of the fellows were beneficed. If this situation is at all typical, it would certainly indicate that the combination of a fellowship and a statutory compatible benefice had become a fairly common attainment for the members of this royal foundation by the late fifteenth century. Presumably, the proportion of beneficed fellows would not have been so high in the earlier period but already, in the first half of the fifteenth century, royal licences were being issued to enable King's Scholars to receive the fruits of benefices valued in excess of the prescribed statutory maximum.[5] It is therefore legitimate to assume that, during the period under special investigation in this chapter, income derived from ecclesiastical benefices held in

---

[1] See e.g. *ibid.* xviii, fo. 119v; xix, fo. 26; xxii, fos. 2, 39; xxiii, fo. 106. On occasion even the college plate was pawned to raise money for building purposes to be redeemed at a later stage (*ibid.* xx, fo. 208v).

[2] *Ibid.* xviii, fo. 91v: 'Deliberacio nobilium erga nundinas concessi sunt per magistrum et socios quod beneficiati non reciperent per biennium et alii non beneficiati haberent unum nobile in anno et ista concessio fuit pro nova edificacione.'

[3] *Ibid.* xviii, fo. 118v.   [4] *Loc. cit.*

[5] See the royal licences granted to Richard Pyghttesley (*Cal. Pat. R.*, 1436–1441, p. 222), Thomas Stokwell (*ibid.* p. 528), Thomas Ardern (*ibid.* p. 564), Stephen Close (*ibid.* 1441–1446, p. 326) and John Filay (*ibid.* p. 461); also the papal dispensation granted to John Bank of 25 March 1439 permitting the tenure of the rectorship of Hildersham, Ely diocese, value not exceeding 20 marks, in conjunction with his King's Hall fellowship (*Cal. of Papal Letters* (ed. J. A. Twemlow, London, 1912), IX, 62).

TABLE 9. *Price tables for wheat and malt barley for the period 1382–3 to 1443–4*

In each table the number of entries upon which the average price was assessed is recorded each year. The processes of extraction, serialisation and annual tabulation were modelled on those outlined by Sir William Beveridge in the introduction to the first volume of *Prices and wages in England* (London, New York and Toronto, 1939). All relevant references to the King's Hall accounts are given at the end.

	WHEAT		MALT BARLEY	
Harvest year	Shillings per quarter	No. of entries	Shillings per quarter	No. of entries
1382–3	5·67	30	4·58	43
1383–4	5·08	46	5·50	48
1384–5	3·83	11	4·17	38
1385–6	3·92	18	3·92	34
1386–7	3·25	19	3·50	36
1387–8	3·17	20	3·25	36
1388–9	3·25	21	3·00	26
1389–90	5·42	18	3·42	29
1393–4	3·50	4	3·67	8
1394–5	5·17	22	4·17	33
1397–8	5·83	38	6·33	65
1398–9	4·58	46	4·25	10
1399–1400	5·25	40	4·25	55
1400–1	6·17	29	4·42	59
1401–2	9·67	56	6·25	84
1403–4	3·67	31	4·58	49
1404–5	3·25	22	3·67	36
1405–6	3·08	14	3·25	29
1406–7	4·42	14	3·17	31
1407–8	4·50	22	3·25	21
1408–9	7·00	38	5·75	34
1410–11	3·92	34	4·17	63
1411–12	3·58	34	2·83	9
1412–13	4·50	25	2·42	4
1413–14	5·00	19	4·42	32
1414–15	3·75	16	4·25	58
1415–16	4·75	28	5·17	57
1416–17	6·83	25	5·50	44
1417–18	4·42	17	4·25	34
1418–19	5·42	29	3·08	28
1419–20	3·92	13	2·75	24
1421–2	5·33	1	—	—
1422–3	—	—	—	—
1423–4	5·33	8	4·33	29
1424–5	5·00	15	3·92	23
1425–6	4·00	3	3·67	7

TABLE 9—*continued*

Harvest year	WHEAT Shillings per quarter	WHEAT No. of entries	MALT BARLEY Shillings per quarter	MALT BARLEY No. of entries
1426–7	—	—	3·67	11
1427–8	3·33	7	3·00	17
1428–9	6·42	6	3·50	7
1429–30	8·67	19	4·92	23
1430–1	5·58	18	4·00	30
1431–2	3·58	25	3·83	35
1432–3	5·67	17	4·67	12
1433–4	5·25	15	4·83	24
1434–5	3·58	15	3·17	38
1435–6	5·42	24	2·75	12
1436–7	5·58	17	2·67	26
1437–8	8·00	14	4·25	15
1438–9	13·83	10	7·08	7
1439–40	10·83	17	6·08	31
1440–1	—	—	2·67	4
1441–2	3·67	9	—	—
1442–3	3·83	7	3·42	3
1443–4	3·67	12	3·00	21

References to wheat and malt barley entries in *K.H. Accts.*: III, fos. 111, 96, 79, 124, 58; V, fo. 2; III, fos. 33, 6; IV, fos. 20, 42, 91, 127; V, fo. 25; IV, fos. 74, 57; V, fo. 69; IV, fo. 119; V, fo. 99; VI, fo. 14; V, fos. 110, 128, 140v, 157v, 180v, 84; VI, fos. 30v, 135v, 49v, 71v, 96, 118v; VII, fos. 15v, 32, 49, 70, 87, 105, 123v, 142; VIII, fos. 13, 31, 54, 79, 104, 128; IX, fos. 18, 49v, 77, 109, 164; X, fos. 15, 42, 66v.

conjunction with fellowships was fast becoming a significant item of a fellow's financial resources: on the other hand, income from the college in the form of dividends appears to have been available only in the mid-fourteenth century and again from the late fifteenth century onwards.

Although adequate information is lacking for an investigation of the incomes of the King's Scholars, we may at least hazard a tentative conclusion concerning their approximate size. The King's Hall statutes state that the maximum income allowable to a fellow and compatible with the retention of his fellowship is to be that derived from an ecclesiastical benefice valued at ten marks per annum (i.e. at £6 13s 4d) or from temporal possessions, pensions or revenues to the annual value of £5.[1] Considering that £5 is the prescribed statutory maximum, we may presume that the average income of a King's Scholar would have been somewhat less. It is true that a King's Scholar was provided with his clothing, lived rent-free and could borrow books from the college library in accordance with his academic needs.[2] Nevertheless, his heavy combined expenditure on commons and sizings together with a variety of miscellaneous expenses such as lecture or degree fees, the purchase of the occasional

[1] See the King's Hall statutes in Rouse Ball, *King's Hall*, p. 68. The similarity of the 'income ceilings' prescribed in the statutes of most English colleges of the fourteenth and early fifteenth centuries suggests that there were fairly uniform rates of allowable personal income which were considered to be compatible with the retention of a college fellowship. Clearly, these conventional statutory rates were adopted at the King's Hall. At Peterhouse, a fellow was required to vacate his fellowship if he was admitted to a benefice, with or without cure of souls, whose income was £5 or more; also if he acquired a life income from pensions, corrodies or rents worth £5 per annum (*Camb. Docs.* II, 34–5); at Michaelhouse, if he acquired temporal or spiritual possessions to the value of £5 per annum (*Stamp*, p. 43; Mullinger, I, 642); at Clare Hall, if he had temporal possessions to the value of ten marks (i.e. £6 13s 4d) for life, or a benefice with cure of souls (*Camb. Docs.* II, 134); at Gonville Hall, if he obtained a benefice with cure of souls of any value, or a benefice without cure of souls or a rural deanery with rents and revenues to the value of £5 per annum (*ibid.* II, 232); at King's College, if he had a permanent income of £5 per annum or if he obtained a benefice with or without cure of souls (*ibid.* II, 562). At Queen's, Oxford, a fellow was obliged to vacate his fellowship if he could realise an income of ten marks per annum from any source, such as patrimony, rents or a benefice (*Statutes*, I, ch. (4), 15); at New College, if he had a permanent income of £5 per annum from any source or if he obtained a benefice with or without cure of souls whose annual value exceeded ten marks (the founder's kin were allowed a benefice with or without cure of souls or temporal possessions not exceeding £20) (*ibid.* I, ch. (5), 64–5). In the case of Trinity Hall, Cambridge, the statutory allowance was slightly lower and a fellow was required to resign his fellowship if he obtained a benefice of any value with cure of souls, or one without cure of souls or a rural deanery with more than an annual income of six marks (i.e. £4 per annum) (*Camb. Docs.* II, 422). Whereas English college founders prescribed fairly uniform allowable rates of income applicable to all fellows, French founders, on the other hand, generally stipulated a scale of statutory rates graded according to academic standing. For instance, at the Paris college of Saint-Michel or Chanac (1343 or 1348) a theologian was required to vacate his fellowship if he received more than forty Paris pounds annually; a decretist, if he received more than thirty Tours pounds; and an artist, if he were in receipt of more than twenty-five Tours pounds from any form of benefice or patrimony. And at the college of Lemoine (1302) a theologian had to resign his burse if he acquired an annual income of more than four silver marks, and an artist if he possessed a revenue of more than three silver marks a year. For the Paris colleges see Gabriel, *The college system*, p. 9.

[2] See below, pp. 248–51.

textbook, personal travelling costs, the maintenance of private guests in college and exceptional outlays on feast days suggests that the average fellow would tend to spend the greater part of his allowable income each year.

The foregoing account would seem to establish that a King's Scholar was only partially subsidised in respect of his maintenance costs and that it was necessary for him to possess substantial private means in order to live in the college from year to year. This peculiar circumstance placed the King's Hall fellow in a unique position vis-à-vis his contemporaries in the medieval English universities. It is hard to avoid the conclusion that the King's Hall was a *collège de luxe* wherein the forces of patronage and money were unduly emphasised at the expense of native ability.

Chapter 5

CONSTITUTIONAL ORGANISATION

Reference has already been made to the singular nature of the constitutional features of the King's Hall, Cambridge; and in this chapter it is proposed to show how and where the organisation of this royal foundation differed from the normal collegiate pattern of the fourteenth and fifteenth centuries. Furthermore, a close study of the King's Hall accounts presents a picture of constitutional evolutionary change and so provides a valuable insight into the growth and development of a medieval academic society. In this connection, the accounts reveal that the balance of power altered within the community in the fourteenth century so that a society which had been ruled by a quasi-monarchical form of government *c.* 1337 had become almost self-governing by 1380. This important constitutional transition was not effected without considerable tensions arising between warden and fellows, and these will be fully investigated. Moreover, an analysis of the annually elected administrative committees of seneschals has furnished useful conclusions concerning the extent to which different categories of the King's Scholars were actively engaged in the governmental process: and the data thus obtained provide a basis for comparison with what is known of 'democratic' arrangements in the more usual type of English college.

The position of the warden of the King's Hall as a Crown appointee is unique among English collegiate establishments of the fourteenth and fifteenth centuries. For in the case of every other college, including the royal foundation, King's College, Cambridge, the important right of electing the warden, master or provost was conferred by statute on the scholars themselves. Although this election usually required confirmation by an external authority, such as the bishop of the diocese or the university chancellor, where this was so it was specified that the confirmation was to be of a purely nominal character.[1] Similarly, most codes of English college statutes make provision for the removal of an unsuitable master: the details

[1] See above, p. 87.

148

vary from code to code but the essential point is that the constitutional machinery existed for this purpose and could be set in motion by the fellows of the college.[1] It is clear that these inviolable statutory rights of election to the mastership and the power of removal vested in the *comitia* (i.e. the collective body formed by all the members on the boards of the foundation) constituted two of the three indispensable pre-conditions of a self-governing medieval collegiate society. In other words, there is here displayed a type of responsible government in which the master is directly accountable to the *comitia* for the conduct of all affairs relating to the society as a whole. In the light of what has been said, it is evident that this basic element of responsibility found little or no expression in the King's Hall. As every warden was appointed by the Crown and held office only during royal pleasure and was removable by the king alone, it is obvious that the King's Scholars did not possess the same ultimate authority over their warden as did their English counterparts elsewhere. For this reason, the King's Hall could never become a self-governing society in the fullest sense of that term as understood and given practical effect in other contemporary collegiate institutions.

The third essential pre-condition of an independent academic society was the right of co-optation of members. In the case of a large number of the Paris colleges of the medieval period, the founder vested control of the patronage in some external body, such as an archbishop, bishop, the head of a religious house, or in the hands of university officers.[2] This French practice found a pale reflection in at least three of the English colleges of the fourteenth century.[3] The

---

[1] See above, p. 88.

[2] For a survey of the Paris colleges see Rashdall, *Universities in the middle ages*, I, 497 ff.; particularly, at p. 508, the patronage arrangements for the college of the Sorbonne (founded *c.* 1257): 'The supreme government of the foundation and the filling up of its "burses" was entrusted to a body of external governors—the archdeacon and chancellor of Paris, the doctors of theology, the deans of the other two superior faculties, and the rector and proctors of the University.' See also the arrangements for the external appointment of the master of the Ave Maria College (Gabriel, *Ave Maria College*, p. 99). In several of the Paris colleges, however, the fellows possessed some measure of democratic control: e.g. at the colleges of Bayeux (statutes, 1315), Cornouaille (1321), Tours (1330–4), Montaigu (statutes, 1499) and Torchi (statutes, 1422), the fellows elected to the mastership. (See Gabriel, *loc. cit.*)

[3] For a discussion of the Parisian collegiate influence on the Oxford colleges of the thirteenth century see Highfield, *The early rolls of Merton College, Oxford, cit.* pp. 67–8.

statutes of 1282 of Dervorguilla, widow of John de Balliol, placed the principal and scholars of Balliol College under the supervision of two external *procurators* (a Franciscan friar and a secular master of arts) who were to confirm the election of the principal, to elect to vacancies, and generally to administer the funds and property of the house.[1] Although their powers steadily diminished, the external *procurators*, or *rectors* as they came to be styled, persisted until the end of the fifteenth century, when, by the new statutes of 1507, their offices were abolished.[2] Similarly, in her first code of statutes, Mary de Valence, countess of Pembroke, subjected her college to the authority of two annually elected external *rectors*, with restricted powers of visitation, but charged with the duty of admitting newly elected fellows. No trace of these *rectors* occurs in the later fourteenth-century code and it is to be assumed that their powers were transferred to the master and fellows of the college, which subsequently developed along purely Mertonian lines.[3] The situation was paralleled at Peterhouse, where at first the bishop of Ely, as founder, retained the patronage of the college for himself; but in 1338 this was partially resigned to the master and fellows by Bishop Montacute, who, nevertheless, reserved to himself and to his successors the right of admitting scholars and of choosing the master from two candidates elected by the college.[4] From these details, it is clear that what measure of French influence there was on early English collegiate development was of a transitory character and so obviously unpopular that the Parisian 'external' attributes were soon discarded in favour of the indigenous Mertonian pattern of complete internal self-government, with full powers of co-optation of members vested solely in the fellows of the college. If a sufficiently wide view is taken of academic history of the pre-Reformation era, it would appear that with respect to patronage arrangements the King's Hall affords the one true lasting parallel with the French colleges; for from the first foundation of the Society of the King's Scholars *c.* 1317 to the dissolution of the college in 1546, the patronage lay entirely in the hands of the kings of England, who appointed every Scholar

[1] See Rashdall, *op. cit.* III, 181; R. W. Hunt, 'Balliol College', *V.C.H.* (Oxford), III, 82; H. W. C. Davis, *A history of Balliol College*, ed. cit. pp. 10 ff.

[2] See Hunt, *loc. cit.*

[3] See A. Attwater, *Pembroke College, Cambridge*, cit. p. 9; Rashdall, III, 305.

[4] H. Butterfield, 'Peterhouse', *V.C.H.* (Cambridge), III, 335.

individually by writ of privy seal.[1] No doubt both Edward II and Edward III were influenced by the 'external' arrangements of the Paris colleges, but perhaps the overriding consideration derived from the fact that as the King's Hall was designed to serve the needs of the royal household and the court, it was essential that the king should exercise a direct, personal supervision over the appointment of his Scholars. And therefore, alone of all English collegiate bodies, the King's Hall was deprived of the power of co-opting its members and accordingly, from this standpoint too, was prevented from emerging as a fully fledged self-governing community.

From the extant writs of privy seal a number of conclusions may be drawn concerning the appointment of the King's Scholars. These documents reveal that one of the important functions of the King's Hall in the fourteenth century was to provide an outlet for royal patronage; for it is evident that the college offered a convenient means both of rewarding superior and inferior household officials in return for good services rendered and of granting the 'patronage' requests of persons close to the king. The procedure for a member of the household who wished to advance his son beyond the level of educa-tion furnished by the grammar school of the chapel royal was to approach the king either in person or more often, it seems, through an influential sponsor (usually a high-ranking household official) who would petition the king on his behalf; if the latter were favourably inclined, the youth would be nominated under writ of privy seal to the next vacancy in the King's Hall. Likewise, the king would often grant a place in the college to the nominee of some high-born patron well connected at court. A few representative examples can be given. On 11 March 1349, the king nominated Thomas de Wodeweston to

---

[1] Writs of privy seal for the appointment of the King's Scholars have not survived for the late fifteenth and sixteenth centuries: fortunately, there exist two pieces of evidence which prove that direct appointment by the Crown continued until 1546. The first is a document dated 13 August 1541 recording a composition made be-tween the college and Thomas Pylson, fellow, in which mention is made of Pylson's appointment letters of privy seal (*K.H. Cabinet*, no. 144). The second fragment of evidence is Archbishop Parker's testimony to the effect that the master and fellows of the King's Hall continued to be appointed by the Crown until the 'translation' of the college (i.e. absorption in Trinity College): '...eiusque magister atque socii a rege sub privato sigillo semper usque ad translationem designati sunt' (M. Parker, *De Antiquitate Britannicae Ecclesiae*, ed. cit. xxvii, lines 45–6).

the first vacancy at the request of the earl of Lancaster;[1] on 30 November of the same year, Thomas, son of Walter the Smith, was nominated at the request of Sir John Darcy for good services rendered by his father at the Tower of London;[2] on 1 February 1350, William, son of William Walkelate, king's sergeant at arms, was nominated, presumably on the supplication of Walkelate the elder;[3] on 18 May of that year, Isabella, mother of Edward III, secured the nomination of William de Walcote to the first vacancy in the King's Hall;[4] on 10 November 1369, Robert de Nicole, cousin of Helmyng Leget, king's esquire and governor of Windsor Castle, was nominated to a vacancy;[5] on 27 May 1385, Richard Lunteleye, a cousin to the bishop of Llandaff, confessor to Richard II, was nominated in place of Edmund Langham, removed on 19 May of that year;[6] and, finally, John Cacheroo secured a place in the college on the resignation of John Frankfield on 8 February 1387, nominated at the request of the confessor of the duke of Ireland.[7] Further examples relating to the king's cook, armourer, and other members of the royal household could be cited, but perhaps sufficient have been supplied for illustrative purposes. From the late fourteenth century onwards, however, fewer purely 'patronage' Scholars of this type can be detected in the records: this, in part, may have been due to the fact that a higher premium came to be placed upon the graduate fellow possessed of a degree in one of the superior faculties and especially in law.[8]

An examination of the extant writs of privy seal for the appointment of all categories of the King's Scholars prompts the following conclusions. The normal procedure acted upon when, for whatever reason, a Scholar vacated his fellowship was that the king nominated a suitable candidate to fill the vacant place either immediately or after a short delay, thereby raising the complement of fellows to the former number. In many instances, however, Scholars were nomi-

---

[1] Writ of privy seal, 11 March 1349, P.R.O. E 101/348/4.
[2] Writ of privy seal, 30 November 1349, *ibid.*
[3] Writ of privy seal, 1 February 1350, *ibid.*
[4] Writ of privy seal, 18 May 1350, *ibid.*
[5] Writ of privy seal, 10 November 1369, P.R.O. E 101/348/12.
[6] Writ of privy seal, 27 May 1385, P.R.O. E 101/348/16.
[7] Writ of privy seal, 8 February 1387, P.R.O. E 101/348/17.
[8] See below, pp. 255 ff.

nated in a general way to be admitted to the Hall when no such vacancy had occurred. The procedure then followed one of two courses: either the nominee was to be admitted to the Society at once (though not replacing any existing fellow) as long as his admission would be deemed compatible with the stipulated number of fellows; or, if this would not be so, he was to remain on the waiting list until such time as a vacancy arose, which, in effect, would mean that he might have to wait for a period ranging from several days to about six months.[1] In every case of nomination recorded in the writs of privy seal it is stipulated that the complement of fellows is to be strictly observed,[2] so that even candidates recommended by such influential patrons as the queen mother or the earl of Lancaster were afforded no preferential treatment over other nominees and were required to await their due turn before being admitted as fellows of the college. In only one of the extant writs is an appointment made for a specified period of time;[3] generally speaking, however, there was no limitation on the number of years for which a King's Hall fellowship might be retained.[4] It is frequently stated that a King's Scholar has resigned his fellowship in favour of a nominee at the top of the waiting list,[5] but there is no evidence to suggest that any

---

[1] Between 1349 and 1417, the gap between nomination and admission ranged from a single day to about twenty-three weeks (figures derived from a comparison of the nomination dates given in the writs of privy seal with the actual admission dates of the Scholars).

[2] Although at least eight Scholars were admitted in the 1340s as supernumeraries (see, conveniently, Stamp, *Admissions to Trinity College, Cambridge*, I, 96–7). The King's Hall statutes made provision for the occasional appointment of such Scholars by special royal mandate: see Rouse Ball, *op. cit.* p. 67. Supernumeraries were no different from other Scholars beyond the fact that they had been admitted after the statutory complement had been filled.

[3] See the case of Laurence de Gryndon, who was nominated for a period of two or at the most three years, writ of privy seal, (?)February 1350, P.R.O. E 101/348/4. The provision was evidently not observed (or was altered) since Gryndon remained in the college from 1 June 1350 until 25 September 1359.

[4] See above, p. 56.

[5] See e.g. writ of privy seal of 30 July 1384 where the master is ordered to accept Nicholas Hethe in place of Thomas de Horston if the latter wishes to resign (P.R.O. E 101/348/15; Horston vacated 15 August 1384); see also writ of privy seal of 30 December 1384 where Nicholas Erlam is allocated the place which the king has been given to understand John Rauf wishes to resign voluntarily (P.R.O. E 101/348/5; Rauf vacated 12 January 1385); see, further, writ of privy seal of 8 October 1386 where it is stated that Henry Spicer, clerk, has resigned in favour of

undue pressure was brought to bear on the outgoing fellow. Indeed, the fact that nominees of even the most influential of patrons had to abide their turns would tend to corroborate this assumption.

Occasionally, these writs of appointment served the purpose of a modern testimonial and contained a character reference to the good qualities of the appointee. In the two writs of this kind which have survived,[1] it is stressed that the Scholar is unaccustomed to wandering abroad at night, is known to be of peaceful habits, and is quite unversed in the arts of the buckler, the baton and the sword.[2] It is perhaps of some significance that both these writs emphasising the pacific dispositions of the fellows appointed belong to the early 1380s: for, as will be seen later in this chapter, this turned out to be the most disturbed period in the history of the Society.[3]

The Tudor historian, Polydore Vergil, was a severe critic of several prevailing aspects of the system of fellowship tenure at the English universities. While fully acknowledging the value of the fellowship as a means towards the furtherance of learning within the academic community, he nevertheless strongly censured what he considered to be its more undesirable by-products. In particular, he criticised the retention of fellowships for life, advocating automatic vacation after a determinate number of years so that those who had already derived sufficient benefit might be released to take up positions elsewhere and those who were unlikely to make any significant progress might be replaced by more promising students.[4] Vergil's second line of attack on the English collegiate system was prompted by the specific example of the College of the King's Hall. In the printed versions of his *Anglica Historia*, though not in the original manuscript, he alleges that the practice of trafficking in fellowships set in at the King's Hall soon after its foundation by Edward III. He claims that, contrary to all law and custom, the selling of college places had taken

---

James de Walsingham, B.C.L. (P.R.O. E101/348/16); see, finally, writ of privy seal of 8 February 1387 stipulating that John Cacheroo, B.C.L., has been nominated upon the resignation of John Frankfield (P.R.O. E101/348/17).

[1] Writs of privy seal of 28 December 1383 and 30 July 1384 (P.R.O. E101/348/15).

[2] '...ne use lart du bokeler, du baston ne de lespee': *loc. cit.*

[3] See below, pp. 170 ff.

[4] See Polydore Vergil, *Anglica Historia* (1st ed. Basle, 1534), p. 103, lines 36–42; (2nd ed. Basle, 1546), p. 107, lines 9–15; also for translation *Polydore Vergil's English History* (ed. by H. Ellis, Camden Society, 1846), XXXVI, 219.

root and that this state of affairs had flourished with the king's overt approval and still persisted even at the time of writing in the first half of the sixteenth century:

[Edward III] alterum [collegium instituit] Cantabrigiae, quod Aulam regiam appelant, deditque facultates, quibus ibi viverent, qui se in bonis exercerent disciplinis. Sed brevi tempore praeter morem atque legem, coeperunt collegae loca vendere. Quod quidem institutum, non vetante rege, cuius auctoritate emptio facta approbatur, etiamnum [*sic*] & durat. . . ¹

Vergil then proceeds to moralise generally upon the ill effects of this practice, contending that those who bought college fellowships were more often disposed to spend their lives in leisure than in devotion to their studies:

. . .saepenumero nonnullis illorum qui de collegiis loca mercantur potius in otio, quam in literis eo loci vitam vivere constitutum est.²

As every King's Scholar was appointed, not by the college, but directly by the Crown under writ of privy seal, Polydore Vergil's censure most probably implies that a candidate could buy his way into a fellowship by offering an agreed sum of money to the college authorities for the support of his candidature with the king. Only in this sense could the fellowship be said to be sold, and the college would be the financial gainer. The sale of fellowships is obviously one of the most damaging accusations which can be levied against a collegiate society and it is imperative to consider just how much reliance can be placed upon Vergil's testimony.

Nowhere in the copious King's Hall material is there a scrap of corroborative evidence for his charge. It might be argued that all references to the sale of fellowships would have been rigorously eliminated from the records: but if, as Polydore Vergil claims, the system had operated with the full approbation of the Crown, there would have been no strong motive for the suppression of the facts. Moreover, deliberate falsification of records for the express purpose of securing a favourable estimate from future historians is not a phenomenon one would expect to find in a medieval collegiate society in an age of poorly developed historical sense: records were

¹ *Anglica Historia* (1st ed.), p. 394, lines 30 ff.; (2nd ed.), p. 399, lines 35 ff.
² *Loc. cit.*

kept for the immediate convenience of the college officials and of the Crown and not for the eyes of unborn generations. It thus seems most likely that if there had been a regular sale of fellowships, the money accruing from such transactions would have appeared unashamedly in the Society's accounts. That it does not, must make us hesitant about the unqualified acceptance of Polydore Vergil's testimony at its face value.

The entry relating to the King's Hall does not occur in the original manuscript of the *Anglica Historia* of *c.* 1512–13[1] but was inserted in the first printed edition of 1534 and appears in all subsequent editions. There would, however, seem to be no particular significance in this since Vergil added more than a dozen passages on the universities and their colleges to the first printed edition which are not included in the manuscript.[2] Nevertheless, of these additions, the King's Hall reference is of special interest because of the element of personal commentary it contains: and it would be rash to deny that there is some substance in his accusation. Polydore Vergil did not easily depart from his relatively high standards of objectivity without good political cause and, as one who moved in court circles, he was singularly well placed to discover the true facts of the situation at the King's Hall. Furthermore, there is nothing to suggest that his critical comments ought to be construed as a piece of Tudor propaganda designed to bring discredit upon the college. As far as is known, neither of the first two Tudors evinced any degree of hostility towards the King's Hall: and we must remember that Vergil alleges that the sale of fellowships was still operating in the reign of Henry VIII and, since the king could have suppressed the practice had he so desired, it is highly improbable that a chronological observation of this kind would have been made in the course of a Tudor-inspired propagandist attack. In the absence of any discoverable motive which might have impelled Polydore Vergil towards a fabrication of the facts, and if we rule out the possibility that he was unwittingly misled by malicious report, we are still faced with the difficulty of squaring his accusation with the conspicuous lack of the slightest trace of supporting evidence in the King's Hall records. For reasons

---

[1] For the dating of the MS. see D. Hay, ed., *The Anglica Historia of Polydore Vergil* (Camden Series, 1950), LXXIV, xiii–xv; also Hay, *Polydore Vergil* (Oxford, 1952), pp. 79–81.

[2] *Polydore Vergil*, p. 119 with details in appendix II, pp. 187 ff.

already stated, this latter circumstance must make us doubt at least the full validity of Vergil's charge and it leads to the suspicion that his comments give us an exaggerated picture of what occasional trafficking in fellowships there may have been at the King's Hall. And it is certainly conceivable that he exaggerated this state of affairs at the King's Hall in order to lend heightened effect to his subsequent general moralising upon the evils arising from the sale of college places at the English universities: beyond this, it would be idle to speculate.

Although I am fully aware of the pitfalls involved in determining geographical origins from surnames derived from place-names,[1] I have thought it worth while to conduct such an inquiry into the surnames of the King's Scholars in the belief that the resultant pattern will provide a rough indication of the areas from which the college recruited its personnel. It was considered desirable to confine the limits of this investigation to the earlier phase of the Society's history because in the late fifteenth and sixteenth centuries surnames become progressively less reliable as guides to geographical origins: and to have included the latter period would undoubtedly have magnified the element of distortion which will inevitably be present in a survey of this kind. Consequently, the examination is restricted to fellows admitted between 1317 and 1443, the latter date being chosen because it forms a natural point of division in the evolution of the college as the year in which the required external exchequer audit came to an end.[2] Bearing in mind the limitations inherent in this type of inquiry, it was found that out of a total of 459 Scholars admitted between 1317 and 1443, 203, on the basis of local surnames, could be assigned with some measure of certainty to single counties; 33 to one of two possible counties; and 66 possessed surnames common to more than two counties and these, for the purposes of the present classification, have been disregarded. Moreover, 139 bore surnames (such as occupational, official or family names) which were not amenable to geographical assignation; 9 possessed names which appear to be place-names but which have not yet been identified; and finally, 7 Scholars had names which are clearly of foreign origin.

The 203 Scholars who may be assigned to single counties are distributed as follows: Norfolk heads the list with 29; Yorkshire

---

[1] See the cautionary remarks of A. B. Emden, *B.R.U.O.* I, xiv.
[2] See above, p. 7; below, p. 162, n. 4.

comes a close second with 23; Lincoln produced 16; Suffolk 13; Essex 10; Buckinghamshire 8; Northamptonshire and Cambridgeshire each yielded 7; Staffordshire and Nottinghamshire each produced 6; 5 Scholars came from each of the seven counties of Berkshire, Devon, Gloucester, Hampshire, Hertfordshire, Huntingdonshire and Middlesex; 4 from each of the counties of Derby, Hereford and Oxford; the counties of Lancashire, Leicester, Shropshire, Somerset and Surrey each yielded 3; Bedfordshire, Cornwall, Kent and Rutland accounted for 2 each; and one Scholar came from each of the counties of Cheshire, Dorset, Durham, Montgomery, Sussex, Westmorland, Wiltshire and Worcester. If these counties are arranged to form natural geographical groupings the pattern becomes clearer, as shown in table 10.

TABLE 10

East Anglia		S. midlands (and Middlesex)		Northern counties	
Lincs.	16	Bucks.	8	Yorks.	23
Norfolk	29	Northants.	7	Lancs.	3
Suffolk	13	Berks.	5	Durham	1
Essex	10	Herts.	5	Westmorland	1
Cambs.	7	Middlesex	5	—	
Hunts.	5	Oxford	4		28 (14%)
	—	Beds.	2		
	80 (39%)		—		
			36 (18%)		

N. midlands (and Montgomery)		S.W.		South-eastern (s. of Thames)	
Notts.	6	Devon	5	Hants.	5
Staffs.	6	Gloucs.	5	Surrey	3
Derby	4	Herefs.	4	Kent	2
Leics.	3	Somerset	3	Sussex	1
Salop	3	Cornwall	2	—	
Rutland	2	Dorset	1		11 (5%)
Cheshire	1	Wilts.	1		
Montgomery	1	Worcs.	1		
	—		—		
	26 (13%)		22 (11%)		

These figures show that by far the largest proportion of this sample of Scholars was recruited from the eastern counties north of the

Thames and that the intake from this region was roughly equal to the combined recruitment from the counties of the midlands and the north. Yorkshire supplied more Scholars than any other county except Norfolk[1] and a significant sprinkling of fellows was apparently drawn from the south-west. The bias towards the eastern, midland and northern counties is further reinforced by the figures for the 'alternative' assignations. For it was found that 48 out of the 66 'alternative' counties from which 33 Scholars might have been drawn were made up of the counties of eastern England north of the Thames, the midlands and the north.

In order to discover how far these figures are representative of the areas of recruitment of the University of Cambridge as a whole, a comparison may be made with the findings of a recent diocesan survey embracing 380 members of the university who petitioned for papal graces in the second half of the fourteenth century.[2] If the counties of the King's Hall inquiry are grouped to form their respective dioceses, a direct comparison of the college and the university samples is thus represented as shown in table 11.

The general pattern revealed by these samples indicates that the King's Hall, like the university, reflected the same recruitment bias towards the dioceses of Lincoln, Norwich and York. To this extent, the college would appear to serve as a microcosm of the university as a whole, with the important qualification that the King's Hall analysis suggests a wider range of derivation than was perhaps usual for the University of Cambridge in the fourteenth and early fifteenth centuries: for the King's Scholars who comprise the remaining 20 per cent of the sample seem to have been drawn from all of the other

---

[1] This is specially interesting because it has been worked out that right throughout the fourteenth century there was a strong connection between the cathedral chapter at York and the central government. A. Hamilton Thompson has shown that from the time of Edward I's chancellor, Robert Burnell, a large proportion of the Englishmen who held prebends or canonries in the chapter at York were royal clerks, many of whom held office in the chancery. (See A. Hamilton Thompson, 'Cathedral Church of St Peter, York', *V.C.H.* (Yorkshire), III, 375 ff. at p. 378; also Hamilton Thompson, ed., 'The medieval chapter' in *York Minster historical tracts 627–1927* (London, 1927), no. 13, and *The register of William Greenfield, archbishop of York (1306–1315)*, I (Surtees Society, CXLV, 1931), xviii; see further K. Edwards, *The English secular cathedrals in the middle ages, cit.*, pp. 86–7.) While Yorkshire is, of course, the largest county, it is possible that this governmental nexus may have had some determining influence upon the composition of the King's Scholars. [2] For this survey see Emden, *B.R.U.C.* xxvi–xxvii.

TABLE II

203 King's Scholars			380 University Scholars		
Diocese	Number	% of 203	Diocese	Number	% of 380
Norwich	42	20½	Norwich	148	39
Lincoln	45	22	Lincoln	82	22
York	33	16	York	52	14
Ely	7	3½	Ely	38	10
London	20	10	London	31	8
Coventry and Lichfield	14	7	Coventry and Lichfield	7	2
Durham	1	½	Durham	4	1
Carlisle	—	—	Carlisle	1	¼
	162 (80% of sample)			363 (95% of sample)	

English dioceses not listed in the table compared with only 5 per cent of the university sample.[1] This wide recruitment basis for the King's Scholars presupposes that the Hall was free of those restrictive geographical preferences imposed by several of the college founders of the medieval period.[2] As a result, there was far less danger that the

[1] Of this 5 per cent, two students were from Ireland and one from Wales (*ibid.* xxvii, n. 1).

[2] For example, at Merton, scholars were to be chosen first from the founder's kin, then from natives of Winchester diocese, and finally from those other dioceses and parishes where the college held property or ecclesiastical benefices (*Statutes*, I, ch. (2), 5, 10, 27); at Exeter College, recruitment of scholars was to be confined to Exeter diocese (Rashdall, *Universities in the middle ages*, III, 202); first preference at Queen's, Oxford, was given to personnel from the counties of Cumberland and Westmorland and second from the places where the college derived its revenues from benefices, manors, land and tenements (*Statutes*, I, ch. (4), 12); like Walter de Merton, Wykeham prescribed that first preference be given to the founder's kin and then to other scholars from Winchester College who were to be chosen according to a lengthy and hierarchical list of preferences (*ibid.* I, ch. (5), 6–7); at Lincoln College, fellows were to be drawn exclusively from the dioceses of Lincoln, York and Bath and Wells (*ibid.* I, ch. (6), 12–13). To cite only one Cambridge example, Bishop Bateman stipulated that in the election of new fellows at Gonville Hall, a preference was to be given to non-beneficed scholars of Norwich diocese (*Camb. Docs.* II, 232). As might be expected, these geographical preferences had, in several instances, the effect of concentrating the government of the college in the hands of a 'county clique' which constituted a ruling oligarchy: see e.g. the discussion of monopoly in Queen's College, Oxford, by R. H. Hodgkin, *Six centuries of an Oxford college* (Oxford, 1949), p. 49. To avoid such dangers, some of the later foundations specifically limited the intake of recruits from single counties or dioceses.

affairs of the college would come to be concentrated in the hands of a group of Scholars from any one county or diocese: and indeed an analysis of the annually elected committees of seneschals, which points to a fairly regular turnover of administrative personnel from year to year, would tend to bear out this conclusion.[1]

Within the space of a few broad generalisations, W. W. Rouse Ball sets out the stages of development through which the Society of the King's Scholars passed from its foundation *c.* 1317 until the end of the fourteenth century.[2] He states that, as long as the first Scholars were boys, 'the warden ruled absolutely, disbursements as well as receipts passing through his hands...'.[3] But, so the argument runs, within a few years of the foundation several of the Scholars were sufficiently mature to manage the internal affairs of the Society. This development was so rapid that:

'In and after 1337 the warden paid all sums received by him into the common chest, and the expenditure was left in the hands of the guardians. From this arrangement a system of self-government soon arose and within half a century the internal affairs of the House were entirely managed by the senior scholars...'[4]

These conclusions were incorporated by P. A. Bezodis in his brief note on the King's Hall in the *Victoria County History*. Citing Rouse Ball as his authority, he writes:

'The management of expenditure and receipt and of the common chest was by 1337 being shared between the warden and six guardians chosen by the members of the Society.'[5]

This is a view of constitutional development which admits of evolutionary change but considers that the main evolutionary movement had come to an end by 1337. The implication is that the lines of government embodied in the statutes of 5 March 1380 had been formulated forty-three years earlier. Allowing for minor adjustments, Rouse Ball and Bezodis have presented a bald and static picture of constitutional arrangements in the period between 1317 and 1380. If they had used the evidence of the King's Hall accounts, however, they would have realised that the structure of internal

[1] See below, pp. 177 ff.   [2] Rouse Ball, *King's Hall*, pp. 27–8.
[3] *Ibid.* p. 27.   [4] *Ibid.* p. 28.
[5] P. A. Bezodis, 'King's Hall', *V.C.H.* (Cambridge), III, 458.

government outlined in the statutes had by no means been fully worked out in 1337 and that the scene in the intervening years, far from being static, was one of exciting evolutionary development.

It is reasonable to assume that financial control will be the key to the distribution of power within a medieval collegiate society: and so, if the administration of the common chest and of all expenditure had really been in the hands of six guardians elected by the Society in 1337, Rouse Ball's conclusions would indeed be hard to refute. Analogous conditions elsewhere in Cambridge might seem to support his view. Fourteenth-century college statutes reveal that control of finance was usually a shared operation between the master and a number of fellows elected for this purpose. Internal audits ensured the responsibility of the warden to the society in all financial matters. At Pembroke, for example, the accounts were audited once a year at Michaelmas;[1] at Peterhouse, Clare and Trinity Hall, the master was bound to render half-yearly accounts at Michaelmas and at Easter in the presence of all or some of the fellows;[2] and at Michaelhouse, quarterly inspections were held before auditors deputed by the fellows.[3] There is, however, nothing in the early King's Hall accounts to suggest that the warden was subject to this measure of financial accountability[4] or that expenditure was controlled by a body of elected Scholars. On the contrary, the accounts disclose that this royal foundation, in the years immediately following 1337, was ruled by a quasi-monarchical and not a responsible form of government.

The common chest was the business heart of the Society, the focal point of its existence, serving the purposes of a modern bank or clearing house through which passed all incoming revenue and outgoing expenditure. Whereas the administration of the chest was

---

[1] *Camb. Docs.* II, 201.   [2] *Ibid.* II, 13–14, 127, 427.

[3] Stamp, *Michaelhouse*, p. 26.

[4] The absence of an internal audit is to be explained by the fact that the Society's accounts were subject to annual external audit at the exchequer. The exchequer audit remained in force until 1443 when warden Richard Caudray secured the release of the Hall from this obligation. Before this date, there were two sets of accounts: the warden's accounts, being carefully prepared statements of the finances of the college submitted annually for audit at the exchequer; and the yearly domestic accounts drawn up by the Society for its own convenience. For the provisions governing the exchequer audit see the statutes of the King's Hall in Rouse Ball, *King's Hall*, p. 69.

from the start in most English colleges a joint enterprise on the part of the master and fellows, the regulation of finance in the King's Hall was at first the exclusive province of the warden. All incoming revenues, whether from the priory of St Neots, Waltham abbey, the abbey of Sautre[1] or the exchequer itself, were received by the warden alone and placed in the chest. The accounts show that it was regular practice for the warden to fetch the money in person, sometimes accompanied by one of the senior Scholars. In 1337–8, for example, a charge of 9s is set against the master's expenses in journeying to St Neots to collect the sum of £41 7s 2d due to the Society for robes and furs: on this occasion, he was escorted by Henry de Chesterfield;[2] the following year, Henry de Gretford acted as his companion.[3] While we must not suppose that the warden fetched all revenues in person, there is enough evidence to confirm the point that at this early juncture in the history of the college he travelled extensively on behalf of its financial business.

The testimony of the accounts militates against Rouse Ball's conclusion that in 1337 revenue received by the warden was automatically handed over to six elected guardians or *custodes* so that they might deposit it in the chest and administer its expenditure. The terminology is self-explanatory. In the early years the form 'Magister liberavit ciste commune . . .' precedes the itemised sum delivered to the chest. Here it is evident that the master was acting alone, and the omission of any reference to *custodes* anywhere in the accounts before 1356 is adequate proof that they were not yet an integral part of the machinery of internal government. In that year, however, occurs the first unequivocal reference to the delivery of incoming revenues by the warden to 'guardians of the chest'; and the account for 1361 produces the first list of six Scholars elected as the administrative officers of the Society (later designated seneschals). By 1361, therefore, the system of personal government by the master had been successfully challenged and the financial affairs of the college were now being administered by the Society through its elected representatives. A close scrutiny of the early accounts provides an insight into what had been happening in the intervening period.

---

[1] These were the bodies upon which the exchequer maintenance award was partially unloaded in the early years of the Society's history.
[2] *K.H. Accts.* I, fo. 10v.   [3] *Ibid.* I, fo. 22.

The first volume of the King's Hall accounts introduces us to a series of *ad hoc* administrative arrangements. The amorphous nature of the records themselves is reflective of the untidy and ill-defined character of internal government at this early stage. By 1337, it is apparent that a number of Scholars were loosely associated with the warden in running the affairs of the Society: these were evidently senior fellows who had been resident for several years. But there is no evidence whatsoever of election and it appears that fellows of this kind had merely 'emerged' as the natural associates of the master in the business of administration. None seems to have held a specific office or to have been assigned permanent duties, but each carried out diversified tasks delegated by the warden. Citations from the accounts will illustrate the point. Both Henry de Gretford, who entered the Society in 1319, and Adam de Wirlyngworth, present in 1332,[1] played prominent parts in internal government in the years immediately following 1337. In 1337–8, for example, Gretford was commissioned by the master to buy shoes for the warden and thirty-two Scholars for five terms. For this purpose the master delivered from the chest the sum of £4 2s 6d.[2] Gretford was also made responsible for the purchase of fur for the lining of the fellows' gowns[3] and for contracting the college's supply of peat-fuel.[4] On one occasion, he was provided with money to pay the wages of workmen engaged in building a new latrine;[5] and, as mentioned above, he sometimes accompanied the master on external business. The duties performed by Wirlyngworth were equally varied. In 1337–8, he was in charge of building operations relating to the hall and fellows' rooms, rendered an account for all expenses incurred, and received money for the workmen's wages.[6] Moreover, it appears that he was associated in the administration of weekly commons because he collected money due for commons from the *extranei* then resident in the college.[7] The examples could easily be multiplied, but sufficient has here been said to indicate the lack of clear division of function within the Society at this juncture. Nevertheless, the *ad hoc* and seemingly casual character of these administrative arrangements, the

[1] Stamp, *Admissions to Trinity College, Cambridge*, I, 84, 91.
[2] *K.H. Accts.* I, fo. 11v. Below is a further payment of £2 11s for shoes for three terms. [3] *Ibid.* I, fo. 22.
[4] *Ibid.* I, fo. 8. [5] *Ibid.* I, fo. 25.
[6] *Ibid.* I, fo. 22. [7] *Ibid.* I, fo. 21v.

natural outcome of a nascent system of delegated authority, constituted the primary phase in the breakdown of the warden's monarchical rule.

The extensive practice of associating senior Scholars in college affairs had already led to a tenuous measure of restraint upon the master's powers. In 1337–8, there are two entries in the accounts concerning the delivery of money to the chest by the warden in the presence of senior Scholars: 'Item magister liberavit ciste commune die...xv li. presentibus Milemet, Secheville, Glaston, Wirlyngworth, Gretford';[1] and below, 'Item magister liberavit ciste commune...presentibus Adamarus [i.e. Wirlyngworth], Glaston et Perrers'.[2] In isolation, these entries may not appear to be very important, but linked with the chain of events culminating in the emergence of the elected body of six guardians in 1361 their combined significance is apparent. From the evidence of the accounts, it is clear that all of the above-named Scholars were engaged in the administrative process but had not yet acquired the formal, technical status of *custodes*. The key point, however, is that on both these occasions a number of Scholars had acted as witnesses to the placing of sums of money in the chest. And the conclusion seems to be that from the practice of associating the senior Scholars in the administration there had evolved the custom whereby the presence of an indeterminate number of Scholars was required to attest to the delivery of revenue to the common chest: this was the first *de facto* limitation on the warden's absolute control over finance.

The 1350s stand out as a turning point in the constitutional relations between the warden and the fellows: but even in the 1340s there are signs of a more active participation by the fellows in financial matters. In 1344–5, for example, a series of payments were made from the chest by John Sautre and Thomas Priour;[3] in 1346–7, by John Perrers and John Conyngton.[4] In the main, these were payments to the manciple,[5] John Repton, and to the master and individual Scholars for expenses incurred while engaged on the Society's business: and, at a slightly later date, appears the *compotus* of Perrers

---

[1] *Ibid.* I, fo. IV.   [2] *Loc. cit.*
[3] *K.H. Accts.* I, fo. 85V.   [4] *Ibid.* I, fo. 99.
[5] The term 'manciple' is used in the earliest accounts but was soon superseded by 'butler' (*pincerna*).

and Conyngton, largely concerned with expenditure relating to Great St Mary's, Cambridge.[1]

From the nature of these payments it is reasonably clear that for periods in 1344–5 and 1346–7 the internal and external finances of the college came under the joint direction of two of the King's Scholars. The payment of the master's expenses to Ely, Hintlesham and other places provides a clue to the capacity in which they were acting. It is obvious that the master was absent from the college for the greater part of these years: and although the office of vice-master may have been in operation by the 1340s,[2] it seems probable that the master had specifically charged two of the Scholars with the management of the college's finances throughout his period of non-residence. While the accounts furnish only brief glimpses of fellow participation in government in the 1340s, one can generally sense that the fellows were gradually acquiring a significant measure of control over the affairs of the Society.

These observations are in the nature of probabilities, and much firmer ground is reached with the accounts for the 1350s. By this time, the earlier *ad hoc* administrative arrangements had become institutionalised, a development which inevitably imposed a substantial limitation upon the warden's powers. Two events had taken place: the number of Scholars associated in the business of administration had come to be fixed at six; and they were now elected by the Society. The folio in which the evidence occurs is headed: 'Assignatio camerarum facta per custodem et *socios per comitivam deputatos* anno xxvij' [i.e. 1353–4].[3] At the foot of the page six names are listed against which is written: 'Sex electi sunt per comitivam pro administratione istius anni.' The additional information is given that two of the six, Wormenhale and Norton, were appointed procurators for Great St Mary's, Cambridge.[4] But beyond the fact that two of the six acted in this capacity, the division of function is uncertain at this stage.[5] It is observable, however, that the *socii deputati* are not yet described as *custodes*: nor has the term hitherto appeared in the accounts. It is therefore a matter of some constitutional im-

---

[1] *K.H. Accts.* I, fos. 102–3.

[2] See the many references to the office of vice-master in the King's Hall statutes in Rouse Ball, *King's Hall*, pp. 64–70; also below, pp. 209–10.

[3] *K.H. Accts.* I, fo. 174 v.   [4] *Loc. cit.*

[5] On the division of function among the seneschals, see below, pp. 207 ff.

portance that only three years after the occurrence of the *socii deputati*, the term *custodes ciste* begins to be found regularly in the records.

The term *custodes* makes its début in the account for 1356. In that year the warden delivered incoming revenues from Scarborough, Swavesey and the abbey of Sautre to the guardians of the chest (*custodibus ciste*),[1] a practice which henceforth became unwavering custom. *Custodes* embraced all of the six elected Scholars because, in the title pages to the accounts of 1361 and those following, the administrative officers for the year are designated either as *custodes* or *senescalli*. And so, when the accounts state that revenue was handed over to the guardians of the chest, this can only mean that the money was delivered, not to one or two Scholars particularly associated with finance, but to the six acting as a body. When this situation is compared with that which existed in 1337, there is but one possible conclusion. Whereas formerly the sole limitation on the warden's control over finance had been the presence of an indeterminate number of Scholars as witnesses to the placing of money in the chest, from at least 1356 onwards the warden was obliged to deliver all incoming revenues *en bloc* to the corporate body of the six elected guardians.

It is apparent that the events of the 1350s constitute a radical shift in the distribution of power within the Society. There can now be little doubt that the relationship between the master and fellows was gravitating towards that which existed in most other contemporary English colleges. In this connection, there is an intriguing paradox. It has already been remarked how the King's Hall could never become a completely self-governing community in the accepted sense of the term and yet, when the constitutional balance was fully worked out between the warden and Scholars, it seems that the latter acquired a more actual control over both internal and external affairs than did their counterparts elsewhere. And one can appreciate how this difference arose.

In most medieval English colleges the fellows were constitutionally involved in the governmental process from the start: the powers of the master were hedged around with effective checks and balances, and the fellows remained reasonably content with the contractual division of authority worked out by the founder. If

---

[1] *K.H. Accts.* II, fo. 14v.

difficulties materialised, minor adjustments could be made within this contractual framework of government. At the King's Hall, however, there was at first no such constitutional division of authority: the master was subject only to the restraint of the Crown and wielded a near-absolute authority over the Society. In the very nature of things, this unqualified exercise of power was bound to meet with resistance. But there was here no contractual framework within which the fellows could operate. Of necessity, they had to take positive action to whittle down the master's authority and to win a *de facto* recognition in the direction of the Society's affairs. In this, they were strikingly successful: they established their own dominant position and reduced the master's power to a shadow of its original strength. Because the King's Hall fellows succeeded in subverting the prevailing monarchical system of government, they were then in a strong position to impose a fresh division of authority on the master which was perhaps more advantageous to themselves than could have been achieved through working within the limits of the contractual form of government functioning elsewhere in Cambridge. For their colleagues in contemporary colleges appear to have been generally satisfied with the sphere of authority allocated to them by founders' statutes; and there do not seem to have been strong driving pressures acting upon them to augment their stake in governmental affairs. It is therefore arguable that if the King's Scholars had been incorporated within the framework of government from the beginning and had been reasonably happy with their powers in this direction, the circumstances would not then have been present which enabled them to achieve their position of impressive constitutional strength realised in the second half of the fourteenth century.

The developments of the 1350s were given definition in 1361–2. On the title page to the account of that year the names of six Scholars are set down under the heading: 'Papirus anni tricesimi quinti quo anno electi sunt infrascript' in custodibus ciste communis videlicet magistri...'[1] Thereafter, every extant title page contains a list of the six elected *custodes* or *senescalli* as they were later called.

If this is to be fitted into the general context of the history of the King's Hall, it is important to establish 1361–2 as a key date. It might be argued that the lack of reference to six elected guardians before

---

[1] *K.H. Accts.* II, fo. 43.

this date is to be explained by the loss of earlier title pages. Fortunately, the title page to the account of 1360–1 is extant.[1] It is in a good state of preservation and bears the heading, 'Papirus anni tricesimi quarti' (i.e. 1360–1); the rest is blank and there is no sign that any writing has been obliterated. There can therefore be little doubt that if the six guardians of the chest had existed as a formally constituted body before 1361–2, their names would have appeared on this title page. That this was not so indicates the following pattern: some time between 1353 and 1356 the six Scholars elected to participate in the administration of the college acquired the status of *custodes*; from 1356 to 1361 *custodes* were managing the finances of the chest as a *de facto* body of guardians; and this arrangement was formally institutionalised in 1361–2.

Thomas Powys, the first warden of the College of the King's Hall, died a victim of the Black Death on 14 September 1361.[2] His successor, John de Schropham, was not formally appointed until 26 October of that year.[3] One can well imagine that life in the college must have sunk to a very low ebb during this hiatus of six weeks. The twenty-eight-year wardenship of Thomas Powys[4] had seen the establishment of the Society of the King's Scholars as an endowed institution. Under his guiding hand, the site had been extended and new buildings erected. In brief, he had witnessed the rise of the Society from precarious beginnings to a position of financial strength and inner cohesion. His removal must have meant a great loss to the college, particularly at a time when it was engulfed by the ravages of plague. Apart from the warden himself, eight Scholars died in the course of the second visitation of the Black Death.[5] The account for 1361–2 reveals the unusually low numbers present,[6] giving an average weekly figure of only about fifteen over the whole year. As the election of the administrative officers took place at the beginning of October, it seems more than a mere coincidence that the first formally constituted committee of elected guardians appeared between the death of Powys and the appointment of Schropham. It is

---

[1] *Ibid.* II, fo. 29.   [2] Stamp, *op. cit.* I, 138.   [3] *Ibid.* I, 139.

[4] Warden of the endowed college from 7 October 1337 to 14 September 1361. Powys had previously been warden of the Society of the King's Scholars from 10 November 1333 and remained as first master of the King's Hall.

[5] Stamp, *op. cit.* I, 101. On plague at the King's Hall, see below, pp. 220 ff.

[6] *K.H. Accts.* II, fos. 43 v–45.

highly probable that the unfavourable circumstances of the moment, the death of Powys, the depleted numbers in the college and the absence of a constituted head, provided the opportunity. In the interests of stable government it was seized, and the strands that had evolved since 1337, the association of a definite number of Scholars in administration, the elective principle and the emergence of the *custodes*, were finally fused and institutionalised.

The breakdown of the authoritarian rule of the warden was accompanied by a marked deterioration in the relations between the master and the fellows. One of the first signs of this is a reference to a lawsuit filed by the college against its ex-warden, John de Schropham.[1] Unfortunately, the nature of the dispute and the outcome of the suit are unknown but the episode would seem to be reflective of the presence of early tensions within the body of the Society. The third warden, Nicholas de Drayton, remained for only one year[2] and the shortness of his tenure of office suggests that all was not well. This is further borne out by the fact that the King's Scholars 'elected' the next two wardens themselves. In the case of Nicholas Roos, this was a permissive election held by virtue of the king's mandate,[3] Roos being required to journey to London to obtain royal confirmation of his position as warden.[4] But in the second case of election, namely that of the fifth master, Richard Ronhale, the permissive nature is not at all certain. For in the royal letters of appointment the phrase 'virtute mandate [*sic*] nostri' is omitted[5] and it is possible that here the Scholars took the initiative in electing Ronhale without first obtaining the royal consent. Nevertheless, the fact that royal confirmation was required in either case shows that the 'elections' were, in reality, designations. But coming as they do in the years immediately following the formal inception of the administrative committees of seneschals, it is tempting to speculate as to whether these 'elections' were in some measure an outcome of the tide of constitutional advance. But if they represent an attempt by the

---

[1] The account for 1366–7 contains an entry for expenses incurred by the Society 'apud London' ad prosequendum contra Magistrum Johanem de Schropham xviijs. vid.' (*ibid.* II, fo. 144v).

[2] Appointed 1 December 1363; resigned 2 December 1364.

[3] P.R.O. *Pat. R.* 38 Ed. III, p. 2, m. 10.

[4] *K.H. Accts.* II, fo. 112: 'Item expense facte circa confirmationem electi in custodem ...per x dies xls.' [5] P.R.O. *Pat. R.* 49 Ed. III, p. 2, m. 12.

King's Scholars to secure a permanent voice in the appointment of their wardens, the effort was doomed to failure. For on Ronhale's vacation in 1377, Simon Neylond, himself a King's Scholar, was appointed without reference to election on the part of the fellows.[1] It would indeed be enlightening to discover if this appointment was made with the willing assent of the fellows or whether Neylond was forcibly imposed upon the Society by the king.

At all events, the appointment proved an unmitigated disaster, because Neylond soon showed himself to be an injurious thorn in the flesh of the community: indeed, with some justification, he could be described as 'the Bentley of the King's Hall'.[2] There can be no doubt that relations between the warden and the vast majority of the fellows were strained to breaking point during his tenure of office, a state of crisis only resolved by his removal from the mastership. The evidence for the distressed condition of the college at this time is contained in the letters patent of Richard II of 14 July 1383[3] whereby the bishop of Ely was commissioned to visit the Hall to investigate the alleged abuses which had sprung up during Neylond's wardenship. In the preamble, it is announced that serious defects had materialised relating both to the actual government of the Scholars and to the buildings themselves, resulting from the carelessness (*incuria*) and negligence (*negligentia*) of the master. It was alleged that the warden had withdrawn legitimate rights pertaining to the Scholars and that he and his 'ministers' had wasted and despoiled the lands, tenements, rents and possessions of the college.[4] Moreover, the king's letters claimed that the master had removed, sold or carried off charters, books, valuables, muniments, goods and chattels belonging to the Society with the result that unedifying disputes, dissensions and discords had arisen between the warden and fellows

---

[1] P.R.O. *Pat. R.* 1 Ric. II, p. 1, m. 16.

[2] The allusion here is to the outstanding classical scholar, Richard Bentley, who was master of Trinity College from 1700 to 1742. Trinity seldom knew peace under his turbulent regime and for the greater part of his mastership a state of civil war raged between Bentley and the majority of the fellows. For a recent study of his colourful and astonishing career see R. J. White, *Dr Bentley* (London, 1965).

[3] See the register of Thomas Arundel (bishop of Ely, 1374–88), fo. 106 v.

[4] 'Et quod iura ad ipsos scolares pertinentia per ipsum custodem subtrahuntur ac diversa terre, tenementa, redditus et possessiones eidem collegio per dictum avum nostrum in pios usus collata per ipsum custodem et ministros suos vastantur et destruntur...': *loc. cit.*

so that the lives of the latter were rendered desolate and they could no longer devote themselves to their studies.[1] It was predicted that if the master were not brought to heel, he would lead the college to the brink of utter destruction.[2]

The letters patent of Richard II depict an academic community confused and divided within itself and brought perilously near the point of complete disintegration by a master who had been criminally negligent of the physical needs of the college committed to his care, who had exploited his office for the sake of personal gain and to the advantage of a few 'interested' fellows, and who had ridden roughshod over the rights of the majority of the members of the Society, thereby threatening the constitutional balance worked out over the preceding forty years. It is abundantly clear that the bishop of Ely had good grounds for believing that the king's allegations were well founded, because the visitation led to the removal of Neyland from the mastership and the deprivation of six of the offending Scholars of their fellowships.[3]

Among Trinity College muniments there is an important notarial instrument which throws further light on this troubled period.[4] The document takes the form of an appeal to the Holy See made by Thomas Mordon,[5] proctor, on behalf of the warden and fellows of the King's Hall. After testifying to the good character of his 'masters', Mordon states that the warden and fellows, the college, and its appropriated churches and other possessions may suffer injury in the near future from certain probable lawsuits:

...ex quibusdam causis probabilibus et verisimilibus coniecturis dictis dominis meis, statui, collegio, ecclesiis aut possessionibus suis premissis grave posse preiudicium generari in futurum.

[1] 'Et cartae, libri, iocalia et alia munimenta necnon bona et cattalla eiusdem collegii per eundem custodem sunt elongata, vendita et asportata quodque ex causis premissis diversa debata, dissensiones et discordie inter ipsum custodem et prefatos scolares sunt suborta per quod iidem scolares vitam ducunt aliter desolatam et ea occasione studiis suis et eruditionis laboribus vacare non possunt ut deberent...': *loc. cit.*

[2] The master's conduct had brought upon the Society '...finalis destructionis periculum': *loc. cit.*

[3] Stamp, *Admissions to Trinity College, Cambridge*, I, 107 (from Foreign Roll, 7 Ric. II).

[4] The document is preserved in *K.H. Cabinet*, no. 44(6). It is attested by Robert de Foxton, clerk of the diocese of Lincoln and notary public.

[5] King's Scholar, admitted 21 November 1376; died 18 September 1416.

To forestall such injury imposed by anyone acting under any authority Mordon makes a direct appeal to the Holy See and craves the protection of the court of Canterbury, in whose name the appeal is made. The note of urgency in the appeal may be gauged from its language. As proctor, Mordon submits his 'masters' (i.e. the warden and fellows), the college, and its appropriated churches and all its possessions to the protection and defence of Rome and Canterbury:

...subiciens dictos dominos meos et me eorum nomine statum, collegium, ecclesias et possessiones sua premissa eiusque sibi adherentes,... protectioni, tuitioni et defensioni sedis et curie predictarum.

The following explanation is suggested. Dating appears to be the key to the interpretation of the document. It will be recalled that on 14 July 1383 Richard II commissioned the bishop of Ely to visit the Hall; on 19 May 1385 warden Simon Neylond and six fellows were removed as a result of the bishop's findings. This notarial instrument bears the date of 16 April 1384. That is to say, the appeal was launched nine months after the king's commission to Arundel and thirteen months before the royal deprivations. From the dating, it is evident that the appeal was made on behalf of warden Neylond, whom the king alleged to be the mainspring of internal disorder. It is therefore clear that the appeal was made either shortly before or shortly after the episcopal visitation.[1] In view of this, is it not most probable that the causes to be raised against the warden and fellows mentioned in the notarial instrument refer to possible disciplinary action which the king might take to rid his college of abuses? If this is so, then the appeal is seen to be a device of warden Neylond and his 'cronies' to insure themselves against the wrath of the king. By throwing themselves upon the protection of the court of Canterbury and, through it, the Holy See, they hoped to range the ecclesiastical powers on their side. The scene was prepared for a struggle which never materialised. For the appeal seems to have gone unanswered as no trace of a papal reply has been found. Perhaps there was insufficient time for the papacy to consider the situation and anyway, after the removal of Neylond and the six offenders, the appeal *ipso facto* would be irrelevant. As far as can be determined, this is the only occasion on which a warden of the King's Hall and several

---

[1] The exact date of the visitation is unknown.

'interested' fellows attempted to by-pass the authority of the king: their action was tantamount to open rebellion.

On the removal of Simon Neylond, Thomas Hetersete was appointed warden after 'election' by the Scholars.[1] As with Roos and Ronhale, the 'election' was, in reality, a designation. This is the last known instance in which the King's Scholars played a part in the appointment of a warden. How then are we to explain these three 'elections', especially in view of the fact that a direct royal appointee was sandwiched between the second and the third? The only explanation which possesses the virtue of consistency derives from a consideration of the state of order within the Society. Given the strained nature of the relations which appear to have existed between the fellows and warden Schropham and perhaps Drayton as well, the Crown may have decided that the best way of allaying tension was to allow the fellows to designate a candidate of their own choosing. The same procedure was adopted in the case of Ronhale. But in 1377, after thirteen years of apparent harmony, the Crown probably considered it safe to revert to its former policy of direct appointment. As this turned out to be an outstanding failure, the king once again permitted the Scholars to designate their warden. Good relations seem to have prevailed from Hetersete's time onwards and this may explain the readiness of the fellows to acquiesce in all subsequent appointments.[2] But amid all the 'ifs' and 'buts' of the situation, it is undeniable that the Scholars had been permitted to play a decisive role in the events leading to the appointment of three wardens and this constituted a recognition by the Crown of their newly acquired status in the government of the college.

The statutes of 5 March 1380 are in the nature of a compromise. On the one hand, the authority of the warden as supreme head of the Society was confirmed; on the other hand, the rights in government acquired by the Scholars between 1337 and 1380 were fully recognised. It is unequivocally stated that the administration of the finances of the college was now to be a joint enterprise on the part of the warden and the elected representatives of the fellows.[3] Although

---

[1] P.R.O. *Pat. R.* 8 Ric. II, p. 2, m. 14.

[2] Of the 30 wardens of the King's Scholars appointed between 1317 and 1546, only 8 were drawn from the ranks of the Society, the other 22 being royal appointees 'imposed' upon the college from outside. See below, pp. 280 ff.

[3] See the King's Hall statutes in Rouse Ball, *King's Hall*, p. 65.

the statutes allow a wide latitude to the master in the ordering of domestic affairs,[1] in all matters affecting the college as a whole the consent of the fellows was obligatory. The common seal was not to be affixed to any document without first obtaining the consent of the majority of the fellows (i.e. members of the *comitia*)[2] and this same consent was required before any important act of business might be undertaken: '...in arduis negotiis et magnis dicte domus prefatus custos sine consensu omnium sociorum vel maioris partis eorum nihil attemptet.'[3] It is therefore indisputable that by 1380 the doctrine of totality of consent was firmly embodied in the constitution of the college. And it is noteworthy that, in the years immediately following the granting of the statutes, several references to the practical registration of this consent occur in the accounts. In 1382–3, for example, a payment of 40*s* was made from the chest 'ex consensu totie comitive' in connection with a legacy left to the college by John de Glaston;[4] two years later, a loan of the same amount was contracted from the university 'de consensu omnium et singulorum sociorum';[5] and in 1413–14, five marks were paid to Stephen, a carpenter, working at the Hall, 'ex consensu omnium sociorum'.[6] One can sense that these references to totality of consent mirror the anxiety of the fellows to give formal expression to their newly acquired rights in this respect: when the novelty had worn off, however, it was felt to be no longer necessary to have them emphasised by repeated registration in the records of the Society.

The statutes of Richard II of 5 March 1380 constitute the only extant code remaining for the King's Hall. It has always seemed implausible that this community had functioned for so long without reducing its customs and constitutional practice to a written form. In the government records of the period before 1380, there is one possible allusion to the existence of an earlier code of statutes. It will be recalled that in the letters patent of Edward III of 1342 the royal commissioners were charged 'to ordain a rule of life for the

---

[1] For example, the warden was responsible for the distribution of the rooms, for the hiring of the servants and for the examination of all the fellows upon entry so that they might be assigned to a course of study commensurate with their academic capabilities. *Ibid.* pp. 65, 67.

[2] *Ibid.* p. 65.
[3] *Ibid.* p. 67.
[4] *K.H. Accts.* III, fo. 113v.
[5] *Ibid.* III, fo. 89v.
[6] *Ibid.* v, fo. 84v.

Scholars'.[1] Nothing is known of the outcome of this, but it is hardly likely that the statutes of 1380 were a direct result of the royal commission of 1342. There is, however, one piece of evidence in the King's Hall accounts which affords conclusive proof for the existence of an earlier code of statutes. The folio upon which the entry is written is clearly dated and belongs to the year 1346.[2] Most of the items of the entry have been crossed out and this may explain why it has hitherto been completely overlooked. The entry is titled 'Puniciones Statutorum anno supradicto' (i.e. 1346): beneath this are set down the names of fourteen Scholars, against each of which is a brief note to the effect that the Scholar has been fined a specified sum for breaking a particular statute. After the phrase 'propter transgressionem statuti', occurs the incipit; but, in all, only four incipits and consequently only four different statutes are cited. The range of fines varied from sixpence to one or two shillings,[3] the money raised in this way being paid into the common chest.[4] There are two points of interest arising from this entry. First, it supplies definite proof for the existence of a code of statutes as early as 1346: and it is possible that this was the code which was the direct outcome of the commission of 1342. Moreover, it is at first sight very surprising to find that in the early years the King's Hall was governed by a code of statutory fines. This was the usual form of punishment employed in the halls or hostels, the customary method in the English colleges being the deprivation of a fellow's commons.[5] The difference is readily explicable. Generally speaking, the halls and hostels attracted a wealthier type of student who paid for his board and lodgings and who could afford the occasional fine. But a hierarchical system of fining was rather unsuited to the colleges[6] as

---

[1] See above, p. 95.   [2] *K.H. Accts.* I, fo. 95.

[3] On one exceptional occasion a fine of 3s 4d was exacted.

[4] Fines were not only imposed for breaking specific statutory regulations but also for general disorderly conduct: for in 1346 a fine of 6d was levied on Harlaston (King's Scholar), 'pro discordia facta cum Ivor' (King's Scholar). *Ibid.* I, fo. 95.

[5] See the remarks of A. B. Emden, *An Oxford hall in medieval times*, p. 201.

[6] Nevertheless, a system of fining for statutory transgressions is found in operation at several of the Paris colleges. See e.g. the statutory provisions relating to fines at the colleges of Upsala (1291) and Skara House (*c.* 1407), founded for the support of Swedish scholars in Paris, in Gabriel, *Skara House at the mediaeval University of Paris* (Texts and studies in the history of mediaeval education, no. IX, Indiana, 1960), pp. 26–8, 94–6.

so many of the fellows were largely dependent on the bounty of the founder and, in such circumstances, deprivation of commons was the more practical form of general punishment. As the majority of the King's Scholars were recruited from the upper strata of society, however, it is obvious that a fining system would be appropriate to a community of this kind. Nevertheless, it appears that the system had been abandoned by 1380 as there are no provisions for fines in the statutes of that year and the accounts shed no further light on the matter.

An analytical study of the personnel of the annually elected committees of seneschals provides valuable information concerning the character of the internal government of the King's Hall. The accounts fortunately permit us to reconstruct fully the composition of no fewer than 113 such committees for the years between 1361-2 and 1543-4.[1] In the case of 500 of the 616 seneschals known to have served on these administrative bodies, the degree held in the year of election to office can be determined either with certainty or with a fair measure of probability.[2] In order that the changing pattern of administrative personnel can be more easily appreciated, it will be convenient to consider this analysis by degrees in two distinct phases. For this purpose, we may select 1443 as the point of division, the year in which the college gained its independence of external exchequer control. The analysis for the period 1361-2 to 1442-3, embracing 41 committees of seneschals, gives the data shown in table 12. One explanatory point needs to be given about this table. Although it presents a total of 34 seneschals whose degrees are

---

[1] There are no records of the personnel of the committees for the following years: 1362-3 to 1364-5, 1366-7 to 1369-70, 1371-2 to 1385-6, 1390-1 to 1392-3, 1394-5 to 1397-8, 1400-1 to 1402-3, 1404-5 to 1405-6, 1407-8 to 1409-10, 1413-14 to 1414-15, 1420-1, 1424-5, 1439-40, 1450-1, 1457-8, 1460-1 to 1464-5, 1466-7 to 1473-4, 1477-8, 1482-3, 1485-6, 1486-7, 1490-1, 1493-4, 1495-6, 1501-2, 1506-7, 1509-10, 1515-16, 1530-1, 1533-4, 1538-9, 1540-1. There are some half-dozen years for which committees can be partially reconstructed, but these have been ignored for the purposes of the present investigation. The names of the seneschals are usually found on the title page of each account, but where this is not so, the committee can often be fully constructed from information contained in the main body of the account: e.g. the later accounts normally itemise the salaries paid to the seneschals of the year.

[2] The information about degrees is derived from Emden, *B.R.U.C.*, and, for the sixteenth century, from J. Venn and J. A. Venn, *Alumni Cantabrigienses*, pt. I, I–IV (Cambridge, 1922–7).

TABLE 12

Number of seneschals who, upon election, held the degree of:[1]

Lic.C.L.	4
B.C.L.	70
B.Cn.L.	6
B.C.L. or B.Cn.L.	12
M.A.	54
B.A.	20
Unknown	34

unknown at the time of election, it must be borne in mind that many of these had, in fact, acquired degrees in later years and may well have held these same degrees when elected into administrative office.

This analysis by degrees firmly attests that the administrative government of the King's Hall was almost entirely the exclusive province of the graduate members of the Society. It is true that in the rather exceptional circumstances which prevailed for a number of years during the latter part of the fourteenth century a handful of young, inexperienced Scholars without degrees were, out of necessity, appointed seneschals of the college with detrimental and perhaps even disastrous consequences.[2] But this situation represents an aberration from the norm, and administrative power was usually vested in the hands of the graduate fellows. Moreover, the analysis reveals that the vast majority of the seneschals had already attained a second degree upon election to office. In the main, this was either the M.A. or the B.C.L. degree, with a sprinkling here and there of degrees in canon law. It will be observed that a small proportion had only B.A. status when elected, which one might imagine to be a patronising concession to the younger element in the Society. There can, however, be no doubt that the composition of these committees was weighted very heavily indeed in favour of fellows with the higher degrees in arts and law. It is equally apparent that long residence was not an essential qualification for election: for, between 1361–2 and 1442–3, at least 10 fellows were elected seneschals within two years of first entry into the college and several more were created officers in their third year. Nevertheless, it would certainly seem fair to

[1] To these ought to be added a number of 'probables': B.C.L.: 2; M.A.: 31; B.A.: 1.
[2] For this, see below, p. 181 and n. 5.

conclude that both a degree (and normally a second degree) and residence of about three to six years constituted the usual kind of requirements for office. On the basis of this study, it may be affirmed that the sizable undergraduate population of the King's Hall took little or no active part in the running of affairs in normal circumstances, irrespective of the fact that they were fully fledged fellows in every technical sense of the term and that some of them were evidently men of mature years.[1] It should also be stressed that it was not at all uncommon for a fellow to remain in the college for periods of twenty years or more without, in any discoverable way, participating in administrative government: for out of a total of 41 fellows admitted between 1337–8 and 1442–3 who retained their fellowships in excess of twenty years, only 26 are known to have served as seneschals.

Significant differences emerge from a similar analysis of the degrees of the members of the 72 administrative committees for which there is information between 1442–3 and 1543–4. The information for this period is summarised in table 13.

TABLE 13

Number of seneschals who, upon election, held the degree of:[2]

D.C.L.	5	B.C.L. or B.Cn.L.	2
B.C.L.	35	D.Th.[3]	2
Sch.C.L.	1	B.Th.	13
D.Cn.L.	5	M.A.	57
Lic.Cn.L.	4	Inc.A.	14
B.Cn.L.	54	B.A.	11
B.C.L. and B.Cn.L.	5	Unknown	82

As before, it is obvious that the overwhelming majority of the seneschals held degrees in arts or law upon election. But there is now detectable a marked increase in canon law degrees. In this later

[1] See above, p. 56.

[2] To these ought to be added a number of 'probables': B.C.L.: 9; D.Cn.L.: 1; B.Cn.L.: 19; D.Th.: 1; M.Th.: 3; B.Th.: 3; M.A.: 55; B.A.: 1.

[3] It would appear that the term 'Theology' should be used in preference to 'Divinity' as a designation for degrees at medieval Cambridge since the latter term is very infrequently employed in documents of the medieval period. On this point, see the remarks of Emden, *B.R.U.C.* p. xxviii.

period, 63 seneschals definitely possessed degrees in canon law when elected (and there were more than a score of 'probables') as opposed to only 6 in the earlier phase. Whatever the reason behind this mushroom growth, it is clear that canon law qualifications had over-taken and outstripped civil law degrees, of which there were 41, with 9 'probables'. Arts degrees continued to lead the field although a considerably reduced proportion of fellows were elected seneschals on the strength of a B.A. status. A wholly novel feature is the emergence of a handful of seneschals with theological qualifications: none, however, seems to have acquired a degree in medicine. It is worthy of remark that the proportion of fellows to be elected to office within two years of first entry into the college is only margin-ally greater than in the earlier period: of the 382 fellows involved, a mere 21 fall into this category and of these 16 were elected in the first half of the sixteenth century. This minimal emphasis upon the utilisation of the talents of the newer entrants may, of course, have been determined by the dictates of conservative caution but may also, to some extent, be explained by the fact that a substantially aug-mented proportion of long-tenured fellows were now taking an active part in governmental affairs. Whereas, in the earlier phase, less than half of those fellows who retained their fellowships for more than twenty years served as seneschals, in this later period the pro-portion has gone up to exactly three quarters (that is, 30 of the 40 long-tenured fellows held administrative office). Considerations of this kind lead one to believe that, in the final century of its existence, the centre of administrative gravity in the King's Hall was now even more firmly than before concentrated in the retentive hands of the senior members of the Society.

These conclusions afford an instructive comparison with what is known of 'democratic' arrangements in other contemporary English colleges. It appears that in most collegiate societies, though not perhaps in all, the organisation was so designed that every fellow would play some small part in the running of college affairs. For example, the statutes of Queen's College, Oxford, enjoin that every fellow, the provost and the doctors in theology and canon law excepted, was to undertake the office of seneschal of the hall for a week.[1] A similar arrangement was in operation at New College[2] and

---

[1] *Statutes*, I, ch. (4), 25.   [2] *Ibid.* I, ch. (5), 42.

also at King's College, Cambridge.[1] These arrangements were obviously contrived to ensure that the administrative burden would fall with equal weight upon the shoulders of every member of the Society. While the King's Hall accounts furnish examples here and there of a fellow engaged in the business of the college who was not himself a seneschal in that year,[2] it is evident that the overwhelming bulk of the Society's administration was conducted in person by its six elected representatives.[3] There are thus very good grounds for supposing that the 'democratic' involvement of the King's Scholars in collegiate government was not nearly so extensive as that which prevailed in the more usual type of English college.

Although the administrative affairs of the King's Hall were concentrated in the hands of the seneschals, this does not necessarily imply that government was oligarchical in character. Quite the reverse, as a detailed study of the administrative committees reveals that throughout the entire history of the college there was a healthy turnover of personnel, which prevented the development of government by a ruling clique as came to be the unenviable situation in not a few medieval English colleges.

At first, the element of continuity in these committees was not very great. Indeed, it seems that in the 1360s, 1370s and early 1380s the turnover of personnel was altogether too excessive to make for orderly stable government. It was probably this situation which moved the Scholars to petition the king for assistance. The petition,[4] which is undated but, from the handwriting, seems to belong to the second half of the fourteenth century, states that owing to a large number of resignations or deaths there was at this time a dearth of mature responsible senior members in the Hall available to undertake the burden of office. Consequently, the running of the college had, of necessity, to be entrusted to young and inexperienced Scholars, some of whom were not likely to take a degree in the university for some time to come.[5] The situation was much stabilised by the late 1380s and from 1386 right down to the 1540s a fairly regular pattern of administrative service can be discerned.

---

[1] *Camb. Docs.* II, 533.   [2] See below, pp. 206–7.
[3] For the way in which the seneschals divided up the work of administration see below, pp. 207 ff.   [4] The petition is preserved in *K.H. Cabinet*, no. 144.
[5] As a result, it was reported that the Hall was 'desolée et destitute de bone gouvernance'.

An examination of the personnel of the committees of seneschals shows that something like a constant balance was maintained between elements of continuity, represented by the repeated re-election of a number of experienced fellows over several years, and elements of new blood, represented by the infusion in most years of one or two members who had not previously served in an administrative capacity.[1] Generally speaking, three or four members of the retiring committee were re-elected for service on the committee of the following year. Of those who were not re-elected some, through death or promotion to a benefice, were no longer available for service; others who were available, but were not immediately re-elected, often reappear on committees several years later. What is, however, most noteworthy is that in most years (though not all) one, two or occasionally three new fellows, who had not previously served as seneschals, were elected into administrative office. As this was the general pattern which persisted unabated all the way down to the mid-sixteenth century, there are substantial grounds for asserting that while the everyday affairs of the college came to be administered almost exclusively by the annually elected committees, their composition was sufficiently balanced and fluid to keep at bay the perils of descent into devitalising, oligarchical rule. Since the pattern of administrative balance is so tenaciously maintained, it is indeed hard to avoid the conclusion that successive generations of King's Hall fellows were ever acutely aware of the contemporary evils of academic oligarchy and consciously determined to prevent it from gaining a stranglehold upon their own governmental councils by ensuring that there would always be reasonable scope for the representation of the newer and younger members of the Society.

The concentration of day-to-day administrative powers in the committees of seneschals was offset by the consideration that ultimate sovereignty resided in all the fellows of the Society acting together as a body or corporation. It has been previously remarked that the doctrine of totality of consent was fixedly embodied in the statutes of 1380 and given practical implementation in the years immediately following.[2] Since it is obvious that consent could only have been registered or withheld through the instrument of a college meeting,

---

[1] It will be appreciated that the evidence is simply too vast to be given in this place.
[2] See above, p. 175.

we must assume that fairly regular meetings of all the resident members on the foundation were held from 1380 onwards. The term used consistently to designate the fellows acting in a corporative capacity is *comitia* or *comitiva*, a word with wide medieval technical and general application ranging in meaning from a county or earldom to a county court or a meeting of parliament and, by extension, to any kind of company or assembly convoked for a specific purpose.[1] The first fully documented college meeting belongs to 1488–9, when the vice-master, John Girton, summoned all the fellows of the King's Hall then present in the university to a meeting held in the recently built college chapel.[2] On this occasion, the business conducted related to perquisites to which fellows were entitled by virtue of their fellowships. Similar assemblies (though the location is not specified) were held in 1517–18,[3] 1524–5[4] and 1529–30.[5] Whether or not meetings took place automatically every year as part of the regular governmental process is impossible to say: on the face of it, the more probable conclusion is that they were convened as the need arose, although meetings of a kind must have been held annually for the specific purpose of electing the seneschals for the year. As earlier indicated,[6] only those matters of particular difficulty, delicacy and importance were submitted to the college meeting and in almost every instance they involved either the expenditure of funds or the contraction of loans. On every recorded occasion, the consent is said to have been unanimous, but it is hard to believe that the element of concord was as great as the official statements imply. Nevertheless, the combination of the ultimate deterrent, the college meeting, and the operative principle of annual election to administrative office shows beyond all reasonable doubt that a system of responsible government was firmly embedded in the constitution of this medieval college.

---

[1] See *Revised medieval Latin word-list*, p. 98.

[2] *K.H. Accts.* xviii, fo. 68 v: 'Memorandum quod anno domini 1488 vicesimo primo die mensis Novembris per Magistrum Gyrton locum tenentem collegii [aule Regis *erased*] istius convocacione facta omnium sociorum dicti collegii in universitate tunc presentium et ibidem existentium in nova capella dicti collegii de consensu unanimi omnium et singulorum predictorum sociorum provisum est et ordinatum pro perpetuo...'

[3] *Ibid.* xxii, fo. 38 v.   [4] *Ibid.* xxiii, fo. 132 v.
[5] *Ibid.* xxiv, fo. 48 v.   [6] See above, p. 175.

Whereas in the majority of English colleges new scholars were elected for a probationary period of one or two years prior to election into full fellowships, there was clearly no such general procedure at the King's Hall. With occasional exceptions discoverable among the ranks of the royal chapel personnel,[1] all new entrants were, *ab initio*, fully incorporated members of the college (i.e. full fellows).

In the fourteenth century, the terms *scolaris* and *socius* appear to be wholly interchangeable and are used, for example, as clear alternatives throughout the King's Hall statutes of 1380.[2] But during the wardenship of John Blakman,[3] nominee of the provosts of Eton and King's, the terms were employed seemingly to indicate a technical distinction such that all new King's Hall entrants were designated *scolares* and remained thus for about four years, at the end of which time their names were transferred to the *socii* grouping in the Society's records. This form of differentiation occurs in the accounts for 1451–2, 1452–3 and 1453–4,[4] but thereafter there was a reversion to the usual practice whereby all new entrants, without exception, were classified as *socii* from the outset. It should not be inferred, however, that the King's Hall *scolares* of the mid-fifteenth century were scholars in the modern 'Oxbridge' sense of members of the university maintained by a college for a guaranteed number of years but without the right of participation in the management of college affairs. At Oxford, it seems that scholars approximating to this type made their appearance first at Magdalen College, where they were known as *demies*.[5] An early prototype of the modern

---

[1] See below, pp. 186–7.

[2] See e.g. the King's Hall statutes in Rouse Ball, *King's Hall*, p. 66: 'In cameris vero prefati scolares absque strepitu et impedimento sociorum studentium conversantur...'; also the remarks of H. E. Salter, *Medieval Oxford*, p. 98.

[3] Warden from 3 December 1452 till 11 July 1457. For details of his career see Emden, *B.R.U.C.* pp. 670–1.

[4] *K.H. Accts.* XI, fos. 99–104, 135–7, 163–5, where the new entrants are separated from the *socii* and are ranged together under the heading of *scolares*. At the end of four years the name of a *scolaris* was moved to the *socii* section. Exceptions are provided by the cases of Thomas Sutton, who, entering the college in 1451–2, was straightway included among the *socii*, and William Cloos, who, admitted in 1451–2, remained a *scolaris* for only about three instead of the usual four years.

[5] The *demies* were thirty in number and lived at the rate of half commons. When elected, they had already received instruction in plainsong and went on to study grammar, logic and sophistry. 'In the early years the *demies* did not often become

scholar may be identified in Bishop Bateman's *scolares*, the provisions for whom the founder of Trinity Hall, Cambridge, outlined in his explanatory statute (or *interpretatio*), given at South Elmham on 14 August 1354.[1] As is the modern practice, the *scolares* of Magdalen and Trinity Hall did not necessarily advance to fellowships;[2] whereas, as far as can be determined, all the mid-fifteenth-century King's Hall *scolares* were transferred automatically from the *scolares* to the *socii* grouping at the expiry of a four-year period.[3] Nor does the evidence warrant the classification of the King's Hall *scolares* as probationary fellows in the New College sense whereby undergraduate entrants might be advanced to fellowships after a sojourn of two years in Oxford.[4] On the contrary, the *scolares* of the King's Hall were fully incorporated fellows of the college from their first admission.

Perhaps the explanation for this terminological distinction made between *scolares* and *socii* is to be sought in the consideration that of the fourteen *scolares* whose names occur in the accounts for 1451–2, 1452–3 and 1453–4, at least seven are known to have been King's Scholars at Eton, nominated and admitted to King's Hall 'scholarships'.[5] Clearly, the term *scolares* would most aptly describe this category of personnel and one can well imagine that for an experimental period the term was extended to cover all new entrants (who

---

fellows, but about the beginning of Elizabeth's reign the custom grew up of admitting them to fellowships by regular succession...': N. Denholm-Young, 'Magdalen College', *V.C.H.* (Oxford), III, 194; see also the statutes of Magdalen in *Statutes*, II, ch. (8), 15–16 and the remarks of Salter, *op. cit.* p. 98. A further account of the *demies* will be found in R. S. Stanier, *Magdalen School* (2nd ed. Oxford, 1958), pp. 8, 17–20, 50–1 and 95–8.

[1] This document is printed in *Warren's Book*, ed. cit. pp. 51–3 and in *Camb. Docs.* II, 436–9. Bateman prescribed that when convenient the college was to admit two or three *scolares* who were to be students in civil law. Each was to receive three marks annually and when the resources of the college would allow, their number was to be increased to seven. It is specifically stated, however, that they were to have no voice in college affairs, and while they were to be given preference over others in the fellowship election, their promotion was clearly by no means automatic.

[2] See above, n. 1, and p. 184, n. 5.

[3] With the exceptions mentioned, p. 184, n. 4.

[4] *Statutes*, I, ch. (5), 16; Salter, *op. cit.* p. 99. For similar probationary arrangements at King's College, see *Camb. Docs.* II, 498.

[5] William Bale (Baghel), John Brayne (Braine), Reginald or Richard Brynkley, William or Thomas Caps (Cappys), William Cloos (Clos), Henry Shalston (Shalleston, Challeston) and John Wode. For further details see below, p. 190, n. 2.

might conceivably be men of mature years with a degree upon entry)[1] to indicate nothing more than a measure of hierarchical distinction between the new fellows and the main body of their established colleagues. The fact that this terminological differentiation was discontinued after Blakman's wardenship would seem to corroborate the conclusion that the distinction was not a fundamental one.

As the Society of the King's Scholars derived originally from the chapel royal, it seems necessary to take further stock of the position and fortunes of the chapel recruits admitted to the college. Generally speaking, the chapel Scholars do not appear to have occupied any specially privileged place within the community: they do, however, provide us with the only known cases of 'probationary' fellows at the King's Hall. Although the majority of the chapel entrants were accorded the status of fully incorporated fellows upon admission, some half dozen of them were evidently appointed in the first instance for a probationary period. In 1402–3, four clerks and two boys were recruited from the chapel royal:[2] but for the space of two years all six remained unincorporated and lived as semi-commoners, their names and rates due for half commons appearing immediately after the list of fellows on the foundation.[3] Two of the chapel clerks, John Cook(e) and William Fraunceys, were created full fellows in 1404–5[4] and the other two, William Bayly and Thomas Penkriche, were likewise upgraded to the ranks of the fellows in 1407–8.[5] But neither of the chapel children John Spar(o)we and John Straunston ever became a full fellow: there is no trace of the former after 1403–4 and Straunston vanishes from the records in the following year. Doubtless these were very young boys who may well have failed to achieve the minimum proficiency in grammar required for entry upon the

---

[1] E.g. William Bale, who first appears as a *scolaris* in 1453–4, had acquired the title of 'magister' by that date, which most probably signifies the possession of an academic degree (Emden, *B.R.U.C.* p. 33).

[2] Chapel clerks: John Cook(e), vacated 17 January 1414; William Bayly, vacated 25 June 1411; Thomas Penkriche, vacated 26 May 1411; and William Fraunceys, vacated 10 May 1424. Chapel boys: John Spar(o)we and John Straunston (*K.H. Accts.* v, fo. 51v). The chapel clerk, John Cook(e), is probably to be identified with the composer, John Cooke, a clerk in the royal chapel of Henry V. (F. Ll. Harrison, *Music in medieval Britain*, pp. 22, 228, 245–6.)

[3] *K.H. Accts.* v, fos. 51v, 67, 67v.

[4] *Ibid.* IV, fo. 116v.   [5] *Ibid.* v, fos. 108, 108v.

arts course proper. It is indeed rather puzzling to understand why the chapel entrants of 1402–3 were relegated to this probationary status at the beginning of their academic careers. The available evidence almost certainly proves that all other chapel recruits of the fourteenth and early fifteenth centuries were created fully incorporated fellows from the outset. A possible explanation may be that the six entrants in question, none of whom ever appears to have acquired a degree, were particularly unpromising students upon admission and were not promoted to the foundation until such time as they could show evidence of satisfactory progress in their studies.

Investigation of the chapel Scholars reveals that neither their academic nor administrative record had much to recommend it. Of the eighteen about whom we possess some detailed information, only four are known to have taken a degree of any kind[1] and no chapel Scholar is recorded as having acquired a degree in any of the superior faculties: while only one, John Bilneye, the future mayor of Cambridge and arch-enemy of the university, served in an administrative capacity as seneschal of the college.[2] Moreover, one of the chapel clerks[3] was singled out by Thomas Arundel, bishop of Ely, as a troublemaker and was forthwith expelled along with the warden and five other offending Scholars in 1385;[4] and another chapel clerk, Robert Gillot,[5] removed himself from the college for the less notorious reason that he had committed the indiscretion of getting married. In addition to this singularly unimpressive record, the chapel element constituted a severe financial drag upon the resources of the college because several of the chapel Scholars were permitted to remain in the Hall for periods of up to twenty years without meeting their bills for commons or paying off the relatively heavy dues levied upon every entrant at admission. As a result, their debts continued to pile up year by year and in 1422–3, for example, there

---

[1] These were: John Bilneye, M.A.; Thomas Aston, M.A.; John Franfield, B.A.; and Richard Shrowsbury, B.A. (see entries in *B.R.U.C.*).

[2] Served as seneschal 1387–8, 1388–9 and 1398–9. For details of Bilneye's eventful career see *B.R.U.C.* p. 62, and below, pp. 297–8.

[3] William Fyssh, 'petit clerk de notre chapelle', admitted 12 May 1382; expelled 19 May 1385.

[4] See above, p. 172.

[5] Admitted 4 October 1410; vacated on marriage 14 February 1420.

still remained unpaid £10 2s 4½d for commons from 1402–3 and 1403–4.[1]

It is reasonable to assume that the king himself would have been answerable for the debts of his chapel protégés: and considering the dismal academic record of most of the chapel Scholars and the financial burden involved in their upkeep, it may have been adjudged that this royal educational investment was not producing an adequate return and had best be discontinued. The last recorded admission from the chapel royal is that for John Fissher, one of the chapel children, who was admitted on 3 December 1417 and vacated on 7 July 1432 without taking a degree.[2] The fact that a depletion in the numbers of the king's choristers is detectable in the last few months of Henry V's reign and in the opening years of the minority of Henry VI[3] may also have been a contributory reason for the breaking of the King's Hall–chapel royal nexus at this point in time. And the links with the college were apparently not revived when Henry VI augmented the ranks of the choristers towards the middle of the century.[4] Thus, the conclusion would seem to be that either in the closing years of the reign of Henry V or in the opening years of Henry VI's minority, the direct connection between the chapel royal (though not the court) and the King's Hall was finally severed, bringing to an end a relationship which had endured for over a hundred years and in which is to be found the real origin of this remarkable medieval college.

In the late 1440s a new but temporary phase in the history of the Society began. Events were set in motion by the letters patent of 26 January 1446 whereby Henry VI transferred the Crown's right of nomination of the King's Scholars to the joint control of the provosts of his recently founded establishments of Eton and King's College, Cambridge.[5] On 24 February 1447, there was added the right of appointment to the King's Hall wardenship to take effect im-

---

[1] *K.H. Accts.* v, fos. 88, 126, 145, 166; VI, fos. 15, 34v, 52v, 73v, 138v; VII, fo. 1.

[2] Stamp, *Admissions to Trinity College, Cambridge,* I, 115.

[3] Harrison, *Music in medieval Britain,* p. 22.

[4] *Cal. Pat. R.,* 1436–1441, p. 452; Harrison, p. 23.

[5] Mr J. Saltmarsh points out that these letters patent have not yet been discovered, nor do they appear in the printed *Cal. Pat. R.*: but their contents have come down to us through a summary in a fifteenth-century calendar preserved in the muniments of King's College (Saltmarsh, 'King's College', *V.C.H.* (Cambridge), III, 379, n. 43).

mediately after the death or resignation of the then warden, Richard Caudray:[1] and on 24 January 1448, the provosts were charged with full powers to examine and reform the King's Hall statutes which allegedly had not been observed of late, to enforce the observance of new or reformed statutes upon the warden and fellows, on pain of expulsion if necessary, and to hold disciplinary visitations.[2] This process of calculated and relentless subordination was completed by the imposition of a most humiliating and severe oath of obedience upon the King's Hall warden who, by its terms, was reduced to little more than a mere cipher.[3] There is not the slightest doubt that these patronage arrangements were intended to be anything other than permanent but, fortunately for the Society, the accession of Edward IV in 1461 brought about a reversal of this inequitable Lancastrian settlement and on 3 February 1462 the former independent status of the King's Hall under the Crown was restored.[4] And this remained the situation until 1546.

How then are we to explain Henry VI's innovatory policy towards the King's Hall? No trace of the emergence of an attitude of royal hostility can be discovered in the earlier part of the reign. On the contrary, as late as 1433, the king had bestowed a signal mark of favour upon the Society through his exceptionally valuable bequest of seventy-seven volumes for the King's Hall library.[5] And yet, within the space of a dozen or so years, the college had so completely fallen from its position of royal grace that it was relegated to the status of a kind of academic makeweight, a powerless entity at the disposal of Eton and King's.

It is generally assumed that the king's purpose was entirely one of administrative convenience: that is to say, the King's Hall was to continue to function as a suitable institution for the absorption of

---

[1] Letters patent printed by Rouse Ball, *King's Hall*, pp. 75–6. Caudray vacated the wardenship on 29 September 1448 but whether or not royal pressure was brought to bear upon his resignation is unknown.

[2] *Cal. Pat. R.*, 1446–1452, p. 121.

[3] The oath is printed by Rouse Ball, p. 76 (transcribed from the original in King's College Muniment Room). The warden had to swear to obey the provosts in all matters arising out of their visitations of the King's Hall and any other injunction or ordinance which they saw fit to impose upon the college: he had also to swear that he would admit *absque examinacione sive contradiccione quacumque* all the nominees of the provosts and none other.

[4] *Cal. Pat. R.*, 1461–1467, p. 103.   [5] See below, pp. 256–7.

surplus Eton Scholars who could not readily be found scholarships at King's.[1] It is indisputable that during this period the King's Hall was extensively utilised for the provision of places for Etonians: the names of thirteen Eton Scholars appointed to scholarships at the King's Hall have been extracted from the Eton records[2] and doubtless the remaining King's Hall personnel appointed between 1446 and 1461 were also the nominees of the provosts of Eton and King's. But having testified to these facts, the picture is still very far from complete because the question inevitably arises that if Henry VI had conceived the idea of linking up the three royal institutions solely for the sake of centralised administrative convenience, then why did he not proceed on the basis of parity? What led him to single out the King's Hall for discriminative and disciplinary treatment? It is surely a matter for some surprise that an institution which had enjoyed a continuous existence for more than a century should suddenly be so humiliatingly subordinated to the heads of two colleges still in their infant stages of development, neither foundation being much more than five years of age. At the very least, one would have expected Henry VI to confer an equality of status upon each of the three academic partners; but failing this, if there was to be a disparity of relationship, one would have thought that headship ought to have devolved naturally upon the King's Hall as the senior and experienced establishment, and certainly during the difficult, formative years of this novel, tripartite, collegiate association.

The available evidence strongly points to the conclusion that the explanation is to be sought in the punitive motives which plainly underlay the policy of Henry VI and his advisers towards the King's Hall in 1446–8. The project envisaged was seemingly to combine these three collegiate societies to form a single administrative unit, and within this framework the King's Hall was to be sentenced to occupy an obviously subordinate role as a college whose recent behaviour had disqualified it from taking an equal place alongside the

---

[1] See the remarks of H. C. Maxwell Lyte, *A history of Eton College 1440–1910* (4th ed. London, 1911), pp. 55–6; also Saltmarsh, *op. cit.* p. 379; Rouse Ball, *op. cit.* pp. 43–5.

[2] Their names and dates are given by W. Sterry, *The Eton College register 1441–1698* (Eton, 1943). Only one Eton Scholar is definitely known to have been appointed to a vacancy at the King's Hall in the period following the end of the tutelage of the college in 1462: there were, however, possibly two others (see Sterry, under the names Cause, Powes and Wotton, pp. 66, 271 and 379).

new foundations. Exactly what had been going on inside the King's Hall is difficult to determine: that there had lately been some form of serious internal disorder can be deduced from the letters patent of 24 January 1448[1] which make reference to the non-observance of the statutes and give powers to the provosts to punish and correct all negligence, excesses and defects, even if this should entail the expulsion of members of the Society. Further evidence of disturbances may be inferred from a royal pardon of 20 April 1458[2] acquired by the master and fellows of the King's Hall and couched in identical terms to a general pardon of 1455 preserved in the *Rotuli Parliamentorum* for that year.[3] As this copious document covers every conceivable crime from petty theft to conspiracy and rebellion, it is not possible to say of which particular offence or offences the King's Scholars had been deemed guilty: but the fact that it had been thought necessary to obtain such a pardon suggests there may have been much unbecoming and perhaps even criminal behaviour to forgive.

In this present context, it is relevant to stress that during Henry VI's reign the finances of the college had fallen into a temporarily unhealthy state. The combined outstanding revenue due to the Society from farmed exchequer sources (£72 10s 8d),[4] from appropriated churches (£137 10s 2d),[5] from fellows and pensioners (£75 9s 7¼d)[6] and from other miscellaneous quarters (£25 5s 8d)[7] had steadily accumulated until *c.* 1454–5 the total for arrears stood at the enormous sum of £310 16s 1¼d.[8] It is impossible to judge whether this represents mismanagement on the part of the senior administrative officers or was due to circumstances beyond their control. Whatever the case, the alarming combination of serious internal disturbances and financial muddle may well have provided the reasons which led Henry VI to the decision that the King's Hall required to be severely disciplined and overhauled, a task which could be most conveniently accomplished under the auspices of his splendid new collegiate foundations. Moreover, there is every likelihood that the king had conducted a personal investigation of conditions

[1] *Cal. Pat. R.*, 1446–1452, p. 121.
[2] *K.H. Cabinet*, no. 105.
[3] *Rotuli Parliamentorum*, v, 283–4.
[4] *K.H. Accts.* XII, fo. 29.
[5] *Loc. cit.*
[6] *Ibid.* XII, fo. 28v.
[7] *Ibid.* XII, fo. 29.
[8] *Ibid.* XII, fo. 29v. For further details of these expenses see *ibid.* XII, fos. 25–29v.

within the college because he visited the King's Hall in 1448-9[1] and in 1452-3,[2] and members of his retinue were present between 1445 and 1447.[3] From these visits, the king must have acquired intimate first-hand knowledge of the disturbing internal situation, and the decision to bring the King's Scholars to heel may well have been one largely of his own making.

There is no proof that the King's Hall was tinged with pro-Yorkist feelings at the time of the withdrawal of its independent status. But the fellows would have been less than human if Henry VI's ruthless treatment of their college had not provoked a measure of anti-Lancastrian sentiment among their ranks. Indeed, the royal pardon of 1458 might conceivably have embraced the crime of pro-Yorkist sympathies, although this has to remain no more than a conjecture. There is, however, in the north-west oriel window of the hall of Trinity College a small adult figure in plate armour bearing the legend 'Ricardus Dux':[4] on the basis of the armour this portrait has been assigned to *c.* 1425[5] and could very well be a representation of Richard, duke of York, father of Edward IV and twice Protector of England. Although proof is unobtainable, it is probable that this window portrait came from the King's Hall, where it may have been cherished as a visible token of Yorkist proclivities. But, apart from the fact that the college had every reason to harbour resentment against the Lancastrians and to feel gratitude towards the House of York, the restorer of its independence, there exists no concrete evidence enabling us to determine with certainty the political orientation of the King's Hall during the Wars of the Roses.

The treatment meted out to the King's Hall by Henry VI was more than counterbalanced by that experienced by King's and Eton at the hands of Edward IV. Whereas Henry VI's punitive policy may have been prompted by a relatively objective appraisal of the troubled

[1] *Ibid.* xi, fo. 39: 'Item in expensis famulorum Regis in tempore adventus sui ixs.; in expensis Petri Ardern principalis Baronis Skaccarii Regis cum famulis suis xiijs. viijd. ob.'

[2] *Ibid.* xi, fo. 124: 'Item in adventu regis xxs.'

[3] In the accounts of 1445-6 and 1446-7 there are several entries for the expenses of the *familiares* and *hospitatores* (i.e. harbingers) of the king: *ibid.* x, fos. 123, 158.

[4] For a description of this see *Royal Commission on Historical Monuments (England) City of Cambridge* (H.M.S.O. 1959), ii, 227, with photograph, plate 230.

[5] *Loc. cit.* This dating has been firmly corroborated by Mr C. Blair of the Victoria and Albert Museum, for whose expert opinion I am indebted.

internal situation at the King's Hall, there can be little doubt that Edward IV's antipathy towards Eton and King's stemmed entirely from their Lancastrian origins, and they found themselves luckless victims of the game of power politics. Henry VI had at least tried to be educationally constructive, however disadvantageous this may have been for the King's Hall; but Edward IV was, in the first instance, wholly destructive in intent. Soon after his accession in 1461, King's College was ordered to pay its revenues into the exchequer.[1] Although the November parliament of that year confirmed the Lancastrian foundations and exempted their sites from the general resumption, their estates were not allowed to escape. King's recovered some of its property later in the reign and more under Henry VII, but much of the founder's endowment was permanently lost. As a result of this pettiness, the income of King's was seriously reduced and the complement of fellows and scholars sadly depleted, not to revive again fully until the mid-sixteenth century. Eton fared even worse. For not only did Edward IV seek to reduce and impoverish the foundation but he evidently entertained the idea of suppressing it altogether and annexing it to St George's Chapel at Windsor.[2] Towards this end, a papal bull was obtained in 1463, although it is uncertain if the scheme was ever fully implemented: later in the reign, Eton recovered the royal favour and the bull was revoked.[3] While Henry VI's radical reorganisation of the King's Hall was obviously ill considered and too extreme to be acceptable on a permanent basis, his projected scheme of a closely integrated, tripartite, academic association shows a far deeper concern for true educational values than that evinced by his Yorkist successor.

[1] For this and the following information about King's see Saltmarsh, *op. cit.* p. 379.
[2] Maxwell Lyte, *History of Eton College*, p. 63.
[3] *Ibid.* pp. 63, 66, 67.

Chapter 6

ASPECTS OF COLLEGIATE LIFE
IN THE KING'S HALL

ADMINISTRATIVE AND BUSINESS ARRANGEMENTS

It has already been stressed that by far the greater proportion of the business of the college was concentrated in the hands of the six elected guardians of the common chest.[1] By the latter part of the fourteenth century, it had become customary for one of the guardians or seneschals to be made responsible for the management of external finances. For in the royal letters of appointment of Nicholas Roos as warden of the King's Hall in 1364, it is directed that, by the common consent of the master and fellows, one of their number is to be given special responsibility for the conduct of the Society's external business.[2] This directive is repeated in the letters of appointment of Richard Ronhale in 1375[3] and in those for Simon Neylond in 1377.[4] It was subsequently incorporated verbatim into the statutes of 5 March 1380.[5] From 1433–4 onwards, this official, termed variously *prosecutor ad forinseca*, *procurator ad negotia forinseca* and *senescallus ad forinseca*, was accorded a status wholly distinct from that of the other seneschals and was henceforth regarded as an independent officer.[6] In general, the *prosecutor* was directly accountable for the receipt of all incoming revenues and for the administration of expenditure relating to extra-collegiate affairs. One of his principal duties was to journey each year to London to negotiate at the exchequer for the

---

[1] See above, p. 181.

[2] 'Excitand'...quod Ricardus Bergh, capellanus, seu alius de commune assensu ipsorum Magistri et Scolarium deputandus ut locum tenens ipsius Magistri ad negotia forinseca dictam aulam tangentia prosequenda et expedienda sit intendens.' P.R.O. *Pat. R.* 38 Ed. III, p. 2, m. 10.

[3] P.R.O. *Pat. R.* 49 Ed. III, p. 2, m. 12.

[4] P.R.O. *Pat. R.* 1 Ric. II, p. 1, m. 16.

[5] Rouse Ball, *King's Hall*, p. 69.

[6] *K.H. Accts.* VIII, fos. 61, 87, 112; IX, fos. 1, 31, 60, 148; X, fos. 1, 28, 51, 82, 117, 153; XI, fos. 1, 118; XV, fo. 29; XVI, fos. 1, 27; XVIII, fos. 26, 48, 151; XXI, fo. 73; XXIV, fos. 98, 110; XXV, fos. 73V, 144V; XXVI, fos. 32V, 71V, 112V, 150.

annual income due to the college[1] and to collect from the king's wardrobe materials, or a monetary equivalent,[2] for the robes and furs of the warden and fellows.

Every year towards Christmas the warden and fellows received from the royal wardrobe cloth and furs for their robes[3] or a monetary equivalent from the exchequer to the combined annual value of forty marks (i.e. £26 13s 4d).[4] At first the warden was supplied with two sets of robes, one lined with fur for winter wear and the other with linen or silk for the summer.[5] By 1361 at the latest, however, the delivery of robes to the master had been commuted into a cash sum of eight marks (i.e. £5 6s 8d) a year, made chargeable to the sheriff of Cambridgeshire.[6] From the inception of the Society *c.* 1317

---

[1] Normally, the greater part of the exchequer income was farmed out (see below, pp. 202 ff.) but it was necessary each year for the *prosecutor* to purchase a series of writs at the exchequer, without the production of which the farmed revenues would not be paid.   [2] See below, p. 196 and n. 7.

[3] The numerous writs of privy seal addressed to the keeper of the great wardrobe and the wardrobe accounts themselves testify to the fact that the annual distribution of robes and furs was usually made at or near the Christmas festival. See e.g. P.R.O. E 101/395/2(A), E 101/409/12, E 101/409/6, where the distribution is made 'contre la feste de Noel'; also the statement in the letters patent of 19 November 1448 that from the time of the college's foundation it had been customary for the warden and fellows to receive vestments of cloth and fur annually 'pro habitu suo clericali erga festum Natalis domini...' (*K.H. Cabinet*, no. 104; *Cal. Pat. R.*, 1446–1452, pp. 206–7). Christmas appears to have been the usual time for the distribution of cloth to members of the royal household (see e.g. writs of privy seal of December 1364 for the delivery of cloth to a serjeant at arms and to a valet of the chamber 'contre la feste de Noel', P.R.O. E 101/395/2(A)): it was doubtless from this consideration that Christmas rather than the beginning of the academic year at Michaelmas was chosen for the delivery of robes and furs to the King's Scholars.

[4] See below, p. 196.

[5] See letters patent of 28 September 1334 granting two sets of robes annually to warden Thomas Powys, one lined with fur (*cum pellura*) and the other with linen (*cum linura*), *Cal. Pat. R.*, 1334–1338, p. 28. See also the parchment compotus roll of 1351 (*K.H. Cabinet*, no. 30): 'Prefatus custos computat pro quatuor robis suis, duabus cum linura et duabus cum pellura, videlicet pro una roba estivali cum linura... et pro duabus robis videlicet una cum pellura et alia cum linura... et una roba cum pellura...' (£10 13s 4d). Evidence that silk was sometimes given as a lining is contained in the writ of privy seal of 2 August 1333 whereby the keeper of the wardrobe is ordered to supply warden John de Langtoft with 'drap pour sa robe... et sendal' (P.R.O. E 101/386/18).

[6] On his appointment as warden in 1361, John de Schropham was provided with eight marks a year for his robes: *Cal. Pat. R.*, 1361–1364, p. 116. See the similar arrangements made on the appointments of Thomas Hetersete, Richard Holme and Robert Fitzhugh, *ibid.* 1385–1389, p. 33; 1416–1422, p. 123; 1422–1429, p. 210.

until 1448, the materials for the gowns and fur linings of the Scholars were paid in kind: but as the keeper of the great wardrobe had defaulted in his deliveries for two or three years in the 1440s, warden Robert Ayscogh and the King's Scholars petitioned Henry VI to commute this customary payment in kind into a fixed annual remuneration of forty marks.[1] Their request was granted and given official embodiment in the letters patent of 19 November 1448 in which the resulting exchequer charge was farmed out to the sheriffs of the counties of London and Middlesex, to be paid in two equal portions at Easter and Michaelmas.[2] In 1462, Edward IV transferred this payment to the prior of Barnwell, who was henceforth bound to find the stipulated forty marks from the revenues of the farmed royal manor of Chesterton,[3] an arrangement subsequently confirmed in the letters patent of Richard III of 9 February 1484,[4] in those of Henry VII of 18 June 1486,[5] and in those of Henry VIII of 4 March 1510.[6]

In the period before 1448, however, there was one brief interlude of a few years immediately following the foundation of the King's Hall in 1337 when a monetary equivalent for robes was given directly from the exchequer or from a farmed exchequer source.[7] During this phase the college itself was responsible for the purchase of the cloth and for its fair distribution among the Scholars. In 1337–8, 253 ells of cloth were distributed among 35 Scholars;[8] and in 1339–40, 33 Scholars received 249¾ ells.[9] At the distribution of

[1] See the terms of this petition reported in the letters patent of Henry VI of 19 November 1448, *K.H. Cabinet*, no. 104; *Cal. Pat. R.*, 1446–1452, pp. 206–7.

[2] *Loc. cit.*

[3] See letters patent of Richard III of 9 February 1484 reciting the letters of confirmation of Edward IV of 3 February 1462, *K.H. Cabinet*, no. 111; *Cal. Pat. R.*, 1461–1467, p. 103.

[4] *Loc. cit.*

[5] *K.H. Cabinet*, no. 112.

[6] *Ibid.* no. 122 (with great seal) and no. 123 (copy with seal of the King's Hall).

[7] In 1338–9, the college received £41 7s 2d for robes from the abbot of Waltham Holy Cross. Of this sum, £28 11s 6½d was expended on the purchase of cloth. The total outlay, including travelling expenses and the costs of preparing the cloth (e.g. the cost of shearing was 1s a length or *pannus*), came to £37 15s 3½d, leaving a balance of £3 11s 10½d (*K.H. Accts.* I, fo. 22). In 1341–2, £33 19s was received from the exchequer for robes: the total expenditure came to £30 17s 2¼d, leaving a balance of £3 1s 9¼d (*ibid.* I, fo. 54).

[8] *Ibid.* I, fo. 13.   [9] *Ibid.* I, fo. 41.

1341–2, the master and 35 fellows received 261¾ ells;[1] and in 1342–3 269½ ells were distributed among the same number:[2] while in 1344–5, when the number present had risen to 38, 273½ ells were purchased.[3] For the purpose of these distributions, the Scholars were grouped into nine or ten divisions to the members of each of which a different length of cloth was assigned.[4] These lengths ranged from 8½, 8¼ or 8 ells to 5¾ or 5½ ells, each division representing a difference of one quarter of an ell and giving an average of just over 7 ells per Scholar. It is not known exactly upon what principles the divisions were made. The Scholars were certainly not arranged in strict order of seniority, and the multiplicity of division rules out the possibility that they were grouped solely according to their degrees. Perhaps the explanation is that each fellow was allocated a length of cloth suitable both for his academic standing and for his physical size. But when, as was the more normal situation before 1448, the distribution was made from the great wardrobe the lengths assigned were such that every fellow possessed of an academic degree received 9 ells and the remainder, the *scolares* (a term which, in this context and in this context only, denoted fellows who had not yet acquired a degree), were supplied with 7 ells.[5]

The cloth went towards the making of the *roba* (i.e. the *supertunica* or body-coat), a gown or tabard[6] suitable to the degree (some-

---

[1] *K.H. Accts.* I, fo. 39v.

[2] *Ibid.* I, fo. 69v.

[3] *Ibid.* I, fo. 96v.

[4] In 1337–8 and 1344–5 there were nine divisions; in 1339–40, 1341–2 and 1342–3, ten divisions, excluding the warden.

[5] In 1439, 9 ells of cloth were supplied to six masters of arts, six bachelors of civil law and three bachelors of arts; 7 ells to thirteen *scolares* or undergraduates (P.R.O. E101/409/6). In 1444, 9 ells were delivered to one inceptor of civil law, eight masters of arts, five bachelors of canon law, three bachelors of civil law and two bachelors of arts; 7 ells were given to eleven undergraduate *scolares* (P.R.O. E101/409/12). These numbers do not represent the full complements of the King's Scholars in these years since robes and furs were supplied only to those actually resident. For this purpose, it was the duty of the *prosecutor* to furnish a list of names of fellows resident for the year. In one or two instances, the names of Scholars at first included in the wardrobe lists are crossed out, with the explanation 'quia absens' written above.

[6] See e.g. writ of privy seal of 20 December 1330 authorising the issue of cloth for robes and tabards for the master and 43 Scholars (P.R.O. E101/385/4); see, further, witness of receipt of 20 February 1334 by warden Powys of cloth for robes with tabards for himself and 31 Scholars (P.R.O. E101/386/18).

times called a *collobium*)[1] and a hood. The furs were given for the lining or trimming of these garments and the type of fur is often an indication of a Scholar's degree. In the wardrobe distribution lists of 1439 and 1444,[2] the hoods of the inceptor of civil law and the masters of arts were lined with miniver. For this purpose, the inceptor received 32 *ventres*[3] of this expensive fur and the masters of arts 24 each.[4] Although these provisions apply to the members of only one particular college, they nevertheless afford proof of the fact that miniver was commonly used in the first half of the fifteenth century as a lining for the hoods of the Cambridge masters, a point which hitherto appears to have been none too clear.[5] In addition to miniver fur, the inceptor and the masters of arts were supplied with *fur' de popull'* (or *papull'*).[6] References to this kind of fur are found in the Merton College accounts for 1342[7] and in the Durham account rolls for 1380–1.[8] Although popel seems to have been in vogue in the fourteenth and fifteenth centuries, its origins remain obscure apart from the possibility, by no means proven, that it may have been a type of squirrel's fur.[9]

Throughout the fourteenth century the legists especially were sup-

---

[1] E.g. on 22 February 1330, William de Brocok witnessed receipt of 7½ ells of cloth for a robe 'cum collobio', P.R.O. E101/385/4; on 23 September 1332, Richard de Wymundeswold received a robe 'cum collobio longo', P.R.O. E101/386/6. On this term, see W. N. Hargreaves–Mawdsley, *A history of academical dress in Europe* (Oxford, 1963), p. 193.

[2] See above, p. 197, n. 5.

[3] 'i caput de xxxij ventr' menev' pur'...': P.R.O. E101/409/12.

[4] 'i caput de xxiiij ventr' men' pur'...': P.R.O. E101/409/6, 409/12. *Ventre* was apparently an area measurement of variable dimensions applied to the white belly patches of animals valuable for their fur (*Du Cange*, VIII (Fr. ed. 1887), 273).

[5] In the draft petition of the University of Cambridge relating to regulations for dress addressed to Henry V *c.* 1415, the kind of fur to be used by regent and non-regent masters in their hoods is not specified; it is merely stated that they may wear 'in suis caputiis fuduraturas de pellura': 'Articuli Universitatis Cantabrigiae', ed. by C. Hardwick, *C.A.S. Communications*, I (1850–9), no. xix, 87. The parliamentary statute of 1533 concerning apparel sheds no further light upon the type of fur to be used. (See Hargreaves–Mawdsley, *Academical Dress*, p. 122.)

[6] The *O.E.D.* defines popel (popil(l), populle, pople) as 'an inferior kind of fur; derivation unknown' (VII, 1119). References are cited ranging from 1327 to 1493.

[7] J. E. T. Rogers, *A history of agriculture and prices in England* (Oxford, 1866), II, 539, where the average cost of one 'furrura de popel' is given as 14s 0¼d.

[8] *Durham Account Rolls* (Surtees Society) (1901), III, 590: 'In una furrura de popill empt' pro d'no Priore 10s.'

[9] From a reference of 1351 quoted in *O.E.D.*

plied with fur of white budge:[1] bachelors in the other faculties as well as all undergraduate members of the Society generally received lambskins.[2] But in the wardrobe lists of 1439 and 1444[3] this distinction is not drawn. On these occasions, every bachelor, irrespective of faculty, was given two white lambskins and every undergraduate Scholar one skin of the same type. This limitation to the use of either budge or lamb's wool was in strict accordance with the university statute *De penulis et pelluris baccalaureorum* of 24 May 1414 which enacted that no bachelor of any faculty, unless of noble family, might use silk or any variety of rich fur for the lining of his hood or tabard.[4]

In the fourteenth and fifteenth centuries, several of the English colleges stipulated the form of dress to be worn by their members: the universities did not at first intervene in these matters beyond issuing from time to time general regulations concerning academic apparel.[5] Like the fellows of Queen's[6] and New College, Oxford,[7] Gonville,[8] Trinity Hall,[9] and King's College, Cambridge,[10] the King's Scholars wore a definite college livery.[11] In the first half of the fourteenth century, the tunics and tabards of the Scholars were of a blue[12] or bluish grey colour.[13] Nothing is known of the colour in the

---

[1] See e.g. writ of privy seal of 20 December 1330 authorising the issue of 'furrures de boge pour chaperons pour cync des ditz Escolers Legistres', P.R.O. E101/385/4; also writ of privy seal of 21 August 1330 whereby Thomas Powys, who was soon to read the Institutes, received budge for his coat and hood, *loc. cit.*; see further writ of privy seal of 23 September 1332 by which Richard de Wymundeswold (D.C.L. by 1338) received fur of white budge for his gown and hood, P.R.O. E101/386/6.

[2] From many examples, see witnesses of receipt by Simon de Bury of 30 lambskins on 26 January 1328, P.R.O. E101/384/2; by Thomas Powys of 27 lambskins on 21 May 1334, P.R.O. E101/386/18; by Richard de Hales of one lambskin on 22 January 1330; and by John Gros of the same on 14 December 1330, P.R.O. E101/385/4.

[3] See above, p. 197, n. 5.   [4] *Camb. Docs.* I, 402.

[5] See the remarks of Hargreaves–Mawdsley, *op. cit.* p. 101.

[6] See Eglesfield's provisions in *Statutes*, I, ch. (4), 14.   [7] *Ibid.* I, ch. (5), 45–6.

[8] *Camb. Docs.* I, 229–30: '...omnes socii Robis unius secte cum longis Tabardis seu Epitogiis talaribus annis noviter singulis induantur...'

[9] *Ibid.* II, 419.   [10] *Ibid.* II, 538–9.

[11] See e.g. writs of privy seal of 20 March 1364, 30 October 1364 and 30 September 1366 directing the delivery of cloth and fur to Scholars upon admission 'de la suite de noz autres escolers': P.R.O. E101/395/2(A), (D).

[12] On 1 September 1326, Aymer Symeon received 7 ells of blue cloth for his livery; and on 23 September 1332, Richard de Wymundeswold, in addition to his doctoral scarlet robe, was supplied with blue cloth for his tunic: P.R.O. E101/382/8, 386/6.

[13] In 1334, Thomas Powys witnessed receipt of cloth of a bluish grey colour (*glaucus*) for robes with tabards for 31 Scholars: P.R.O. E101/386/18.

second half of the century, but in the wardrobe list of 1444 all the Scholars, that is to say, the inceptor of civil law, the masters of arts, the bachelors of civil and canon law and of arts, as well as the under-graduate members of the Society, received lengths of blue material for their robes.[1] That this blue livery was royal livery is proved by the wording of the letters patent of Henry VI of 19 November 1448: here it is reported that since robes have not been delivered for two or three years, a King's Scholar cannot easily fulfil his statutory obligation to attend masses in memory of benefactors, to perform scholastic acts or to appear in public places properly and decently attired '...in habitu clericali *de liberata* [sic] *regia* secundum gradum suum quem in scolis habuit'.[2] It would therefore seem that the Society of the King's Scholars was the only academic body at the English universities to wear the king's livery.

In addition to the annual supply of robes, each Scholar, upon admission, received a bed out of the royal wardrobe: the practice of bed-giving was maintained throughout the fourteenth century but was probably discontinued in the fifteenth.[3] The wording of several of the writs directed to the keeper of the great wardrobe indicates that a frame was supplied along with the materials for a bed: in others, however, the terminology, though ambiguous, suggests that materials alone were given. In one or two cases, these latter are particularised. On 18 February 1332, John de Langtoft, upon his appointment to the wardenship,[4] received a bed with a worsted coverlet, 21 ells of English linen and 12 ells of canvas:[5] for the beds of the ordinary Scholars the doles were somewhat less. In 1330, Richard de Hales and John Gros each received one worsted coverlet, 12 ells of linen and 8 ells of canvas:[6] the same lengths of material were supplied to Thomas Wasteneys on 11 December 1332.[7] These measurements appear to have been typical of the first half of the fourteenth century, although there were exceptions as in the case of

---

[1] *Blodius* or *blodeus* is here the adjective translated as blue.
[2] *K.H. Cabinet*, no. 104; *Cal. Pat. R.*, 1446–1452, pp. 206–7.
[3] No evidence has survived for the delivery of beds after the end of the fourteenth century: perhaps by this time a sufficient stock had been accumulated to serve the needs of the Society.   [4] Appointed 8 October 1331.
[5] Wardrobe account of 18 February 1332, P.R.O. E101/386/6.
[6] P.R.O. E101/385/4.
[7] Writ of privy seal of 11 December 1332, P.R.O. E101/386/6.

Terry de Colonia, who was given 14 ells of Paris linen in place of the usual 12.[1] The wardrobe accounts and writs of privy seal of the second half of the century do not normally specify the materials:[2] but one such writ of 18 January 1387[3] details the items delivered to Richard Maudeleyn when first admitted as a King's Scholar.[4] In this instance, the keeper of the great wardrobe was directed to supply a bed with a coverlet and tester (i.e. a canopy), 8 yards of blanket, 24 ells of linen cloth and 15 ells of canvas. Maudeleyn may have been a specially favoured Scholar, but if these measurements are at all representative it would seem that by the latter part of the century the ordinary materials allowance was almost double what it had been before 1350.

This practice of the provision of a bed to every Scholar is yet another manifestation of the strong nexus between the Society and the court. For it was customary medieval procedure for a member of the royal household to be given a bed from the wardrobe on special occasions, such as knighthood. The wardrobe accounts abound in such cases and the issue of beds to the King's Scholars ought perhaps to be seen as an extension of this peculiar form of household endowment.[5]

On the occasion of his visit to the exchequer in connection with the Society's business the *prosecutor*, as the warden's representative and in accordance with the statutory requirement,[6] presented, for

---

[1] Colonia witnessed receipt of robes and a bed on 11 December 1333, P.R.O. E101/386/18.

[2] They simply record that a bed has been or is to be delivered to a Scholar suitable to his estate (*estat*) upon his first entry (*pour son primer(s) entre(s)*). See e.g. writs of privy seal of 30 October and 20 March 1364, 21 August 1366, 17 and 18 October 1368 and 9 November 1369, P.R.O. E101/395/2(A), (B), (D), (E).

[3] P.R.O. E101/401/10.

[4] Admitted 20 August 1386. In this case, there was a delay of about five months between admission and the issue of the writ for robes and a bed.

[5] In this matter of the provision of beds, the English kings of the fourteenth century might possibly have been influenced by continental example. For although English college founders (apart from the king) do not appear to have practised this highly utilitarian form of endowment, there can be no doubt that several of the Paris founders were in the habit of supplying their bursars with well-equipped beds. (Details are given in Gabriel, *Ave Maria College*, p. 96, n. 17.)

[6] 'Statuimus quod quamdiu et quotiens custos...ratione officii...de vadiis receptis nomine Scolarium...compotum ad scaccarium nostrum reddere teneatur, tamdiu et totiens expense per ipsum custodem rationabiliter facte circa dictum compotum fideliter reddendum...' (King's Hall statutes in Rouse Ball, *op. cit.* p. 69.)

the purpose of the external exchequer audit, the carefully compiled account of yearly income and expenditure. The *prosecutor's* business usually lasted from between six to eight weeks;[1] and, as well as being lengthy, it was expensive. Apart from the college's attorney at the exchequer, who received an annual fee of £1 6s 8d,[2] there were also government clerks to be paid: the auditor and his clerk for auditing the warden's account; the exchequer clerk who enrolled the account on the pipe roll; the underkeeper and the doorkeeper of the wardrobe.[3] Further expenses were incurred for the purchase of writs of privy seal and other types of writs necessary for the conduct of the college's affairs[4] and for the provision of breakfasts for exchequer, wardrobe and chancery clerks.[5] Moreover, the cloth for the Scholars' liveries had to be sheared, packed and transported to Cambridge at the Society's expense.[6] And, finally, to these charges must be added the *prosecutor's* maintenance costs during his residence in London. While the costs of all these items are not recorded every year, a comparison of charges over a lengthy period indicates that the *prosecutor's* expenses in London came to about six or seven pounds per annum.[7]

For the greater part of the Society's history, the exchequer allowance was farmed out to several bodies from which the college collected its income upon presentation of the appropriate writs. A brief survey of the *ad hoc* financial arrangements made for the King's Hall will illustrate the numerous shifts and expedients resorted to by the Crown for the maintenance of this royal Society.[8]

It has already been stressed that the original endowment proved wholly inadequate towards meeting the permanent requirements of

---

[1] *K.H. Accts.* VI, fo. 127 v; VII, fos. 9, 117 v, 136.

[2] *Ibid.* V, fos. 76 v, 118 v, 132, 172 v; VI, fos. 21, 105 v, 127 v; VII, fos. 9, 25, 40, 136; VIII, fo. 25.   [3] *Loc. cit.*

[4] *Ibid.* IV, fo. 112 v; V, fos. 93, 105 v, 118 v; VII, fos. 9, 136.

[5] *Ibid.* VII, fo. 99: 'Item in diversis jantaculis factis diversis clericis privati sigilli et garderobe xiijd. ob.'; see also VII, fo. 136; VIII, fo. 7.

[6] E.g. *ibid.* V, fo. 132; VI, fos. 21, 110 v; VII, fo. 9.

[7] Typical annual expenses: attorney's fee £1 6s 8d; attorney's clerk 1s 8d; auditor 6s 8d; auditor's clerk 1s 8d; underkeeper of wardrobe 3s 4d; doorkeeper of wardrobe 1s 8d; clerk of the pipe 6s 8d; clerk's assistant 3s 4d; *prosecutor's* maintenance costs c. £3; miscellaneous (purchase of writs, provision of breakfasts and transport costs) c. £1. Total: £6 11s 8d.

[8] Some of the information about the exchequer revenue has been given by Rouse Ball, *op. cit.* pp. 15–16, 23–4, 42–3 : but all available sources have been independently consulted.

the college.[1] This consisted of the house of Robert de Croyland, the advowson of the church of St Peter, Northampton, together with its chapels and leave to appropriate the same, and an exchequer allowance calculated at the rate of twopence per Scholar per day to be paid from the issues of the counties of Cambridge and Huntingdon.[2] By 1340, it was plain that the sheriff of these counties could not meet this financial obligation and on 1 May of that year £55 of this burden was levied on the abbot of Waltham Holy Cross, who owed this sum to the exchequer for the farm of the town of Waltham: the residue of a cash endowment of £109 10s (i.e. £54 10s) was to be supplied by the sheriff.[3] This arrangement lasted until 1 August 1346 when the sheriff's financial obligation was transferred to the alien priory of St Neots,[4] the remaining £55 to be exacted from the abbot of Waltham as before.[5] By letters patent of 1 December 1351,[6] the financial arrangements of the college were again reorganised. The whole of the sum due from the prior of St Neots and part of the payment due from the abbot of Waltham were now transferred to the abbot of Sautre,[7] proctor of the alien abbot

---

[1] See above, p. 93.

[2] See letters patent of 7 October 1337, *K.H. Cabinet*, no. 8; *Cal. Pat. R.*, 1334–1338, p. 541. On 10 March 1338, the grant of the advowson of the church of St Peter was revoked.

[3] *Cal. Pat. R.*, 1338–1340, p. 511.

[4] The Benedictine priory of St Neots was a dependency of the abbey of Bec-Hellouin. Along with the other alien houses of Bec, it was seized by Edward II in 1324, restored by Edward III in 1327, taken again at the outbreak of the Hundred Years War, and temporarily restored in 1361. In 1370 it was once more in the king's hands, but was given back during the opening years of the reign of Henry IV. Its dependency upon Bec came to an end in 1409 when it received a charter of denization. See W. Dugdale, *Monasticon Anglicanum*, ed. cit. III, 460–84; also M. M. Morgan, 'The abbey of Bec-Hellouin and its English priories', *Journal of the British Archaeological Association*, 3rd series, V (1940), 33 ff.

[5] *Cal. Pat. R.*, 1345–1348, p. 159. The King's Hall derived further financial benefit from the retention of alien houses during the Hundred Years War when, a year later, in order to ease the burden of heavy building costs, the king assigned to the college the sum of £20 which the preceptor of the house of La Maudeleyn in Lokhay, Derbyshire, of the Order of St Lazarus of Jerusalem, was bound to render annually at the exchequer by reason of the yearly tribute due to the superior house in France: *ibid.* pp. 408, 429.

[6] *Cal. Pat. R.*, 1350–1354, p. 190.

[7] The Cistercian abbey of Sautre (Saltrey, Sautrey) in Huntingdonshire, founded in 1147. See Dugdale, *op. cit.* V, 521–6; M. D. Knowles and R. N. Hadcock, *Medieval religious houses* (London, 1953), p. 114.

of Bon Repos, for the keeping of the churches of Fulbourn and Honyngham, and to the prior of the alien priory of Swavesey, Cambridgeshire,[1] and to the burgesses of Scarborough for the farm of the manor of Waldesgrave, so that the abbot of Sautre henceforth paid £40, the prior of Swavesey £33 6s 8d, the abbot of Waltham £7 10s 8d and the burgesses of Scarborough £22 11s, making a total of £103 8s 4d, which remained the exchequer cash endowment until the mid-sixteenth century.

While the total remained constant, the distribution of the finances underwent further adjustment. On 12 May 1355, twenty of the forty pounds due from the abbot of Sautre was transferred to the issues of the counties of Bedford and Buckingham;[2] and on 4 February 1364, the combined revenues due from the alien priory of Swavesey and from Sautre (i.e. £53 6s 8d) were made a direct charge on the exchequer by virtue of the fact that the restoration of peace had withdrawn the priories from the king's hands.[3] Although these arrangements were confirmed at the accession of Richard II,[4] the exchequer obligation was again farmed out: £33 6s 8d was assigned to the abbot of Sautre[5] and £20 to the prior of Barnwell due for the farm of Chesterton.[6] In 1381, this latter payment was transferred to the burgesses of Scarborough.[7] From this date, the distribution of revenues remained fixed and was confirmed by letters patent of 1399[8] and 1413:[9]

Farmed exchequer sources

	£	s	d
Burgesses of Scarborough	42	11	0
Abbot of Sautre	33	6	8
Sheriff of Beds. and Bucks.	20	0	0
Abbot of Waltham Holy Cross	7	10	8
	£103	8	4

---

[1] The Benedictine priory of Swavesey was dependent upon the monastery of St Sergius and St Bachus at Angiers until it was conveyed, towards the end of the fourteenth century, to the Carthusian monks of St Anne near Coventry. Dugdale, VI, pt. ii, 1001.

[2] *Cal. Pat. R.*, 1354–1358, p. 219.

[3] *Ibid.* 1361–1364, pp. 458–9.

[4] *Ibid.* 1377–1381, p. 20.

[5] *Ibid.* p. 259.

[6] *Loc. cit.*

[7] *Cal. Pat. R.*, 1377–1381, p. 602.

[8] *Ibid.* 1399–1401, p. 21.

[9] *Ibid.* 1413–1416, p. 41.

In order to arrive at the approximate total cash income of the Hall, the revenues accruing from its appropriated churches have to be estimated. Such an estimate has to be confined to the fourteenth and first half of the fifteenth century: because of the altered nature of the accounts in the later period it would be impossible to glean reliable information about receipts from appropriated churches. Of the four churches appropriated in the fourteenth century, by far the most lucrative was the parish church of Felmersham in Bedfordshire. Although the advowson of this church with leave for its appropriation was granted in 1342,[1] the appropriation was not effected until 1365–6.[2] From the start, it was the custom of the college to appoint a vicar with stipend (£1 6s 8d per annum)[3] and farm out the rectory at a fee of between forty and fifty marks a year.[4] The annual net income derived from Felmersham ranged from £26 13s 4d to £33 6s 8d,[5] which gives an average sum of about £30. This was substiantially larger than the income realised from Great St Mary's, Cambridge, appropriated to the college in 1343.[6] Although annual receipts varied as much as from £10 to £26, in most years the net income was somewhere in the region of £18.[7] As with Felmersham, the church of Grendon, Northamptonshire, was earmarked for appropriation to the King's Hall in 1342, but was not finally appropriated until 1365–6,[8] after which a vicar with stipend was appointed to administer the clerical work of the parish.[9] From Grendon the college drew a fixed income of twenty-five marks (i.e. £16 13s 4d)

---

[1] See letters patent of 25 July 1342, *K.H. Cabinet*, no. 25; *Cal. Pat. R.*, 1340–1343, pp. 495–6.

[2] See the printed account of expenses relating to the appropriations of Felmersham and Grendon, 1365–6, in Rouse Ball, *King's Hall*, pp. 71–4.

[3] This stipend had definitely become fixed at two marks by 1406–7 and was paid in half-yearly instalments at Michaelmas and Easter (*K.H. Accts.* v, fos. 75 v, 104 v; vi, fos. 7 v, 62, 85, 109, 126). Before this date, the pension was subject to fluctuations.

[4] See examples of agreements made between the seneschals and the two farmers of Felmersham, *ibid.* v, fos. 143 v, 184 v.

[5] *Ibid.* IV, fos. 44, 60 v, 77, 94, 111 v, 130 v; v, fos. 29, 43 v, 59, 92 v, 104 v, 117 v, 170 v; vi, fos. 7 v, 40, 62, 109, 144 v; vii, fos. 7 v, 23 v, 39, 60 v, 78 v.

[6] See letters of confirmation of the bishop of Ely, *K.H. Cabinet*, no. 28.

[7] See e.g. *K.H. Accts.* I, fos. 80 v, 118 v, 119 v, 135; III, fos. 8, 80, 114; IV, fos. 23, 44, 59, 107, 129; v, fos. 28, 43, 58, 92 v, 104, 117 v, 130 v; vi, fos. 6 v, 40, 61 v, 84 v, 108, 144; vii, fos. 6, 23, 39, 59 v, 73, 97 v, 115 v.

[8] See above, n. 2.

[9] *K.H. Accts.* III, fo. 114 v; IV, fos. 25, 130; v, fos. 44, 59, 111 v, 131 v; vi, fos. 19 v, 40; vii, fo. 39 v.

per annum:[1] this sum was more than three times the fixed amount of eight marks (i.e. £5 6s 8d)[2] derived from the parish church of Hintlesham in Suffolk, appropriated to the college some time between 1361–2 and 1363–4.[3] When the combined net revenues from these four churches are added to the exchequer allowance, it would seem that the average annual cash income of the college between the late fourteenth and mid-fifteenth century came to about £170 or £175.

The collection of the farmed exchequer revenues was normally a shared operation involving two or three of the seneschals and occasionally a Scholar who was not at the time an elected officer.[4] Sometimes, it is true, this burden fell upon the *prosecutor* alone,[5] but as the travelling entailed was so considerable it was found necessary in most years to delegate the task. Similarly, the collection of revenues from Grendon, Felmersham and Hintlesham and the delivery of rents due from the college usually lay with one or two of the fellows who might or might not be seneschals at the time. Great St Mary's was a case apart, for its affairs relating to the college were conducted through two *procurators* elected annually from among the fellows: in some years, both of these officers were seneschals;[6] in

[1] See e.g. *ibid.* v, fos. 75v, 105, 117v, 131v, 149; vi, fos. 7, 19v, 40, 62v, 85v, 109v, 126v, 145; vii, fos. 7v, 24, 39v, 60v, 78v, 116v, 134v.

[2] See *ibid.* ii, fo. 125v; iv, fos. 30, 44, 60, 77, 96, 130; v, fos. 43v, 59, 74v, 92v, 104v, 117, 131, 149, 170v; vi, fos. 7, 19v, 40, 62, 85, 109, 144v; vii, fos. 6, 23.

[3] In the account for 1361–2, the expenses incurred by the master and two fellows journeying to Hintlesham to take possession of the church are recorded (ii, fo. 53); so also are the expenses of Richard Hamecotes and William Wysbech during a visit to London to expedite business concerning the appropriation (ii, fo. 56). In 1363–4 occurs the first reference to the farmers of the church (ii, fo. 74) and in the following year the first receipts were drawn (ii, fo. 100). On 27 April 1387, however, the bishop of Norwich awarded all the rights pertaining to the church to John Hadlee, alderman of the city of London, subject to the payment to the college of an annual pension of eight marks until such time as it should be in receipt of ten marks from another source. Thus, from 1387 onwards, the King's Hall received a fixed annual income of eight marks. A copy of the bishop's award is preserved in *K.H. Cabinet*, no. 44 (7).

[4] See e.g. *K.H. Accts.* v, fos. 76, 93, 132, 150, 172; vi, fos. 8v, 20v, 41v, 63v, 86, 110, 127v, 145v; vii, fos. 40, 99.

[5] E.g. in 1428–9 the *prosecutor*, William Elot, is the only fellow named in connection with the collection of all the revenues: *ibid.* vii, fo. 117.

[6] E.g. in 1365–6 John Lirlyng and Simon Multon each combined the offices of seneschal and *procurator* of Great St Mary's (*K.H. Accts.* ii, fo. 123); in 1427–8, these dual functions were performed by William Elot and John Petit (*ibid.* vii, fo. 97v); and similarly by John Druell and John Pyville in 1429–30 (*ibid.* vii, fo. 134v).

others, we find one steward acting jointly with a fellow who held no further administrative appointment;[1] and occasionally, neither of the *procurators* was a seneschal.[2] These officers were immediately responsible for all income and expenditure relating to the church and for which they accounted directly to the six guardians of the common chest. But the special case of Great St Mary's apart, the general procedure was that sums collected from all sources were received by the *prosecutor* and handed over by him to the other five stewards for deposition in the chest, a bill of indenture being drawn up testifying to the payment of these sums on specified dates.[3]

The other five guardians were responsible for the work of internal administration which, in English colleges, would now be concentrated in the hands of junior bursars, stewards and numerous college committees. Two of the guardians were elected seneschals of the bakehouse (*senescalli pistrine*) and exercised authority over that department and its sub-departments, the brewery and the mill; two were elected seneschals of the kitchen (*senescalli coquine*) with jurisdiction over the kitchen and the vegetable and fruit garden attached; and the remaining guardian served as seneschal of the pantry or butler's department (*senescallus promptuarii*).[4] The stewards exercised a general supervision over the domestic staff and each was concerned with the provisioning and stocking of his allotted department. For example, it was the duty of the seneschals of the bakehouse to contract for the purchase of sufficient quantities of wheat and malt barley to maintain the Society in bread and ale throughout the year and for the necessary fuel required in the baking and brewing

---

[1] E.g. in 1428–9 John Pyville, seneschal, acted with William Waynflete, who was not one of the stewards that year (*ibid*. VII, fo. 115 v); in 1430–1 seneschal Pyville served with John Garland, not then one of the stewards (*ibid*. VIII, fo. 5 v).

[2] E.g. none of the *procurators* in 1425–6 and 1426–7 (Thomas Hesill, John Sutton (both years) and John Pyville) were seneschals (*ibid*. VII, fos. 59 v, 73).

[3] One of these indentures has survived: it belongs to the early fifteenth century and testifies to the fact that Thomas Waryn, *prosecutor ad forinseca*, has, on various dates, handed over to the seneschals the revenues collected from all sources with the exception of Great St Mary's. The indenture is inserted between folios 58 and 59 of vol. IX of the *K.H. Accts*.

[4] All these offices are for the first time set against the names of the seneschals at the opening of the Michaelmas account of 1444–5 (x, fo. 82). From numerous references scattered throughout previous accounts, it seems clear that the general distribution of offices specified in 1444–5 had been in operation from the second half of the fourteenth century.

processes; similarly, it fell to the seneschals of the kitchen to buy the other food items, such as fish, spices and seasonings, used in the preparation of the fellows' meals; and the steward of the butler's department was charged with the custody and renewal of the stock of plate and napery used in the hall. The available evidence indicates that there was a tendency for seneschals to specialise in one office over a number of years with perhaps short relief periods in another department.[1] But to think in terms of a rigid division of function would be to misunderstand the essential *ad hoc* character of this medieval Society: for clearly the seneschals were not strictly limited to the business of their own special departments as each, on occasion, might act for any of the others.[2]

Before 1450, the King's Hall seneschals did not receive remuneration for their services but were required by statute to regard administrative office as an obligation to be undertaken willingly by whomsoever the Society in its wisdom should deem to elect.[3] In the course of the latter half of the fifteenth century stipendiary payments were gradually introduced, and from 1499–1500 onwards every seneschal was in regular receipt of a salary of 4s a year payable at Christmas.[4] Beginning apparently in 1505–6, there was added an annual allowance of 2s *pro piliis*, which can perhaps best be rendered

---

[1] E.g. John Pyville, who with the exception of three years (1429–30, 1430–1, 1434–5) served as seneschal from 1427–8 to 1438–9, acted each year as steward of the bakehouse, apart from 1431–2, when he served as seneschal of the butler's department (VII, fos. 108v, 129; VIII, fos. 39v, 59, 138; IX, fos. 59v, 91); similarly, John Paston, seneschal from 1432–3 until 1443–4 (1436–7 and 1438–9 excepted), served as steward of the bakehouse with the exception of one year, 1435–6, when he acted as seneschal of the kitchen (VIII, fos. 59, 85, 138v; IX, fos. 91v, 122v).

[2] This same fluidity in the division of function has been detected in baronial household accounts. See e.g. the remarks of M. W. Labarge, *A baronial household of the thirteenth century* (London, 1965), especially pp. 54, 63–4.

[3] 'Statuimus si...contingat aliquem...de scolaribus...ad aliquod officium...seu ad aliaque ipsius Domus negotia prosequenda eligi, nominari aut deputari...quod non liceat sic electo...quomodolibet recusare...' See statutes in Rouse Ball, *op. cit.* pp. 67–8. At Cambridge, stipends for fellows holding administrative posts first occur in the King's College statutes (*Camb. Docs.* II, 525, 527). At Oxford, stipends are recorded in the Oriel and New College statutes (*Statutes*, I, ch. (3), 15, ch. (5), 37, 38, 82–3). Rates of payment to college officers are recorded in the New College Bursars' Rolls where there is an exact correspondence with the statutory levels: see e.g. the Bursars' Rolls of 1394–5 and 1415–16, preserved in New College, Oxford.

[4] *K.H. Accts.* XIX, fos. 147, 178; XX, fos. 28, 150v; XXI, fos. 37v, 70v, 124v, 157v; XXII, fos. 65, 80v; XXIII, fos. 25v, 69v, 97v, 125, 160v, 193v; XXIV, fos. 27, 98, 154v, 179; XXV, fos. 33, 73v, 144v; XXVI, fos. 32v, 71v, 112v, 150, 196v.

in English as 'cap money' and was paid in September during Stourbridge Fair.[1] In all, then, the seneschal of the sixteenth century
received his expenses and the rather niggardly salary of 6s per
annum. This cannot have represented much more than a token remuneration and implies that the real guiding principle behind administrative service was still the appeal to the individual's sense of duty
despite the nominal adoption of the concept of salaried office. The
financial position of the *prosecutor ad forinseca* is harder to determine.
From at least the late fifteenth century, this key official was allocated
a fixed stipend of 6s 8d per annum.[2] In several of the years of the
sixteenth century, it was supplemented with the aforementioned
sums to which every seneschal was now entitled, thus bringing his
meagre salary up to the more respectable level of 12s 8d: nevertheless, in a significantly large number of years there was no supple-
mentation, so that only the basic fee was given; and the evidence,
clear-cut and unambiguous in itself, provides no clue to why the
office of *prosecutor* was subject to these puzzling differences in rates of
payment.[3]

The vice-mastership was not in itself a stipendiary office, but from
time to time the vice-master acted as *prosecutor ad forinseca* for the
year and in this capacity received the accompanying fee.[4] His
principal functions appear to have been to co-ordinate the administrative work of the seneschals and to convoke and preside over
meetings of the college. He was normally styled *locum tenens
magistri* (*custodis*) and in one document of 1452 he was also designated
presidens of the King's Hall.[5] Nothing is known definitely about the
process of his selection. If he had been democratically elected by
the Society, this would almost certainly have been registered in the
accounts. A more likely inference is that he was chosen by the
seneschals after consultation with the master. In some years, the vice-
master was himself one of the elected stewards,[6] although this was

---

[1] *Ibid.* xx, fo. 116; xxi, fos. 37v, 70v, 118v, 156v; xxii, fos. 65, 80v; xxiii, fos. 25v,
44v, 97v, 160v, 193v; xxiv, fos. 27v, 98, 154v, 179; xxv, fos. 33, 73v, 144v;
xxvi, fos. 32v, 71v, 112v, 150.

[2] *Ibid.* xv, fo. 128; xvi, fo. 74v; xix, fo. 147.

[3] Payments to the *prosecutor* will be found in most of the references given above,
p. 208, n. 4.   [4] *K.H. Accts.* xxii, fos. 38v, 80v; xxiii, fo. 97v; xxv, fo. 33.

[5] *K.H. Cabinet*, no. 130.

[6] E.g. John Hall combined the offices of vice-master and seneschal in 1452–3 and
William Buckmaster did so in 1534–5.

more the exception than the rule. As the masters of the college became increasingly non-resident after the fourteenth century,[1] the vice-master must then have emerged as the chief *de facto* dignitary in the day-to-day life of the Society.

The jurisdiction of the stewards did not extend to the administration of the two private loan chests[2] instituted by fellows of the college. The earlier of these, the Berkyng Chest, was established about the middle of the fourteenth century from a sum left for this purpose by Thomas de Berkyng, fellow from 1337 to 1349.[3] As the chest is known to have contained £67 3s 4d in March 1389,[4] the original capital endowment may well have been one hundred marks (i.e. £66 13s 4d). This was more than three times the value of the loan chest founded by John Dunmowe, fellow from 1395 to 1412, who left £20 in his will for the establishment of a chest after the manner of that of Berkyng:[5] in 1448–9, the capital endowment was still £20, of which £11 3s 4d was in gold and silver.[6] Before the institution of these private chests, loans were made to the fellows from the funds of the common chest. In 1342–3, for instance, no fewer than twenty fellows borrowed sums ranging from 5d to 1s 6d: the money was borrowed in the forty-first week of the year to enable the Scholars to settle arrears in commons before the Long Vacation period.[7] On this occasion, no charge or pledge was exacted. But judging from another list of the same year, it appears that when money was borrowed for purposes other than the payment of commons a standard charge of 1s was to be exacted if the sum loaned was not repaid by a specified date.[8] After the establishment of the

[1] See below, p. 281.

[2] For a list of medieval Cambridge university and college loan chests see G. Pollard, 'Mediaeval loan chests of Cambridge', *B.I.H.R.* XVII (1939–40), 113 ff.; for a more general discussion on Cambridge university chests see S. M. Leathes, ed., *Grace Book A* (Luard Memorial Series, Cambridge, 1897), xlii–xliii.

[3] Emden, *B.R.U.C.* p. 56. It is only an assumption that the chest was established soon after Berkyng's death. The earliest reference to this chest that I have found in the accounts is for 1363–4 (II, fo. 70) where it is stated that £5 was extracted 'principio anni de cista de Berkyng'.   [4] *K.H. Accts.* III, fo. 28.   [5] *Ibid.* V, fo. 144v.

[6] See the indenture of 12 February concerning the administration of the chest, *K.H. Cabinet*, no. 147.

[7] *K.H. Accts.* I, fo. 64v. Most of the loans were for 6d or 1s.

[8] *Ibid.* I, fo. 69. Under the heading 'Debitores ciste de pecunia eis mutuata' is a list of fellows against whose names are set the sums borrowed and the dates by which they are to be repaid under penalty of 1s.

Berkyng Chest, however, no further lists of borrowings from the common chest are recorded in the accounts.

No information has survived about loans made to individual fellows from the private chests: their records and the statutes determining the lending scale and the value of the pledges were not entered in the main accounts but were kept separately by the administrators of the chests and are unfortunately no longer extant. In times of urgent financial need, however, the master and fellows, as a collective body, might borrow from these chests, in which case the loans would be entered in the Society's accounts. On one such occasion, the college borrowed £26 13s 4d from the Berkyng Chest on 6 March 1389 and a further £40 later in the year (leaving only 10s in the chest) in order to defray heavy building costs arising from the construction of the new dining hall.[1]

An insight into the management of these loan chests is afforded by two isolated indentures of 1429–30 and 1448–9.[2] From these documents, it is clear that each chest was administered by three keepers who, as a body, were quite distinct from the six seneschals,[3] although individual fellows might serve in both capacities. The indentures reveal that new keepers were elected for both chests on 12 February of each year; and that before the new keepers took office the accounts of the retiring guardians were subjected to a careful audit by three fellows, elected auditors for this purpose. Only after the outgoing keepers had been acquitted by the auditors and a statement of outstanding loans handed to their successors were the new keepers permitted to enter upon their charge. These arrangements are similar to those prescribed for the administration of the Michaelhouse private loan chest,[4] founded *c.* 1380 by William de Gotham, master of that college in the late fourteenth century.[5]

---

[1] *Ibid.* III, fo. 28.

[2] See indentures relating to the Berkyng and Dunmowe Chests, *K.H. Cabinet*, nos. 144, 147.

[3] Of the retiring keepers of the Berkyng Chest in 1429–30 one, William Hull, was also a seneschal that year; of the new administrators William Elot alone was a steward (*ibid.* no. 144). Two of the outgoing guardians of the Dunmowe Chest in 1448–9, Henry Cossey and John Garland, were seneschals, as were two of the new keepers, Nicholas Druell and John Fylay (*ibid.* no. 147). In 1388–9, none of the three administrators of the Berkyng Chest (James Walsingham, William Rolf and John Essex) was a seneschal (*K.H. Accts.* III, fo. 28).   [4] A. E. Stamp, *Michaelhouse*, p. 34.

[5] Occurs as master in Otryngham's list in 1369 and 1379 (Stamp, p. 49).

One of the main tasks of the King's Hall seneschals was to contract annually for the items of food, fuel and building materials required throughout the year. With the exception of wheat and malt barley, most of the food provisions were bought at Stourbridge Fair, which, in the fourteenth century, was the largest and most important in England.[1] Something of the range of goods offered for sale is reflected in the diversified nature of the purchases: from the fair the Society bought several varieties of fish, such as hard fish (*piscis durus*), salt fish (unspecified), ling (*lengis*), sperling (a kind of sprat), stockfish (or croplyng), salmon, eels and barrels of red and white herring; spices such as saffron, currants, raisins, figs, pepper, rice, cloves, almonds, cinnamon and mustard seed; and other miscellaneous items such as onions, peas, salt and occasionally live oxen and cows.[2] Although unspecified, it is very likely that most of the domestic articles and utensils were purchased from the extensive choice of hardware goods displayed on the Stourbridge booths.

While there is no information concerning the business relations between the seneschals and the Stourbridge dealers, the King's Hall accounts furnish copious details of contracts made between representatives of the college and farmers and merchants of Cambridgeshire and surrounding districts for the supply of wheat, malt barley, hay and turves, sedge, coal and wood for fuel.[3] The general procedure followed was that an *obligatio* or binding agreement was drawn up covering the purchase and delivery of the goods: this stated the name of the dealer, the quantity of the commodity required, the projected date of delivery and the terms of payment. A copy of the *obligatio*, the *exemplar*, was taken and both this and the original contract were normally deposited in the common chest. Generally speaking, contracts were made about one to five months in advance

---

[1] For an account of Stourbridge Fair see Rogers, *Agriculture and prices in England*, I, 141–4; also C. Walford, *Fairs, past and present* (London, 1883), pp. 54–163; see further L. F. Salzman, *English trade in the middle ages* (Oxford, 1931), pp. 144–5, 157. The fair, which was opened on 18 September and lasted three weeks, was held under the authority of the corporation of the town of Cambridge.

[2] Since references are copiously distributed over 26 volumes, they are too numerous to specify here.

[3] The accounts provide relatively full details of at least 284 contracts for wheat, 250 for malt barley, 50 for turves, 15 for sedge; and give more limited information about a sprinkling of hay, coal and wood contracts.

of the delivery date.[1] Sometimes the college gave payment in full shortly after the agreement was made; sometimes in part at the time of the *obligatio*, with full payment upon delivery; and sometimes withheld it until a specified date or made it over in a series of instalments. In a sizable number of cases, a guarantor or *fideiussor* is named who was either supplied by the dealer or furnished by the college.[2] The responsibility for the provision of the guarantor or sponsor appears to have been determined according to how the weight of obligation was distributed between the contracting parties. Although there are apparent inconsistencies, it seems to have been general practice that if the college made full payment at an early stage, the obligation lay with the dealer to find a guarantor to stand surety for the delivery of the goods (or a monetary equivalent); but that if the obligation lay with the college to make payment after the delivery of all or the greater part of the consignment, the *fideiussor* was normally one of the contracting seneschals.[3] In the former case, it was customary for a dealer to act as guarantor in a contract involving one of his colleagues,[4] who would not always necessarily

[1] Delivery dates were normally fixed at saints' days and festivals. Among the most common were: Michaelmas, All Saints', the feasts of St Martin and St Andrew, Christmas, the Purification, Easter, Pentecost and the feasts of the birth of St John the Baptist and of St Peter ad vincula.

[2] For *fideiussores* of wheat, malt barley and turf contracts see e.g. *K.H. Accts.* IV, fo. 120v; V, fos. 2, 70v, 85v, 100v, 112v, 125v, 142, 163v; VI, fos. 52, 120v, 137v; VII, fos. 8, 51v, 70v, 128; VIII, fos. 17, 83; XII, fos. 53, 147v; XIII, fo. 114v; XIV, fo. 56; XV, fos. 15, 25, 51; XVI, fos. 64, 95; XVII, fos. 69, 93; XVIII, fos. 20, 145; XIX, fos. 95, 168v; XX, fos. 112v, 137; XXI, fos. 59v, 113v; XXII, fos. 27v, 28; XXIII, fos. 21, 60v; XXIV, fos. 25, 95, 150v, 176v. It is possible that *fideiussores* were appointed for all college contracts. When entering details from the original contracts into the Society's accounts, the primary concern would have been with quantities, costs and delivery dates. Thus, the fact that *fideiussores* are sometimes specified and sometimes omitted perhaps indicates nothing more than inconsistent copying practice.

[3] E.g. *K.H. Accts.* V, fos. 112v, 142; VI, fo. 120v; VIII, fos. 17, 83; XIX, fo. 168v; XXIV, fo. 95, where it is known that a seneschal acted as *fideiussor*. Exceptions do occur. In 1413–14, John Bateman, described as 'socius collegii' and not a seneschal that year, acted as guarantor of a wheat contract made with Roger Trot of Harlton (V, fo. 85v); similarly, magister Sawser and magister Sylvester, ordinary fellows of the college, were *fideiussores* in contracts of 1475–6 and 1491–2 respectively (XV, fo. 51; XVIII, fo. 145); and in 1416–17, ex-fellow Robert Attilbrigge, who had resigned in 1397, is named as guarantor of a wheat contract made with Robert Grenlane (VI, fo. 52).

[4] E.g. *ibid.* V, fo. 163v; VI, fos. 52, 137v; VII, fos. 8, 128; XIX, fo. 95; XX, fo. 138; XXIII, fo. 21; XXIV, fo. 95.

be of the same parish.[1] Sometimes a close relative, a brother or a father, served as *fideiussor*[2] and, from time to time, two or more guarantors were appointed.[3] Where the college made a joint contract with two parties, it was usual for one of the dealers to act as sponsor for the other.[4] When the weight of obligation lay with the college, it is unlikely that the contracting seneschal acted as King's Hall representative in his capacity as *fideiussor* since the Society, as a royal foundation, could not presumably be sued for breach of contract.[5] For this reason, it would have been necessary for an officer of the college to take upon himself personal liability for default of payment.[6]

Without exception, wheat, malt barley and turf contracts were made with farmers and dealers of Cambridgeshire and the Isle of Ely. Wheat was purchased from at least forty parishes,[7] enclosing an area bordered on the east by the parishes of Burwell, Cheveley and Brinkley, on the west by Elsworth, Eltisley and Croydon cum Clopton, on the north by Haddenham and Stretham, and on the south by Balsham, Babraham, Stapleford, Shelford, Shepreth and Orwell. The malt barley area was equally extensive, comprising in all forty parishes[8] and extending on the east to Burwell, Dullingham

---

[1] E.g. *K.H. Accts.* XII, fo. 147v; XIII, fo. 114v; XIV, fo. 56; XXIV, fo. 95v.

[2] *Ibid.* XV, fo. 51; XVII, fo. 69.

[3] *Ibid.* XV, fo. 51v; XVI, fo. 64; XX, fo. 138; XXIV, fo. 95.

[4] *Ibid.* XVI, fo. 95; XXIV, fo. 95v: 'et unus est fideiussor pro altro'.

[5] If he had acted as a representative of the college the purpose behind the guarantee would, *ipso facto*, have been nullified.

[6] There is no reference to a broken contract anywhere in the King's Hall accounts. *Fideiussores* do not occur in the series of college building contracts printed by L. F. Salzman, *Building in England*, cit., but several contain a pecuniary guarantee in the form of single (i.e. a pledge by one party only) or mutual (i.e. a reciprocal pledge) bonds of specified amounts for performance of contract. See building contracts for Peterhouse, Queens' and King's College, *op. cit.* pp. 501, 528, 564, 570.

[7] Babraham, Balsham, Bottisham, Brinkley, Burwell, Cambridge (borough), Chesterton, Cheveley, Comberton, Coton, Croydon cum Clopton, Dry Drayton, Elsworth, Eltisley, Eversden, Fulbourn, Girton, Grantchester, Haddenham, Hardwick, Harlton, Haslingfield, Histon, Impington, Kingston, Lode, Lolworth, Madingley, Orwell, Rampton, Shelford, Shepreth, Stapleford, Stow cum Quy, Stretham, Swaffham (Bulbeck and Prior), Teversham, Trumpington, Waterbeach and Wilbraham.

[8] Babraham, Balsham, Bottisham, Boxworth, Brinkley, Burwell, Cambridge (borough), Chesterton, Comberton, Conington, Coton, Cottenham, Dry Drayton, Dullingham, Elsworth, Eversden, Fen Ditton, Fulbourn, Girton, Grantchester, Haddenham, Harlton, Haslingfield, Histon, Impington, Kingston, Little Gransden, Lolworth, Long Stanton, Madingley, Oakington, Orwell, Papworth, Rampton,

and Brinkley, on the west to Conington, Papworth and Little Gransden, on the north to Haddenham, Willingham and Cottenham, and on the south to Balsham, Babraham and Orwell. By contrast, the turf region was far more circumscribed and was confined to the three parishes of Waterbeach, Swaffham and Bottisham lying in a semi-circular arc to the north-east of the town of Cambridge. Sedge was purchased from Cambridge, Ely, Chesterton, Burwell, and Lakenheath in Suffolk;[1] coal from Haverhill and Cowlinge in Suffolk and from Shalford and Radwinter in Essex;[2] and supplies of faggots were occasionally bought from the south-eastern Cambridgeshire parishes of Stetchworth, Dullingham, Burrough Green and Brinkley.[3] Hay was obtained from a variety of places including Grantchester and Boxworth.[4]

Examination reveals that of the forty 'wheat' parishes, the college contracted most regularly with dealers from Swaffham, Madingley, Comberton, Burwell, Grantchester, Fulbourn, Dry Drayton, Bottisham, Elsworth, Coton, Wilbraham, Histon, Chesterton, Babraham and Haddenham. Of the forty 'malt barley' parishes, Grantchester, Chesterton, Histon, Fulbourn, Oakington, Elsworth, Burwell, Swaffham, the borough of Cambridge, Wilbraham, Trumpington and Haddenham furnished the principal sources of supply. A noticeable difference in purchasing procedure was that whereas the year's quota of wheat was generally derived from several parishes, there was a tendency to contract for much larger quantities of malt barley from dealers of the same parish. Longstanding business relations with dealers in wheat, malt barley and turf, sometimes extending for periods of up to ten and fifteen years, were by no means uncommon.[5]

Stow cum Quy, Swaffham (Bulbeck and Prior), Teversham, Trumpington, Wilbraham and Willingham.

[1] *K.H. Accts.* II, fo. 136; IV, fo. 120v; V, fos. 85v, 124v; XIX, fos. 68, 125v; XX, fo. 19; XXI, fos. 58v, 113; XXV, fo. 31v; XXVI, fo. 188.

[2] *Ibid.* XVIII, fos. 19, 65, 113v; XIX, fo. 133v; XXI, fo. 58v.

[3] *Ibid.* V, fo. 112v; VII, fos. 24, 91v; XVIII, fo. 113v; XX, fo. 136v; XXII, fo. 60.

[4] *Ibid.* XVI, fo. 62v; XXVI, fo. 70.

[5] E.g. the college contracted regularly with William Amory of Waterbeach for turf between 1403–4 and 1414–15 (IV, fo. 120v; V, fos. 70v, 100v, 112v, 124v, 142; VI, fo. 32v); with John Cross(e) of Waterbeach between 1403–4 and 1415–16 (IV, fo. 120v; V, fos. 70v, 100, 112v, 124; VI, fo. 137v); with David Butler of Waterbeach between 1410–11 and 1424–5 (V, fos. 85, 142; VI, fo. 145; VII, fos. 8, 24, 32v, 51v); with John Syd(de) of Waterbeach between 1425–6 and 1435–6 (VII, fos. 70v, 91v, 98v, 146; VIII, fos. 17, 129); with William Crast of Madingley for wheat between

Building materials were drawn from a rather wider area, embracing the counties of Cambridge, Lincoln, Norfolk and Suffolk. In the fifteenth century, loads of stones were brought to the college from quarries in Hinton, Barrington and Burwell.[1] Carters from Cambridge, Stapleford and Hinton were hired for their transport.[2] Among the widely assorted types of worked or shaped stones supplied to the King's Hall are to be found ashlars ('asshelers', regularly shaped blocks of stone used for the outer surfaces of walls or for thin structures, such as parapets),[3] beckets ('bekets', 'bekettes', jamb stops, curved bosses on either side of a door),[4] coprons ('coporones', 'copperons peces', a kind of coping stone or cornice),[5] coynes (angle or corner stones),[6] doblettes (an angle piece like a chevron),[7] docelettes (a kind of worked stone not yet identified),[8] jambs ('champys', 'chambys', side pieces of doorways, windows or fireplaces),[9] jointable ('joyntabyl', probably a kind of thin stone slab),[10] kingstable ('kyngestable', probably another variety of flat stone slab),[11] leggements (a type of thin flat stone),[12] mantel stones ('maun-

---

1403–4 and 1411–12 (IV, fo. 120 v; v, fos. 70 v, 112 v, 142, 163 v); with John Evinsray of Comberton between 1403–4 and 1413–14 (IV, fo. 120 v; v, fos. 70 v, 85 v); and with John Chapman of Hou(w)s between 1402–3 and 1415–16 (IV, fo. 120 v; v, fos. 70 v, 100 v; VI, fo. 137 v).

[1] For details of these contracts see *ibid.* IV, fo. 87 v; v, fos. 124 v, 163; VI, fos. 74 v, 98; VII, fos. 124, 125 v.

[2] E.g. in 1427–8, Thomas Chapman of Cambridge was hired to carry 100 loads of stones from Hinton for a fee of £1 16s (i.e. 4¼/4½d a load), food to be provided midway (VII, fo. 108 v); in 1428–9, John Parson of Stapleford was hired for the carriage of 40 loads of stones from Hinton at the rate of 4½d a load (food not specified, VII, fo. 127 v); in the same year, John Bochrer and Thomas Hunderder of Chesterton agreed to carry 100 loads from Hinton at the rate of 5d a load (VII, fo. 127 v).

[3] Salzman, *op. cit.* p. 88; *K.H. Accts.* VII, fos. 124, 142 v; VIII, fos. 16, 59.

[4] *Ibid.* p. 113; VI, fos. 50 v, 74 v; VII, fos. 125 v, 143 v.

[5] *Ibid.* p. 109; VIII, fos. 32 v, 34.

[6] *Ibid.* pp. 101, 105; III, fo. 24 v; v, fos. 10 v, 163; VI, fos. 50 v, 74 v, 75, 76, 97 v; VII, fos. 107 v, 124 v, 145.

[7] W. D. Caröe, 'King's Hostel', *C.A.S.* (quarto publications), new series, no. 11 (1909), p. 21; *K. H. Accts.* VI, fo. 50 v.

[8] Caröe, *loc. cit.*; VII, fos. 125 v, 143 v; VIII, fo. 34.

[9] *K.H. Accts.* VI, fos. 50 v, 74 v, 75, 75 v, 76; VII, fos. 106 v, 124, 142 v, 143.

[10] Salzman, p. 106; v, fo. 85; VI, fo. 31 v; VII, fos. 106 v, 124 v, 142 v; VIII, fo. 16.

[11] Caröe (p. 21) suggests that kingstable might have been used for steps. The term appears to have been peculiar to East Anglia (Salzman, p. 107); *K.H. Accts.* IV, fo. 12; v, fo. 181 v; VI, fos. 32, 42, 119 v; VII, fos. 106 v, 124, 144; VIII, fo. 33 v.

[12] Salzman, pp. 89, 106; VII, fo. 106 v.

tell', pieces over a chimney),[1] moynells (mullions),[2] scoinsons ('sconchons', 'schowchouns', 'skonchonys', a form of angled stone),[3] serches ('serches', 'seerghys', 'sergh', unidentified),[4] somers ('somers', 'somours', 'somerpecys', pieces of stone supporting the end of a beam),[5] soyles,[6] squarpieces ('squarpeces', unidentified),[7] sqwynchuncrests (angle-cresting or coping stones as on a polygonal turret)[8] and voussoirs ('vowsers', 'vowses', 'vousers', wedge-shaped stones used in the construction of arches).[9] For 'rough walling' purposes, large quantities of 'roghwall' or 'ragstone' (broken stones or rubble) and clunch (white limestone used for filling walls) were bought, the latter mainly from Burwell.[10] Slates were purchased from Stamford in Lincolnshire,[11] timber from Haverhill and Worlington in Suffolk,[12] tiles from Wiggenhall in Norfolk,[13] and lime from Reach in Cambridgeshire.[14] Sand and daub for building appear to have been bought locally.[15]

[1] *K.H. Accts.* v, fo. 162v; vii, fo. 143v.

[2] *Ibid.* vi, fos. 50v, 75; vii, fos. 107v, 125v, 144.

[3] Salzman, pp. 104–5; vii, fo. 144.

[4] *Ibid.* p. 109; iv, fo. 11; vi, fos. 50v, 75; vii, fos. 124, 125v, 142v, 144; viii, fo. 32v.

[5] Caröe, p. 21; v, fo. 84v; vii, fo. 125; viii, fo. 34.

[6] Caröe (p. 21) gives soyl-table as 'the ashlar course between plinth and base-course'; vi, fo. 74v; vii, fo. 124v.

[7] *Ibid.* p. 21; vi, fo. 32; vii, fo. 124.

[8] Caröe, *loc. cit.*; vii, fo. 144.

[9] Salzman, p. 115; *K.H. Accts.* iii, fo. 24v; iv, fos. 10v, 11v, 12; vi, fos. 50v, 74v, 75, 76; vii, fos. 106v, 124v, 142v; viii, fo. 32v.

[10] *K.H. Accts.* iii, fo. 25; iv, fo. 10v; v, fos. 38v, 118v, 162v; vi, fos. 50v, 128; see also P.R.O. E101/348/22, 27, 31. For clunch see v, fos. 85, 161v, 182. Details of contracts for clunch for 1412–13 and 1413–14 are given, v, fos. 85, 182.

[11] Details of 4 slate contracts for 1399–1400, 1411–12, 1412–13 and 1427–8 are given, v, fos. 40v, 163, 182; vii, fo. 107.

[12] For timber contracts see v, fo. 182; vi, fo. 31v; vii, fo. 107.

[13] *Ibid.* v, fo. 85. It was quite common practice for Cambridge colleges to dispose of their surplus building materials among themselves. For example, in 1416–17, the King's Hall purchased 45 crests (i.e. ridge tiles) from Trinity Hall at a cost of 2½d each (vi, fo. 50v): and the accounts of 1410–11, 1411–12 and 1412–13 contain lists of persons or institutions to whom supplies of wall-tiles and lime were sold, among them the college of Michaelhouse and the neighbouring Hospital of St John the Evangelist (v, fos. 143, 165, 182).

[14] *Ibid.* vii, 125.

[15] In 1428–9, a contract was made with Andrew Sharp for digging 100 loads of sand 'iuxta Castrum' (presumably Cambridge castle) for 5s (vii, fo. 127v).

INTERNAL ARRANGEMENTS RELATIVE TO
ENTERTAINMENTS; STAFF AND SERVANTS;
STUDIES AND THE LIBRARY

The fellows, pensioners, guests, private servants and perhaps also the
liveried domestic servants ate together in the hall. By 1353, there
were at least two tables, a high table (*alta tabula* or *mensa*) and a table
for the servants (*tabula servientum*).[1] In an indenture of 1405–6, however, secondary tables are now mentioned in addition to the principal
one.[2] In 1523–4, the dimensions of two tables newly purchased for
the hall are supplied, each being 16 feet long, 3 feet wide and 2½
inches thick.[3] It is impossible to determine if both of these served as
high tables for the fellows or if one was used as a table for the
servants. At high table, the fellows seem to have been assigned places
fixed in strict accordance with academical status.[4] Linen napkins and
tablecloths with diaper patterns and bearing the stamp or seal of the
college[5] were in use at all the tables.[6] The floor of the hall was strewn
with rushes which were frequently changed and especially for feast
occasions such as All Saints, Christmas, the Purification, Easter,
Pentecost, St John the Baptist, at the celebration of the exequies of
the founder, Edward II,[7] and in preparation for a royal visit.[8] The
regular entries concerning napkins, tablecloths and rushes for the

[1] See indenture of 1353 made between the college and John de Glaston, former
Scholar and then rector of Hintlesham, *K.H. Cabinet*, no. 44 (1). In return for the
surrender of the church of Hintlesham to the King's Hall for one year, Glaston was
to receive a pension of 12 marks and be given a room in the college and commons
for a year with the right to sit at the high table: his clerk was to be granted first
place 'ad tabulam servientum cum clerico Custodis'.

[2] See indenture of 1405–6 made between the King's Hall butler and the college,
K.H. Accts. v, fo. 98 v: 'Item viij mappe pro secundis tabulis...Item vij manuter-
giis pro secundis tabulis...'   [3] *Ibid.* XXIII, fo. 78.

[4] Glaston was to be permitted to sit at the first place after the warden and doctors, a
stipulation which indicates that there were fixed hierarchical seating arrangements.

[5] E.g. *K.H. Accts.* XIV, fo. 6 v: 'Item pro signata [*sic*] mapparum in turri vid.'

[6] See the indenture of 1405–6, *cit.*: 'In primis iij mappe nove panni linei pro alta
mensa...iiij mappe diapr' pro alta tabula...ij manuterg' pro secundis tabulis...
viij mappe pro secundis tabulis...'

[7] E.g. *K.H. Accts.* II, fos. 97, 121; III, fo. 86 v; VII, fos. 100, 118, 137; VIII, fos. 8, 26, 49.
At first a mixture of straw and rushes was used but after 1360 this was superseded
by rushes alone.

[8] E.g. *ibid.* X, fo. 127 (in preparation for a visit by Henry VI): 'In primis pro cirpis in
adventu Regis viijd.'

floor indicate that close and salutary attention was given to matters of cleanliness. This healthy attitude compares favourably with the keen hygienic sense displayed by the founders of the Paris colleges of the thirteenth and fourteenth centuries.[1] Indeed, contrary to popular belief, it seems very probable that medieval academic standards of personal cleanliness were higher than those which prevailed in university colleges from the Reformation to the end of the eighteenth century.[2]

The napery, eating utensils and valuable items of plate set out on the tables came under the immediate jurisdiction of the butler and were stored in chests in his pantry. From time to time indentures were made, with the butler witnessing the delivery of new pieces into his safe keeping and giving detailed inventories of the items in stock.[3] Additions to the latter were made on five or six occasions throughout the year.[4] As with the linen, the communal dishes evidently bore a college mark, for in 1427–8 two marking irons were bought 'ad signand' vasa Collegii'.[5] Identically with the practice in the medieval halls and hostels,[6] the Scholars had to pay for personal breakages or loss: in 1342–3, for instance, Weylond was charged 3d for a broken mortar and Plumpton 4d for breaking a table;[7] and in 1441–2, Robert Swanland paid 3s 4d through the medium of the butler for the loss of a valuable spoon.[8]

The statutes enact that the responsibility for the distribution of the rooms among the fellows rested with the warden.[9] Three surviving lists in the accounts of the early fourteenth century reveal that two fellows were normally assigned to each room but that in the larger chambers three, four or six were to be found.[10] 'Studies' were erected

[1] On this subject see Gabriel, *Ave Maria College*, pp. 225–6.
[2] A similar view with regard to life in upper-class medieval households is expressed by M. W. Labarge, *A baronial household of the thirteenth century*, pp. 26–7.
[3] See indenture of 1405–6, p. 218, n. 2.
[4] Entries for the renewal of stock such as cups, spoons, basins and napery occur under the head of butler's department. See, from a multitude of examples, VII, fos. 118, 137; VIII, fos. 8, 26, 49.
[5] *Ibid.* VII, fo. 100.
[6] Emden, *An Oxford hall in medieval times*, p. 213.
[7] *K.H. Accts.* I, fo. 62.   [8] *Ibid.* X, fo. 24v.
[9] See statutes in Rouse Ball, *King's Hall*, p. 65.
[10] Summaries of these lists are given by Willis and Clark, *Architectural history*, II, 431, 433–4, 435. The first of these lists, dated 1337, has been printed in full by A. E. Stamp, *Admissions to Trinity College, Cambridge*, I, 94–5.

within several of the rooms which, from later analogies, were doubt-less partitioned-off areas commanding a source of light.[1] The increasing need for these 'studies' in the course of the fifteenth century is shown by the fact that some of the entrance dues of newly admitted fellows which would otherwise have gone towards the provision of a breakfast for the members of the Society were now being diverted for the construction of chamber 'studies'.[2] Meals provided by the college might not be taken in private rooms except in the case of illness or by special licence of the master;[3] and no unruly or noisy conduct would be tolerated which might have a disruptive effect upon the studies of neighbouring fellows.[4]

The statutes do not make specific regulations covering the illness of fellows. From the King's Hall accounts, however, it is clear that in the fourteenth century an indisposed fellow was given a varying sum each week designed apparently to pay for the full cost of his commons.[5] At a later stage, in the fifteenth century, a fellow who fell ill was allocated only the minimum statutory commons allowance calculated at the rate of 1s 2d a week:[6] and there are instances where only 1s a week was provided.[7]

Even by medieval standards, Cambridge was notorious both for the insalubrity of its air and for the unhealthiness of its climate. It is therefore not surprising that it was particularly susceptible to the ravages of plague and diseases of the fever variety, and the King's Hall accounts furnish a morbid reminder of these unsavoury features of

---

[1] For a detailed examination of 'studies' at English colleges see Willis and Clark, *op. cit.* III, 304–27; see also the discussion by W. A. Pantin, 'The halls and schools of medieval Oxford: an attempt at reconstruction', in *Oxford Studies presented to Daniel Callus* (Oxf. Hist. Soc., new series, XVI (1964)), 31 ff. at pp. 86–7 and p. 89; see further E. Miller, *Portrait of a college*, p. 26, on the erection of 'studies' at St John's, Cambridge, in the seventeenth century.

[2] In 1439, for example, dominus Thomas Stafford 'fecit studium in camera sua pro commutacione jantaculi', *K.H. Accts.* IX, fo. 93 v; in 1441 there is a similar entry for Richard Laverok: 'Item dñs Ric' Laverok fecit studium in camera sua pro commutacione jantaculi', *ibid.* X, fo. 1 v.

[3] Statutes in Rouse Ball, *op. cit.* p. 65.

[4] *Ibid.* p. 66.

[5] See the varying payments made to John Sechevill, Richard Hales and Philip de Stoke (*quia infirmus*) for a series of weeks in 1338–9, *K.H. Accts.* I, fo. 20 v; also the sickness rates paid to Robert Caumpe in 1394–5, *ibid.* IV, fo. 38 v, when he received 1s 7½d, 1s 8d and 1s 6d for weeks 10, 11 and 12 respectively.

[6] See e.g. the fixed rates of 1s 2d a week paid to fellows during illness, *ibid.* IX, fos. 121 v, 171 v; XIV, fo. 87.   [7] *Ibid.* X, fo. 164 v; XI, fo. 46 v.

the medieval scene. Sixteen of the King's Scholars fell victims of the Black Death in 1349,[1] and during the second visitation of 1361–2 the warden, Thomas Powys, and eight of the fellows died.[2] There is as yet, in the fourteenth century, nothing to suggest that the King's Scholars attempted to take evasive action by retiring from Cambridge to a rural retreat. Most probably this was because plague epidemics of the fourteenth century appear to have embraced widespread areas of the countryside as well as the towns,[3] with the result that the incentive to evacuate would not have been very strong; and indeed, a recent study cannot find evidence of urban evacuation before the first half of the fifteenth century.[4] In the course of this century, however, the pattern of plague outbreaks is seen to change and they begin to assume a predominantly urban character, so that from the mid-fifteenth century onwards a country sanctuary had become a desirable proposition for all who were in the fortunate position of being able to move to regions of comparative safety.[5] This applied no less to the university populations of Oxford and Cambridge, and a fair number of the King's Scholars sought rural refuge during the reigns of the first two Tudors. Little is heard of plague in the King's Hall records for the greater part of the fifteenth century, but between 1498–9 and 1525–6 they provide an intriguing insight into the extent to which Cambridge was subjected to repeated visitations of plague or sweating sickness,[6] with all the attendant miseries of interrupted studies, disease and death which are so poignantly brought home to us in the Cambridge letters of Erasmus.[7] References to plague or sweating sickness are recorded in the accounts of 1498–9, 1499–1500, 1500–1, 1502–3, 1505–6, 1508–9, 1513–14, 1516–17, 1517–18, 1520–1 and 1525–6:[8] a further plague reference is given in 1541–2.[9] At no time during these troubled years did the King's Hall, as a corporate body, go into voluntary dissolution, and

---

[1] Stamp, *Michaelhouse*, I, 99. [2] *Ibid.* I, 101; and above, p. 169.

[3] J. M. W. Bean, 'Plague, population and economic decline in England in the later middle ages', *Econ. Hist. Rev.* 2nd series, xv (1962–3), 423 ff. at pp. 430–1.

[4] *Ibid.* p. 430. [5] *Ibid.* pp. 430–1.

[6] Much interesting information on sweating sickness or the English Sweat will be found in C. Creighton, *A history of epidemics in Britain*, I (Cambridge, 1891), 237–81.

[7] The Cambridge letters of Erasmus have been translated and edited in *Erasmus and Cambridge* (by D. F. S. Thomson and H. C. Porter, Toronto, 1963).

[8] *K.H. Accts.* xix, fos. 143 v, 177, 207; xx, fos. 59, 149, 212 v; xxi, fo. 68 v; xxii, fos. 37 v, 133 v; xxiii, fo. 168 v; xxvi, fo. 172 v. [9] *Ibid.* xxvi, fo. 39 v.

removal from Cambridge was clearly a matter for individual choice. At a rough estimate, perhaps about a third to a half of the fellows would choose to leave the college in plague years for unspecified destinations[1] and sometimes the proportion was seemingly much less.[2] The college does not appear to have had fixed points of retreat to which Scholars could migrate as a group, as did, for example, Merton College, which made use of the Oxfordshire villages of Cuxham and Islip:[3] presumably, each King's Hall fellow made private arrangements. Length of absence varied from a few weeks to as much as five months,[4] with one or two months perhaps the most representative period. As plague and fevers were rampant generally during the warmer months of the year, the evacuations were seasonal and occurred in spring, summer and autumn. In 1513–14, for example, they began in May[5] and in 1525–6 at some time before Easter.[6] Every absent fellow was supported by the college to the extent of 1s 2d a week, his basic commons allowance. No detailed figures can be derived about the mortality rate; but as references to death from plague are only occasionally recorded, it would seem that the practice of evacuation proved to be quite efficacious.

The royal household character of the King's Hall is in no way better reflected than in the unusually prominent place occupied by minstrel entertainments in the life of the Society. For the accounts prove that individual or small groups of minstrels visited the college regularly on the main festivals of the ecclesiastical year. They were especially common on the feasts of the Epiphany, the Purification of the Blessed Virgin Mary, Easter, All Saints, Christmas, and Holy Innocents' Day, and on 5 May to participate in the celebration of the exequies of the founder, Edward II. In point of time the copious references extend from 1342–3 to the final extant account of 1543–4,[7]

---

[1] E.g. in 1517–18, 17 of the fellows left because of the plague and 11 did so in 1520–1 (*K.H. Accts.* XXII, fos. 37v, 133v).

[2] In 1505–6 only 5 appear to have absented themselves and only 6 in 1525–6 (XX, fo. 149; XXIII, fo. 168v).

[3] See P. D. A. Harvey, *A medieval Oxfordshire village, Cuxham 1240 to 1400* (Oxford, 1965), p. 91; also Creighton, *Epidemics in Britain*, I, 283.

[4] In 1513–14, John Barow was provided with commons for five months' absence because of the plague (*K.H. Accts.* XXI, fo. 68v).   [5] *Loc. cit.*

[6] *Ibid.* XXIII, fo. 168v.

[7] See, from a multitude of references, *K.H. Accts.* I, fos. 58v, 146v; II, fos. 3v, 149v; III, fos. 7, 59; IV, fos. 21, 43; V, fos. 26, 117; VI, fos. 19, 125v; VII, fos. 7, 115v; IX,

furnishing a rich fund of material bearing upon the heterogeneous but all too often concealed nature of the indoor secular entertainments commonly staged in this English collegiate institution. An impressively wide compass of medieval minstrelsy is embraced in the diversity of the terms used in the course of these two hundred years: those which most often recur are *ioculator, iugulator, me(i)ne(i)strallus, mimus, histrio, lusor, ludens, tripudians, fistulator, buccinator, tubicens, wayt* and *pleyar*. It is notoriously difficult to separate medieval categories of entertainers the one from the other or to identify each with a particular form of dramatic performance;[1] and these considerations apply equally to the King's Hall material. From the mere occurrence of minstrel terms in the accounts it is not possible to decide if ensemble playing is ever implied as opposed to a series of individual turns. His profound researches on this subject convinced E. K. Chambers that several of the minstrel names, and especially *ioculator, me(i)ne(i)strallus, mimus* and *histrio*, were in fact equivalent terms.[2] He also expressed reservations as to whether or not words such as *mimus, histrio* and *lusor* could justifiably be rendered in English as meaning actor.[3]

But there is now some general agreement that terms of this kind can usually be legitimately translated in the sense of professional or semi-professional actors[4] as long as it is understood that the meaning is fluid and does not embody any precise, technical definition. In the light of this, it is evident that we cannot easily differentiate within the shadowy assemblage of itinerant minstrels who frequented the King's Hall. For the vast majority of them, there is no concrete information concerning their specialities in entertainment: there can be little doubt, however, that *fistulator* (piper), *buccinator* and *tubicens*

---

fos. 37, 66; x, fos. 33, 88; xi, fos. 39, 156; xii, fo. 131; xiv, fo. 6; xv, fos. 94, 112; xvi, fos. 10, 91; xvii, fo. 58; xviii, fo. 104; xix, fo. 187v; xx, fos. 127, 164; xxi, fos. 8, 137; xxii, fos. 18, 74; xxiv, fos. 40v, 117v; xxv, fos. 1v, 119v; xxvi, fos. 39v, 180v.

[1] E. K. Chambers, *The mediaeval stage* (2 vols., Oxford, 1903), II, 230–3.

[2] *Ibid.* II, 232; but see also the qualifying remarks of C. R. Baskervill, 'Dramatic aspects of medieval folk festivals in England', *Studies in Philology*, xvii (1920), 19 ff. at pp. 80–1.

[3] Chambers, II, 185–6 n. 1, 232–3.

[4] G. Wickham, *Early English stages 1300 to 1660* (2 vols., London and New York, 1963), I, 185; R. E. Alton, ed., 'The academic drama in Oxford', in *Malone Society Collections* (Oxford, 1960), v, 35.

(trumpeters) are used meaningfully to denote different kinds of musical performers. Moreover, the expenses for *tripudiantes* are almost invariably connected with the staging of *tripudia*[1] in the Cambridge churches of Great St Mary's and All Saints in Jewry on the days of their respective dedications.[2] As with *me(i)ne(i)strallus* and *ioculator*, it is unclear if *pleyar* is used in a general or a specific sense; but there is every likelihood that the *wayts*[3] of the accounts refer to troupes of minstrels in the service of the municipal corporation[4] and are probably synonymous with the *histriones ville* which appear with great regularity in the records of the college. Like *lusor*, *ludens* is a fifteenth- and sixteenth-century term[5] and occurs twice in the accounts in entries for 1490–1 and 1520–1.[6] It usually carries the specific meaning of actor but Chambers has found evidence to show that it may sometimes be employed in a more general sense.[7]

Apart from these small and presumably unattached groups of itinerant minstrels, the college received visits from parish, municipal, royal and noble troupes of entertainers: they included the folk players of All Saints parish, Cambridge,[8] the town minstrels[9] (almost certainly a liveried body licensed by the corporation of Cambridge),[10]

---

[1] A term covering a variety of revels commonly held by the inferior clergy in medieval cathedrals and churches: Chambers, *op. cit.* I, 275.

[2] E.g. *K.H. Accts.* IV, fo. 128; V, fos. 92, 117, 170v; VI, fos. 19, 125v; VII, fo. 115v; XV, fos. 94, 138.

[3] *Ibid.* XX, fos. 69v, 127; XXI, fo. 8; XXII, fo. 18; XXIII, fo. 6; XXIV, fo. 1v; XXVI, fo. 39v.

[4] See the remarks of Chambers, I, 51.

[5] *Ibid.* II, 233.

[6] *K.H. Accts.* XVIII, fo. 104; XXII, fo. 117v.

[7] Chambers, II, 233.

[8] 'Item pro parochianis nostris tripudiantibus ijd.' (1342–3): *K.H. Accts.* I, fo. 59. This entry was included in the series of single-line extracts culled at random from the first volume of the *K.H. Accts.* and printed in *Hist. MSS. Com.*, I, 82 ff. at p. 84. Baskervill cites this entry (*art. cit.* p. 82) as one of the earliest surviving instances of a medieval institution opening its doors to folk players.

[9] E.g. *K.H. Accts.* IV, fos. 43, 92, 93, 110v, 128; V, fo. 170v; IX, fo. 7; XI, fo. 39.

[10] See the remarks of Chambers, I, 51: 'Minstrels are also found, from the beginning of the fifteenth century, in the service of municipal corporations...They received fixed fees or dues, wore the town livery...' Cambridge is not included in Chambers' list of corporations; but, from the King's Hall accounts, it would seem that Cambridge possessed its own troupe of minstrels from at least as early as 1394–5 (the first entry for town minstrels is for this year: 'Item pro ministrallis ville ijs.'; *K. H. Accts.* IV, fo. 43).

the king's household minstrels,[1] the queen's minstrels,[2] troupes maintained by the dukes of Norfolk,[3] Exeter[4] and the earl of Salisbury[5] and, in 1342, a local group attached to Richard de Goldynton, a King's Hall commoner and future chancellor of the university.[6] On occasion, individual performers from aristocratic and royal households were sent. In 1468–9, for example, an unspecified entertainment was given in the college by a *mimus* of the duchess of York;[7] and in 1532–3, the college expended 2*s* 6*d* for the services of the king's conjuror (*prestigiator Regis*),[8] perhaps identifiable with *braunden the kyngs jogular* on whom 2*s* 11*d* was spent two years later.[9]

The most lavish feast occasions of the year involving minstrels were undoubtedly those which took place over the Christmas period and especially the one held on Holy Innocents' Day. At this festival, the company of fellows and pensioners might be augmented by the invited presence of townsmen, university dignitaries, tenants of the college, friars and other members of the medieval floating population. The expenditure incurred was often quite considerable. In 1468–9, the entertainment bill for performers and guests combined came to £2 2*s* 9*d*, accounted for as follows: £1 12*s* 5*d* for food and wine for the mayor of Cambridge, twelve townsmen and their retinue; 4*s* for the services of *histriones*, *lusores* and *mimi* with a like sum for King's Hall tenants and their wives; 2*s* for domestic servants;

---

[1] See *K.H. Accts.* IX, fo. 7 (1436–7): 'Item pro histrionibus regis iijd.'; x, fo. 33 (1442–3): 'Item in expensis ministrallorum Regis et Comitis Sarum is. xd.; in regardo et prandio ministrallorum Regis is.'; XXIV, fo. 40v (1529–30): 'Item in regardo lusoriis [*sic*] regiis xxijd.'; XXV, fo. 45v (1535–6): 'Item pro mimis regiis xxd.'; XXV, fo. 81v (1536–7): 'Item lusoribus regiis iiijs. viijd.'; XXV, fo. 119v (1537–8): 'Item pro lusoribus regiis in regardo vs.' In 1500–1, a troupe of the king's musicians gave a performance in the college: 'Item pro buccinatoribus domini regis ijs.' (XIX, fo. 187v). There are also various payments to individual royal minstrels (e.g. IV, fo. 58; XIX, fo. 187v).

[2] *Ibid.* x, fo. 88 (1444–5): 'Item in prandio trium histrionum Regine vid. Item in reward' eisdem xiid.'

[3] *Ibid.* XI, fo. 39 (1448–9): 'Item in repastis mimorum ducis norfolchie et histrionibus ville vs. ijd.'

[4] *Ibid.* XI, fo. 156 (1453–4): 'Item remuneratum est histrionibus ducis Excestre iiijd.'

[5] See above, n. 1.

[6] *K.H. Accts.* I, fo. 70v: 'Item liberabantur menestrallis in communibus Magistri Ricardi goldington iijs.' For Goldington see below, p. 279.

[7] *Ibid.* XIV, fo. 6v: 'Item in repastis mimi ducesse Eboraci.'

[8] *Ibid.* XXIV, fo. 117v: 'Item prestigiatori Regis ijs. vid.'

[9] *Ibid.* XXV, fo. 1v: 'Item to braunden the kyngs jogular ijs. xid.'

1s for the university bedels and another for the porterage of organs to the college.[1] Perhaps the expenses for the Holy Innocents' feast are untypically high this year but they do give some indication of the lavishness and scale of the entertainments which this secular-minded and pleasure-loving Society could stage as the occasion demanded.

The accounts unfailingly record the expenditure incurred for the payment of fees to minstrel entertainers or for the provision of their meals, although it is often impossible to differentiate between fees and maintenance. It would be rash to generalise with any hope of certitude but a typical payment to an individual minstrel for a single performance might be somewhere in the region of 6d to 8d, comprising 2d or 3d for refreshments and 4d or 5d for his reward or fee. Visiting groups of two, three or four minstrels are very common in the fourteenth and fifteenth centuries,[2] a circumstance which firmly corroborates a recent supposition that it would be misleading to think of the average minstrel troupe at this time as being numerically large.[3] Numbers are rarely indicated in the late fifteenth- and sixteenth-century accounts: this might well point to the emergence of a slightly augmented minstrel grouping although it is fair to add that, with the exception of royal minstrel troupes, the fees paid are not significantly higher. As the sums spent on minstrels are so diverse and the numbers hired so variable, it would not be easy to estimate

TABLE 14

Year	Expenditure on minstrels		Year	Expenditure on minstrels	
	s	d		s	d
1350–1	2	4	1477–8	3	4
1361–2	2	0	1511–12	1	8
1365–6	16	7	1514–15	1	8
1383–4	4	6	1517–18	5	4
1389–90	7	0	1529–30	1	10
1412–13	5	1	1535–6	3	0
1436–7	1	7	1543–4	1	0
1448–9	8	4			

[1] For these expenses see *K.H. Accts.* xiv, fo. 6.
[2] E.g. *ibid.* ii, fos. 121, 138v, 149v; iii, fos. 58v, 59, 87; iv, fos. 21, 58; vi, fo. 125v; ix, fos. 7, 37; x, fo. 88; xi, fo. 39; xii, fo. 131; xvi, fo. 91.
[3] Wickham, *Early English stages*, i, 267.

the annual average expenditure on these performers. Expenditure for a random selection of years (table 14) will illustrate this diversity.[1]

Perhaps the chief historical significance of the entries relating to medieval minstrelsy stems from the consideration that they occur so early and so frequently in the records of an English collegiate institution. While minstrels are found at Winchester College from 1400 onwards,[2] evidence of minstrel entertainments in the university colleges dates largely from the late fifteenth century.[3] But the King's Hall material proves conclusively that rudimentary forms of secular entertainment were staged in at least one English college from the first half of the fourteenth century. Moreover, the presence of diversionary activity of this kind in the King's Hall from its earliest years calls to mind the flavour and atmosphere of the court from which it derived and emphasises the intensely secular nature of this royal foundation, whose statutes enjoin only a minimal stress upon the religious functions of its fellows.[4]

Of equal importance is the evidence relating to the occasional performance of classical plays at the King's Hall in the early years of the sixteenth century. Three entries, belonging to 1503–4, 1507–8 and 1508–9,[5] contain the term *ludi*, which may very well denote a form

---

[1] These figures were compiled from entries in *K.H. Accts.* I, fos. 146v, 148v; II, fos. 53, 121, 121v; III, fos. 7, 97; V, fo. 170v; IX, fo. 7; XI, fo. 39; XV, fo. 138; XXI, fos. 8, 98v; XXII, fo. 18; XXIV, fo. 40v; XXV, fo. 45v; XXVI, fo. 124v.

[2] See the extracts from the *computi* of Winchester College printed in Chambers, *op. cit.* II, 246 ff.

[3] See the assembled evidence for the appearance of minstrels in the Oxford colleges in *Malone Society Collections*, V, *cit.* 40 ff.; see also the evidence relating to the Cambridge colleges in *ibid.* II, pt. ii (ed. G. C. Moore Smith, Oxford, 1923), 150 ff. The ceremony of the 'Boy Bishop' was evidently a regular feature at Winchester, New College, Eton and King's for some time before the introduction of minstrel entertainments (Chambers, I, 364–6).

[4] The only religious duty recorded in the statutes was the obligation on the part of the warden and fellows to celebrate weekly mass for the souls of the founder and subsequent kings of England and for the well-being of the state of the realm (statutes in Rouse Ball, *King's Hall*, p. 65). This contrasts very markedly with the heavy devotional duties imposed by the founders of several of the English educational institutions of the fourteenth and fifteenth centuries (e.g. Eton and King's College, Cambridge; Queen's, New College and All Souls, Oxford). An excellent discussion of this theme is provided by F. Ll. Harrison, 'The Eton Choirbook', *Annales Musicologiques*, I (1953), 151 ff.

[5] *K.H. Accts.* XX, fo. 69v (1503–4): 'Item pro clerico et ludo xvid.'; XX, fo. 164 (1507–8): 'pro mimis xijd. pro ludo xijd.; item lusoribus pro ludo xijd.'; XX, fo. 196 (1508–9): 'Item pro ludo xijd.'

of ensemble playing, although one must remember Chambers' warning that *ludus* embraces a wide variety of revels and does not necessarily imply a dramatic performance.[1] However this may be, there exists unequivocal evidence that a comedy by Terence was staged in the college in 1510–11. The crucial entry reads: 'Item solutum est pro comedia Terencii—vis. viijd.'[2] In 1516–17, there appears a further reference to a production of a play (*ludus*) by Terence, on this occasion staged by the 'boys' of master Thorpe, then vice-master of the college: 'Item in regard' m̄ro thorpe [*sic*] pro ludo puerorum suorum therencii—iijs. iiijd.'[3] It would be reasonable to interpret the 'boys' of this entry as meaning those pupils assigned to Thorpe as tutor. Within the context of the history of English drama these entries are of cardinal importance because they rank among the earliest known references to the staging of classical Latin plays in English medieval colleges.[4] No further references of this nature occur in the accounts before the dissolution of the Society in 1546, entertainment, as previously, being represented by the whole gamut of minstrel terminology. From this circumstance, we may suppose that the pioneer presentation of Terence's comedies was an experimental venture, an exploratory response to the stirrings of the humanist movement which was slowly and sporadically making its impact felt in the English universities in the late fifteenth and early sixteenth century. The actual edition of the comedies used by the King's Hall cannot now be discovered but a wide selection was in European circulation by 1510–11.[5] It might not perhaps be too fanciful to see the college's productions as in some measure the practical outcome of the teaching of the Italian *poeta*, Caius Auberinus, who, in his capacity as a Cambridge lecturer, is known to have lectured specifically on the comedies of Terence at least as early as the 1490s.[6] The comedies appear to have been rela-

---

[1] Chambers, *op. cit.* I, 392–3.   [2] *K.H. Accts.* XXI, fo. 137.

[3] *Ibid.* XXVI, fo. 180v.

[4] See the discussion of early plays in English colleges by F. S. Boas, *University drama in the Tudor age* (Oxford, 1914), ch. I.

[5] See e.g. the editions of Terence listed in *Bibliothèque Nationale*, CLXXXIII (Paris, 1955), 186, and in H. M. Adams' forthcoming *Catalogue of sixteenth-century foreign printed books in Cambridge* under the heading *Terentius (Publius) Afer*.

[6] T. Warton, *The history of English poetry* (3 vols., ed. R. Price, 1840), II, 553; R. Weiss, *Humanism in England during the fifteenth century* (2nd ed., Oxford, 1957), p. 163.

tively new to Cambridge society when these productions were being staged in the King's Hall whereas, at Oxford, congregation registers reveal that they had already become part of the official grammar syllabus in the opening years of the sixteenth century.[1] It is certainly conceivable that the King's Hall did something to stimulate further interest in classical studies in a centre of learning which was even more laggard than Oxford in coming to terms with the impulses of European humanism.[2] And the growing popularity of Terence at Cambridge in the next few years can be deduced from the fact that by at least 1523-4, and possibly earlier, one of the three lectureships instituted by Sir Robert Rede in 1518 was devoted specifically to the study of this author.[3]

The King's Hall was evidently subject to the colourful medieval parish custom of 'hocking'. Hock-tide was a term applicable to the Monday and Tuesday following the second Sunday after Easter.[4] On Hock Monday, the parish women roamed the streets 'hocking' or 'capturing' members of the public with ropes for the purpose of exacting forfeits, usually in the form of money; on Tuesday, it was the turn of the men. The funds raised in this manner were put to the general use of the parish. Between 1480-1 and 1537-8 the King's Hall accounts record a number of payments made to women or 'wyfs' on Hock Monday. It is true that the first four entries, those for 1480-1 and 1483-4, do not actually mention the Hock-tide season and merely itemise sums paid out to 'gaggles of women'.[5] But it is more than likely that these entries are to be associated with those of the sixteenth-century accounts fifty years or so later which

---

[1] On this see J. K. McConica, *English humanists and Reformation politics* (Oxford, 1965), p. 87.

[2] On the beginnings of Cambridge humanism see Weiss, *op. cit.* ch. XI.

[3] See *Grace Book B*, pt. II (ed. M. Bateson, Luard Memorial Series, Cambridge, 1905), p. 114.

[4] On Hock-tide and 'hocking' see Chambers, I, 155-8; J. Brand, *Observations on popular antiquities* (2 vols., revised by H. Ellis, London, 1813), I, 156 ff. at p. 161, n. *d.*; S. Denne, 'Memoir on Hokeday', *Archaeologia*, VII (1785), 244 ff.

[5] *K.H. Accts.* XVI, fo. 33 v (1480-1): 'In gagulis mulierum iiijs.; In gagulis mulierum iiijs.'; XVI, fo. 107 (1483-4): 'Item pro gagulis mulierum iiijs.; Item in gagulis et expensis mulierum iiijs.' *Gagula* is clearly a Latinised form of gaggle (gagul, gagyll, gagulle, gagel, etc.), one of the many artificial collective nouns coined in the fifteenth century and one of the few to survive in common usage as applied to geese or women (*O.E.D.* IV, 9; *Middle English Dictionary*, pt. G, I (ed. S. M. Kuhn and J. Reidy, Michigan, 1963), p. 9, dates 'a gagalle of wymmene' from ante 1450).

always specify that the payments were made to the women on Hock Monday.[1] Presumably, these women or 'wyfs' refer to the collectors of the Cambridge parish of All Saints in Jewry in which the college was situated: men collectors on Hock Tuesday are nowhere mentioned. What then do these payments represent? They may simply record the contributions of the King's Hall towards this annual parish event; on the other hand, part of the expenditure incurred may have been used to provide refreshment for the wives in the college. Analogous evidence elsewhere shows that it was customary for the parish to supply a meal for the women when the day's collecting was over.[2] It is therefore a distinct possibility that the King's Hall now and then fulfilled this charitable function for the parish of All Saints. Indeed, one of the late fifteenth-century entries gives a positive lead in this direction. In 1483-4, a portion of the payment was used to cover the women's expenses,[3] which, in this context, most probably signifies the provision of a meal in the King's Hall. The sums expended are quite large at first, no less than 8s being paid out in both 1480-1 and 1483-4.[4] These are much reduced in the sixteenth century and all payments in the entries between 1531 and 1538 are either for 1s or 8d.[5] Whether or not the fellows of the King's Hall actually participated in the general merriment which usually accompanied these frolics and allowed themselves to be 'hocked' by the women is a matter which the impersonal business records of the college do not choose to elucidate. It would also be of considerable interest to discover if the King's Hall was the only Cambridge college to which 'gaggles of women' had direct access, bearing in mind the very stringent regulations of most academic societies designed to safeguard their fellows from all contact with the opposite sex.[6]

[1] *K.H. Accts.* XXIV, fo. 73 v (1531-2): 'Item in hoke monday mulieribus xijd.'; XXIV, fo. 117 v (1532-3): 'Item on Oke monday pro mulieribus xijd.'; XXV, fo. 1 v (1534-5): 'Item for the wyfs of hok monday viijd.'; XXV, fo. 25 (1535-6): 'Item pro hoke monday pro mulieribus viijd.'; XXV, fo. 81 v (1536-7): 'Item on hokemondaye mulieribus viijd.'; XXV, fo. 119 v (1537-8): 'Item pro hokke mondey mulieribus xijd.'

[2] Brand, *op. cit.* I, 164, n. *k.*: in 1526 the parish of St Giles, Reading, 'paid for the wyv's supper at Hoctyde xxiiijd.'; in 1496 the church of St Mary at Hill in London spent 10d on 'the wyves that gaderyd money on *Hob Monday*'.

[3] See above, p. 229, n. 5.

[4] *Loc. cit.*

[5] See above, n. 1.

[6] I know of no other references to Hock-tide collectors in English academic records.

Judging from the impressive lists of servants prescribed by English college founders, it would certainly seem that the average English fellow enjoyed superior service facilities and higher standards of personal comfort than did his French medieval counterpart. Whereas in the typical Parisian college of the fourteenth century it was by no means uncommon to find only one servant provided for the entire complement of fellows,[1] in England all but the poorest of colleges were able to furnish a whole array of domestics who relieved the fellows of most of the essential chores and maximised the time available for study. The copious evidence of the King's Hall accounts relating to domestic staff allows us to construct a far more detailed and evolutionary picture of the servant situation within an English college than would otherwise be possible from statutory sources alone.

The domestic staff is not specified in the King's Hall statutes but is listed year by year in the accounts. During the course of more than two hundred years there were naturally marked variations in the numbers employed and in the wages paid. The earliest domestic list, of 1337–8, reveals that the regular staff then comprised a butler, cook, laundress, barber and one other who probably filled the office of baker;[2] by 1347–8, however, a servant who combined the functions of baker and brewer had quite definitely emerged as a permanent member of the domestic body.[3] In the fifteenth century, the positions of baker and brewer were sometimes distinct and held by different persons and were sometimes discharged by the same servant: but from *c.* 1472–3 until the dissolution of the college separate bakers and brewers were regularly employed each year. An undercook or kitchen knave appears in 1349–50,[4] 1350–1[5] and in 1361–2,[6] after which the office became a permanent one. An underbaker is first found as a recognised servant in 1394–5,[7] appears in most of the annual lists up to the mid-fifteenth century, but thereafter was employed only occasionally on a regular basis, the duties attached to this office being for the most part performed by means of casual labour. The position of janitor was assigned to a specific servant between 1492 and 1495[8] and was subsequently combined with the

[1] Gabriel, *The college system*, p. 16.   [2] *K.H. Accts.* I, fo. 8 v.
[3] *Ibid.* I, fo. 117 v.   [4] *Ibid.* I, fo. 134 v.   [5] *Ibid.* I, fo. 149 v.
[6] *Ibid.* II, fo. 54.   [7] *Ibid.* IV, fo. 48.
[8] *Ibid.* XVII, fo. 11 v; XVIII, fo. 162; XIX, fo. 12 v.

office of barber;[1] and this had probably been the situation before 1492. Perhaps the most colourful domestic functionary to modern ways of thinking was the book-bearer (*portitor* or *lator librorum*), a servant hired to carry the fellows' books to and from the schools of the university. This position was instituted at the King's Hall in 1356-7:[2] the office was a fairly regular one in the fourteenth and early fifteenth centuries but became less so during the remainder of the period and, on occasion, the functions of book-bearer were fulfilled by other members of the domestic staff—for example, by the baker in 1443-4[3] and by the barber in 1449-50.[4] One can well imagine that 'book-bearing' arrangements were particularly necessary at the King's Hall because of the emphasis placed there upon legal studies.[5] As there seems to have been a strong university obligation for students taking courses in the faculty of law to possess their own copies of a proportion of the required bulky texts,[6] the provision of adequate transport facilities between the college and the lecture rooms would have been a much-appreciated luxury:[7] and apart from the texts which individual fellows may have owned or borrowed from wealthier colleagues in the university, many of the volumes carried to and from the schools would have come from the fairly extensive corpus of legal books provided in the unchained section of the King's Hall library. In addition to the regular servants mentioned above, gardeners,[8] extra staff for the bakehouse and kitchen, assistants

[1] *K.H. Accts.* XIX, fos. 117v, 160.

[2] *Ibid.* II, fo. 12, where a quarterly payment of 3*s* is made to Hugo Bukbereher.

[3] *Ibid.* X, fo. 62.   [4] *Ibid.* XI, fo. 71v.   [5] See above, pp. 54-5; see below, pp. 251 ff.

[6] The possession (i.e. ownership or extended loan) of legal texts is not specifically stipulated in the Cambridge statutes (as at Oxford, see S. Gibson, ed., *Statuta Antiqua Universitatis Oxoniensis* (Oxford, 1931), pp. 43, 44, 46) as a necessary requirement for the fulfilment of the conditions leading to degrees in civil and canon law. But as it was a statutory provision at Oxford, it is highly probable that Cambridge students reading for legal degrees would have been obliged to possess at least a minimal corpus of the essential texts.

[7] See the description of the functions of book-bearer in the statutes of All Souls in *Statutes*, I, ch. (7), 58-9: 'Ordinamus quod...sit semper unus sufficiens et idoneus ad deferendum libros sociorum et scholarium juristarum maxime ad scholas...' (In this case, the office of *lator librorum* was to be combined with that of gardener.) See also the entry for book-bearer in the statutes of King's College, *Camb. Docs.* II, 596.

[8] In 1383-4 and 1384-5, a gardener was employed as a full-time liveried servant. He was paid stipends of 8*s* and 6*s* 8*d* and provided with a tunic and cap (*K.H. Accts.* III, fos. 89v, 92v): apart from these exceptional years, the garden was worked by means of casual labour.

for the laundress,[1] labourers and poor scholars[2] were hired on a casual basis.

The staff for the permanent domestic offices were engaged annually by formal written agreements (*conventiones*), drawn up between the seneschals and the contracting servants.[3] These agreements state the office for which the servant was hired and the yearly salary to be paid quarterly in arrears at the terms ending at Christmas, Easter, the feast of St John the Baptist, and Michaelmas. Sometimes they furnish details of the liveries supplied. Until the late fifteenth century, there were six liveried servants (i.e. the butler, cook, baker, book-bearer, undercook and underbaker): by 1474–5, however, the barber, who had previously been *sine liberatura*, had been elevated to the ranks of the liveried staff. As befitting the high dignity of his office only the butler was in receipt of a robe (*roba*),[4] on one occasion described as a full robe (*integra roba*):[5] the remaining servants were supplied with gowns and caps, the former being variously designated as *gouna*, *gipon* and *tunica*,[6] the latter as *pilii*.[7] In some years, the liveries were made up partly of striped or rayed material (*pannus stragulatus*)[8] and partly of cloth of a uniform colour (*pannus coloris*);[9]

---

[1] E.g. *ibid.* I, fo. 37v: 'Item pro ancilla lotrice vid.'

[2] E.g. *ibid.* III, fo. 96: 'Item solut' viij pauperibus scolaribus laborantibus in orto viijd.'; XXVI, fo. 180: 'Item Johani paupero [*sic*] scolario [*sic*] pro labore suo laborando in orto iijd.'

[3] For examples of *conventiones* see *K.H. Accts.* VII, fos. 10v, 81v; XII, fo. 137v; XIII, fo. 112v; XV, fo. 72v.

[4] *Ibid.* III, fos. 10v, 38v, 90, 92v, 133.   [5] *Ibid.* III, fo. 38v.

[6] It is uncertain if these terms are interchangeable or if they denote a measure of hierarchical distinction of dress. In 1383–4, the cook and baker each received a *gouna*, while the book-bearer, undercook and gardener were each supplied with a *gipon* (III, fo. 92v). But in 1384–5, the cook, baker and undercook were each given a *gouna* and the book-bearer and gardener a *tunica* (III, fo. 90). In the following year, a *gouna* was issued to all of these servants (III, fo. 133). A liberal supply of footwear and hose was given to the undercook in 1445–6, comprising three pairs of shoes (*sotulares*) at 5d a pair and hose (*calligae*) to the value of 10d (X, fo. 128v): it is, however, impossible to determine if these items formed a regular part of the livery each year.

[7] E.g. *ibid.* XVII, fo. 40 (1515–16): 'Item pro pilliis emptis pro servientibus iiijs. viijd.'; XX, fo. 126v; XXI, fo. 101.

[8] *Du Cange*, VI (Paris, 1846), 383, defines *stragulatus pannus*: 'diverso colore variatus'. In 1411–12, 12 yards of this striped material were bought at 1s 3½d a yard; in 1415–16, 12 yards were purchased at 1s 6d a yard (*K.H. Accts.* V, fo. 151v; VI, fo. 127v).

[9] E.g. in 1430–1, a mixture of striped and blue cloth was issued to the King's Hall domestic staff, *ibid.* VIII, fo. 8v. See the remarks of Rogers, *Agriculture and prices in*

and in other years, they were evidently composed entirely of woollen cloth of a single hue—green,[1] grey[2] or tawny.[3] The quantities issued are twice particularised. In 1419–20, the butler received a mixture of plain and striped material measuring 4 yards long and 1 yard wide, the variegated cloth apparently containing twenty-four rays or stripes:[4] the baker, cook and book-bearer were each supplied with 3¾ yards of plain and striped material, the latter having twenty stripes to the yard's width:[5] and the undercook and underbaker each received 6 yards of 'narrow' cloth (*strictus pannus*) of unspecified breadth.[6] In 1421–2, the amounts distributed were the same except that the baker, cook and book-bearer were each given 3½ yards of plain and striped cloth instead of the 3¾ yards issued two years previously.[7] Judging from the fact that at New College, Oxford, college servants were given only about a yard and three quarters of the cheaper variegated cloth,[8] the King's Hall doles for domestic staff are, by comparison, strikingly liberal. Livery was also supplied to the master's personal servant at the Society's expense;[9] but the laundress remained a non-liveried servant who was not permitted to reside in the college. As with the fellows, the cloth for the domestic liveries was bought and made up under the direction of the *prosecutor ad*

England, I, 578, concerning cloth purchased by New College from a London cloth-merchant: 'The cloth is either "coloris" or "stragulatus", that is, it seems, of one uniform colour or variegated...the rayed or variegated cloth being the cheaper...'

[1] E.g. in 1486–7, 37 yards of green cloth (*de colore virid'*) were bought for the servants' livery at a cost of 40s 7d (*K.H. Accts.* XVIII, fo. 12v).

[2] E.g. in 1458–9, three dozen yards of 'mustardefelyys' provided the domestic livery (*ibid.* XII, fo. 96v). This was a kind of mixed grey woollen cloth deriving its name from the town of Montivilliers in Normandy (*O.E.D.* VI, 795); see also *K.H. Accts.* XIII, fo. 11.

[3] In 1496–7, 21 yards 'de le tawny' were purchased for the livery at a cost of 49s (*K.H. Accts.* XIX, fo. 72v).

[4] *Ibid.* VI, fo. 110v: 'Item...pincerne xxiiij stragul' et pann' coloris viz latitud'is unius virge iiij virge.' *Du Cange*, VI, 383, cites one example showing that striped material was sometimes described by the number of stripes or rays it contained: 'Et predictus Ricardus habebit de prefato Willelmo Skrine...pannum stragulatum continentem xx rayes...'

[5] *K.H. Accts. loc. cit.*

[6] *Ibid.*

[7] *Ibid.* VI, fos. 145v, 146.

[8] Rogers, *op. cit.* I, 578–9.

[9] E.g. *K.H. Accts.* VI, fos. 87v, 147; VII, fo. 100v. In 1418–19, 8s was paid for his livery; in 1421–2, 6s 8d.

forinseca at an average annual cost of between two and three pounds.[1]

Taking wages only into consideration, the highest paid servant in 1337–8 was the laundress, engaged at a stipend of 16s a year.[2] This varied subsequently from 10s to 20s until 1399–1400,[3] but between 1400–1 and *c.* 1465 the rate was fixed at 20s per annum.[4] In 1466–7 it was raised to 25s[5] and further augmented to 26s 8d in 1475–6,[6] and was stabilised at this level until the mid-sixteenth century. The King's Hall rate was by no means exceptional: in terms of cash payment, laundresses were among the most highly paid of English college servants. At Merton, for example, the laundress was paid 20s a year[7] and at New College, where wage rates were unusually high, the laundress was hired at 40s a year.[8] Most medieval codes of college statutes stipulate that, as far as is possible, all domestics employed within the precincts of the college are to be males.[9] Where a laundress has, of necessity, to be hired, elaborate precautions are to be taken to ensure that personal contacts with the fellows are kept to an absolute minimum.[10] In the statutes of New College and King's College it is specifically stated that the laundress is to live in the town.[11] As the King's Hall laundress was a non-liveried servant only rarely in receipt of refreshments at the Society's expense, it is likely that she was always boarded out in Cambridge.[12] Perhaps this residential

---

[1] E.g. *ibid.* IV, fo. 112v; V, fos. 76, 118v, 132; VI, fos. 64, 86v, 105v; VII, fos. 25, 40, 99, 136; VIII, fo. 7; XII, fo. 9v; XIV, fos. 101, 128; XV, fos. 73, 141v; XVI, fos. 9v, 33, 66, 109v; XVII, fos. 10v, 57v, 79v; XIX, fo. 158; XX, fo. 126v; XXI, fo. 101.

[2] *Ibid.* I, fo. 8v.

[3] *Ibid.* I, fos. 26v, 55v, 63, 80, 92v, 101, 117v, 134v, 149v, 171v; II, fos. 12, 28, 54, 101, 111; III, fos. 10v, 38v, 67, 112v, 133; IV, fos. 30v, 48, 101, 131v; V, fo. 33.

[4] See, from many possible references, *ibid.* V, fos. 45v, 60, 107, 119v, 134v, 175; VI, fos. 9v, 87v; VII, fos. 100v, 119, 137v; VIII, fos. 8v, 49v, 122; IX, fos. 11v, 71, 157; X, fos. 10, 37, 62, 93, 128v; XI, fos. 12v, 41v, 71v, 97v, 129v; XII, fos. 70v, 99v, 137v; XIII, fo. 47v.

[5] *Ibid.* XIII, fo. 136v.   [6] *Ibid.* XV, fo. 43.

[7] See e.g. Merton College Bursars' Rolls for 1400, 1411 and 1429 (M.R. 3727, 3737, 3750) preserved in Merton College Library.

[8] See e.g. New College Bursars' Rolls, *cit.*, for 1393 (although in 1383 the laundress was hired at a salary of 26s 8d a year).

[9] See e.g. the statutes of Merton (1270 and 1274), Oriel and New College in *Statutes*, I, ch. (2), 19–20, 36–7, ch. (3), 15, ch. (5), 94; also the statutes of Peterhouse and King's in *Camb. Docs.* II, 30, 596.

[10] *Ibid.*

[11] *Statutes*, I, ch. (5), 94; *Camb. Docs.* II, 596.   [12] See below, p. 241.

consideration partly explains why college laundresses were seemingly so highly paid in relation to other domestic servants. For their stipends presumably contained an assessed monetary equivalent for the college board and lodging from which they were precluded by reason of their sex.

In 1337–8 the butler's stipend was only 13*s* 4*d*[1] but rose to 18*s* in 1340–1.[2] Between 1350 and 1360 it remained at 16*s*[3] and increased to 20*s* in 1361–2.[4] By 1383–4 it had risen to 30*s*[5] and maintained this level until 1386–7, when it dropped to 26*s* 8*d*.[6] In 1389–90, the maximum rate of 40*s* was reached,[7] but this fell once more to 30*s* in 1393–4.[8] During the remainder of the 1390s the rate was fixed at 33*s* 4*d*:[9] from 1399–1400 to the 1540s, however, the stipend was stabilised at 26*s* 8*d*.[10] Although these rates are lower than those paid at New College[11] and at Merton,[12] where stipends of 40*s* are regularly recorded, they are nevertheless probably more than double the usual rates found in the smaller English colleges.[13]

The butler's duties extended from time to time into other domestic spheres. In 1363–4, for instance, an extra remuneration was given for assuming responsibility for kitchen operations during the Christmas festivities[14] and in 1422–3 the office of butler was temporarily combined with that of cook[15] and with that of barber in 1486–7.[16] Opportunities evidently existed for the promotion of servants from the lower to the superior domestic positions and at least two of the King's Hall butlers had started service as book-bearers. Thomas

---

[1] *K.H. Accts.* I, fo. 8 v.

[2] *Ibid.* I, fo. 35.

[3] *Ibid.* I, fos. 149 v, 171 v; II, fos. 21 v, 28.

[4] *Ibid.* II, fo. 54.

[5] *Ibid.* III, fo. 92 v.

[6] *Ibid.* III, fos. 89 v, 133, 67.

[7] *Ibid.* III, fo. 10 v.

[8] *Ibid.* IV, fo. 30 v.

[9] *Ibid.* IV, fos. 48, 101, 131 v.

[10] From many possible references see *ibid.* V, fo. 33; VI, fo. 9 v; VII, fo. 26; VIII, fo. 8 v; X, fo. 62; XI, fo. 45 v; XII, fo. 99 v; XIII, fo. 15 v; XIV, fo. 103 v; XV, fo. 43; XVI, fo. 86 v; XVII, fo. 60 v; XVIII, fo. 34; XIX, fo. 38 v; XX, fo. 11 v; XXI, fo. 166; XXIII, fo. 25; XXIV, fo. 178 v; XXV, fo. 74; XXVI, fo. 112.

[11] See e.g. New College Bursars' Rolls for 1383 and 1393.

[12] See e.g. M.R. 3727, 3737 and 3750.

[13] Information concerning the wages of domestic staff is rarely given in collegiate statutory codes. At Trinity Hall, however, it is stipulated that the steward or butler is to receive a robe and 10*s* a year (*Camb. Docs.* II, 430).

[14] *K.H. Accts.* II, fo. 75 v.

[15] *Ibid.* VII, fo. 10 v: agreement was made with Thomas Hayton 'ad gerend' officium pincerne et coci per annum et habetur per annum pro utroque officio xls.'.

[16] *Ibid.* XVIII, fo. 12 v.

J(Ch) esse appears as *portitor librorum* in 1393–4[1] and still retained that post in 1405–6.[2] His name is absent from the staff list for 1406–7 but re-appears as butler in 1407–8,[3] an office which he continued to discharge until 1415–16.[4] The second case is that of John Stykney, book-bearer in 1431–2,[5] who was engaged as butler in 1434–5.[6] Promotions of this kind occur in other departments: Galfridus Bukden, for example, hired as underbaker in 1428–9,[7] became principal baker the following year[8] and retained this position until 1441–2.[9] While opportunities for 'domestic mobility' were clearly present, it is doubtful if any significant proportion of the superior servants was in fact recruited from the lower ranks. A few members of the staff did indeed give several years of continuous service to the college[10] but, generally speaking, tenurial periods were brief and the turnover of personnel rapid. Because of this, the college does not appear to have had a large pool of experienced labour from which to draw for appointments to the higher domestic offices.

Not all medieval English colleges made permanent provision for the offices of baker and brewer.[11] In the King's Hall, however, where the Society's bread and ale were baked and brewed on the premises, these servants necessarily occupied key positions in the sphere of domestic economy. In the fourteenth century, brewing and baking activities were discharged by the same servant. Between 1347–8 and 1364–5, the stipend of the baker/brewer ranged from 10s to 15s, though in most years it was fixed at 13s 4d:[12] by 1383–4, however, it had doubled to 26s 8d.[13] In the fifteenth century, the offices of baker and brewer were sometimes distinct and sometimes combined, but after *c.* 1472–3 they were entirely separate. When a baker was employed in the fifteenth century, his stipend varied from 16s to 26s 8d[14]

---

[1] *Ibid.* IV, fo. 30v.   [2] *Ibid.* V, fo. 95.   [3] *Ibid.* V, fo. 107.

[4] *Ibid.* V, fos. 119v, 134v, 175; VI, fo. 22.   [5] *Ibid.* VIII, fo. 26v.

[6] *Ibid.* VIII, fo. 98.   [7] *Ibid.* VII, fo. 119.   [8] *Ibid.* VII, fo. 137v.

[9] *Ibid.* VIII, fos. 8v, 26v, 98, 122; IX, fos. 42, 102, 157; X, fo. 10.

[10] See the cases of J(Ch) esse and Bukden cited.

[11] See the statutes of Balliol, New College, Lincoln and All Souls, where no provision is made for the employment of a regular baker, in *Statutes*, I, ch. (1), 19–20, ch. (5), 94, ch. (6), 23, ch. (7), 58.

[12] *K.H. Accts.* I, fos. 117v, 134v, 149v; II, fos. 12, 21v, 28, 54, 101.

[13] *Ibid.* III, fo. 92v.

[14] *Ibid.* IV, fo. 78; V, fo. 45v; VI, fos. 9v, 87v; VII, fos. 26, 81v; X, fos. 62, 93; XII, fos. 70v, 99v; XIII, fos. 15v, 47v; XV, fos. 43, 114v; XVI, fos. 36, 56v; XVII, fo. 81; XIX, fos. 60v, 88v.

and was fixed at the latter rate in the first half of the sixteenth century.[1] As previously mentioned, an underbaker did not have a regular place upon the staff until almost the end of the fourteenth century and for the next fifty years he received a stipend of 8s or 10s with the exception of two years when wages of 6s 8d were paid:[2] after 1450, bakehouse assistants were hired for only a handful of years at rates varying from 10s to 16s.[3] Separate brewers made their appearance early in the fifteenth century at a salary of 26s 8d and, from *c.* 1472–3 onwards, a brewer was hired each year as a regular servant at this stipend:[4] indeed, the brewer was the only domestic whose wages remained constant throughout.

The bakehouse/brewhouse was perhaps the most efficiently and economically managed of all the domestic departments. Each year the by-products of the baking and brewing processes (i.e. bran and drass[5]) were sold for animal foodstuffs,[6] the cash realised from this source being ploughed back into the department and used generally for the purchase and repair of necessary utensils.[7] Careful accounts of cash income and expenditure were kept and the profit or loss recorded;[8] and by comparison with the very elementary techniques employed in other departments, bakehouse/brewhouse accounting appears to have attained a fairly high level of sophistication and comprehensiveness.[9]

---

[1] E.g. *ibid.* XX, fos. 11 v, 103 v; XXI, fo. 140; XXII, fo. 25; XXIII, fo. 44; XXIV, fo. 28; XXV, fo. 74; XXVI, fo. 150 v.

[2] *Ibid.* VI, fo. 43; VII, fo. 26 (1416–17 and 1423–4).

[3] E.g. *ibid.* XII, fo. 137 v; XIII, fos. 47 v, 113, 136 v.

[4] E.g. *ibid.* XI, fos. 12 v, 129 v; XII, fo. 99 v; XIII, fo. 62 v; XIV, fo. 70 v; XV, fo. 18; XVI, fo. 13 v; XVII, fo. 81; XVIII, fo. 135; XIX, fo. 12 v; XX, fo. 11 v; XXI, fo. 166; XXII, fo. 76; XXIII, fo. 25; XXIV, fo. 67; XXV, fo. 145; XXVI, fo. 112.

[5] A term used to describe the residue of malt barley left after the ale has been extracted. (See *Du Cange*, II, 939.) Perhaps the same as *drasch* mentioned by Rogers, *op. cit.* I, 336–7, and used as a cheap foodstuff for pigs. Bran was also used for this purpose.

[6] Sales of bran and drass are entered in the accounts under the heading of *Exitus pistrine*. E.g. *K.H. Accts.* II, fos. 2 v, 75, 89, 109, 127 v; III, fos. 73, 100 v, 114 v; V, fo. 173 v; VI, fo. 21 v.

[7] References as in previous note.   [8] E.g. *ibid.* II, fo. 58.

[9] In the accounts all items of expenditure relating to the various departments are grouped under the appropriate headings (*pistrina, coquina, promptuarium* and *aula*). It is clear that the bakehouse was the only domestic department to possess an income additional to the monetary sum allocated to all departmental seneschals from the King's Hall funds to cover the payment of staff, provisions and running costs.

Fluctuations in the wages of the principal cook ran roughly parallel with those of the baker. Between 1337–8 and the 1360s the stipend varied from 7s to 13s 4d:[1] it had been increased to 26s 8d by 1383–4[2] and until the mid-fifteenth century rates of 20s, 23s 4d and 26s 8d are recorded.[3] From 1457–8 until the end of the period, however, the stipend was permanently fixed at this latter sum.[4] The wages of the undercook were, from the end of the fourteenth century, almost identical with those of the baker's assistant. In the second half of the fifteenth century his stipend was subject to pronounced fluctuations but was stabilised at 16s in 1518–19.[5]

Of the remaining servants, the book-bearer occupied a position on the domestic scale midway between the ranks of the superior and inferior servants. Between 1356–7 and 1384–5 his stipend ranged from 6s 8d to 8s.[6] It rose steadily throughout the second half of the 1380s: it was 9s in 1385–6,[7] 10s in 1386–7, and 15s in 1388–9 and 1389–90.[8] By 1393 it had fallen slightly to 13s 4d,[9] which became the standard rate until the 1440s and was the same as that paid to the *lator librorum* at New College.[10] As already indicated, the book-bearer ceased to be a regular servant in the second half of the fifteenth century and more than once his functions were discharged by other members of the domestic staff.[11] But in those years when separate book-bearers were employed wages show an upward trend: for example, a stipend of 18s was paid in 1447–8[12] and of 26s 8d in 1487–8.[13]

The wages of the barber/janitor reveal a similar upward trend over the whole period. In 1337–8, the stipend was fixed at 4s[14] and remained so until 1363–4 when it was raised to 6s 8d.[15] It had been

---

[1] *K.H. Accts.* I, fos. 8v, 26v, 101; II, fos. 21v, 28, 54, 75v.

[2] *Ibid.* III, fo. 92v.

[3] E.g. *ibid.* IV, fos. 48, 101, 131v; V, fos. 45v, 60; VI, fo. 22; VII, fo. 26; VIII, fo. 8v; X, fo. 62; XI, fo. 45v.

[4] E.g. *ibid.* XII, fo. 70v; XIII, fo. 15v; XIV, fo. 103v; XV, fo. 43; XVI, fo. 56v; XVII, fo. 60v; XVIII, fo. 34; XIX, fo. 12v; XX, fo. 11v; XXI, fo. 21; XXII, fo. 76; XXIII, fo. 95v; XXIV, fo. 28; XXV, fo. 74; XXVI, fo. 32.

[5] E.g. *ibid.* XXII, fo. 64v; XXIII, fo. 25; XXIV, fo. 67; XXV, fo. 112; XXVI, fo. 72.

[6] *Ibid.* II, fos. 12, 21v, 54, 101; III, fos. 90, 92v.   [7] *Ibid.* III, fo. 133.

[8] *Ibid.* III, fo. 67.   [9] *Ibid.* III, fos. 10v, 38v.

[10] New College Bursars' Rolls for 1383 and 1393.   [11] See above, p. 232.

[12] *K.H. Accts.* XI, fo. 12v.   [13] *Ibid.* XVIII, fo. 34.

[14] *Ibid.* I, fo. 8v.   [15] *Ibid.* II, fo. 75v.

further increased to 8*s* by 1384–5[1] and had doubled to 16*s* in 1435–6.[2] Until 1450 the rate fluctuated from 13*s* 4*d* to 16*s*[3] but increased to 20*s* in 1451–2[4] and remained at this level until 1495–6, when it became permanently fixed at 26*s* 8*d*.[5]

The King's Hall servants evidently had to be versatile and prepared to fill a gap as the need arose. The intermittent 'book-bearing' activities of the barber and baker have already been alluded to and in 1486–7 the barber had to step in temporarily to fill the office of butler for a year.[6] Moreover, servants were sometimes called upon to transact college business: in 1468–9, for example, the barber journeyed to London on behalf of the King's Hall[7] and in 1505–6 the barber was dispatched to purchase wheat for the college in place of one of the contracting seneschals.[8] During illness, members of the domestic staff were cared for at the college's expense[9] and, in conjunction with the fellows, were given allowances for their commons when absent from Cambridge because of plague visitations.[10]

Towards the middle of the fifteenth century the King's Hall acquired a number of tenements situated near by in the parish of All Saints in Jewry. On 9 May 1449 the property known as Tyled Hostel (so called from its style of roofing), a building in the High Street in All Saints parish, was sold to the king by its then owner, ex-King's Hall fellow Richard Pyghttesley, who had vacated his fellowship in the previous year.[11] The king subsequently conveyed the property to the King's Hall and the college (not the king) paid Pyghttesley £33 6*s* 8*d* for the sale of the hostel.[12] At about the same time the college rented two tenements, formerly in the possession of Pyghttesley and adjacent

---

[1] *K.H. Accts.* III, fo. 90. [2] *Ibid.* VIII, fo. 122.

[3] *Ibid.* IX, fos. 11 v, 42, 71, 102, 157; X, fo. 10. [4] *Ibid.* XI, fo. 97 v.

[5] E.g. *ibid.* XIX, fo. 38 v; XX, fo. 11 v; XXI, fo. 166; XXII, fo. 64 v; XXIII, fo. 25; XXIV, fo. 28; XXV, fo. 24; XXVI, fo. 112.

[6] *Ibid.* XVIII, fo. 12 v.

[7] *Ibid.* XIV, fo. 6. [8] *Ibid.* XX, fo. 127.

[9] E.g. *ibid.* XI, fo. 124 (1452–3): 'Item in expensis circa custodiam pistoris infirmi. In primis in prandio custodientium xd. Item in expensis circa sepulturam eiusdem' [no entry]; see also *ibid.* XII, fo. 94 (1458–9): 'Item in repastis unius famuli tempore infirmitatis vid.'; *ibid.* XXVI, fo. 180 (1516–17): 'In regardo pandoxatori nostro tempore infirmitatis sue xxd.'

[10] *Ibid.* XX, fo. 196 (1508–9): 'Item pro communibus servientium in tempore pestis iiijs. xd.'; XXIII, fo. 136 v (1525–6): 'Item in tempore pestis Petro pandoxatori pro communibus xxd.'

[11] Willis and Clark, *Architectural history*, II, 426. [12] *K.H. Accts.* XI, fo. 57 v.

to Tyled Hostel, from the White Canons of St Edmund of Sempring-ham,[1] who had first settled in Cambridge in 1290. For a short duration, another house once owned by Pyghttesley was rented from the Benedictine nuns of St Rhadegund.[2] In *c.* 1449, the college acquired a further messuage in the parish of All Saints formerly belonging to Margaret Maste, a Cambridge widow.[3] For the next eighty years or so, these properties were rented out to a variety of townspeople and to a goodly proportion of the college's domestic servants. Indeed, the need to find satisfactory accommodation for the domestic staff may well have been the principal *raison d'être* for the acquisition of the All Saints holdings. Whatever the case, a whole succession of King's Hall servants including butlers,[4] bakers,[5] brewers,[6] cooks[7] and laundresses[8] were installed at various times as tenants of the college. Sometimes, husband and wife teams were involved: for example, Thomas Kelsay and his wife, baker and laundress to the King's Hall, inhabited one of the tenements for a number of years.[9] Before the mid-fifteenth century most of the unmarried staff had presumably lived in the college. If so, accommodation must neces-sarily have been cramped and a continual headache to the King's Hall authorities; but the establishment of outside living quarters was an arrangement which neatly combined the advantages of having an external safety valve to absorb the domestic overspill while at the same time providing an additional source of income.

Apart from catering for staff actively engaged in service, the All Saints tenements were also apparently utilised for housing servants who had vacated their domestic duties: in 1457–8, for example, John Gylmyn, who ceased to serve as King's Hall butler in that year, leased one of the holdings for a twelve-year period at an annual rent of 40s.[10] A small proportion of the tenants appear to have been married servants and it sometimes happened that when the husband

---

[1] *Ibid.* XI, fo. 94; XIII, fos. 108, 132 v: the rent was 6s 8d a year.

[2] *Ibid.* XI, fo. 94: the rent was 2s 4d a year.

[3] *Ibid.* XI, fos. 41, 83 v, 94, 112 v. In 1452 the college leased this property for a twelve-year period at a rent of 50s 8d to Thomas Pynnok, brewer, of Cambridge, and to Isabella, his wife (*K.H. Cabinet*, no. 130).

[4] E.g. *K.H. Accts.* XII, fos. 113 v, 157 v; XIII, fos. 34, 76 v, 107 v; XVIII, fo. 58 v.

[5] *Ibid.* XX, fos. 36, 69.   [6] *Ibid.* XX, fos. 9, 36.

[7] *Ibid.* XIII, fos. 76 v, 100 v, 107 v; XVI, fo. 32.

[8] *Ibid.* XVIII, fos. 9, 34, 56, 77, 103, 132.

[9] *Ibid.* XIX, fos. 132, 157 v.   [10] *Ibid.* XII, fo. 85 v.

died his widow retained the tenancy for several years after his decease. The non-domestic tenants were a motley crew embracing, for the most part, tradesmen of the town of Cambridge and included brewers,[1] bakers,[2] cloth cutters,[3] a cobbler[4] and a tiler[5] as well as a vicar of All Saints Church,[6] an ostler of the Dolphin inn[7] and Philip Morgan, the distinguished university bedel[8] and possibly physician to Lady Margaret, countess of Richmond and Derby.[9] As in the case of the Bellamy holdings *ultra pontem*, receipts from the All Saints tenements came to an end in 1528–9. On 12 March 1529 an indenture of lease was drawn up whereby one of the All Saints properties was let to Henry Jugge and his wife for thirty years, Jugge and his executors to have full liability for all repairs over the entire period.[10] The King's Hall accounts contain no record of rent received and there must remain some doubt as to whether the agreement was ever implemented. The subsequent history of this and the remaining properties is shrouded in oblivion.

Most sets of academic records tell us little or nothing about the number of private servants maintained by fellows of medieval colleges. Was the retention of a personal servant the exception or the rule and was the pattern substantially different in the sixteenth century from what it was in the fourteenth and fifteenth centuries? Fairly definite answers to these questions can be supplied for the particular case of the King's Hall, although they cannot be taken as necessarily representative of English medieval colleges in general.

The King's Hall accounts yield what is seemingly accurate information concerning the numbers of private servants maintained by the fellows throughout the greater part of the history of the college. Data can be derived for 124 years extending, with a few unfortunate

[1] *K.H. Cabinet*, no. 130; *K.H. Accts.* XVIII, fo. 132.
[2] *Ibid.* XIII, fos. 100v, 159v; XXII, fo. 72v; XXIII, fo. 76v.
[3] *Ibid.* XX, fo. 101; XXII, fos. 72v, 102v; XXVI, fo. 165v.
[4] *Ibid.* XXIV, fos. 6, 164.
[5] *Ibid.* XXIII, fo. 140v.
[6] *Ibid.* XVIII, fo. 132.
[7] *Ibid.* XXIV, fo. 6: there were two inns by this name in medieval Cambridge; one was situated at the Bridge Street end of All Saints' Passage, now part of Whewell's Court, Trinity, and the other was in the High Street on the site of Corpus Christi. (See *Cambridge borough documents*, cit. I, 138.)
[8] *K.H. Accts.* XIX, fo. 157v (1499–1500).
[9] For his career see Emden, *B.R.U.C.* p. 411.   [10] *K.H. Cabinet*, no. 139.

gaps, from 1383–4 to 1543–4.[1] Taking this period as a whole, it would appear that the year 1460 marks a real point of division. Before that date it was evidently quite exceptional for fellows to keep personal servants: in no single year prior to 1460 did the total number of private servants maintained exceed three; while, in about two-thirds of those years for which there is information, there were none at all. The relevant data for this period may be summarised thus: of the 64 years between 1383–4 and 1459–60 for which figures can be obtained, a total of three private servants is recorded in each of four years,[2] two in each of five,[3] one in each of fifteen[4] and none in each of the remaining 40 years.

After 1460 the pattern begins to change quite appreciably and there is now detectable a marked increase in the number of servants retained annually, giving average numbers of 4, 11 and 18 for the three periods set out in table 15.

TABLE 15

Period	Annual average no. of fellows with servants	Annual average no.[5] of fellows	No. of years within period for which data are obtainable
1460/1–1478/9	4	33	11
1486/7–1499/1500	11	34	12
1500/1–1543/4	18	34	38

In the first half of the sixteenth century, the annual average figure of 18 servants was exceeded in 15 individual years. The peak period for private servants was clearly the ten years between 1514–15 and 1523–4, when the average number was 23, with the exceptionally

[1] Reliable data are unobtainable for: 1384–5, 1390–1 to 1392–3, 1395–6, 1396–7, 1400–1, 1406–7, 1409–10, 1420–1, 1450–1, 1454–5, 1455–6, 1461–2 to 1463–4, 1469–70, 1474–5, 1475–6, 1479–80 to 1485–6, 1492–3, 1493–4, 1506–7, 1512–13, 1530–1, 1533–4, 1538–9, 1540–1.

[2] 1387–8, 1388–9, 1389–90 and 1398–9. (*K.H. Accts.* v, fos. 15–17; III, fos. 40–1; III, fos. 15–17; IV, fos. 134–6.)

[3] 1386–7, 1393–4, 1402–3, 1411–12 and 1418–19. (*Ibid.* III, fos. 69v–72; IV, fos. 32–4; v, fos. 49–50v; v, fos. 154v–156v; VI, fo. 95.)

[4] 1385–6, 1394–5, 1397–8, 1399–1400, 1403–4, 1404–5, 1405–6, 1407–8, 1408–9, 1412–13, 1439–40, 1448–9, 1456–7, 1458–9 and 1459–60.

[5] These averages are based on the number of fellows whose names are inscribed on the boards of the college each year and do not take non-residence into account.

high complement of 29 servants recorded in 1522–3.[1] The remaining 'high' years were 1534–5 with 22,[2] 1535–6 with 20[3] and 1527–8, 1532–3 and 1536–7 with 19 each.[4]

It has emerged from this investigation that the retention of private servants was an exceptional practice in the period before 1460, occurring in only a handful of years and confined to not more than three fellows in any one year. The keeping of personal servants began to figure as a regular feature of a fellow's life from the late fifteenth century onwards: and, as we turn into the sixteenth century, there can be no doubt that it had become common for about half, and in some years two-thirds, of the fellows to support private servants in the college. These findings may not necessarily be reflective of conditions elsewhere but, for the King's Hall, they are indicative of the evolution of higher standards of comfort and ease which were the accompaniment of the life of the average fellow in the twilight phase of the history of this royal foundation.

The first reference to a dovecot (*columbarium*) appears in the account for 1414–15.[5] In that year it was stocked with four dozen pigeons[6] and for a space of more than fifteen years the numbers of pigeons bred and sold are recorded. They were fed mainly on peas, barley, wheat (occasionally), cummin-seed and salt in the form of salt-cat.[7] The annual yield was high and in some years a good profit was realised. In 1415–16, 1416–17 and 1417–18, 308, 687 and 773 young pigeons were sold at 4*d* or 5*d* a dozen, giving returns of 10*s* 7*d*, £1 3*s* 9½*d* and £1 6*s* 11½*d*.[8] The figures for 1418–19 are incomplete, but in the following year 830 young birds were produced for sale, the largest total recorded for any single year.[9] From this time onwards the yield began to fall: in 1421–2 it was 786;[10] in 1422–3 381

---

[1] *K.H. Accts.* XXIII, fos. 56–58v.   [2] *Ibid.* XXV, fos. 22–26.

[3] *Ibid.* XXV, fos. 65–67v.

[4] *Ibid.* XXIV, fos. 172v–174v, 142–6; XXV, fos. 99v–104v.

[5] *Ibid.* VI, fo. 31. All the Cambridge colleges are known to have possessed pigeon-houses, with the possible exceptions of Clare, Magdalene and Sidney Sussex. (Willis and Clark, *Architectural history*, III, 592.)

[6] *K.H. Accts.* VI, fo. 53: 'Item pro remuneracione portatorum columbarum ad mbare iiij dussen iiijd. ob.'

[7] *Ibid.* VI, fos. 31, 50, 71v, 96v, 119, 136; VII, fos. 16, 32v, 45v, 87, 105; VIII, fo. 13. Cummin-seed was a popular 'lure' for pigeons. Salt-cat, a mass of salt and other matter such as gravel, lime and cummin-seed, was also used for this purpose.

[8] *Ibid.* VI, fos. 136, 50, 71v.   [9] *Ibid.* VI, fo. 119.   [10] *Ibid.* VI, fo. 151.

(though it is suspected that here the figures are incomplete);[1] in 1423–4, 551;[2] in 1424–5, 444;[3] and in 1426–7, 375.[4] Although the accounts continue to list sales of pigeons,[5] the entries are not sufficiently comprehensive to permit us to draw up accurate totals. The recipients of the sales are not specified but were presumably either individual fellows or buyers from outside the college.

Swans are first mentioned in the account for 1433–4, where it is recorded that a quarter of oats was bought for feeding purposes.[6] In most subsequent years the kitchen expenses contain entries for barley and oats for these birds. It is known that the college maintained eight swans in 1437–8,[7] and in 1451–2 occurs the first reference to a swanherd.[8] Henceforth, the accounts contain copious entries for the capture,[9] inspection[10] and marking of the swans.[11] Between 1460 and 1467 the office of *custos signorum* was held by one William Say,[12] who, in addition to his wages, was provided with a toga: between 1486 and 1489 the swanherd was named Webster.[13] Judging from the fact that the entries for swans are recorded under the head of kitchen expenses, it seems likely that the kitchen department assumed overall responsibility for their care and that they were kept on some part of the river near the college. Swans were also bought for immediate consumption and these are listed separately in the section for stores.[14] It seems, too, that a number of swans were maintained privately as there are entries in the accounts for the purchase of swans and for their foodstuffs by warden Richard Caudray and three of the fellows in 1437–8.[15]

Bees were also kept by the college and the accounts list the purchase of eight beehives, three in 1399–1400 and five in 1402–3.[16]

[1] *Ibid.* VII, fo. 16.
[2] *Ibid.* VII, fo. 32v.
[3] *Ibid.* VII, fo. 45v.
[4] *Ibid.* VII, fo. 87.
[5] E.g. *ibid.* XVI, fo. 55v; XXIV, fo. 150.
[6] *Ibid.* VIII, fo. 60v.
[7] *Ibid.* IX, fo. 41.
[8] *Ibid.* XI, fo. 92: 'Item remuneratum est uni pro custodia signorum viijd.'
[9] E.g. *ibid.* XI, fos. 92, 155v.
[10] E.g. *ibid.* XI, fo. 92; XII, fo. 131.
[11] E.g. *ibid.* XII, fo. 40: 'Item in expensis circa signacionem cignorum xixd.'
[12] *Ibid.* XIII, fos. 14, 129.
[13] *Ibid.* XVIII, fos. 10, 57.
[14] E.g. *ibid.* VIII, fo. 122; IX, fo. 156v; X, fo. 9v.
[15] *Ibid.* IX, fo. 42: warden Caudray owed 20s for twelve swans, John Pyville owed 3s 4d for two and Richard Pyghttesley and John Bank each owed 1s 8d for one swan.
[16] *Ibid.* v, fo. 26: 'Item pro iij alveis pro apibus xd.'; v, fo. 46.

Although there are further expenses for bees and hives in 1477–8[1] and 1492–3,[2] nothing is known of the honey yield, which was presumably confined to domestic consumption since sales are nowhere itemised.[3]

The new King's Hall library, begun in 1416–17,[4] was designed to supersede an older one which was in existence by the latter part of the fourteenth century. In the account for 1397–8, under the heading of *Expense circa librariam*, there are entries for the purchase of 24 chains and for a lock with 33 keys, that is to say one each for the master and 32 fellows;[5] in 1399–1400, a payment of £1 13s was made to a bookbinder (*ligator librorum*) to cover the costs of his expenses, salary and commons incurred in the course of work performed in the old library over a period of about eight weeks;[6] and in 1410–11 there is a further entry for the purchase of chains for library books.[7] The new library was evidently completed by 1421–2[8] and thereafter the accounts supply details of the interior fittings and of the binding and placing of the books. Twenty-four pairs of clasps were bought in 1421–2[9] and seven more in 1424–5.[10] During the early 1420s assorted types of skins were acquired for the covering of the books. In 1421–2, 24 calfskins, 8 sheepskins and 4 red skins were purchased;[11] in 1423–4, 12 calfskins, 5 skins of white leather, one white sheepskin and one red skin were bought;[12] and in the following year there are entries for 12 sheepskins, 9 calfskins and one red skin.[13] In addition to these, 8 parchment skins were procured for the use of the keeper of the library:[14] on these would be written the titles of all

---

[1] *K.H. Accts.* xv, fo. 138.   [2] *Ibid.* xviii, fo. 161 v.

[3] In 1479–80, the college sold six of its beehives to its butler, Richard Holmes (*ibid.* xvi, fo. 26v).

[4] Willis and Clark, *Architectural history*, ii, 441–3.

[5] *K.H. Accts.* iv, fo. 86: 'In primis pro xxiiij catenis viijs. Item pro j cera et xxxiij clavis vs. vid.'

[6] *Ibid.* v, fo. 39.

[7] *Ibid.* v, fo. 141 v. On this occasion seven chains were bought for 3s 4d.

[8] Willis and Clark, *loc. cit.*

[9] *K.H. Accts.* vi, fo. 152: six pairs of clasps were bought at 2s 1d; six more at 2s and twelve at 3s 9d.

[10] *Ibid.* vii, fo. 52v.

[11] *Ibid.* vi, fo. 152. In addition, eight skins were purchased for the fireplace for the greater comfort of the seneschals.

[12] *Ibid.* vii, fo. 31.

[13] *Ibid.* vii, fo. 52v.   [14] *Ibid.* vii, fo. 72v.

the books in his care, thus making up the official library register.[1] By 1423-4 the carpentry work and binding operations were sufficiently advanced for the books to be entitled on the outside and chained into their places.[2]

The contents of the King's Hall library were built up in part from private donations but largely from a series of royal bequests. The first of the latter was made by Edward II, who granted a number of books on civil and canon law which were subsequently reclaimed by Queen Isabella after Edward's death:[3] although Edward III did not restore these actual volumes, he gave in their stead the sum of £10 in 1332 to Simon de Bury, warden of the King's Scholars, in recompense for their loss.[4] An incomplete inventory of the possessions of the Society in 1361-2 reveals that the college then owned fourteen civil law texts, comprising different parts of the Institutes, the Digest, the Code and the *Parvum Volumen*, and two commentaries, one by Azo and the other by Odofredus, on the *Digestum Vetus*:[5] the additional information is supplied that three of the texts had been sent by the king from Calais.[6] In the same year is recorded the gift of a theological work given by warden Thomas Powys:[7] and four years later two canon law commentaries, the *Rosarium* of Archidiaconus (Guido de Baysio, archdeacon of Bologna, *d.* 1313) and the *Speculum Judiciale* of Guilielmus Durantis (written by 1276), also left to the Society by Powys, came into the possession of the college.[8] The last recorded bequest of Edward III was a gift of five civil law texts made through his chancellor, William of Wykeham, in 1368 for the special benefit of Walter de Herford, one of the King's Scholars.[9]

It is not possible to estimate the size of the library stock before the appearance of the first complete catalogue in 1391: it seems fairly

---

[1] For the use of parchment for the compilation of a library register see the undated ordinance (probably late fifteenth century) for Pembroke College, Cambridge, concerning the appointment and duties of the librarian, quoted in Willis and Clark, III, 396-7. At the King's Hall, the master or his deputy appears to have acted as librarian.

[2] *K.H. Accts.* VII, fo. 31: 'Item pro titulacione librorum et catenacione eorumden [*sic*] vd.'

[3] This information is contained in the Issue Roll of 2 Oct. 6 Ed. III (*Issues of the exchequer* (ed. F. Devon, London, 1837), pp. 142-3): the number of books is unspecified. An abstract of this entry is given by C. E. Sayle, 'King's Hall Library', *C.A.S. Proceedings*, XXIV, old series, no. lxxii (1921-2), p. 54.

[4] Sayle, *loc. cit.*   [5] *K.H. Accts.* IV, fo. 6; Sayle, p. 55.

[6] *Loc. cit.*   [7] *K.H. Accts. loc. cit.*; Sayle, p. 56.

[8] *Ibid.* II, fo. 121 v; Sayle, *loc. cit.*   [9] See above, p. 64 and n. 7.

certain, however, that between 1377 and 1383, during the wardenship of Simon Neylond, the collection of books was sadly depleted.
This information is contained in the letters patent of 14 July 1383
commissioning the visitation of the King's Hall by the bishop of
Ely:[1] there it is stated that by virtue of the neglect and bad govern-
ance of the warden a host of charters, books, valuables and other
muniments had been dissipated, sold or carried off.[2]

As information concerning the borrowing habits of fellows of
medieval colleges is rather difficult to come by, it is most fortunate
that the King's Hall accounts contain parts of four library lending
lists: one belonging to 1386–7, one to some date between 1385 and
1391, the third to 1390–1, and the fourth to 1392–3.[3] These record the
name of the fellow to whom the book was loaned, the author, the
incipit (the opening words of the second folio) and, in the case of the
second of these lists, the monetary value placed upon the book.
These values, which are expressed usually in marks but sometimes in
shillings, range from £6 13s 4d to 10s,[4] the most highly priced book
being the *Rosarium* of Archidiaconus, the lowest, a work of the
glossator Placentinus (*d.* 1192). No borrowing dates are specified
and, apart from the liability for the payment of the assessed price of
the book in case of loss or severe damage, no pledges seem to have
been exacted.

In the list for 1386, 80 volumes were distributed among the warden
and twenty-two Scholars so that the warden and one of the fellows
had 11 each, two had 7, one had 5, two had 4, three had 3, nine had 2
and the remaining four fellows one each.[5] The second list is much
briefer and records the distribution of books among the warden and
seven Scholars: in this instance, the warden had 6 books, two of the
fellows had 2, and the rest one volume apiece.[6] Apart from one or
two medical treatises and the occasional work on grammar, logic
and theology, the vast majority of the books borrowed were either
the basic civil and canon law texts or else commentaries upon these

[1] See above, p. 171.   [2] See above, p. 172, n. 1.

[3] The first, third and fourth of these lists are printed by Sayle, *art. cit.* pp. 62–3, 67–8,
69–70: the second list was missed by Sayle and is to be found in *K.H. Accts.* III, fo.
104.

[4] Thirteen such prices (*pret(c)ia*) are listed.

[5] *K.H. Accts.* III, fo. 19; Sayle, pp. 62–3.

[6] *K.H. Accts.* III, fo. 104.

subjects. Analysis of the remaining lists yields information of a similar nature.

When these borrowing lists are correlated with the seemingly almost complete library catalogue of 1391,[1] it becomes possible to discover the approximate extent of the lending part of the library as opposed to the chained or reference department. This catalogue lists a total of 101 books, one of which is reported missing. The books are divided into six classes as shown in table 16.

TABLE 16

	No. of volumes	No. chained
Libri grammaticales	11	5
Libri dialectici	5	1
Libri de medicina	16	—
Libri juris civilis	48	7
Libri theologie	5	1
Libri juris canonici	16	8
	101	22

It is thus clear from the table that only about one-fifth of the books were chained[2] and that the rest were available for lending purposes. At Peterhouse in 1418, where the stock of books was three times as large, just under half were chained, a proportion of the others being assigned for division among the fellows.[3] At Merton, the chained books were much less numerous than those kept for the personal use of the fellows.[4] Although it may be that the reference section in most English college libraries would generally be smaller than the lending department, there can be no doubt that the King's Hall library was overwhelmingly a borrowing one.

Wykeham's statutes for New College had enacted that only those books which remained after the fellows had made their selection

[1] This catalogue is printed by Sayle, pp. 64–7. The contemporary borrowing lists reveal a number of volumes not entered in the catalogue (see below, p. 251).

[2] This proportion is almost the same as that found at the Sorbonne in 1338: the catalogue of that year records 1,722 books, of which 330 are described as *cathenati* (F. M. Powicke, *The medieval books of Merton College* (Oxford, 1931), p. 9).

[3] A numerical analysis of this catalogue is given in Willis and Clark, *Architectural history*, III, 403; see also B. H. Streeter, *The chained library* (London, 1931), p. 8.

[4] Powicke, *Medieval books of Merton College*, pp. 7–8; Streeter, *loc. cit.*

were to be chained in the library.[1] The essence of this enactment was incorporated in the statutes of King's College, Cambridge.[2] In the statutes of All Souls of 1443, however, it is decreed that the fellows may select from only those books left over after the removal of the books to be chained.[3] Willis and Clark regarded this as having 'the importance of an original enactment'.[4] It is repeated, with variations, in the statutes of Magdalen,[5] Brasenose,[6] Corpus Christi[7] and Cardinal College.[8] The King's Hall statutes are silent on library arrangements; but judging from the fact that the chained books in the catalogue of 1391 are indicated in the margin by the abbreviation *cath* (i.e. *cathenati*) against each such volume, it is clear that here also in the fourteenth century it was customary to make a definite choice of books for the reference department prior to the selection of books by the fellows.

The diversity displayed in the library lists as to the number of volumes borrowed per fellow suggests that books might be borrowed according to immediate academic needs and that no rigid limitation was placed upon the number or kind of book required. Nor was borrowing restricted to the books of a fellow's current faculty. In the lending list of 1386–7 it is recorded that Simon Godrich, B.C.L., had taken out a total of eleven volumes, seven of which were parts of the Digest and the Code, one was a commentary of Azo, and the remaining three were medical treatises:[9] in the same list it is stated that William Waltham, B.C.L., had borrowed two medical works in addition to three of the 'extraordinary' books of the Code.[10] The later lists reveal similar combinations. Very occasionally, it seems, a book normally kept chained in the library might be loaned out.[11] In 1391, for instance, Nicholas Depyng borrowed the commentary of Jacobus de Ravanis on the *Digestum Novum* and two years later that of Cynus on the Code.[12] But these

---

[1] *Statutes*, I, ch. (5), 98; Willis and Clark, III, 391–2.

[2] *Camb. Docs.* II, 601–2; Willis and Clark, III, 392.   [3] *Statutes*, I, ch. (7), 54–5.

[4] Willis and Clark, *loc. cit.*   [5] *Statutes*, II, ch. (8), 61.

[6] *Ibid.* II, ch. (9), 35.   [7] *Ibid.* II, ch. (10), 90.

[8] *Ibid.* II, ch. (11), 112.   [9] See the list in Sayle, p. 62.

[10] *Ibid.* p. 63. The 'extraordinary' books of the Code are books X–XII.

[11] Powicke cites one such instance at Merton where, in 1452, a book described as 'in *libraria*' is included in an *electio* or distribution list of that year: Powicke, *Medieval books of Merton College*, p. 11.

[12] See the lists of 1390–1 and 1392–3 in Sayle, pp. 67, 69.

were evidently exceptional happenings and the distinction between the reference section and the circulating library was generally observed. Moreover, it is apparent that books might be renewed and indeed retained for as long as a Scholar had legitimate need, subject always to their production for inspection by the keeper of the library after each loan period,[1] a practice which serves to underline the unrestrictive character of the library as an eminently practical working institution.

As may be seen from the details given of the contents of the library catalogue, about half of the entire stock was composed of books on civil law. The basic texts comprised different sections of the Institutes, the Digest, divided into the *Digestum Vetus*, the *Digestum Infortiatum* and the *Digestum Novum*, the Code and the *Parvum Volumen*, in all twenty-eight volumes. This policy of division was no doubt maintained to ensure that students working on different sections of the texts might have more ready access to the appropriate parts. Among the commentaries were works by such distinguished glossators as Placentinus (*d.* 1192) and Azo (including the *Summa* on the Code), and by Odofredus (*d.* 1265), one of the last jurists of the school. What is especially noteworthy, however, is that the post-glossators or commentators should be so well represented. For in the catalogue of 1391 are found works by Jacobus de Ravanis (Jacques de Revigny) on the three parts of the Digest (*c.* 1250), by Jacobus de Belvisio (1270–1335), and by Cynus de Pistoia on the Code (written *c.* 1312–14) and on the *Digestum Vetus* (before 1329): and, while not specified in the list of 1391, it is known from the lending lists that the college also possessed works by Dinus (*d.* 1300), by Petrus de Bellapertica (Pierre de Belleperche, *d.* 1308) and by Jacobus Buttrigarius (1274–1348) on the *Digestum Vetus*. When to these are added, from a later list of 1435,[2] commentaries by Bartolus de Sassoferrato (1314–57) on the *Digestum Novum* and by Johannes Faber (Jean Faure, early fourteenth century), something of the range, variety and voguishness of civil law studies at the King's Hall can be gauged.

[1] The recurring phrase 'exhibet et rehabet' used throughout the borrowing lists clearly refers first to the exhibition of the book for inspection and second to the renewal of the loan. In the list of 1392–3, the term 'reliberavit integre' (or 'plene') appears to be substituted for 'exhibet' (Sayle, pp. 69–70).

[2] See below, p. 257.

In this respect, comparison with contemporary college and university library lists is most illuminating. A study of such Cambridge catalogues as have survived prompts the following conclusions: first, the ratio of civil law volumes to the total stock is elsewhere much smaller than at the King's Hall; and, second, in no other list do we find such a comparable range of jurist commentaries. In the list of books presented by Bishop Bateman to Trinity Hall in 1350,[1] civil law volumes represent less than one-fifth of the total bequest: moreover, with the exception of commentaries by Cynus and Rainerius de Forlivio and one, possibly, by Petrus de Bellapertica, all of these books comprised basic civil law texts. The earliest book list for Corpus Christi College, which forms part of a general inventory begun in 1376, contains the substantially greater proportion of 18 civil law manuscripts out of a total of 55;[2] but it is important to add that in the later catalogue of 76 books bequeathed to the college by Thomas Markaunt[3] in 1439, civil law studies are represented solely by a single volume of the Code.[4] For our knowledge of the contents of the medieval library of Pembroke we must, of necessity, rely mainly upon an incomplete list of donations extending from 1347 to 1487:[5] here, out of a total of 158 manuscripts only 9, or just possibly 10, are concerned with civil law. Similarly, of the 302 volumes enumerated in the Peterhouse catalogue of 1418 there are but 29 books on civil law,[6] and three of these had already been sold by this time. It would appear that this exceedingly low proportion

---

[1] These books are listed by G. E. Corrie, *C.A.S. Communications*, II (1864), no. vi, 73 ff.

[2] This list is printed by M. R. James, *A descriptive catalogue of the manuscripts in the library of Corpus Christi College, Cambridge*, I (Cambridge, 1912), ix–xi.

[3] Fellow of Corpus Christi College from 1413–14 until his death in 1439.

[4] The list is printed by M. R. James, 'Catalogue of Thomas Markaunt's library from MS. C.C.C. 232', *C.A.S.* (octavo series), no. xxxii (1899), pp. 76–82.

[5] Printed by M. R. James, *A descriptive catalogue of the manuscripts in the library of Pembroke College, Cambridge* (Cambridge, 1905), xiii–xvii; see also G. E. Corrie, 'A list of books presented to Pembroke College, Cambridge, by different donors, during the fourteenth and fifteenth centuries', *C.A.S. Communications*, II (1860–4), no. iii, 13–23.

[6] The old catalogue of 1418 together with the lists of subsequent donations up to 1481 is printed by M. R. James, *A descriptive catalogue of the manuscripts in the library of Peterhouse, Cambridge* (Cambridge, 1899), pp. 3–26. For a convenient numerical analysis of the original catalogue see Willis and Clark, III, 403. Among the commentaries are works by Azo, Roffredus, Odofredus, Petrus de Bellapertica, Cynus and Bartolus.

remained static until at least 1481; for by this date some 137 manuscripts had been added to the library by private donation and not
one of these pertained to the discipline of civil law.[1] Out of a total of
111 manuscripts listed in an inventory of Clare College of *c.* 1440[2]
there are to be found only 13 works on civil law, 10 of which are
basic texts and 3 commentaries by Azo, one on the Institutes and two
on the Code:[3] a supplementary list of 55 donations extending to *c.*
1440[4] adds about another half-dozen, as does a register of the un-
bound books in the library of 1496.[5] In the earliest library catalogue
remaining for King's College, dated *c.* 1452, civil law studies find
no representation whatsoever among the 175 manuscripts listed;[6]
nor are any civil law books known to have been given by private
bequest throughout the remainder of the fifteenth century.[7] Moreover, it is rather surprising to find that not a single civil law text or
commentary is listed in the Cambridge University Library catalogue
of *c.* 1435, containing 122 volumes,[8] although it is known that an
unspecified number of civil law books had been bequeathed *c.* 1415:[9]
the catalogue appears to be complete and the lack of reference to any

[1] For these additional MSS. see James, *Catalogue of Peterhouse, cit.* pp. 3–26.

[2] This inventory is printed by R. W. Hunt, 'Medieval inventories of Clare College
Library', *Transactions of the Cambridge Bibliographical Society*, I (1950), 110–16.

[3] *Ibid.* 111–12. By comparison, there are 43 items on canon law (113–14).

[4] *Ibid.* 116–18.

[5] *Ibid.* 119–21. Eighty-seven works are here listed, most of which belong to theology
and philosophy or are of a miscellaneous character.

[6] The catalogue is printed by M. R. James, *A descriptive catalogue of the manuscripts
other than oriental in the library of King's College, Cambridge* (Cambridge, 1895), pp.
72–83; for the dating of the entries see J. Saltmarsh, *V.C.H.* (Cambridge), III, 393,
n. 60.

[7] See the examination of fifteenth-century wills containing bequests of books to
King's College by A. N. L. Munby, 'Notes on King's College library in the
fifteenth century', *Trans. Camb. Bib. Soc.* I (1951), 280 ff.

[8] This list is printed by H. Bradshaw, 'Two lists of books in the University Library',
C.A.S. Communications, II (1864), no. xxii, 242–57; for the dating of this list see the
additional remarks of Bradshaw, 277–8; see also Willis and Clark, III, 404.

[9] Bequeathed by William Loryng, brother of Sir Nigel Loryng, chamberlain of the
Black Prince, *d.* as canon of Salisbury by February 1416. (For his career see Emden,
B.R.U.C. pp. 373–4.) The bequest is contained in his will, dated 14 December 1415
and proved 20 March 1416, in *Reg. Chichele* (ed. E. F. Jacob with the assistance of
H. C. Johnson), II (Oxford, 1938), 81: 'Item volo quod omnes libri mei iuris
civilis remaneant in communi libraria scolarium universitatis Cantebrigg' imper-
petuum.' Only one of these volumes remains in the University Library: CUL, MS.
Dd.7.17 (*Codex* of Justinian, containing the *glossa ordinaria*).

work on civil law or even to a sectional heading for this discipline is indeed puzzling.[1] Nor is the civil law content in the later catalogue of 1473 very impressive, there being only a dozen or so volumes on this subject out of a total of 330 listed works.[2] The lengthy catalogue for Queens' of 1472, which enumerates 224 volumes, contains one civil law book;[3] and in the late fifteenth-century list for St Catharine's College, this discipline appears to be represented solely by a copy of the Institutes.[4]

In the light of this investigation, it is indisputable that of all the Cambridge colleges the King's Hall was the best equipped for the pursuit of civil law studies. The practical outcome of this for the university in terms of civil law graduates will be discussed below, but first it is necessary to complete the analysis of the library catalogue of 1391. In marked contrast to the impressive stock of works on Roman law, the King's Hall catalogue contains only 16 volumes on canon law. The standard texts comprised parts of the *Decreta* (i.e. Gratian), the *Decretales* and the *Liber Sextus*: the commentaries included works by Vincentius Hispanus on the Decretals (early thirteenth century), the *Speculum Judiciale* of Guilielmus Durantis (written by 1276), the *Rosarium* (composed between 1296 and 1302) and a commentary on the *Liber Sextus* (compiled between 1299 and 1312) by the Archidiaconus, and the writings of Innocent IV, Dinus and Johannes Andreae (d. 1348). From the list of 1435[5] must be added works by Roffredus Epiphanii (d. 1243), Goffredus de Trano (d. 1245), Guilielmus de Mandagoto (d. 1312) and Guilielmus de

---

[1] The catalogue lists 23 volumes on canon law under a separate sectional heading.

[2] The list is printed by Bradshaw, *op. cit.* 258–76. This catalogue of 1473, and presumably the earlier one of *c.* 1435, refer to the common library (*libraria communis*) or great library (*libraria magna*) as opposed to the more private chancellor's library (*libraria domini cancellarii*).

[3] The catalogue is printed by W. G. Searle, *C.A.S. Communications*, II (1864), no. xv, 168–81.

[4] The catalogue is printed by G. E. Corrie, *C.A.S.* (quarto publications), I (1840), 1–5. At Oxford, the Oriel catalogue of 1375 contains several civil law texts but no commentaries (C.L.Shadwell, *Collectanea* (ed. C. R. L. Fletcher, Oxf. Hist. Soc., 1885), I, 67); that for Merton has a few texts and commentaries (see the references to civil law books in the index, Powicke, *op. cit.*); the New College list displays a fairly wide range of both texts and commentaries (A. F. Leach, *Collectanea* (ed. M. Burrows, Oxf. Hist. Soc., 1896), III, 240–2); but the most extensive civil law section appears to be that contained in the list of All Souls *c.* 1440 (E. F. Jacob, 'An early book list of All Souls College', printed as an appendix to 'The two lives of Archbishop Chichele', *B.J.R.L.* XVI (1932), 469–81). [5] See below, p. 257.

Monte Lauduno on the *Liber Sextus* (before 1343). Medicine seems to have figured more prominently in the studies of the King's Scholars than might otherwise be suspected. For the catalogue of 1391 itemises as many books on medicine as there were on canon law: and the lending lists testify to the fact that medical treatises were regularly borrowed. In the medical section were works by Hippocrates, Galen, Isaac the Jew, Constantinus Africanus, Avicenna and Thomas Aquinas as well as several anonymous and unidentifiable tracts. Of the remaining subjects, grammar was served by the books of Priscian, Papias, Cassiodorus, Isidore and the dictionaries of Hugucio of Pisa and John Balbi of Genoa (i.e. the *Catholicon*, 1286): the small section on theology comprised only five works, one of which was a complete Bible.[1]

Concrete evidence for the position of the King's Hall as a cradle of civil law studies within the Cambridge *studium* is afforded by a numerical comparison of the college's output of civil law graduates with the total output from the university in the same period. In order to keep the data within manageable proportions and also because the evidence is not sufficiently copious or reliable in the later period, especially in the sixteenth century, this comparison has been confined to the years between 1317 and 1450. It has been shown

---

[1] As far as is known not a single manuscript or early printed book from the King's Hall library has passed into the present Trinity College collection. (See the remarks of R. Sinker, *A catalogue of the fifteenth-century printed books in the library of Trinity College, Cambridge* (Cambridge and London, 1876), p. vi.) The only surviving remnants from the King's Hall library appear to be two fifteenth-century MSS. now in the British Museum (N. R. Ker, *Medieval libraries of Great Britain* (2nd ed. London, 1964), p. 26). Trinity College Library seems to contain only one text from the medieval period, an early sixteenth-century printed edition of Petrus Comestor's *Historia scholastica*, formerly in the possession of Michaelhouse: *Historia scholastica* (Strassburg, pr. G. Husner, 1503), Trinity College Library, C.15.2, bearing the inscription of provenance on the fourth folio. The disappearance of the King's Hall library need occasion no especial surprise as the greater parts of all the libraries of medieval Cambridge colleges have vanished. M. R. James thought that the prime responsibility for this lay with the commissioners appointed by Edward VI to reform the universities: James, 'The sources of Archbishop Parker's collection of MSS. at Corpus Christi College, Cambridge', *C.A.S.* (octavo series), no. xxxii (1899), p. 4. R. W. Hunt, however, believes the more probable explanation to be that 'the collections of manuscripts were regarded as out of date and useless, that they were no longer taken care of and were allowed to disintegrate, and that the remnant was finally thrown away or disposed of to bookbinders' (Hunt, *art. cit.* 109).

above that over this selected period at least 53 of the King's Scholars are known to have taken degrees in civil law while still fellows of the Hall, the vast majority of them between 1350 and 1450.[1] An analysis of the entries in A. B. Emden's *A biographical register of the University of Cambridge* has revealed that from the late thirteenth to the mid-fifteenth centuries at least 198 civil law degrees were taken by university students who were neither King's Scholars nor King's Hall pensioners, with an additional 27 degrees which are probably of Cambridge origin. These figures indicate that over the specified period the King's Hall supplied about a fifth of the university's output of legists. But as this reckoning includes the latter years of the thirteenth century (before the institution of the Society of the King's Scholars) and the first half of the fourteenth century when the King's Hall was largely undergraduate in composition, it would be more profitable to compare the figures for the hundred years following 1350. For this period, the number of civil law degrees taken within the university (excluding, as before, those of King's Scholars and King's Hall pensioners) was about 173, with 23 'probables': the corresponding figure for the King's Hall is 48.[1] Again, this indicates that the college furnished about a fifth of all Cambridge civilians in this hundred-year period. As the proportion has remained constant, it follows that the university's output of civil law graduates from the middle of the fourteenth century onwards must have increased in roughly the same proportion as at the King's Hall.

It is not at all easy to estimate the individual output of the other Cambridge colleges as we do not possess lists of fellows comparable to that for the King's Hall: for this reason only very rough computations can be made. It would seem, however, that Trinity Hall ranks next to the King's Hall as far as civil law studies are concerned but with only a quarter of the output of the royal foundation; Peterhouse comes next and is closely followed by Clare; Pembroke, Gonville and Corpus Christi find representation but the numbers involved are now so few that no further meaningful distinctions can be drawn.

It is apparent that successive English kings had attempted to foster civil law studies at the King's Hall right from the early fourteenth century. This legal emphasis was given specific verbal expression in an indenture of 2 July 1440 relating to the handsome gift of 77

---

[1] For 1317–50 see above, p. xiii, note (*e*); for 1350–1450 see above, pp. 54–5.

volumes made to the college five years previously by Henry VI. The grant was the direct outcome of a supplication presented to the king by Richard Caudray, warden of the King's Hall, in which it was stated that the library was insufficiently stocked with books necessary for the proper advancement of the studies of the Scholars.[1] As in the case of the former royal bequests, that of 1435 was significantly weighted towards Roman law, there being no fewer than 28 volumes on civil law comprising 23 texts and 5 commentaries.[2] The indenture testifying to the delivery of the books was made between Ralph Cromwell, treasurer and chancellor of the exchequer, and warden Richard Caudray. In the preamble, it is asserted that these volumes had been presented for the better erudition of the King's Scholars so that the king and the state might be better served, especially in civil law: '...pro meliori erudicione Scolarium Regis in dicto Collegio commorant' ac ut Regi et rei publice melius de eisdem *potissime in Jure civili* imposterum deserviatur tradidit et deliveravit...libros infrascriptos...' This piece of evidence appears to be an unequivocal statement of the value of this academic institution from the monarchical standpoint. For it now seems clear that English kings had come to regard the King's Hall, their own highly exclusive university possession, as a college whose primary function was the output of civil law graduates who would constitute, so to speak, a corps of

---

[1] The essence of this petition is reported in the indenture of 2 July 1440 preserved in *K.H. Cabinet*, no. 102.

[2] This list of 1435 is printed by Sayle, *art. cit.* pp. 71–2. Henry VI's generous bequest of 77 volumes to the King's Hall in 1435 was paralleled five years later in 1440 by a similar grant of 27 books given out of the exchequer to the recently founded Oxford college of All Souls (R. Weiss, 'Henry VI and the library of All Souls College', *E.H.R.* LVII (1942), 102 ff.); of the 27 books, 4 were on civil law, 5 on canon law, 17 on theology and one on philosophy (p. 104). For our knowledge of the library collections of medieval English kings we have to rely upon a few scattered lists of books found among wardrobe and exchequer records. Evidence of the earliest known collection dates from John's reign (V. H. Galbraith, 'The literacy of the medieval English kings', *Proceedings of the British Academy*, XXI (1935), 201 ff. at pp. 214–15). Although the first properly constituted royal library appears to date from the reign of Edward IV (G. F. Warner and J. P. Gilson, *Catalogue of western manuscripts in the old Royal and King's collections* (London, 1921), I, xi), it is evident that all medieval English kings, at least from Edward II onwards, possessed a store of books at their disposal; and judging from the substantial nature of the grants made to the King's Hall and to All Souls, in all totalling 104 volumes, it would certainly seem that during the reign of Henry VI this royal stock of exchequer books was indeed very considerable.

legally trained 'king's men'. And this royal emphasis at the King's Hall upon the discipline of Roman law with its concomitant theories of theocratic kingship might well come within the category of those periodic attempts on the part of the monarchy to free itself from the limitations imposed upon it by feudal law. The stress laid by English kings upon the theocratic nature of kingship as opposed to its more predominant feudal character is a recurring theme and stands at the root of the series of constitutional crises from the reign of John to Richard II.[1] In his *De Laudibus Legum Anglie* Sir John Fortescue makes a general reference to those English kings who had attempted to assert the primacy of civil law over the English common law so that they might 'rule regally' over a subject people.[2] And, generally speaking, with the ever-present example before them of the highly developed theocratic monarchy in France, English kings had, to a lesser or greater degree, tried to harness to their support Romanist governmental teachings and the more 'mystical' attributes of kingship: Edward II's *imitatio regis Francorum* concerning the supposedly miraculous oil of Thomas Becket is a good illustration of this latter point.[3] In the light of these considerations, it is perhaps not unimportant to find that under direct royal patronage and stimulation the King's Hall, Cambridge, was evidently playing a leading part in the perpetuation of civil law studies at the English universities in the medieval period.[4] While Roman law never succeeded in supplanting English common law, though it may well have come within an ace of doing so for a time in the sixteenth century, by ensuring its continuance at the universities through such institutions as the King's Hall the English monarchy appears to have been striving to engender and nourish a climate of thought in the country which would be generally favourable towards the accentuation of the more theocratic aspects of kingship.

[1] For a very full discussion of the feudal and theocratic elements of English kingship see W. Ullmann, *Principles of government and politics in the middle ages* (2nd ed., London, 1966), pp. 150 ff.

[2] *De Laudibus Legum Anglie* (ed. S. B. Chrimes, Cambridge, 1942), pp. 79–80.

[3] W. Ullmann, 'Thomas Becket's miraculous oil', *J.T.S.* VIII (1957), 129 ff.

[4] Added incentives for the output of trained civilians from the English universities were doubtless provided by the increased diplomatic activity arising out of the Hundred Years War and by the widespread conciliar movement in Europe in the late fourteenth and early fifteenth centuries. This whole subject, however, awaits a historian.

EX-FELLOW PENSIONERS, COMMONERS AND
SEMI-COMMONERS

As in most contemporary collegiate institutions, the King's Hall made provision for a number of residents who were not on the foundation. These *extranei* divide fairly naturally into two main categories. There were those who may be described conveniently as ex-fellow pensioners, comprising fellows who had vacated their fellowships but continued to reside in the King's Hall as pensioners paying full rates for board and lodging. The second category consisted of residents who had never at any time been 'on the boards' of the foundation and were admitted to the college either as commoners taking full commons or as semi-commoners who paid only half the commons rate in return for meals of a lower standard. Each of these classes will be considered in turn.

The term *pensionarius* is not found anywhere in the King's Hall accounts. It is nevertheless justifiable to use this term with reference to all the ex-fellow residents and to a sizable proportion of the other commoners both by virtue of the *pensio* or rent charged for their rooms and because of the later prevalence of this designation at Cambridge in the early sixteenth century.[1] In the Society's annual records, the entries for all commoners and semi-commoners occur immediately after the list of *socii* or resident fellows of the college.[2] Each entry is headed by the surname of the *extraneus* and contains the sums due to the college for his commons and sizings for each week or parts of a week as well as for those of servants, clerks, priests or relatives attached to his person and for whom he was financially responsible to the accounting officers of the college. At this juncture is also set down the *pensio* for his room or rooms and any other miscellaneous item for which the college was entitled to be reimbursed.[3] On the basis of the number of entries for weekly commons

---

[1] See below, p. 262 and n. 3.

[2] With one or two exceptions where fellows are described by their Christian names, only the surnames of the King's Scholars are entered in these lists, proving that reference by surname was a well-established collegiate practice by the early years of the fourteenth century.

[3] E.g. ex-fellow pensioner John Wittilsey rented a small fuel-house (described variously as 'parva domus', 'wodhows' and 'domus focalium') from the college at a rent of 2s a year: *K.H. Accts.* v, fo. 82v; vi, fos. 28, 47v, 69v, 92, 116, 133v,

the amount of residence each year of most of the academic *extranei* can be fairly accurately calculated.

The King's Hall *extranei* are not at first accorded technical designation in this annually recurrent section of the records. They are, however, classified in a series of accounts for weekly commons stretching from 1364 to 1398–9. On these occasions, personnel not on the foundation are referred to variously as *commensales, sojournants* or *commorantes. Commensales* first occur in the account of 1364–5,[1] *sojournants* and *commorantes* in that of 1382–3.[2] There is no evidence that these terms can be differentiated in any meaningful way[3] beyond the fact that, of the three, *commensales* is by far the most commonly employed; although, from later analogy, it is just possible that they denote different methods of boarding.[4] In the period immediately following 1389–90 information about academic *extranei* is only rarely entered in the accounts for weekly commons. A few references to *commensales* are found in 1393–4,[5] 1394–5[6] and 1398–9[7] but after this

150; VII, fo. 15. The accounts contain numerous entries for the purchase by commoners of fuel and food commodities such as flour, almonds and other types of spices: e.g. *ibid.* XI, fo. 16 v; XII, fos. 103 v, 142 v; XIII, fo. 69.

[1] *Ibid.* II, fos. 91–3. The form is always the same: in the entry for weekly commons the number present for that week is given followed by the statement: (number) de quibus (unus, duo, tres, etc.) sunt commensales.

[2] *Ibid.* III, fos. 108–110 v.

[3] From many examples see the series of weeks, eleven to sixteen inclusive, in the commons account for 1382–3 (III, fo. 108 v) where the following terms are used: week 11: *comorantes*; week 12: *soj(i)ournants*; week 13: *comorantes*; week 14: *comorantes*; week 15: *commensales*; week 16: *commensales. Soj(i)ournant*, meaning guest, visitor or lodger, was a term in vogue in England in the fourteenth and fifteenth centuries. See e.g. the letter of Jane Stonor to her husband (*c.* 1470) informing him that she would 'raythere breke up housallde than take sugiornantes...' (*The Stonor letters and papers, 1290–1483* (ed. C. L. Kingsford for the Camden Society, 3rd series, XXIX, London, 1919), I, 110); also John Paston's letter to Margaret Paston of 3 February 1478 in which he writes, 'your doughter of Sweynsthorpp and hyr sojornaunt E. Paston recomandyth hem to yow...' (*The Paston letters, 1422–1509* (ed. J. Gairdner, 6 vols., London and Exeter, 1904), V, 312). For further examples of *soj(i)ournants* in the accounts see *K.H. Accts.* III, fos. 55 (week 7), 121 (week 1), 122 (week 7).

[4] For example, at Oriel in the early sixteenth century 'a *batellarius* paid for the food that he ordered, and ate it in his room; a *commensalis* or *communarius* had his food in hall, and paid a fixed sum each week according to contract' (*The Dean's Register of Oriel, 1446–1661* (ed. G. C. Richards and H. E. Salter, Oxf. Hist. Soc., LXXXIV, 1926), 56, n. 4).

[5] *K.H. Accts.* IV, fo. 16 v (week 12).   [6] *Ibid.* IV, fo. 39 v (week 22).

[7] *Ibid.* IV, fo. 124 v (week 24, erroneously numbered 34).

date the term largely disappears from the records.[1] By the middle of the fifteenth century, however, the King's Hall *extranei* had acquired more uniform terminology. After the list of resident fellows in the accounts of 1451–2, 1452–3 and 1453–4, all commoners are classified as *communarii*[2] and those who lodged at the rate of half commons are designated *semicommunarii*.[3] These terms are used consistently until the last quarter of the fifteenth century, when the general word *perhendinantes* is frequently substituted to embrace all gradings of academic *extranei*.[4]

The diversity of these entries for academic lodgers reflects the amorphous state of the nomenclature for commoners in the pre-Reformation era. At University College, Oxford, the terms *commensales* and *commorantes* are found;[5] at Oriel, lodgers were known as *commorantes* in the fifteenth and *commensales*, *communarii* or *batellarii* in the sixteenth century;[6] rooms were let to *commorantes* at Canterbury College,[7] and at Exeter and Queen's *communarii* and *commensales* are the terms employed.[8] At Merton *communarii* had a peculiar and puzzling application[9] and at Eton College the *commensals* were privileged commoners who were given free tuition provided that they

---

[1] In 1430–1, there is an entry concerning the arrears for commons of ex-fellow pensioner John Bank (fellow, admitted 11 July 1424; resigned 5 March 1428) in which the term *commensalis* is used: 'Item John Bank debet collegio pro communibus tempore quo fuerat commensalis [£3 15s 3½d]...' (*ibid.* VIII, fo. 1).

[2] *Ibid.* X, fos. 101, 102, 133v–134v, 165–166.

[3] *Ibid.* X, fos. 102v–104, 135–137, 166–167.

[4] *Ibid.* XV, fo. 117; XVI, fos. 17, 60, 114v; XIX, fo. 42.

[5] A. Oswald, 'University College', *V.C.H.* (Oxford), III, 63.

[6] W. A. Pantin, 'Oriel College and St Mary Hall', *ibid.* III, 120; see also specifically the references cited in the *Dean's Register of Oriel*, pp. 51, 56, 61–2; for *commorantes* see *Oriel College Records* (ed. C. L. Shadwell and H. E. Salter, Oxf. Hist. Soc., LXXXV, 1926), 52, 55–6.

[7] Rashdall, III, 213, n. 1.

[8] Salter, *Medieval Oxford*, p. 100. Among the *commensales* of Queen's in the late fourteenth century were John Wyclif, Nicholas of Hereford and John Trevisa; see R. H. Hodgkin, *Six centuries of an Oxford college*, pp. 27–38.

[9] The Merton *communarii* appear to have been youths who were maintained for several years in return for the performance of specified duties. They were never to exceed four in number and were to be reduced to three or two if the college income fell below a stipulated minimum level. These *communarii* were therefore a charge upon the finances of Merton whereas elsewhere they were usually a source of revenue. (*Registrum Annalium Collegii Mertonensis, 1483–1521*, ed. cit. xv–xvii; also Rashdall, III, 200, n. 2.)

paid for their board and lodging.[1] On the other hand, the word most commonly used in Cambridge college statutes of the fourteenth and fifteenth centuries to denote lodgers is *per(h)endinantes*,[2] a term which does not appear in the Oxford codes of the same period. *Pensionarius* is for the first time used in place of *perendinans* in the statutes of Christ's College, Cambridge, of 1506[3] and henceforth, in the sixteenth-century codes, *pensionarii* and *commensales* are the terms usually found.[4] There would seem to be little doubt that it was the prevalence of the designation *pensionarius* among the Cambridge colleges of the sixteenth century which led to its adoption after the Reformation to describe that class of undergraduate commoners who were not on the foundation but resided in college, paying their way for board, lodging and all necessary expenses.[5]

Of the 600 or more King's Scholars on the boards of the college between 1337 and 1546, at least 52[6] are known to have lived at some time in the Hall as pensioners either immediately or shortly after the vacation of their fellowships and for lengths of residence ranging from several years[7] to brief spells of a few weeks or days. It is certain that 34 of them resided for an appreciable part of one or more years

[1] H. C. Maxwell Lyte, *A history of Eton College, ed. cit.* p. 19; for an analysis of the relevant statutory provisions regarding *commensales* see appendix A, p. 582.

[2] E.g. the statutes of Peterhouse in *Camb. Docs.* II, 27, and the statutes of Queens', *ibid.* III, 37.

[3] See the statutes of Christ's College, *De Pensionariis intra Collegium admittendis*, *ibid.* III, 208. The term *pensionarii* is recorded in the first quarter of the sixteenth century in the earliest extant Bursar's Book of Gonville Hall: see J. Venn, *Early collegiate life, cit.* pp. 68–9, where a list of *pensionarii* is cited for the year 1513; also J. Venn, *Gonville and Caius College* (College Histories Series, London, 1910), p. 30.

[4] From many examples see the statutes of Clare of 1551 in *Camb. Docs.* II, 164; also the Edwardian statutes of Trinity College of 1552, *cit.* cap. XVI, pp. 20–1. However, *perendinant* is sometimes retained as a sectional heading in the statutes: see e.g. the early sixteenth-century statutes of Jesus College, *De admissione commensalium sive perhendinantium*, in *Camb. Docs.* III, 120–1; this point is made by Willis and Clark, *Architectural history*, I, xc.

[5] The equivalent of the Oxford 'commoner'. For a discussion of the post-Reformation pensioner at Cambridge see D. A. Winstanley, *Unreformed Cambridge* (Cambridge, 1935), pp. 200–1.

[6] There may well have been more than 52 since consideration must be taken of the several gaps in the records of the fourteenth century. No accounts at all have survived for the period 1370–1 to 1381–2 and, while a few folios remain, the full accounts are missing for 1354–5, 1355–6, 1357–8 and 1358–9.

[7] E.g. John Wittilsey remained a pensioner for fifteen years; Richard Lyes for twelve; Peter Stukely for eleven; and Simon Baret for nine.

during which they remained as pensioners, staying for periods extending from a minimum of ten[1] to a maximum of fifty weeks: the rest were only occasional visitors or 'birds of passage' who came up to Cambridge to live in the college for a number of weeks or days at a time.[2] The distribution of ex-fellows over the whole period was as follows: four became pensioners between 1337 and 1350; eleven between 1350 and 1400; twenty-seven between 1400 and 1450; and ten between 1450 and 1500–1. Apart from Sokeborne in 1500–1, no other fellow is recorded as a pensioner in the sixteenth century before the dissolution of the college in 1546. The marked increase in the number of pensioners in the first half of the fifteenth century is doubtless linked with the substantial growth in non-residence detectable among the senior members of the Society in the same period.[3] Indeed, unless this latter circumstance had prevailed, the college could not possibly have provided the accommodation necessary for the reception of such an enlarged influx of lodgers. The apparently direct connection between non-residence among the seniors and the growth in the number of pensioners is strikingly demonstrated by reference to the figures for one exceptional year. In 1421–2, when the number of fellows in residence had fallen to the very low yearly average of ten present per week,[4] the corresponding number of ex-fellows who resided at intervals throughout the year attained the unusually high figure of nine. Moreover, if the figures are examined for all the years of 'low residence' between 1419–20 and 1426–7,[5] when the average numbers of fellows present per week were only 17, 10, 15, 19, 22, 20 and 17,[6] the analogous figures for ex-fellow pensioners were 6, 9, 4, 4, 5, 5 and 5 compared with the average number of three or four present per annum in the first half of the fifteenth century.

Whereas 52 of the King's Hall pensioners were ex-fellows, at least

[1] A minimum of ten weeks has been selected to represent an 'appreciable' period of residence since this is roughly equivalent to a university term: it must be stressed, however, that figures quoted in this chapter indicating lengths of residence may denote either periods of consecutive weeks or numbers of weeks distributed throughout the year. It has seemed unnecessary to make the distinction in each case.

[2] See e.g. below, p. 266.

[3] See above, p. 55 and n. 2.

[4] See above, table 5 (pullout), column 4.

[5] With the exception of 1420–1 for which there is no account.

[6] See above, table 5 (pullout), column 4.

four of the fellows were ex-commoners. Boynton, who became a fellow in 1461–2, had been present as a commoner for 13 weeks of the previous year;[1] Screne was admitted as a fellow in 1461–2 after residence as a commoner for three weeks in 1460–1;[2] John Derby, who was re-admitted as a fellow in 1468–9, was a commoner for 11 weeks in 1465–6, 44 weeks in 1466–7, 43 weeks in 1467–8 and 9 weeks in 1468–9;[3] and Thomas Pykering, incorporated as a fellow on 17 July 1492, had been a commoner for 33 weeks in 1490–1 and 30 weeks in 1491–2.[4] It is not improbable that here we have instances of candidates who had been promised fellowships at some future date and who preferred to enter the college as pensioners until such time as the necessary vacancies should arise. Perhaps it was felt that concrete attachment to the college in this capacity would enhance their chances of later incorporation.

This same pattern of academic promotion was repeated at the semi-commoner level. The accounts reveal that as early as the fourteenth century opportunities evidently existed for a member of this class to be elevated to the ranks of the fellows. Four such cases are recorded, in each of which the future fellow lived as a semi-commoner prior to incorporation into the Society. On 12 December 1357 John de Grimesby was admitted as a fellow, having been present as a semi-commoner for the greater part of 1356–7;[5] Geoffrey Asteley, charged as a semi-commoner in 1436–7, 1437–8 and for nine weeks in 1438–9,[6] was admitted as a fellow on 15 December 1438; William Soole was present as a semi-commoner for 24 weeks of 1436–7 and for seven weeks of 1437–8,[7] after which he was incorporated as a fellow of the college; and lastly, John Coo, a semi-commoner between 1422–3 and 1425–6,[8] is most probably to be identified with one John Coo appointed a fellow on 17 July 1432. The fact that these were promotions from the semi-commoner ranks suggests that ability rather than wealth or background was here the operative criterion. It would, however, be misleading to equate the semi-commoners of the King's Hall with the sizars and sub-sizars found in Cambridge colleges in the post-Reformation era.[9]

[1] *K.H. Accts.* XIII, fo. 19v.
[2] *Loc. cit.*
[3] *Ibid.* XIII, fos. 70, 118, 142; XIV, fo. 18v.
[4] *Ibid.* XVIII, fos. 108, 139.
[5] *Ibid.* II, fo. 9v.
[6] *Ibid.* IX, fos. 29v, 47v, 75.
[7] *Ibid.* IX, fos. 29v, 47v.
[8] *Ibid.* VII, fos. 15v, 31v, 47, 67v.
[9] On the subject of sizars see D. A. Winstanley, *op. cit.* pp. 201–2.

Whereas the latter were poor youths, often of great ability, who were permitted to live at very low cost, paying their way by the performance of menial services, the King's Hall semi-commoners were not an economically depressed class but persons of some consequence who lived at a rate not much below the full commons level at most contemporary English colleges.

While a degree of academic mobility thus undoubtedly existed for members of both gradings of the commoner class, the available evidence does not bear out the conclusion that promotions of this kind occurred on any really significant scale: on the contrary, they appear to have been occasional happenings making sporadic breaches in the solid wall dividing foundation members from the motley assembly of tolerated lodgers. There is no reason to suppose that these findings are untypical of the situation elsewhere.

The diversity in the residential habits of the ex-fellow pensioners can best be illustrated by means of concrete examples. It is clear that the majority of these fellows had vacated their fellowships upon promotion to benefices and that some, such as John Albon, were subsequently granted episcopal licence to study at a university for a specific number of years.[1] As might be expected, ex-fellows of this type lived in the college for the greater part of each year of residence when studying for degrees in the superior university faculties.[2] Others, such as John Wittilsey, John Metefeld (Metford), Robert Leek and John Hole (Hoole), during the time that they were King's Hall pensioners, participated in an official capacity in diocesan administration: Wittilsey, charged as a commoner between 1412–13 and 1426–7, was an official of the archdeacon of Ely in 1411 and still held that position in 1415;[3] Metefeld, a pensioner from the vacation of his fellowship in 1389–90 until at least 1390–1,[4] was admitted as chancellor of the bishop of Ely on 25 October 1389 and was acting in that capacity in 1407;[5] Robert Leek, accounted for as a commoner in 1421–2[6] and again in 1424–5,[7] served as vicar general of the

---

[1] Emden, *B.R.U.C.* p. 5.
[2] Albon is accounted for 18 weeks in 1405–6, 49 weeks in 1406–7, 46 weeks in 1407–8 and 50 weeks in 1408–9: *K.H. Accts.* v, fo. 97v; vi, fo. 13; v, fos. 109, 122.
[3] Emden, *op. cit.* p. 644.
[4] *K.H. Accts.* III, fo. 20. There is no information available for pensioners for the years 1391–2 and 1392–3 but Metefeld had ceased to be a commoner by 1393–4.
[5] Emden, p. 404. [6] *K.H. Accts.* VI, fo. 150. [7] *Ibid.* VII, fo. 47v.

bishop of Lincoln in 1421;[1] and John Hole, pensioner from 1496 to 1499,[2] was a canon of York and prebendary of Riccall in 1496–7, archdeacon of Cleveland from March to May of 1497 and archdeacon of the East Riding from May 1497 until his death in 1500.[3] As already indicated, several ex-fellows who technically may be designated pensioners were so only in the sense that they made occasional and usually brief visits to the Hall. We may select the case of John Grym as an example of personnel belonging to this category. Grym vacated his fellowship upon promotion to a benefice on 10 March 1419 and in the years immediately succeeding held the rectorship of Fen Drayton, Cambridgeshire, the wardenship of St John's Hospital, Armston, Northamptonshire, and the vicarship of Terrington St Clement, Norfolk.[4] Although he appears to have devoted most of his time to his various livings, Grym visited his old college regularly each year between 1418–19 and 1427–8, residing for periods extending from a week to as long as a month in 1425–6.[5] Other members of this 'visiting' category of pensioners came much less frequently. John Lynne, for example, who vacated his fellowship in 1437–8, returned to the college solely to attend the Christmas festivities of 1440–1, apparently at the invitation of the master and fellows.[6]

It would be of some value to discover how those ex-fellow pensioners who concurrently held ecclesiastical benefices apportioned their time between the college and their charges. A certain amount of information can be derived from an examination of several individual cases but, as will be seen, it would be dangerous to draw too many generalised conclusions about this matter.

We may first of all consider the case of Simon Baret, accounted for as a pensioner between 1410–11 and 1419–20,[7] but who seems to have spent most of his time away from the college. It is not known if Baret held a benefice during the first three of these years;[8] on 16 November 1413, however, he was admitted as rector of Brent Eleigh, Suffolk, and retained this living until May 1419.[9] Apart from

---

[1] Emden, *B.R.U.C.* p. 361.
[2] *K.H. Accts.* XIX, fos. 63, 91, 120v.
[3] Emden, *op. cit.* pp. 310–11.
[4] *Ibid.* p. 274.
[5] *K.H. Accts.* VI, fos. 93v, 117v, 150v; VII, fos. 15, 30v, 47, 67, 85v, 103.
[6] *Ibid.* IX, fo. 160.
[7] *Ibid.* V, fos. 143v, 166, 179, 83; VI, fos. 134v, 48, 94, 117.
[8] For details of his early career see Emden, *op. cit.* p. 37.
[9] *Loc. cit.*

a period of seven weeks in 1415–16[1] and a few days every year, Baret was clearly non-resident throughout the whole of this time, although he continued to pay rent for his room in the King's Hall. After the vacation of his benefice in 1419,[2] he returned to the college and resided for eight weeks in the latter part of 1418–19[3] and for thirty-five weeks during 1419–20.[4] His connection with the college was permanently severed upon his admission into the rectorship of Great Snoring, Norfolk, on 1 January 1421.[5] From evidence of this kind it appears that a King's Hall pensionership could be utilised merely to provide a convenient base between the vacation of one benefice and the retention of another. There were, however, ex-fellow pensioners, of whom Peter Stewkley is representative, who divided their time unequally between the college and ecclesiastical livings. Stewkley vacated his fellowship on 8 October 1411 and is charged as a commoner from 1413–14 to 1423–4. During his first four years as a pensioner, Stewkley resided in the Hall for 18, 22, 6 and 25 weeks of each respective year.[6] On 11 November 1416 he was admitted as rector of Walsoken, Norfolk, a charge which he retained until November 1433.[7] In the first year of tenure of this benefice he continued to live in the college for about half of the year, but during the next two years he was wholly non-resident, returning in 1419–20 and 1421–2 for periods of thirty-five[8] and twenty-four weeks.[9] In 1422–3, he was again non-resident, and during his last recorded year as a pensioner resided in the Hall for seventeen weeks.[10] It cannot be assumed with certainty that the greater part of the time spent away from the college by beneficed pensioners would automatically be devoted to their livings but, in the absence of evidence to the contrary, it seems a reasonable enough supposition to make. Like Stewkley, Robert Ware appears to have divided his time irregularly between the Hall and a benefice. Ware vacated his fellowship on 16 November 1417, having been admitted as rector of Westley, Suffolk, a year previously,[11] and retained this living until his death in 1450.[12] He was charged as a pensioner from 1417–18 to 1425–6 and,

[1] *K.H. Accts.* VI, fo. 134 v. [2] Emden, *loc. cit.*
[3] *K.H. Accts.* VI, fo. 94. [4] *Ibid.* VI, fo. 117.
[5] Emden, *loc. cit.* [6] *K.H. Accts.* V, fo. 82 v; VI, fos. 28 v, 134, 47 v.
[7] Emden, p. 555. [8] *K.H. Accts.* VI, fo. 116 v.
[9] *Ibid.* VI, fo. 150. [10] *Ibid.* VII, fo. 29 v.
[11] Emden, p. 617. [12] *Loc. cit.*

during the first two years of tenure of his benefice, thirty weeks of 1417–18 and thirteen weeks of 1418–19 were spent in the college.[1] Thereafter, until 1425-6, he seems to have concerned himself with ecclesiastical business because he resided in the Hall for only a week or parts of a week each year. A final example is provided by John Derby, who ceased to be a fellow in 1432–3 and was admitted to the rectorship of Sandy, Bedfordshire, on 1 December 1432,[2] a living which he retained until at least 1439.[3] In the accounts, Derby is charged as a pensioner from 1432–3 to 1434–5 and again from 1440 onwards. A substantial part of each of the three years following his promotion to a benefice was spent in the college.[4] Between 1434–5 and 1439–40, however, he absented himself from his academic environment; and resumed short spells of residence after 1440–1.[5]

It would be of little avail to multiply examples since additional information does not substantially alter the pattern revealed by these selected cases. This inquiry has found that beneficed ex-fellow pensioners do not appear to have neglected their charges through excessive residence in the King's Hall: at most, time and energies were divided irregularly between college and living and, in some instances, the pensionership served the utilitarian purpose of a base in the interim period between the tenure of different benefices. For the majority of ex-fellows, life as a pensioner was clearly not an end in itself: it was regarded either as a means by which a former fellow might be conveniently housed while continuing his studies in the university or as affording a congenial Cambridge lodging place, retained for intermittent use by those actively engaged in ecclesiastical administration.

The King's Hall accounts do not indicate which of the college's rooms were occupied by pensioners. They do, however, permit us to determine the rates charged for rent and they provide tantalisingly concise information concerning the sub-letting of rooms by non-residents not on the foundation.

The customary rent charged for a single room was 6*s* 8*d* per annum[6] and 13*s* 4*d* for a set consisting of two chambers, one of

[1] *K.H. Accts.* VI, fos. 70, 93.   [2] Emden, *op. cit.* p. 184.
[3] *Loc. cit.*   [4] *K.H. Accts.* VIII, fos. 53 v, 76 v, 101 v.
[5] *Ibid.* IX, fo. 160; X, fos. 13, 40 v.
[6] See e.g. *ibid.* v, fos. 82 v, 178; VI, fo. 93; VII, fo. 122; X, fo. 12.

which probably served the functions of a study.[1] There was, in addition, a third rating of 10*s* a year which, like that of 6*s* 8*d*, represented the rent of a single room. For in 1365–6 dominus John Clerevaus, a commoner from 1363–4 to 1365–6,[2] paid £1 for the rent of his room for two years of residence.[3] Similarly, magister Edmundus, a pensioner who was present with a companion named Bonworth between 1411–12 and 1419–20,[4] was charged 10*s* a year for a room shared with his associate[5] until, in 1419–20, an additional room was acquired for Bonworth at an annual rent of 6*s* 8*d*.[6] And, finally, Peter Stewkley was charged 5*s* for the rent of a room for half a year[7] and Thomas Wilton and John Derby hired single rooms at 10*s* per annum in the second half of the fifteenth century.[8]

Judging from the rates charged elsewhere, the King's Hall rentals, assessed presumably on the basis of the number, size and quality of the rooms, were of a moderate character. For example, when John Wyclif and Nicholas of Hereford lived as *commensales* at Queen's College, Oxford, in the latter half of the fourteenth century, they were charged 20*s* for their rooms;[9] at Oriel, until Thomas Gascoigne was granted a rent-free room for life in 1449, he had apparently been paying an annual rent of 20*s* for more than twenty years;[10] the bursars' roll of University College of 1392 records that room rentals in that year varied from 6*s* 8*d* to 20*s*;[11] and in a general survey of Oxford *commensales* H. E. Salter cites typical room rents fixed at 10*s*, 13*s* 4*d*, 16*s* and 20*s*.[12] By comparison, then, the rates charged at the King's Hall were relatively low, and this tends to corroborate the

---

[1] *Ibid.* v, fos. 83, 143v, 166; vi, fo. 134v; vii, fos. 85, 121, 140; viii, fos. 11, 29; ix, fos. 29v, 46v, 106; x, fos. 40, 40v, 64, 165v; xii, fo. 27v; xv, fo. 22v.

[2] *Ibid.* ii, fos. 81, 129.   [3] *Ibid.* fo. 129.

[4] *Ibid.* v, fos. 157, 178v, 82; vi, fos. 27v, 133, 47, 69, 92, 115v.

[5] E.g. *ibid.* vi, fo. 133 (1415–16): 'Memorandum quod Magister Edmundus soluit pro pensione unius camere xs.'

[6] *Ibid.* vi, fo. 115v.   [7] *Ibid.* fo. 47v.

[8] *Ibid.* xii, fo. 28; xiv, fo. 18.

[9] Wyclif paid 40*s* for two rooms in 1365–6; in 1374–5 and 1380–1 he paid 20*s*. Nicholas de Hereford paid 20*s* for a room in 1380–1 and one Britell paid an annual room rent of 20*s* in 1374–5. (See J. R. Magrath, *The Queen's College, cit.* i, 122 and notes; also R. H. Hodgkin, 'The Queen's College', *V.C.H.* (Oxford), iii, 133.)

[10] See the *Dean's Register of Oriel*, p. 370: 'Item in trahendo moram in collegio nostro per viginti annos et amplius solvendo annuitim pro camera sua xxs...'

[11] W. Carr, *University College* (College Histories Series, London, 1902), p. 49.

[12] Salter, *Medieval Oxford*, p. 100.

conclusion drawn below that in this Cambridge college the maintenance of pensioners was not primarily a profit-making concern.[1]

Of the 52 ex-fellow pensioners present in the Hall from 1337 to
1546, 33 retained one or more private servants during residence.[2]
This naturally poses the question of their accommodation. There is
no specific information on this point, but the fact that pensioners
did not pay rent on their behalf when they accounted for the
commons and sizings of their servants doubtless signifies that all
private servants, clerks or boys (*garciones*) attached to their persons[3]
occupied the same premises as their masters.

In the King's Hall accounts there is evidence of an interesting
practice of sub-letting whereby a pensioner who was largely non-
resident might retain his rooms without incurring financial loss. For
example, in 1413–14 both the rooms of ex-fellow Simon Baret, non-
resident for the whole of this year,[4] were retained in his name; but
the rent of 13*s* 4*d*, owing by virtue of this retention, was defrayed by
letting one of the chambers to ex-fellow pensioner John Wittilsey,
for which a rent of 6*s* 8*d* was exacted, and the other to William
Paynell, who remained a fellow until 1419.[5] This arrangement
lasted until 1416–17 when Baret once again began to pay rent for his
rooms and Wittilsey acquired another room to replace that which
now reverted to Baret.[6] Whether or not Paynell found a substitute
is a point which cannot be determined; perhaps, upon giving up
Baret's room, he remained content with the shared accommodation
to which he was entitled under the terms of his fellowship. That the
acquisition of an extra room by a fellow was not an isolated occurrence is proved by an entry for 1441–2 where it is recorded that
Thomas Waryn, a fellow from 1436 to 1445–6, rented a private

[1] See below, pp. 272–3.
[2] The general term *famulus* is the one usually employed to denote a servant but sometimes *garcio* and *clericus* are found.
[3] Occasionally, an ex-fellow pensioner maintained a small entourage. For about ten
weeks in 1424–5 Robert Leek lived in the Hall in the company of two servants and
a priest. The servants were each boarded at the rate of half commons (i.e. at 9*d* or
10*d* per week) and the priest received commons at the average rate of 1*s* 5*d* per
week: *K.H. Accts.* VII, fo. 47 v.   [4] *Ibid.* v, fo. 83.
[5] *Loc. cit.*: 'Memorandum quod Baret soluit pro pensione camerarum suarum xiijs.
iiijd. de qua summa Wyttylsey soluit vis. viijd. et Paynell soluit vis. viijd.'; *ibid.*
VI, fo. 28 (1414–15): 'Memorandum quod Wittlesey soluit xiijs. iiijd. pro pensione
camere sue et unius camere Baret'; *ibid.* VI, fo. 133 v (1415–16).
[6] *Ibid.* VI, fo. 47 v.

room at 6*s* 8*d* a year.[1] Evidently, then, there was scope for a fellow or pensioner with expansionist tendencies to acquire additional accommodation, and if his need dovetailed with the sub-letting desire of a non-resident pensioner a settlement might be made to the advantage of both parties.

The ex-fellow pensioners paid full commons rates for themselves and the rate of half commons for their servants. These rates were subject to the same fluctuations as those levied on the fellows and consequently need not be further analysed. But whereas the fellows actually paid only a varying proportion of the commons rate from their own pockets,[2] the ex-fellow, with no subsidies to his credit, was required to meet the full levy from the resources of his private income. As a result, a substantial spell of residence in the King's Hall must have been for a pensioner a rather expensive business. For if we take 1*s* 11*d* as a typical rate for full commons in the fifteenth century,[3] it follows that an ex-fellow who resided for a year would incur a bill of about £5 for his commons alone. To this must be added an allowance for personal sizings which might range in cost from a farthing to a shilling or more per week. If the round sum of sixpence is adopted as representing an average weekly expenditure on luxury items, this means that about £1 6*s* would be spent on sizings per annum. Moreover, if a pensioner retained a servant at the rate of half commons, the cost of maintenance for the year would be about £2 3*s* 4*d*.[4] And, finally, to these expenses must be added the rent of his room or rooms which, in most cases, appears to have been 13*s* 4*d*. These average sums give a total of £9 3*s* 4*d* and this indicates very roughly that it must have cost the average ex-fellow pensioner about 3*s* 6*d* a week for maintenance in the King's Hall. When this rate is compared with those deduced for the average King's Hall fellow,[5] it is seen that the maintenance costs for an ex-fellow were approximately three or four times as great, a consideration which applies equally to all other members of the full-commoner class.

[1] *Ibid.* x, fo. 12.
[2] See above, pp. 129 ff.
[3] This figure was arrived at by calculating the average amount charged to each pensioner for his commons per week per annum. The results bore a close resemblance to the equivalent average charges levied on the fellows for their commons.
[4] For the purposes of this calculation 10*d* has been selected as the average rate for half commons. [5] See above, pp. 129 ff., particularly pp. 135, 137.

It is generally supposed that the English colleges regarded the intake of pre-Reformation commoners as a means towards augmenting their revenues. However this may have been elsewhere,[1] it is unlikely that the King's Hall derived much financial benefit from the admission of pensioners. As their commons rates appear to have been assessed on the same principles as those of the fellows, which were designed not to make a profit but merely to cover week by week the costs of the basic food requirements used in the preparation of the meals,[2] it follows that these charges would not have constituted a source of profit for the college. There is just a possibility that a small surplus was realised from the retail of extra food and drink commodities which came collectively under the heading of sizings;[3] but this, if any, would have been of negligible proportions. Similarly, even if the costs of upkeep are disregarded, the income accruing from room rentals assessed at, say, 13s 4d per annum would only have brought in about threepence a week. In the light of such considerations, it seems that the admission of pensioners was not, on the whole, a very lucrative practice, yielding at most only a marginal profit:[4] and even this is doubtful because it assumes that the commoner system was efficiently administered and that income due from this category of personnel was in fact realised. But if the situation during the reign of Henry VI is anything to go by, it was seemingly not uncommon for pensioners to reside for long periods of time without

---

[1] See e.g. the remarks of W. Carr, *University College, cit.* p. 49, on the admission of *commensales* to University College: 'The admission of these *commensales* was in the first instance due to no educational zeal or desire to open the gates of learning to a larger class, but simply to secure such monetary assistance as might be derived from their payments for board and lodging.' The profit motive behind the maintenance of commoners or pensioners was written into the statutes of several of the French colleges of the fourteenth century: e.g. A. L. Gabriel cites from the statutes of the college of Narbonne (1379) where the fellows are warned not to harm their lodgers because they bring both riches and honour to the society (domus lucretur et honoretur per tales): Gabriel, *The college system*, p. 15.

[2] See above, p. 126.

[3] Since the college bought its food in bulk it is just conceivable that 'extra commons' or luxury items were retailed at a slight profit: this, however, is only an inference and cannot be proven.

[4] R. H. Hodgkin casts doubt upon the profitability of the practice of maintaining pensioners (*commensales*) at Queen's, Oxford, in the fourteenth century because of the 'unbusinesslike methods of the college officials' (Hodgkin, *Six centuries of an Oxford college*, p. 28, n. 1). Unfortunately, no detailed evidence is cited in support of this contention.

squaring their debts which, in several instances, were very considerable. By 1454–5 the arrears of eleven commoners owing for commons, sizings, room rents and servants amounted to £63 3s 10¼d with individual debts ranging from 4s 10¼d to £24 9s 3½d.[1] Perhaps it was this kind of financial drag, which the commoner system could evidently impose upon the college, that was largely responsible for the marked curtailment in commoner intake in the second half of the fifteenth century and which culminated in the complete disappearance of this class in the sixteenth century.[2] Whatever the truth of this matter, the evidence certainly does not indicate that a profit motive lay at the basis of the King's Hall pensioner system and it is possible that the prime consideration was no more than a desire to fill vacant accommodation with men of approved character who could be trusted to fit in harmoniously with the fellows and who were thought capable of deriving benefit from a period of residence in a university environment.

This cautionary emphasis upon the suitability and trustworthiness of academic *extranei* is one common to most codes of college statutes of the pre-Reformation era.[3] Although it is similarly reflected in the King's Hall statutes,[4] this did not deter the college from admitting a strikingly large number of commoners and semi-commoners who had not previously had any connection with the Society. It is possible to give reliable numerical evidence for the commoner population but it is not always easy to distinguish the academic semi-commoners from the private servants and clerks maintained by members of the Society. For this reason, only broad indications of the size of the semi-commoner community will be advanced and no detailed figures will be attempted.

Between 1337 and 1500 at least 68 commoners are known to have

---

[1] See the entries for the arrears of John Derby, Richard Lyes, John Whyte, Richard Moresby, John Bank, Robert Fereby, Stephen Close, Robert Ayscogh, Adam Copyndale, William Alnewyk and Thomas Wilton, *K.H. Accts.* XII, fos. 26–8.

[2] See below, p. 274.

[3] E.g. the statutes of Peterhouse in *Camb. Docs.* II, 27; the statutes of Michaelhouse in Stamp, *Michaelhouse*, p. 44; the statutes of Clare and King's in *Camb. Docs.* II, 136–7, 534–6; the statutes of Merton in *Statutes*, I, ch. (2), 13 (1270), 26 (1274); the statutes of Balliol, Oriel, Queen's and New College *ibid.* I, ch. (1), 20, ch. (3), 8, ch. (4), 18, ch. (5), 43.

[4] See the statutes in Rouse Ball, *King's Hall*, p. 66: 'Extraneos vero vel propinquos ad morandum inter ipsos [fellows] absque licentia dicti custodis non introducant...'

been admitted by the college: as in the case of the ex-fellow pensioners, commoner entrance appears to have been discontinued in the
sixteenth century since no fresh entry is recorded after 1492–3. The
commoner population was distributed as follows: 10 commoners
entered the Society in the period 1337 to 1350; 12 between 1350 and
1400, although in view of the fact that several accounts are missing
for this period the intake was almost certainly higher; 30 entered
between 1400 and 1450; and 16 in the second half of the fifteenth
century. When to these are added the corresponding figures for ex-
fellow pensioners, the overall distribution of all known full-
commoner personnel is as represented in table 17.

TABLE 17

Period	Commoners (excluding ex-fellow pensioners)	Ex-fellow pensioners
1337–50	10	4
1350–1400	12	11
1400–50	30	27
1450–1500	16	10
	—	—
	68	52

The semi-commoner intake reached proportions of considerable
magnitude. There are about one hundred persons in the King's Hall
accounts to whom the designation semi-commoner could be legitimately applied and who seem to be distinct from dependent *clerici*
and *famuli*.[1] Only eleven of these are to be found in the period 1337
to 1400 but thereafter until the mid-fifteenth century there was a
significantly large entry of somewhere in the region of 70 semi-
commoners of the self-supporting type. But apart from a handful
who resided for an appreciable number of years, lengths of residence
were on the whole brief and the turnover of personnel fairly rapid.
The numbers of commoners, semi-commoners, ex-fellow pensioners

---

[1] Details regarding 78 independent semi-commoners can be supplied for the period
up to 1441–2. After that date, the forms of entry in the accounts are such that it
becomes impossible to distinguish between self-supporting semi-commoners and
dependants. It is, however, reasonable to assume that a proportion of the semi-
commoners admitted after 1441–2 would be of the self-supporting type, thus
bringing the total independent semi-commoner intake up to or near the hundred
mark.

and resident fellows do not add up each year to a constant total, although the issue is here impossibly complicated by the fact that
members of each of these several categories were present for differing
parts of each year. Though a full analysis cannot be given, the main
importance of this evidence from the point of view of academic
history is the known presence of so large a commoner element in a
medieval college in the fourteenth and fifteenth centuries: and,
moreover, the division of the King's Hall *extranei* into two distinct
gradings, commoner and semi-commoner, affords adequate proof
of the fact that the origins of the stratified commoner system are,
on the basis of this evidence, to be placed at least as early as the first
half of the fourteenth century. It is an intriguing paradox that the
King's Hall, which had harboured a substantial commoner element
for so long, should have abandoned it in the sixteenth century just at
the time when most English colleges were adopting the commoner
system on a significant scale.

As in the case of the King's Hall fellows, the commoner and semi-
commoner intake appears to reflect a similar bias towards the eastern
counties north of the Thames and towards Yorkshire. Forty-six of
the members of this category possess surnames which may be
assigned with a fair degree of probability to single counties. For
reasons already stated, no exact total can be given for the combined
commoner and semi-commoner population, but this figure perhaps
represents a proportion of between a quarter and a third. The
resultant geographical distribution both by counties and by dioceses
is shown in table 18.

Comparison with the inquiry conducted into the surnames of the
King's Scholars[1] reveals that the same three counties, Lincoln, Yorkshire and Norfolk, come out top of the list and that the dioceses of
Lincoln, York, Norwich and London occupy the first four places in
both cases.

Our knowledge of the King's Hall academic *extranei* does not, in
many instances, extend beyond surnames, periods of residence and
rates paid for commons. Nevertheless, the few who can be further
identified illustrate the mixture of types to be found in the college.
Several of the commoners were rectors who had presumably come
up to Cambridge University to take a 'refresher' or an advanced

----

[1] See above, pp. 157–61.

TABLE 18

Counties		Dioceses	
Lincs.	9	Lincoln	14
Yorks.	8	York	12
Norfolk	7	Norwich	7
Cambs.	3	London	4
Essex	2	Ely	3
Hants.	2	Winchester	2
Herts.	2	Coventry and	
Lancs.	2	Lichfield	1
Northants.	2	Hereford	1
Notts.	2	Canterbury	1
Beds.	1	Durham	1
Bucks.	1		—
Hereford	1		46
Kent	1		
Leics.	1		
Northumb.	1		
Salop	1		
	—		
	46		

course of study, and some of them were of noble birth, such as Gilbert, rector of Halsall, Lancashire,[1] Richard Moresby, with diverse rectorships to his credit,[2] and John and William, the natural sons of the earl of Huntingdon, both of whom were rectors at the time of admission.[3] There were other commoners of noble lineage who did not hold ecclesiastical office upon entry to the college. Examples are William Bardolf, brother of Thomas, fifth Lord Bardolf[4] and one of the *nobiles* on the Colville roll, the Cambridge University roll of petitions for benefices sent to the papal curia *c.* 1390;[5] and Sir Henry Huntingdon, who succeeded to the earldom of Huntingdon and the

[1] For details of Halsall's career see Emden, *B.R.U.C.* p. 282.
[2] Moresby was of noble birth by both parents: Emden, *op. cit.* p. 410.
[3] Emden, p. 322. Both were accounted for as commoners in 1440–1 and 1441–2: *K.H. Accts.* IX, fos. 161 v, 162; X, fo. 13 v.
[4] Bardolf was charged as a commoner between 1387–8 and 1389–90 (*ibid.* III, fos. 74 v, 43, 19). Upon his first entry it is recorded (III, fo. 74 v): 'In die sancti vincentii Magister Wilhelmus Bardolf intravit hora prandii et pro illa septimana xjd.'
[5] Emden, p. 36; see also E. F. Jacob, 'Petitions for benefices from English universities during the Great Schism', *T.R.H.S.*, 4th series, XXVII (1945), 58.

dukedom of Exeter in 1447.[1] A number of commoners whose position at the time of admission is uncertain were admitted to rectorships either during or soon after their sojourn in the Hall, suggesting that their study at Cambridge had been undertaken in order to qualify for future ecclesiastical promotion.[2] Although there were almost certainly many more, at least two and probably three of the King's Hall commoners are known to have received episcopal licence to study at an English university: dominus Hugo (Hugh) Wymundeswold, granted permission to study at a university for one year on 26 September 1344,[3] selected Cambridge and resided as a King's Hall commoner during 1344–5;[4] Thomas Barbur, vicar of Kenninghall, Norfolk, who was granted licence to study at Cambridge on 11 May 1411,[5] lived as a semi-commoner for parts of 1439–40;[6] and Robert Ayscogh, canon of Sarum, prebendary of Charminster and Bere and rector of Campsall, Yorkshire, obtained leave of absence for three years from his rectory on 8 March 1456[7] in the midst of his period of residence as a King's Hall commoner.[8]

With one or two possible exceptions,[9] the King's Hall commoners and semi-commoners appear to have been men of mature years and most of them were probably of graduate status.[10] In these respects,

[1] Emden, *op. cit.* p. 321. Sir Henry Huntingdon was charged as a commoner from 1439–40 to 1441–2: *K.H. Accts.* IX, fos. 106v, 162; X, fo. 13v.

[2] E.g. dominus John Clerevaus, charged as a commoner between 1363–4 and 1365–6, attained the degree of B.Cn.L. and was rector of Banham, Norfolk, in 1371 (*ibid.* II, fos. 81, 129; Emden, p. 138); John Careway, accounted for as a semi-commoner in 1400–1 and 1401–2, had acquired the degrees of M.A. and B.Cn.L. by 1422 and became rector of St Vigor's, Fulbourn, in 1429 (*ibid.* IV, fos. 84v, 66v; Emden, p. 123); and Thomas Martyn(s), charged as a commoner between 1491–2 and 1493–4 and again in 1495–6, was admitted as rector of Papworth St Agnes, Cambs., on 16 June 1497 (*ibid.* XVII, fo. 17v; XVIII, fos. 139, 166v; XIX, fo. 41v; Emden, p. 394).

[3] Emden, *B.R.U.O.* III, 2121.

[4] *K.H. Accts.* I, fo. 91v.

[5] Emden, *B.R.U.C.* pp. 35–6.

[6] *K.H. Accts.* IX, fo. 106v.

[7] Emden, *B.R.U.C.* p. 27.

[8] Charged as a commoner 1447–50, 1451–3, 1454–5, 1457–9, 1460–1: *K.H. Accts.* XI, fos. 17v, 48v, 74v, 101v, 133v; XII, fos. 13, 74v, 103v; XIII, fo. 20.

[9] E.g. William Bardolf had not yet attained the degree of B.A. when his name appeared on the list of petitioners for benefices on the Colville roll (Jacob, *art. cit.* p. 58); Thorneton, accounted for as a semi-commoner in 1366–7(?), was evidently only a young boy receiving grammatical instruction within the college (see above, pp. 76–7).

[10] E.g. Gilbert Halsall was M.A., B.Th. upon entry; Richard Moresby had the degrees of B.Cn.L. and B.C.L.; and Thomas Martyn(s) was of M.A. status (Emden, pp. 282, 410, 394).

they conform to what has been discovered about the commoner class elsewhere[1] and therefore the subject need not be further pursued. There is a strong likelihood that several of them were related to fellows of the college. The connection is certain in the case of dominus Hugo (Hugh) Wymundeswold, the elder brother of Richard Wymundeswold, a King's Scholar from 1329 to *c.* 1338, and in the case of the brother of Ralph Gartside, fellow from 1472–3 to 1491–2, who resided for short spells as a commoner in 1478–9 and 1479–80.[2] In other instances, the relationship can only be inferred from the coincidence of surnames. For example, it seems probable that Ripon,[3] Romeseye,[4] Appilton[5] and Pyghttesley[6] were related to the fellows of the same name. And the brief spells of residence of these latter commoners indicate, not a serious academic purpose, but merely social visits on the part of relatives.

Most of the academic *extranei* who paid the rate of full commons could be technically described as pensioners by virtue of the rent or *pensio* charged for their accommodation. In the case of a few of the commoners and all of the semi-commoners, there is no record of such a charge. The exceptions in the former instance may be due to incomplete documentation and it is indeed highly probable that all members of the full-commoner class were charged rent for their rooms. But semi-commoners, without exception, appear to have been exempt from this payment and this poses the problem of the location and style of their living quarters. As all meals and sizings were taken in the college, it is not very likely that semi-commoners would have been boarded out in the town. A more plausible explanation is that humble and necessarily crowded accommodation was provided in the Hall for which no *pensio* was exacted.

From the circumstances of their division into two gradings, commoner and semi-commoner, it naturally follows that the differences among commoner personnel who were not ex-fellow pensioners would be more pronounced than among those who were. Some, such as dominus Clerevaus, lived in grand style, maintaining one or

---

1 See the remarks on medieval commoners by Salter, *Medieval Oxford*, p. 100.
2 *K.H. Accts.* xv, fo. 117; xvi, fo. 17.
3 A commoner present for 14 weeks in 1346–7 (*ibid.* I, fo. 104).
4 A commoner present for 2 weeks in 1346–7 (*ibid.* I, fo. 104).
5 A commoner for a week and a day in 1425–6 (*ibid.* vii, fo. 68).
6 A semi-commoner for just over two weeks in 1426–7 (*ibid.* vii, fo. 86).

more servants, taking regular sizings and expending large sums of money on feast occasions: Richard de Goldyngton, a future chancellor of Cambridge University,[1] was sufficiently wealthy to entertain the Society with his private troupe of minstrels.[2] At the other end of the scale, the typical semi-commoner, after meeting the cost of half commons, could not afford to retain a servant and was only very rarely in receipt of sizings. Moreover, whereas about 63 per cent of the ex-fellow pensioners supported one or more servants,[3] only about 31 per cent of the other full commoners did so,[4] and only one semi-commoner.[5] And, as already indicated, the incidence of regular sizings among the commoner element was much less frequent than among ex-fellow personnel and consequently the luxury margin was significantly smaller.

Thus, an investigation of the King's Hall academic *extranei* reveals that ex-fellows were accorded no preferential treatment with respect to commons, sizings or room rents over those members of the commoner ranks who had never at any time been on the foundation. It is also apparent that while the living standards of the former were fairly uniformly high, among personnel of the latter class there were wide variations reflective of the diversified composition of this shadowy academic population.

---

[1] Goldington is not included in the list of chancellors in *V.C.H.* (Cambridge), III, 331–3, but ought to be inserted between Thomas de Northwood (1344) and John de Crakhall (1346–8). On this point see Emden, *B.R.U.C.* p. 264.

[2] Goldington was charged as a commoner in 1340–1 and 1341–2 (*K.H. Accts.* I, fos. 48, 60). For the reference to minstrels see above, p. 225 and n. 6.

[3] See above, p. 270.

[4] Only 21 of the 68 full commoners maintained servants.

[5] Alexander, a semi-commoner who remained for 6 weeks of 1432–3 and maintained a servant for part of that time.

Chapter 7

CAREERS OF THE WARDENS AND SOME OF THE NOTABLE SCHOLARS

A definitive examination of the post-university careers of the King's Scholars lies beyond the scope of this present study. Nevertheless, for the sake of completeness, it is necessary to give some broad indication of the variety and nature of the employments into which the King's Hall fellows and their wardens were absorbed in the course of more than two hundred years. This task has been made possible only by the timely appearance of Dr Emden's monumental *Biographical register of the University of Cambridge to 1500* which provides much of the basic material upon which the following analysis depends.

Between 1317 and 1546, thirty wardens or masters presided over the destinies of the Society of the King's Scholars and the endowed College of the King's Hall. Of these, only eight had come through the ranks of the Society in the sense that they were either King's Scholars or ex-King's Scholars at the time of their appointment.[1] The vast majority, therefore, were external choices, without any previous connection with the Society, imposed upon the fellows by the Crown. It is not really surprising that five of the 'internal' selections fall within the confines of the fourteenth century. This is readily intelligible in view of the fact that in the early years the warden was very much the key figure in the government of the Society and it was obviously politic to appoint masters with a deep personal knowledge of its business. But once the King's Scholars had acquired full democratic rights of participation in their own affairs, and conciliar government by annually elected committees of seneschals had replaced the former monarchical structure, there was then clearly less need for the master to possess the same intimate contact with the

---

[1] These were: Thomas Powys (warden, 1333–61); John de Schropham (1361–3); Nicholas de Drayton (1363–4); Nicholas Roos (1364–75); Simon Neylond (1377–85); Robert Ayscogh (1448–9); Christopher Urswick (1485–8); John Blythe (1488–98).

college as had before been almost obligatory. Thus we find that from the late fourteenth century onwards there was a marked tendency for the King's Hall wardens to become increasingly non-resident dignitaries whose energies were for the most part absorbed in the burdens of royal service and high ecclesiastical office. This does not mean that they necessarily neglected the college or looked upon the mastership entirely as a sinecure. They continued to take an active interest in the major problems confronting the Society and there can be little doubt that the external involvement of its wardens in influential governmental and ecclesiastical circles served as a positive asset to the college, enhancing its social standing and academic prestige. But, inevitably, the frequent and lengthy absences of the later masters further entrenched the *de facto* sovereign powers of the fellows and, in effect, made of the mastership a distinct estate set above the Society by the Crown and no longer forming an integral part of its daily life and business.

A study of the careers of the majority of the fourteenth-century wardens shows conclusively that where engagement in royal service was involved, it was confined to the period either preceding or following the tenure of the wardenship, once more underlining the point that at this early juncture in the history of the college the master was required to devote the greater part of his attention to its affairs. A few examples will illustrate this career division. John de Langtoft, who served as the third warden of the King's Scholars from 1331 until 1333, was evidently drawn into royal service in the years succeeding the vacation of his mastership: for in 1338 he was granted protection on going overseas on the king's business and had become a chancery clerk by 1340.[1] The sixth warden, Nicholas de Drayton, who was already a king's clerk at the time of his appointment in 1363, entered royal service as a baron of the exchequer in 1376,[2] twelve years after his resignation as warden in 1364. Richard Ronhale, also a king's clerk with a salary of fifty marks a year when appointed eighth master of the King's Scholars in 1375, vacated the wardenship in 1377 and spent the remainder of an extremely busy life in the employ of Richard II. In 1382, he was made a chancery clerk of the first form and subsequently took a leading part in numerous royal diplomatic missions to France, Portugal, Bavaria and

---

[1] Emden, *B.R.U.C.* p. 351.   [2] *Ibid.* p. 194.

Scotland and, in addition, frequently served as special king's commissioner for appeals from the chivalry and admiralty courts.[1] The final example is provided by the case of the infamous Simon Neylond, who served as a member of Edward III's council until his appointment as the ninth warden in 1377.[2]

This brief investigation points to a sharp demarcation between that portion of the career devoted to the mastership and that concerned with royal employment. Indeed, it seems that for the greater part of the fourteenth century only ecclesiastical duties were considered compatible with the tenure of the wardenship. It was common practice for the warden to hold one or more rectorships in conjunction with his office and at least two of them discharged important diocesan functions: Nicholas Roos, warden from 1364 to 1375, was acting official of the bishop of Ely in 1373[3] and Thomas Hetersete, who succeeded Neylond in 1385, was archdeacon of Sudbury in 1389.[4] Clearly, however, the initial phase of the history of the King's Hall mastership is characterised by the severe curtailment of onerous external functions which might serve to distract the warden from his collegiate duties.

The appointment of Ralph Selby as the Society's eleventh warden in 1391 brought about a radical transformation in the nature of the mastership. Selby's wardenship constitutes a real turning point and inaugurates a long succession of celebrated masters whose common distinguishing feature was the combination of academic office with notable careers in the royal and ecclesiastical sphere. From this time forward, the King's Hall warden is usually a far more important public figure than most of his fourteenth-century counterparts. He might be a king's secretary, chaplain or almoner, a keeper of the privy seal, a master of the rolls, a dean of the chapel royal or a bishop or he might be extensively utilised in the royal diplomatic service. Whatever the particular circumstances, the King's Hall mastership now becomes only one of several concerns to its holder and, in most cases, presumably a subordinate one. The careers of these later wardens are of such general historical interest that some measure of individual treatment seems called for.

---

[1] Emden, *B.R.U.C.* pp. 487–8.   [2] *Ibid.* p. 425.
[3] *Ibid.* p. 488.
[4] *Ibid.* p. 296. Hetersete was also confirmed chancellor of the university in 1386.

Ralph Selby,[1] warden from 1391 to 1398, was a member of Richard II's council and a trusted royal agent and diplomat. Before his appointment as warden he had been official of the archdeacon of Ely and a canon and subdean of York. Less than three years after he became master of the King's Hall, he was made a privy councillor and, in the same month, a third baron of the exchequer, combining these governmental positions with that of the archdeaconry of Buckingham. He was employed on diplomatic missions to France and to Rome and, like his predecessor, Richard Ronhale, served as a special royal commissioner in appeal cases from the court of chivalry. In 1398, Selby resigned the wardenship in order to enter the Benedictines at Westminster Abbey, where he remained until his death in 1420, having successfully survived a charge of conspiracy brought against him in 1410.

Selby was succeeded by Richard Dereham,[2] who was warden first from 1399 until 1413 and again from 1415 until his death in 1417. Before his appointment, Dereham had acquired a wealth of experience in many different spheres. Originally a fellow of Gonville Hall, he had become chancellor of the university by 1404 and represented Cambridge in that capacity at the council of Pisa in 1408–9. During the reign of Richard II, he had laboured hard for the revocation of the Statute of Provisors so as to enable the university to continue to send collective rolls of petitions for benefices to the papal curia and appears to have achieved some modification of the statute in the university's favour. In the reign of Henry IV, Dereham became the trusted chaplain and diplomatic agent of the king, so much so in fact that in 1404 parliament demanded his dismissal from the royal household. He was employed by Henry IV on missions to Denmark and to the Roman curia and, during his second term as warden, was apostolic protonotary of the English nation at the council of Constance in 1415–16. Throughout his diversified career he held several canonries, prebends and rectorships, was dean of St Martin's le Grand, London, archdeacon of Norfolk and, on occasion, served as justice of the peace for Cambridge: in 1400 he was summoned to preach before Henry IV and the Byzantine emperor during the latter's visit to England.

[1] Emden, *B.R.U.C.* p. 517.
[2] *Ibid.* pp. 184–5; see also E. F. Jacob, 'English university clerks in the later middle ages: the problem of maintenance', *B.J.R.L.* XXIX (1946), 318–20.

Sandwiched between Dereham's first and second spells of office was John Stone,[1] warden from 1413 to 1415. Stone, who was a king's clerk by 1404, was secretary to Henry V at the time of his appointment and apparently retained this position until his death in 1419. Little more is known of his career except that he held a variety of canonries and prebends and, in conjunction with the mastership, the archdeaconry of Northampton and the deanery of St Martin's le Grand, London.

Richard Holme,[2] who was appointed warden in 1417 following Dereham's second term of office, was extensively engaged in the service of the first two Lancastrians. He had become a king's clerk under Richard II in 1397, was a member of Henry IV's council by 1408, and appears as the king's secretary in 1412, presumably being the immediate predecessor to John Stone in that office. He was widely utilised for diplomatic activity by both Henry IV and Henry V and participated in missions to France, Scotland and Burgundy. Throughout his career he held a number of canonries, prebends and rectorships, acted as proctor of the bishop of Sarum at the Roman curia in 1391, was an abbreviator of papal letters by 1397 and commissary general of the bishop of Durham in 1406: and, like Ronhale and Selby, he gave frequent service as a royal judicial commissioner between 1394 and 1413. Holme retained the mastership of the King's Hall until his death in 1424.

Holme was succeeded by Robert FitzHugh,[3] son of the king's chamberlain, Sir Henry FitzHugh of Ravensworth Castle, Yorkshire. FitzHugh remained warden from 1424 until his appointment as bishop of London in 1431. His first four or five years as warden were combined with the chancellorship of the university, to which he had been elevated in 1423. He was, however, constantly nonresident owing to his position as Henry VI's proctor at the Roman curia and because of diplomatic service elsewhere. For example, he was sent as an envoy to treat for an alliance with the king of Aragon in 1429. In the course of his lengthy career FitzHugh held an impressively large number of ecclesiastical positions including the

[1] *B.R.U.C.* pp. 559–60; J. Otway-Ruthven, *The king's secretary and the signet office in the fifteenth century* (Cambridge, 1939), pp. 153, 168–9.
[2] *B.R.U.C.* pp. 311–12; Otway-Ruthven, pp. 153, 167–8.
[3] *B.R.U.C.* pp. 231–2.

chancellorship of St Patrick's, Dublin, the mastership of St Leonard's Hospital, York, the archdeaconry of Northampton, and the bishopric of London. Three years after his resignation of the King's Hall wardenship he was appointed ambassador to the council of Basel in 1434.

FitzHugh was followed in 1431 by Richard Caudray,[1] who retained the wardenship until his resignation in 1448. Of noble birth, Caudray had qualified as a notary public by 1414 and in this and the succeeding year was in the employ of the archbishop of Canterbury. Later in the reign of Henry V, he was engaged in diplomatic negotiations with the French and by 1420 had risen to the position of king's secretary: in the early part of the reign of Henry VI he served as clerk of the council. As warden of the King's Hall he was also chancellor of the university between 1433 and 1435 and justice of the peace for Cambridge between 1437 and 1440. In 1435 he was in the service of John Kempe, archbishop of York, and, in conjunction with the wardenship, held the archdeaconries of Norwich and Lincoln, the deanery of St Martin's le Grand, London, as well as numerous canonries and prebends.

Upon Caudray's resignation in 1448 Robert Ayscogh,[2] brother of William Ayscogh, bishop of Sarum, was appointed to the mastership, which he vacated shortly before his death in 1449. At the time of his appointment Ayscogh had been a fellow of the King's Hall, chancellor of the university and dean of the chapel royal and continued to hold these last two positions until his death. He was a pluralist of some magnitude and, in association with the offices of warden and dean of the royal chapel, held the archdeaconries of Colchester and Dorset, the canonries of York and Southwell, the rectorship of Campsall, Yorkshire, and the Sarum prebends of Charminster and Bere.

Nicholas Close[3] succeeded Ayscogh in 1449 both as master of the King's Hall and as chancellor of the university. Close was one of the foundation fellows of King's College in 1441 and won the king's high regard for the leading part he took in the supervision of the

[1] *Ibid.* pp. 126–7; Otway-Ruthven, pp. 154, 169–70; A. H. Thompson, ed., *Visitations of religious houses in the diocese of Lincoln* (Lincoln Record Society, 7), I (1914), 176–8 and index (resignation date of wardenship and years of tenure of chancellorship erroneously stated, p. 177).
[2] *B.R.U.C.* p. 27.   [3] *Ibid.* p. 142.

erection of the buildings in the initial stages. By 1448 he had become chaplain to Henry VI and was employed as a commissioner to treat with the Scots in 1449. He held the archdeaconry of Carlisle in 1448 and was made archdeacon of Colchester in 1449 but vacated both on his appointment as bishop of Carlisle in 1450. In 1452, Close was created bishop of Coventry and Lichfield, resigned the wardenship of the King's Hall, and died later in the year.

Following the loss of the college's independent status under the Crown, the first warden to be appointed by the provosts of Eton and King's was John Blakman,[1] master from 1452 until 1457. He had previously been a fellow and subwarden of Merton College and a fellow of Eton from *c.* 1443 until his transference to the wardenship of the King's Hall. Blakman was a bachelor of theology and a notary public by 1452 and, while warden, held at different times the rectorship of Sapperton, Gloucestershire, and the deanery of Westbury-on-Trym in the same county. He vacated the mastership in July 1457 in order to enter the Carthusians but whether as a *clericus redditus* or as a monk is uncertain: he lived until 1485 and was the author of the celebrated memoir on the life of Henry VI.

The provosts next offered the wardenship to William Towne, a foundation fellow of King's College, but it was probably declined, for he does not appear to have acted. Their choice then fell upon Richard Scrope,[2] younger son of Richard, third Lord Scrope of Bolton: he accepted and retained the mastership until 1463, having been confirmed in his appointment by Edward IV on the restoration of the independence of the King's Hall in February 1462. During his period of office he served as chancellor of the university and as justice of the peace for Cambridge and shortly after his vacation was consecrated bishop of Carlisle in 1464.

On Scrope's resignation, Edward IV appointed his chaplain, Thomas St Just, who held the position until his death in 1467. St Just is the first known recipient of the doctoral degree in music at Cambridge and was admitted D.Mus. in 1461–2.[3] He combined the wardenship with several canonries and prebends and, in addition,

---

[1] *B.R.U.C.* pp. 670–1.

[2] *Ibid.* pp. 514–15.

[3] *Ibid.* p. 503; see also W. J. Smith, *Five centuries of Cambridge musicians* (Cambridge, 1964), p. 2. His argument that St Just was granted the degree in 1464 and not in 1461 I find hard to understand.

held the deanery of St Chad's, Shrewsbury, and the archdeaconry of Chester.

St Just was succeeded as warden in 1467 by John Gunthorpe,[1] the distinguished English humanist scholar, statesman and diplomatist. Gunthorpe appears to have received his early education at Cambridge and was certainly an M.A. of the university by 1452 and served as junior proctor in 1454–5. He later went to study in Italy and by 1460 was a student at the school of Guarino de Verona at Ferrara and attended his lectures in rhetoric. While there, he mastered Greek and probably associated with his fellow English humanist, John Free. He then seems to have visited Padua and Rome and returned to England after Free's death in 1465. His scholarship and knowledge of foreign countries well equipped him for governmental and diplomatic service and he was extensively and continuously engaged in the employ of Edward IV, Richard III and Henry VII. In the year of his appointment as King's Hall warden, he was secretary and chaplain to the queen and had recently also been chaplain to Edward IV. He was created king's almoner in 1468 and clerk of parliament in 1471. In 1481 he was made dean of the chapel royal and was keeper of the privy seal in the reign of Richard III: in reward for his services he received numerous ecclesiastical offices including the deanery of Wells and the archdeaconry of Essex. During his many visits abroad he collected a valuable manuscript library and was one of the small group of scholars who tried to promote the study of Greek in fifteenth-century England. Gunthorpe's career well illustrates the growing awareness in England of the importance of humanistic scholarship as a valuable qualification for governmental service in the latter phase of the fifteenth century—a circumstance which had been recognised in Italy some three-quarters of a century before. Although Gunthorpe may not have contributed as much as some of his predecessors towards the well-being of the college and the promotion of its interests, he must certainly rank as one of its most distinguished masters.

The next warden was Roger Rotherham,[2] brother of Thomas Rotherham, archbishop of York and chancellor of England from 1474 until his deprivation in 1483. Rotherham was appointed in 1473

---

[1] *B.R.U.C.* pp. 275–7; Weiss, *Humanism in England, cit.* pp. 122–7 and index.
[2] *B.R.U.C.* p. 489.

and remained master until his death in 1477. Not a great deal is known of his career beyond the fact that he was a doctor of civil law by 1471 and combined the wardenship with several canonries and prebends and the archdeaconry of Leicester, and with service as justice of the peace for Cambridge in 1475.

On Rotherham's death the Crown appointed the newly elected provost of Eton, Henry Bost,[1] as warden of the King's Hall. Bost retained the former position until his death in 1504 and the latter until 1485. In 1483 he also acquired the provostship of Queen's College, Oxford, of which he had formerly been a fellow, and thus for two years contrived to be the common head of three collegiate institutions, an instance of academic pluralism not easily, if ever, paralleled in the annals of English university history. There is perhaps some significance in the combination of the headships of Eton and the King's Hall in the person of Bost in 1477. This occurs just at the time when the twin Lancastrian foundations of Eton and King's were gradually recapturing the royal favour and it is certainly conceivable that the temporary linkage of the former with the King's Hall was a deliberate device on the part of Edward IV to impose a greater measure of amity upon the academic scene.

Bost was followed by Christopher Urswick,[2] an ex-fellow of the King's Hall, who remained warden from 1485 until 1488. Urswick had been chaplain and confessor to the Lady Margaret, mother of the future Henry VII, and appears to have acted as her agent in negotiations with bishop Morton, then an exile in Brittany, for the marriage between her son and Elizabeth of York. He subsequently became Henry's chaplain and confessor and landed with him in England in 1485: in the September of that year he was made king's almoner and in November he was appointed warden of the King's Hall. But Urswick rarely resided at the college because he was frequently called away on diplomatic business. He held a multitude of canonries, prebends and rectorships and, at various times, the archdeaconries of Richmond, Huntingdon, Norfolk, Oxford, Surrey and Wiltshire and the deaneries of Windsor and York. Another

---

[1] *B.R.U.C.* pp. 74–5; Bost is said to have been confessor to Jane Shore (see C. J. S. Thompson, *The witchery of Jane Shore* (London, 1933), p. 84).

[2] *B.R.U.C.* pp. 605–6; J. K. McConica, *English humanists and Reformation politics*, cit. pp. 70–2; D. Hay, 'The manuscript of Polydore Vergil's 'Anglica Historia',' *E.H.R.* LIV (1939), 240 ff. at pp. 246, 251.

important facet of Urswick's career was his prominent contribution to the English humanist movement. He was a close friend of Erasmus and commissioned a large number of translations or copies of valuable texts ranging from the writings of the early Fathers (and especially Chrysostom) to works by Savonarola and Luther.

Urswick was succeeded by John Blythe,[1] nephew of Thomas Rotherham, archbishop of York. Blythe had been a King's Hall fellow from 1476–8 and an ex-fellow pensioner from 1478 to 1480 and retained the wardenship from 1488 until 1498. During his tenure of office he was master of the rolls between 1492 and 1494 and became both chancellor of the university and bishop of Sarum in 1494. In addition, he held the archdeaconries of Huntingdon and Richmond, both of which he vacated upon his promotion as bishop. He died on 23 August 1499.

John Blythe was followed in 1498 by his brother, Geoffrey Blythe, who remained warden until 1528. He was educated at Eton and King's and became dean of the latter in 1492–3. While warden, he was consecrated bishop of Coventry and Lichfield in 1503 and had previously held numerous canonries, prebends and rectorships, the archdeaconries of Cleveland, Gloucester and Sarum, the deanery of York and the wardenship of St Nicholas Hospital, Salisbury. In 1502 he was engaged as an envoy to Ladislaus II, king of Hungary and Bohemia, to cement a league against the Turks. He was cleared of a charge of treason in 1509 and was lord president of the council of Wales from 1512 until 1524. He died in London in 1530.

Very little is known about his namesake successor, Geoffrey Blythe,[2] warden from 1528 until 1541. He was probably the nephew of the last two wardens: he received his educational training at Eton and King's and appears to have studied for a spell at Louvain. He attained a doctoral degree in civil law and is credited with having preached against Hugh Latimer at Cambridge.

The thirtieth and last warden of the King's Hall was John Redman,[3] appointed on 13 March 1542, who, upon the dissolution of the college in 1546, provided continuity as the first master of Trinity.

---

[1] *B.R.U.C.* p. 68. [2] *D.N.B.* v (1886), 278.

[3] *Ibid.* XLVII (1896), 382; L. V. Ryan, *Roger Ascham* (Stanford, 1963), pp. 15, 17–19 and index; A. Tilley, 'Greek studies in England in the early sixteenth century', *E.H.R.* LIII (1938), 439.

Redman was a highly eminent theologian and a Greek and Latin scholar of great reputation who had studied at Oxford's principal centre of humanist learning, Corpus Christi College, and at Paris before becoming a fellow of St John's, Cambridge, in 1530. There, he was a prominent member of a distinguished circle of Greek scholars, among them Robert Pember, John Cheke and his close friend, Roger Ascham,[1] who has left us a eulogistic account of Redman's qualities as a scholar. In 1537 Redman attained a doctoral degree in divinity and henceforth devoted himself to theology. He subsequently became chaplain to Henry VIII and was Lady Margaret Professor of Divinity from 1538 to 1544. According to Bishop Burnet, he was by now 'esteemed the most learned and judicious divine of that time'[2] and stood high in the regard of Cranmer. In association with Matthew Parker (then vice-chancellor) and William Mey, president of Queens', Redman conducted the crucial royal commission of inquiry into the state of the Cambridge colleges in 1546 whose favourable outcome resulted in the specific exemption of the colleges from the terms of the Chantries Act of 1547. Although the full circumstances will probably never be discovered the available evidence suggests that Redman was a major influence in bringing to fruition Henry VIII's magnificent conception that became Trinity College, Cambridge.

The multifarious activities of the King's Scholars almost defy neat classification and only indications along very general lines can here be given. Because of the inadequacy of the data, it is impossible at this juncture to estimate with any precision the proportion of King's Scholars who were directly utilised in the service of the Crown. The signs are, however, that it was fairly substantial. King's Scholars are found in the ranks of the chancery,[3] the exchequer,[4] the king's council,[5] and the royal diplomatic service:[6] they were employed in

---

[1] E. Miller, *Portrait of a college*, p. 12.

[2] G. Burnet, *The history of the reformation of the Church of England* (Oxford, 1816), I, pt. i, 521.

[3] E.g. the careers of Roger Basset and John Derby, *B.R.U.C.* pp. 43, 184.

[4] E.g. the careers of Nicholas de Drayton and Richard de Medford, *ibid.* pp. 194, 399.

[5] E.g. the career of Simon Neylond, *ibid.* p. 425.

[6] E.g. the careers of Richard Maudeleyn, Nicholas Hethe, John de Wormenhale, Richard de Medford, Thomas Barowe, Christopher Urswick and Cuthbert Tunstall, *ibid.* pp. 397, 303, 650, 399, 40, 606, 597–8.

the queen's household,[1] as royal bailiffs and keepers of the forest,[2] and as judicial commissioners;[3] at least three held the office of master of the rolls, one was a keeper of the privy seal, another a king's secretary, and one rose to the position of keeper of the great seal of England.[4] Since considerations of space exclude the possibility of presenting in detail the careers of all King's Scholars known to have engaged in royal service, the careers of three of the most pre-eminent of them, drawn from the fourteenth, fifteenth and sixteenth centuries, must suffice by way of illustration.

The fourteenth-century example is provided by Richard de Medford,[5] King's Hall fellow from 1352 to 1378, who became one of the inner circle of advisers to Richard II. By 1375, while still a fellow, he had acquired the status of king's clerk and is later specifically designated a clerk of the chapel royal. Five years after the vacation of his fellowship he was appointed chirographer of the common bench and was king's secretary by June 1385. From this time onwards, he was in constant attendance on the king's business until his deprivation by the lords appellant in 1388. In 1390 he was consecrated bishop of Chichester and in 1394 was appointed treasurer of the exchequer in Ireland. He was made bishop of Sarum in 1395 and, as such, was one of the 'courtier bishops' so unpopular with the opposition to Richard II. Medford survived the deposition of 1399 and died in 1407 still as bishop of Sarum.

Thomas Barowe,[6] educated at Eton and the King's Hall, where he was a fellow from 1457 to 1473, came to prominence with the accession of Richard III. He was already chancellor to Richard, duke of Gloucester, in 1483, and when the latter became king Barowe was appointed master of the rolls in the September of that year. He was employed in a diplomatic capacity and was engaged, for example, in peace negotiations with Scotland in 1484. Upon the vacation of

---

[1] E.g. the careers of Robert de Imworth, Adam Davenport and Roger Radcliff, *ibid.* pp. 326, 178, 469.

[2] E.g. the career of John Godrich, *ibid.* p. 261.

[3] E.g. the career of John Derlyngton, *ibid.* p. 185.

[4] See above, the career of John Blythe, p. 289; and for the careers of Richard de Medford, Thomas Barowe and Cuthbert Tunstall, see text.

[5] *B.R.U.C.* pp. 398–9; A. Steel, *Richard II* (reprinted, Cambridge, 1962), pp. 113, 116–17, 143, 161, 218, 220, 261.

[6] *B.R.U.C.* pp. 40–1; *D.N.B.* III (1885), 272–3.

the chancellorship of John Russell on 29 July 1485, Barowe was made keeper of the great seal for the short period until Bosworth. Under Henry VII, Barowe was obliged to resign his position as master of the rolls but retained a mastership in chancery granted by Richard III. He last appears in governmental activity as a receiver of petitions in the parliament of 1496, and died three years later.

The sixteenth-century example is furnished by Cuthbert Tunstall,[1] fellow of the college from 1496 to 1500, and certainly one of the most distinguished of all the King's Scholars. He received his early education at Oxford and is alleged to have migrated to Cambridge because of an outbreak of plague. He later studied at Padua and became one of the most influential of English humanist scholars of his age: indeed, Cardinal Pole regarded him as the greatest of all.[2] After his return from Italy, Tunstall gained rapid ecclesiastical preferment culminating in the bishopric of London in 1522 and of Durham in 1530. His advancement in the king's service was equally rapid. From 1516 to 1522 he was master of the rolls, from 1523 to 1530 he served as keeper of the privy seal, and he acted as president of the king's council in the north from 1530 to 1538. Throughout his career he was busily engaged in diplomatic activity: for example, in 1525 he was sent as an ambassador to the Emperor Charles V; he accompanied Wolsey on an embassy to France in 1527, was one of the negotiators of the Treaty of Cambrai in 1529 and, under Elizabeth, was one of the commissioners appointed to treat with the Scots in 1559.

The careers of these three King's Scholars were evidently of exceptional prominence and are not representative of the average level of participation in governmental business. Nevertheless, the available evidence points to the conclusion that the King's Hall provided a fairly regular stream of university-trained personnel for absorption in the king's administration and diplomatic service: this latter circumstance may have been due to the preponderant emphasis placed by the college upon the attainment of degrees in civil law, which were generally recognised to be among the best qualifications (along with theology) for this type of work. Although later discoveries may enable us to build up a more detailed picture of the deployment of the King's Scholars within the governmental structure, there can be little doubt that the King's Hall, whose fellows continued to be ap-

---

[1] *B.R.U.C.* pp. 597–8.   [2] A. Tilley, *E.H.R.* LIII (1938), 224.

pointed directly by the Crown right down to 1546, constituted one of the principal academic reservoirs at the permanent disposal of the king.

In terms of ecclesiastical offices, the King's Hall produced three bishops,[1] at least twenty-one archdeacons,[2] some of whom held two or more archdeaconries at a time, ten bishops' officials,[3] three archdeacons' officials,[4] an archiepiscopal secretary,[5] two episcopal chancellors,[6] an episcopal chaplain[7] and a number of bishops' commissaries and vicars general.[8] Some small proportion of these offices were discharged in conjunction with fellowships, but most were undertaken in the course of the post-university career and combined with employment in other capacities. An analysis of the diocesan distribution of ecclesiastical livings (rectorships, vicarages, deaneries, canonries and prebends) held by King's Scholars either with their fellowships or immediately after their vacation or in subsequent years shows a marked correlation with the results obtained for the areas of geographical recruitment of fellows based upon surname evidence. The data for ecclesiastical livings held by King's Scholars between 1317 and 1500 are extremely copious and comprise well over 1,600 positions. When these are grouped according to dioceses, the order of the first six is Lincoln, London, Norwich, York, Sarum and Ely. With the exception of Sarum, this diocesan concentration is the same as that for the geographical recruitment of fellows spanning the period 1317 to 1450.[9] These results, which of necessity can only

[1] Richard de Medford, John Blythe and Cuthbert Tunstall.
[2] See *B.R.U.C.* for the careers of Robert Ayscogh, Thomas Barowe, John Blythe, Edmund Bothe, Joachim Bretoner, William Chaundry, John Cheyne, Stephen Close, John Derlyngton, John Hole, Richard Maudeleyn, Richard de Medford, Roger Radcliff, Robert de Ragenhill, Peter Stewkley, John Stubbes, John Treguran, Cuthbert Tunstall, Christopher Urswick and William Waltham; for Baughe, see Venn and Venn, pt. I, I, 110.
[3] See *B.R.U.C.* for the careers of John Cheyne, John Derlyngton, John Derby, Thomas de Gloucester (Gloucestre), Richard Laverok, Robert Leek, Roger Radcliff, Robert de Ragenhill, Nicholas Roos and John de Wormenhale.
[4] William Fynderyn, Roger de Harlaston and John Wittilsey (*B.R.U.C.*).
[5] John Lathum, secretary to John Kempe, archbishop of York (*B.R.U.C.* p. 354).
[6] John Metefeld and John Rowclyff (see *ibid.* pp. 403–4, 492).
[7] Stephen Close, chaplain to Marmaduke Lumley, bishop of Carlisle (see *ibid.* pp. 142–3).
[8] See e.g. *ibid.* for the careers of John Albon, John Cheyne, John Druell, Robert Leek, Thomas de Gloucester, James de Walsingham and John de Wormenhale.
[9] See above, table 11, p. 160.

be of the roughest kind, indicate that King's Scholars who acquired church livings did so primarily in the eastern counties north of the Thames and in Sarum diocese towards the south-west: but while these were the main concentrations, it is equally clear that King's Hall fellows found livings in every diocese of England with the possible exception of Carlisle. Thus, as in the case of the investigation of recruitment areas, the coverage was national in scope but reflects that same pronounced bias which one would expect to find in England's eastern university. For the period 1500 to 1546 we are without the benefit of the herculean efforts of Dr Emden and reliance has to be placed upon the *Alumni Cantabrigienses* of J. and J. A. Venn. Only about fifty livings were culled from this source: once again, however, the same six dioceses, with the addition of Coventry and Lichfield, lead the field and we may safely assume that there was no significant alteration in the pattern in the first half of the sixteenth century.

The remaining aspects of the careers of the King's Scholars are so kaleidoscopic in character that they had best be treated together and illustrated by way of specific example.

There are only six known instances of King's Scholars vacating academic life for the purpose of entering a religious order and all six are to be found in the first half of the fourteenth century: four of these joined the Franciscan Order at Cambridge[1] and the others may possibly have done so.[2] After the last recorded case, of 1352, King's Hall fellows, seemingly without exception, confined themselves to the ranks of the secular clergy: all further contact with the Cambridge Franciscans took the inglorious form of a bitter and lengthy dispute over the possession of part of a conduit running through King's Hall territory, which the Friars Minor had built in the early fourteenth century to convey water to their convent on the site of the present Sidney Sussex College. A compromise solution was evolved in the reign of Henry VI and the entire conduit was given over to Trinity College by Henry VIII in 1546.[3]

Several of the King's Scholars were evidently drawn directly into

[1] Hugh de Sutton, Philip de Stoke, Peter le Scoteler and William de Walcote (*B.R.U.C.* pp. 567, 557, 364, 610).
[2] Alexander de Saunford and John de Sturtone.
[3] For this episode see Willis and Clark, *Architectural history*, II, 427–30.

the papal service if the careers of Thomas Paxton and William Radclyff are anything to go by. Paxton, a fellow by 1342 and still in 1346, was a papal chaplain and auditor in 1362 (still in 1370)[1] and William Radclyff, fellow from 1436 to *c.* 1445, became a papal chamberlain in 1447 and was an abbreviator of apostolic letters in 1451. A year later, he combined this office with that of chamberlain of the English Hospital of St Thomas the Martyr in Rome.[2] And apart from those actually attached to the curia, many of the King's Scholars made temporary contact through their diplomatic capacities.

At least two of the King's Scholars relinquished academic life in order to embrace a military career during the Hundred Years War. These were Stephen de Byneau, who became a fellow in 1344, and Thomas, son of Walter, the king's smith, admitted as a fellow in 1349.[3] Both appear to have gone overseas together and did so without the warden's permission and, for their exuberant patriotism, were removed from the boards of the foundation in 1360. Another fellow, William Goldwin, combined his fellowship with the occupation of physician. He had received his earlier education at Oxford and had been a fellow of All Souls before his migration to Cambridge, where he became a King's Hall fellow in 1480-1. He incepted in medicine and, at the time of his death in 1482, was a physician in London.[4]

The contribution made by the King's Hall to the life of the university is a barometer of its standing within the academic community. No fewer than eight of its wardens became chancellors of the university, one in the fourteenth century and seven in the fifteenth:[5] moreover, Robert Ayscogh had already been elected chancellor while still only a fellow of the King's Hall and before his promotion to the wardenship in 1448. In the first half of the sixteenth century, four of the fellows, Robert Dussing, William Buckmaster, John Young and Edmund Cosyn,[6] became vice-chancellor at a time when the chancellorship was often held by a non-resident dignitary, such as Thomas Cromwell, and when the vice-chancellor was in every way the *de facto* head of the *studium*. Furthermore, ten of the King's

---

[1] *B.R.U.C.* p. 445.   [2] *Ibid.* p. 469.   [3] *Ibid.* pp. 114, 581.
[4] *Ibid.* pp. 263-4.   [5] See above, p. 282, n. 4 and pp. 283-9.
[6] See Venn and Venn, pt. I, II, 78; I, 248; IV, 493; I, 400.

Hall fellows are known to have served as proctors of the university,[1] and there were certainly many more, since the proctorial lists are lamentably very far from complete. In addition, the King's Hall was a coloniser of other Cambridge colleges and provided masters for at least six different societies. John de Chatterys, fellow from 1350 to *c.* 1365, became master of Clare Hall in 1366;[2] Henry Costessy was admitted as master of Gonville Hall following the vacation of his fellowship in 1472–3;[3] Richard Wyott, fellow from 1492–3 to 1501–2, became master of Christ's College in 1506;[4] Thomas Larke was made master of Trinity Hall in 1517, having almost certainly been a King's Hall fellow in 1508–9;[5] John Young, a fellow from 1542–3 and one of the original fellows of Trinity, was elected master of Pembroke in 1554;[6] and, finally, Reginald Bainbridge, fellow from 1524 to 1529, and Edmund Cosyn, fellow from 1540–1, each became master of St Catharine's, in 1529 and 1554 respectively.[7] Nor must the association of the King's Hall with the promotion of humanist studies in the university be overlooked. Reference has already been made to the institution of elementary instruction in Greek by 1517–18, and the careers of Urswick and Tunstall, both fellows of the college and two of the most celebrated of the English humanists, have been detailed above. To these must be added the name of Robert Pember, who, at a late stage in his career, came to be linked with the King's Hall and Trinity College. With Redman, Pember had been a member of the brilliant circle of Greek scholars at St John's, where he was one of Roger Ascham's tutors. He migrated to a fellowship at the King's Hall in 1542–3, remained as one of the foundation fellows of Trinity, and was the college's first reader in Greek between 1546 and 1560.[8] Another distinction held by the King's Hall is that it furnished the first occupant of the Regius Professorship of Divinity in 1540. The appointment is a rather puzzling one in that theologians of the calibre of Ridley and Parker

---

[1] John de Kent, John de Chatterys, Richard Morgan, Thomas Swayn, Richard Wyott (*B.R.U.C.* pp. 336, 132, 411, 570, 661); Reginald Bainbridge, John Cheeswright, John Denne, Thomas Blythe, Edmund Cosyn (Venn and Venn, pt. I, I, 69, 328; II, 32; I, 171, 400).   [2] *B.R.U.C.* p. 132.

[3] *Ibid.* p. 161.   [4] *Ibid.* p. 661.

[5] See Venn and Venn, pt. I, III, 48.   [6] *Ibid.* IV, 493.

[7] *Ibid.* I, 69, 400.

[8] *Ibid.* III, 338; see also Mullinger, *University of Cambridge*, II, 42, 84.

were passed over for an elderly theological fellow of the King's Hall, Eudo Wigan, who had formerly been subdean of Wolsey's chapel and is not known to have possessed reformist views.[1] Perhaps a 'safe' appointment in a period of religious turmoil was considered desirable.

Although the King's Hall produced a succession of scholars who played a constructive role in the manifold affairs of the *studium*, it must also bear responsibility for harbouring John Bilneye, the future formidable mayor of Cambridge and arch-enemy of the university.[2] Bilneye had been a clerk of the chapel royal and was recruited to the college in 1382. He gave administrative service as a seneschal and appears to have taken an M.A. degree by 1388-9, but relinquished academic life *c.* 1400 and embarked upon a long trouble-filled career in Cambridge municipal politics. He served as mayor in 1406-7, 1414-15, 1416-17 and 1433-4 and was M.P. for Cambridge in 1415, 1417 and 1419. By 1415 a bitter dispute had broken out between Bilneye and the university authorities, the cause apparently being his refusal to allow the conversion of one of his houses into a hostel for scholars. The quarrel engendered extreme behaviour on both sides and, on one occasion, scholars attacked his house and threatened to kill him. The original dispute soon blossomed out into a wrangle of vast proportions with the mayor and the university bombarding the king's council with petitions and counter-petitions. The upshot was that Bilneye was excommunicated and in 1420 the university published a schedule of twenty-five articles of complaint which summarised the main points at issue.[3] Here Bilneye is accused of everything from perjury to threatening resistance to the chancellor's authority with a hundred armed men. There was one clause which had a particular relevance for his old college, the King's Hall. By long-established custom, the university claimed exemption from all tolls on the transportation of building materials, fuel and victuals for the use of the university and of any college or house within it. Bilneye was accused of violating this privilege and the case which prompted the charge was one involving the King's Hall. In 1420 the warden and fellows of the King's Hall

---

[1] Venn and Venn, pt. I, IV, 402; Mullinger, *op. cit.* II, 53.
[2] For Bilneye see *B.R.U.C.* p. 62; J. M. Gray, *Biographical notes on the mayors of Cambridge* (reprinted from *Cambridge Chronicle*) (1921), pp. 16-17.
[3] See Cooper, *Annals of Cambridge*, I, 164-6.

complained to the chancellor that the municipal authorities had unlawfully exacted tolls from carriers of timber and other materials necessary for building work at the college. At their special request, a congregation of regents and non-regents was convened on 2 May 1420 by the chancellor, John Rykynghale, wherein reinforced testimony was recorded to the university's right of exemption from any such tolls imposed by the mayor and bailiffs.[1] Bilneye's mayoralty clearly precipitated one of the darkest chapters in town–gown relations in the history of medieval Cambridge. Allowance must doubtless be made for propagandist excesses on the part of the university but, on balance, the burden of guilt seems to have lain with the municipal authorities.

There still remains a fair proportion of King's Scholars about whose careers there is at present no information at all. In many instances, the evidence either does not permit us to see beyond the initial phase of the career or else introduces us to it at an advanced stage, leaving an exasperating gap to be accounted for. Because of these limitations, it has been possible at this juncture to give only the most general indications of the nature and variety of the adopted careers of the King's Scholars. But even this is considerably more than can be realised for most medieval colleges. Such a comparable well-nigh complete list of fellows as that for the King's Hall, stretching as it does from 1317 to the last extant account of 1543–4, survives for very few European collegiate institutions: indeed, it may well be the fullest European compilation that can now be evolved. And so, for the majority of medieval colleges, one of the basic problems is the absence of sufficiently comprehensive lists of fellows to provide even a starting point for career analysis of personnel, at least before the late fifteenth and sixteenth centuries. While this circumstance obviously heightens the historical value of anything that can be discovered about the careers of the King's Scholars, it should be stressed that they are not necessarily representative of the fellows of the more typical medieval college. Because of the royal household origins of the King's Hall, its court associations and the unique method of Crown appointment to fellowships, we may suppose that a far higher proportion of King's Scholars would be utilised in the king's service than would be the case with the fellows of the

[1] See *K.H. Cabinet*, no. 99; Cooper, *Annals*, I, 163–4.

average college of humbler status and fewer numbers. Just how far the Crown's deployment of the King's Scholars compared with that of the members of other untypically large English colleges, such as Merton, New College and King's College, is a matter deserving of the closest investigation if we are ever to work out the full extent of the relationship which persisted between the central government and the English universities in the later middle ages.

CONCLUSION

Since the appearance in 1895 of Rashdall's monumental three-volume work on the medieval universities, a great deal of new research has been completed, necessitating both major and minor readjustments to this classic of university history. The need for these revisions can be partly explained by the discovery of fresh sources of information; but partly also because of the valuable new light thrown upon the functioning of the universities by the many peripheral studies which have recently appeared in areas closely allied to, though not directly concerned with, university history.

It is the fortunate survival of no fewer than twenty-six volumes of the King's Hall accounts which, on the one hand, has made it possible to reconstruct the history of a unique university college from the inside and, on the other hand, has enabled us to cast a revisionary slant on the medieval *studium* of Cambridge itself. There can no longer be any doubt that Cambridge had achieved advanced organisational maturity, embodying features of indigenous growth, at a much earlier date in the thirteenth century than had hitherto been supposed. Her ability to attract scholars of European renown is not any more a legitimate topic of dispute. A re-examination of the crucial letter of Pope John XXII of 1318 indicates that there is every justification for classifying Cambridge with those universities of the highest European status, such as Paris, Bologna, Padua and Oxford, which had attained their positions as *studia generalia* by widespread customary acclaim and not by formal papal or imperial enactment. Recent research trends of this kind underline the urgent need for a more balanced re-appraisal of English academic history. Although Oxford appeared as the larger of the two English universities, the standing and reputation of Cambridge were not thereby affected.

The colleges of the medieval universities do not always receive the emphasis they deserve. From relatively insignificant beginnings they grew to have a fundamental impact upon the direction and character of the old-established universities of Paris, Oxford and Cambridge. For in the later middle ages the English and Parisian colleges were the heirs to the system of public instruction of the university schools, a system which seems to have degenerated in varying degrees for reasons which are still not yet fully explored. We know the effect of this degeneration of university instruction—largely in the shape of the rise of the colleges to a position of dominance—but we know very little of the causes which set this process in motion. The emergence of colleges as self-sufficient educational units completed that movement whereby teaching came to be entirely decentralised in the colleges, which then became the real focal points of secular academic life on both sides of the Channel. At the same time, it would be no exaggeration to claim that several of the fourteenth- and fifteenth-century universities in Germany and Scotland might not have survived at all but for the stabilising effects of collegiate establishments. It is therefore of paramount importance that in any survey of the medieval universities the European collegiate movement should be assigned a position commensurate with its historical role and not, as is sometimes the case, dismissed with subordinate and cursory treatment. And the royal College of the King's Hall assumes in this context its pronounced importance and historical significance.

The King's Hall, Cambridge, stands out as an institution *sui generis* among English academic societies of the middle ages. It had its origins in an extension or arm of Edward II's chapel royal set in the University of Cambridge. For over two centuries the King's Hall remained the intensely personal instrument of the Crown: the Society was supported throughout by direct exchequer grant, and successive English kings retained the patronage entirely in their own hands, every fellow and warden being a direct Crown appointee. These peculiar constitutional features decisively set apart the King's Hall from all other categories of English colleges with royal associations. Edward II's academic stimulus, manifesting itself in the Society of the King's Scholars and later in the endowed College of the King's Hall, was a vital landmark in English university history. For it brought into being the first royal colony of clerks to be established in a university setting and effected the first institutional link between the royal household and the English universities. This tie was later expanded to embrace all 'royal' colleges at Oxford and Cambridge: but because of its unique relationship to the royal household the King's Hall remained the sheet-anchor of this nexus between the universities and the court right throughout the middle ages. For these reasons, the King's Hall has to be evaluated not only within the realm of academic history but also in relation to royal household government, of which it properly forms a part.

As a kind of educational supplement to the household and to the court, this royal Society had, apparently, as one of its principal aims the provision of a reservoir of educated personnel for service in the church and in government departments. It is therefore highly significant that civil law was, and remained, the main academic concentration in the superior faculties; and right from the early fourteenth century English kings had deliberately fostered this discipline at the King's Hall. Their success can be gauged from the fact that the college became the most important single cradle of civil law graduates in Cambridge, accounting, on a conservative estimate, for about one fifth of the university's total output of legists. Under direct royal patronage and stimulation, the King's Hall was obviously intended to play a central role in the perpetuation and renaissance of civil law studies at the English universities. Royal manipulation of this nature may well have been prompted by the need to satisfy the increased demand for civil law graduates arising from movements such as the Hundred Years War and European conciliarism: but it may also have been part of a monarchical policy designed to engender and nourish a climate of legal thought generally favourable to the accentuation of the more theocratic aspects of kingship. And further research into this matter may reveal that the King's Hall was only one of several such instruments utilised by the Crown to promote civil law studies in medieval England.

Until the foundation of New College, Oxford, in 1379, Merton and the King's Hall were the two largest and most celebrated colleges in England. At Cambridge, the King's Hall retained its position of primacy until rivalled by King's College in the mid-fifteenth century: even so, and until its dissolution in 1546 and amalgamation with Michaelhouse to form Trinity College, Cambridge, contemporary opinion still regarded the King's Hall as the 'oracle' of the university. In many respects, the King's Hall stood in the forefront of institutional change and showed itself to be finely geared and adaptable to the academic needs of the age. It was undoubtedly the first English college to make regular provision for the admission of undergraduates and so constitutes the earliest prototype of those mixed collegiate societies which were to characterise the colleges of post-Reformation England: that is to say, the King's Hall brought together an association of undergraduate and graduate scholars sharing a life in common and engaged in study at their own particular levels. For the first time in English university history provision had been made for a scholar to pass through the entire educational gamut within the walls of the same institution.

The King's Hall records also furnish vital clues for a feature of university life—the tutorial system—which came to have an overriding importance for English academic development. Very little is as yet known of the early growth of the tutorial system and it is therefore particularly fortunate that the King's Hall accounts can yield valuable information on this matter. For they reveal in operation a rudimentary form of tutorial organisation involving pupils (i.e. commoners) introduced into the college for private tuition at the hands of individual fellows. This appears to be the earliest available evidence for an English college concerning that type of tutorial arrangement whereby the entire regulation of the pupil's finances is vested in a fellow in his capacity as tutor. It was this kind of arrangement which was to become one of the main distinguishing features of the English collegiate teaching system in the late sixteenth and seventeenth centuries.

These academic innovations do not yet exhaust the historical significance of the contributions which the King's Hall made to the life of the university. The available evidence points to the conclusion that the King's Hall initiated at Cambridge the fully fledged college lectureship as a form of academic instruction within the university. Moreover, the King's Hall showed itself keenly alert to the educational importance of the rising tide of humanism when, by means of both lectures and classical plays, it took an active part in the promotion of humanist studies in Cambridge at a time when the English universities were only just beginning to come to grips with the academic re-orientation stemming from European humanism.

It would also seem advisable to draw especial attention to what might well be called the fertilising effect of the King's Hall's establishment at Cambridge. For the coming of royal patronage to Cambridge in the form of the Society of the King's Scholars had a pronounced and vitalising effect upon the development of the university.

It appears to have been the introduction of this royal community into Cambridge which attracted the patronage of college founders and benefactors who might otherwise have expended their wealth upon the University of Oxford. This found concrete expression in the first great wave of collegiate expansion—unsurpassed anywhere else—which was unleashed at Cambridge in the early fourteenth century. On this reckoning, the university seems to have derived far more substantial benefit from this royal Society as a more efficacious stimulus to its collegiate development than from Peterhouse, the solitary college foundation of the thirteenth century. Further, an investigation of the whole complex of events surrounding the inception of the King's Scholars in Cambridge indicates that the fortunes of the university were closely intertwined with the political tensions and personalities of the reign of Edward II, serving as a salutary reminder that academic history can rarely be divorced from the mainstream of national events. The history of the King's Hall amply proves how much it fructified the development of the University of Cambridge itself as well as that of other academic institutions: this history also demonstrates how a medieval college could make a positive and constructive contribution to some of the most exciting academic movements of the age.

In the past, the college history has often amounted to little more than an evaluation of the founder's statutes, a biographical survey of its *alumni* and a description of its architectural features. As the colleges were destined to occupy such a dominant position in the universities of northern Europe, they deserve better treatment than this. But it is not always the historian who has been at fault: in so many cases, the sheer poverty of the source material has made the 'pious memorial' approach almost a necessity. Even where lengthy sets of college documents survive, they often deal mainly with estate management and yield little or no information on the internal situation. The historical value of the magnificent set of twenty-six volumes of the King's Hall accounts derives from two main circumstances: first, they form the longest sequence of paper collegiate records in England, and probably also in Europe, and so are accessible to sustained analytical inquiry over a significant period of time; secondly, the matter of the accounts is principally concerned with internal affairs. These continuous records have made possible a detailed examination not only of internal collegiate economy but also of the constitutional, administrative and business organisation of a medieval college. The rich profusion of the material enables one to obtain glimpses into almost every aspect of collegiate life and to draw conclusions supported by a mass of distilled evidence. Apart from economic, constitutional, administrative and business matters, one can derive information on everything from minstrel entertainments to plague visitations, from the book-borrowing habits of the fellows to the composition of the motley crew of commoners who so enriched and diversified the academic community and whose history has yet to be written. From these accounts even the modern sociologist might well extract that kind of reliable information which would enable him to draw a portrait of an academic community for which no fully comparable set of sources seems to exist. This is one of the worlds we have not yet lost.

It is only right that the medieval college should receive the same kind of exhaustive treatment which has been lavished upon the monastery or the baronial household. For the colleges were the main secular supports of the students in the superior faculties and, in company with the mendicant orders, harboured generations of the abler and most creative spirits in the universities. These were the students with the greatest potential social and professional value: and before we can properly evaluate the role of the university as a functional entity in medieval society we shall have to know far more about the colleges which housed them than we do at present. Only when European collegiate organisation and life have been microscopically examined shall we be in a position to estimate the conditions in which the majority of the advanced students of the medieval universities had to live and work. The King's Hall, however important a link this college was in English academic development, is only a segment of the general medieval academic movement of which the colleges form an integral and constitutive part. Not until their history and their contributions have been properly evaluated can we know enough of the medieval universities of which we are today the heirs.

APPENDIX

FIVE TYPICAL EXAMPLES OF THE KING'S HALL ANNUAL ACCOUNTS FOR WEEKLY COMMONS

ENGLISH EXPLANATIONS OF COLUMN HEADINGS

In septimana	Weeks of harvest year (i.e. from Michaelmas to Michaelmas).
Presentes	Number of fellows present per week.
In pane	Total college expenditure on bread for fellows' commons per week.
In cervisia	Total college expenditure on ale for fellows' commons per week.
In coquina	Total college expenditure on kitchen per week (running costs, etc.).
In stauro	Total college expenditure on stores and fuel per week.
Summa totalis	Total college expenditure on fellows' commons per week.
Cōes Sociorum [Communes sociorum]	Amount charged by college to each fellow for commons per week.
In repastis	Total amount spent on sizings by fellows per week.

20-2

Account for weekly commons of 34 Edward III, i.e. 1360–1 (*King's Hall Accts.* II, fos. 30–31 v)

COMMUNES SOCIORUM

(1) In septimana	(2) Presentes	(3) In pane (s d)	(4) In cervisia (s d)	(5) In coquina (£ s d)	(6) In stauro (£ s d)	(7) Summa totalis (£ s d)	(8) In repastis (s d)
1	7	3 0	6 3	6 6½	4	16 1½	1 9
2	10	4 0	4 4	9 0	4	17 8	2 4
3	12	5 10	7 0	8 8	4	1 1 10	2 5½
4	19	6 8	10 0	12 11	9	1 10 4	4 3
5	22	8 6	12 6	13 7½	1 4	1 15 11½	3 11
6	21	8 0	11 0	15 0	1 5	1 15 5	4 8½
7	19	7 4	10 0	14 0	1 4	1 12 8	4 4
8	18	8 0	11 0	16 6	1 3½	1 16 9½	5 1
9	21	8 8	10 0	13 1	1 1	1 12 10	3 9
10	23	9 0	10 0	14 7½	2 1	1 15 8½	5 2
11	22	8 0	9 8	14 11	1 2	1 13 9	4 8
12	23	8 0	9 6	17 10	1 4	1 16 8	6 7
13	19	8 8	17 6	1 7 11½	5 8	2 19 9½	6 0
14	20	11 8	18 6	1 1 6	5 0	2 16 8	8 8
15	19	9 0	12 4	1 0 0½	2 8	2 4 0½	5 0
16	19	8 0	10 0	13 9½	2 6	1 14 3½	6 1
17	23	11 4	13 0	16 8½	2 8	2 3 8½	8 0
18	24	9 0	11 0	18 3	1 10	2 0 1	5 6

19	24	10 9	13 2	1 0 7	2 9	2 7 3	8 2
20	26	10 0	13 6	1 0 0½	11 0½	2 14 7	8 9
21	25	11 0	15 2	11 8½	15 0	2 12 10½	8 2
22	27	10 2	15 0	14 1	12 6½	2 11 9½	8 10
23	27	13 6	16 8	13 1	1 0 9½	3 4 0½	7 8
24	28	13 0	15 8	16 9½	1 0 8½	3 6 2	9 8
25	27	11 0	14 0	13 4	16 4	2 14 8	10 0
26	23	13 0	10 0	13 4½	7 7½	2 4 0	5 7½
27	19	11 0	13 0	19 8	2 4	2 6 0	5 7
28	21	11 3	12 4	16 3¾	2 6	2 2 4¾	6 7
29	20	8 6	12 0	14 0	2 3	1 16 9	6 5½
30	21	9 3	9 6	16 3	2 4	1 17 4	5 8½
31	23	9 0	15 5	15 5½	1 8½	2 1 7	5 2
32	23	9 0	14 4	18 4	4 5½	2 6 1½	4 6½
33	23	8 8	14 0	16 0	2 3	2 0 11	6 8
34	22	6 6	10 4	15 4	2 2½	1 14 4½	5 10
35	17	6 0	11 0	12 0	1 8	1 10 8	5 2
36	18	8 0	13 0	13 9	1 8½	1 16 5½	5 0
37	20	8 0	14 0	14 9½	1 10	1 18 7½	7 8
38	19	10 0	15 0	17 4	1 6½	2 3 10½	7 0
39	20	13 0	17 0	1 1 7	1 6	2 13 1	9 4
40	19	11 0	15 6	19 1	2 8½	2 8 3½	7 9½
41	19	8 0	11 4	13 3½	2 4	1 14 11½	6 10½
42	17	7 2	11 4	15 6½	2 6½	1 16 7	5 6
Totals (supplied)	869	£18 19 5	£25 15 10	£32 16 8¼	£8 15 9½	£86 7 8¾	£12 15 11
Weekly averages	21	9 0½	12 3½	15 7½	4 2¼	£2 1 1½	6 1

Account for weekly commons of 6 Richard II, i.e. 1382–3 (*King's Hall Accts.* III, fos. 108–110v)

COMMUNES SOCIORUM

(1) *In septimana*	(2) *Presentes*	(3) *In pane*	(4) *In cervisia*	(5) *In coquina*	(6) *Summa totalis*	(7) *Cōes sociorum*	(8) *In repastis*
		s d	£ *s d*	£ *s d*	£ *s d*	*s d*	*s d*
1	24	6 6	8 0	18 10½	1 13 4½	1 1½	6 2½
2	23	7 6	11 8	1 0 6½	1 19 10½	1 2	12 2
3	25	7 0	11 0	1 1 9½	1 19 11½	1 2	8 8
4	28	7 0	12 7	1 2 2½	2 2 0½	1 2½	7 11
5	29	7 0	12 8	1 2 4	2 2 7	1 2	8 5
6	30	8 0	12 8	1 6 10	2 9 1	1 3	10 11½
7	32	8 8	12 0	1 3 8	2 4 10	1 3	4 6½
8	32	8 6	11 0	1 2 9½	1 14 1½	1 0½	9 4
9	32	8 6	12 8	1 4 0	2 5 6	1 3	4 8
10	32	8 8	12 8	1 4 4½	2 6 0½	1 2½	7 0
11	32	7 0	11 0	1 5 4	2 3 10	1 2½	5 2½
12	32	8 2	10 8	1 6 2	2 5 8	1 3½	3 10¾
13	32	8 0	13 6	2 0 11	3 6 5½	1 9	10 6
14	30	9 0	12 0	2 1 2	3 5 4	1 10	10 9
15	30	9 6	11 3	1 9 3½	2 13 6½	1 6	7 11½
16	32	9 0	11 6	1 3 5½	2 4 5½	1 3	4 10½
17	32	8 6	10 8	1 4 2	2 3 0	1 3	3 7
18	32	8 6	10 0	1 5 0	2 3 3	1 3	2 5
19	31	9 0	13 0	2 1 1	2 1 1	1 8½	10 0½
20	32	8 0	12 0	1 1 3½	2 1 7½	1 2	3 9
21	32	7 0	12 0	14 6	2 3 4	1 2	5 5½
22	33	8 0	12 0	14 4½	2 5 4½	1 2	6 10½
23	32	7 0	12 0	14 7	2 5 0	1 2½	5 2
24	31	7 0	12 0	13 2	2 2 1	1 2½	4 1½
25	29	6 0	10 0	15 8½	1 16 8½	1 2	2 10½
26	29	7 0	11 0	1 11 0½	2 10 9½	1 6½	5 7
27	28	7 6	11 0	1 1 2	1 19 10	1 2½	5 0
28	30	7 0	11 0	1 4 1	2 2 5	1 3½	3 0½

29	30	7 6	10 0	1 3 10½	2 2 4½	1 3	3 9
30	29	6 6	10 0	1 2 11½	1 19 11½	1 3	3 9½
31	28	8 0	12 0	1 9 0	2 9 9½	1 6	7 4½
32	29	6 0	10 0	1 3 11½	2 0 1	1 3	3 9½
33	26	6 0	10 0	1 10 10½	2 7 2½	1 7	5 11½
34	27	7 0	13 0	1 8 1	2 8 5	1 6	7 8½
35	29	6 0	11 0	1 2 0	1 19 2	1 3	2 11
36	29	6 0	11 0	1 2 10½	2 0 0	1 3	3 2½
37	29	6 0	12 0	1 1 4	1 19 6	1 3	3 9½
38	29	6 0	12 0	1 2 6½	2 0 8½	1 3	3 6
39	29	6 0	11 0	1 4 0	2 1 2	1 3	4 3
40	30	6 0	12 0	1 0 2	1 18 4	1 0½	6 9
41	30	7 0	1 1 0	1 9 7½	2 18 7½	1 10	4 6½
42	29	5 0	11 8	1 4 1	2 0 11	1 2½	5 11
43	28	5 0	11 0	1 2 5½	1 18 1½	1 3	3 2
44	27	5 0	12 0	1 1 0½	1 18 2½	1 2½	3 11
45	26	4 6	11 0	1 0 1½	1 15 9½	1 3	2 8½
46	24	5 0	10 6	18 11½	1 14 5½	1 2½	4 8½
47	28	6 6	11 0	1 2 0	2 0 1	1 3	4 8
48	27	6 0	11 0	1 1 1½	1 18 1½	1 2½	4 9
49	18	4 0	9 9½	16 9	1 10 6½	1 4	5 4½
50	14	4 8	8 0	11 9	1 4 5	1 6	2 8
51	19	6 0	12 6	1 1 3½	2 0 1½	1 4½	12 9
52	17	3 0	8 6	12 6	1 4 6	1 2½	3 0
Totals (supplied)	1,477	£17 17 2	£29 15 5	£60 7 3½	£112 1 0	£3 15 1½	£14 15 11¼
Weekly averages	30	6 10½	11 5½	£1 3 2½	£2 1 6½	1 5¼	5 8¼

Annual college expenditure on stores for fellows' commons = total annual college expenditure on fellows' commons – (annual college expenditure on bread and ale for fellows' commons + annual college expenditure on kitchen costs incurred in providing fellows' commons)

= £112 1*s* – (£17 17*s* 2*d* + £29 15*s* 5*d* + £60 7*s* 3½*d*)

= £112 1*s* – £107 19*s* 10½*d*

= £4 1*s* 1½*d*

∴ average weekly expenditure on stores and fuel = £4 1*s* 1½*d* ÷ (52)

= 1*s* 6¾*d*

Account for weekly commons of 10 Henry IV, i.e. 1408–9 (*King's Hall Accts.* v, fos. 114–116v)

COMMUNES SOCIORUM

(1) In septimana	(2) Presentes	(3) In pane	(4) In cervisia	(5) In coquina	(6) Summa totalis	(7) Cōes sociorum	(8) In repastis
		s d	£ s d	£ s d	£ s d	s d	s d
1	23	13 4	9 0	17 5	2 3 6	1 9	2 6
2	23	9 8	13 8	17 9½	2 5 10½	1 10	3 3½
3	26	10 6	11 4	19 4	2 5 11	1 8	2 5
4	26	11 6	12 0	18 11	2 7 2	1 7½	3 10
5	27	12 0	13 0	1 7 7	2 18 5	1 11½	5 5
6	25	14 0	12 0	1 0 1	2 11 5	1 11	3 6
7	24	11 0	11 0	1 0 3½	2 7 1½	1 11	1 11
8	28	12 4	13 0	1 1 11	2 12 8	1 9	3 5½
9	29	16 8	16 0	1 3 8	3 2 8	1 10½	7 4
10	31	12 0	18 0	1 7 1	3 1 3½	1 10	3 0½
11	30	12 0	12 0	1 6 8½	2 15 11½	1 9½	2 2
12	28	10 8	17 6	1 2 0½	2 14 11	1 10½	1 10½
13	29	13 0	13 3	2 9 7	4 4 5	2 10	2 6½
14	27	13 0	15 3	1 11 2	3 7 3	2 5	2 6½
15	27	11 0	13 9	1 11 10½	3 4 5½	2 0½	9 5
16	30	13 0	14 6	1 5 1½	2 18 11½	1 10	1 9½
17	30	12 0	17 0	1 6 10½	3 1 8½	1 11½	3 3½
18	31	14 0	16 0	1 3 10½	2 19 7	1 9½	4 4½
19	27	13 6	16 0	1 9 5½	3 5 10½	2 2½	5 2½
20	27	12 6	12 0	1 1 3	2 11 5½	1 10	2 0½
21	29	14 0	11 6	1 4 7½	2 16 5	1 10½	2 0½
22	29	12 0	15 6	15 9½	2 17 5	1 10	2 9½
23	28	11 0	17 0	15 4½	2 15 6	1 10½	2 8
24	30	15 0	16 0	15 9	2 18 9½	1 10½	1 1½
25	29	11 0	14 0	12 5½	2 12 6	1 8½	3 4

26	27	9 6	16 0	16 2½	2 11 0	1 9	3 5
27	21	11 6	12 0	17 1½	2 8 6½	2 2	2 7
28	23	11 2	15 0	1 9 5	3 0 0½	2 6	2 9½
29	22	10 2	17 0	1 0 4½	2 12 3½	2 2	3 1½
30	29	14 0	18 0	1 4 4	3 0 7	2 0	2 7½
31	27	11 8	16 0	1 3 6	2 15 5	1 11	2 11
32	27	9 6	18 0	1 3 11½	2 15 9½	1 11½	2 4½
33	29	9 6	17 0	1 5 10½	2 18 2	1 10	4 4
34	30	11 0	19 6	1 4 6½	2 19 9½	1 10½	2 7
35	24	11 0	16 0	1 12 6	3 4 6½	2 6½	2 6
36	21	9 0	16 6	1 2 0	2 12 1½	2 4	2 9
37	27	9 0	1 1 0	1 3 10	2 18 5½	2 1	2 2½
38	27	12 0	19 0	1 6 4	3 1 8	2 2	2 0
39	28	12 0	19 0	1 8 5½	3 3 8	2 1½	4 1½
40	27	11 6	1 1 0	1 5 6½	3 2 5	2 0½	7 6
41	26	12 0	1 1 0	1 4 4½	3 2 1	2 1	6 0½
42	26	11 9	19 0	1 2 7½	2 18 3½	2 0½	5 9
43	26	10 0	18 0	1 3 9	2 16 8	2 1½	1 8½
44	26	11 0	17 0	1 1 2½	2 13 1	1 11	3 8
45	26	10 0	16 0	1 2 0	2 11 5½	1 10	1 9
46	27	9 4	15 0	1 1 0½	2 9 3	1 9	1 9
47	23	9 0	14 6	18 0	2 5 4	1 10	2 2
48	24	8 9	17 6	1 0 3	2 5 4½	2 0½	1 9
49	22	8 6	14 6	18 8½	2 5 3½	2 0	1 3½
50	25	8 8	18 0	19 2½	2 9 5	1 10½	2 9½
51	26	10 2	18 0	1 3 0½	2 14 8½	1 10	6 7
52	21	8 6	15 0	17 8	2 5 6	2 1	1 0
Totals (supplied)	1,381	£29 10 10	£40 14 9	£60 1 11	£145 2 3	£5 2 9	£8 8 0
Weekly averages	27	11 4¼	15 8	£1 3 1¼	£2 15 9¾	1 11¾	3 2¾

Annual college expenditure on stores and fuel for fellows' commons = (£145 2*s* 3*d* – £130 7*s* 6*d*)
= £14 14*s* 9*d*

∴ average weekly expenditure on stores and fuel = 5*s* 8*d*

Account for weekly commons of 3 Henry VI, i.e. 1424-5 (*King's Hall Accts.* VII, fos. 35-37v)

COMMUNES SOCIORUM

(1) In septimana	(2) Presentes	(3) In pane		(4) In cervisia		(5) In coquina			(6) Summa totalis			(7) Cões sociorum		(8) In repastis	
		s	d	s	d	£	s	d	£	s	d	s	d	s	d
1	19	4	0	9	8		14	2½	1	11	5½	1	5½	3	3
2	20	5	8	8	11		14	9½	1	12	3	1	5	3	4
3	21	5	10	9	5	1	2	2½	2	1	1½	1	8	5	8
4	23	5	0	11	0	1	2	0½	2	1	8½	1	6½	5	7
5	21	4	0	9	0	1	11	9½	2	7	11½	1	11	7	11
6	22	6	8	10	0	1	3	2½	2	3	6½	1	8½	5	7½
7	25	8	6	11	6	1	6	4	2	9	4	1	8	7	0½
8	28	8	0	12	6	1	6	0½	2	10	8½	1	4½	12	0½
9	27	6	0	11	10	1	7	3	2	8	10	1	6	7	9½
10	26	7	0	10	10	1	11	3	2	12	10½	1	8	8	10
11	27	7	7	9	10	1	1	7	2	3	2	1	4	6	10
12	23	6	8	10	6	1	1	7	2	2	5	1	5½	9	6
13	21	7	6	13	6	2	11	6½	2	11	6½	3	0½	18	4½
14	21	3	10	10	0	1	11	7½	2	13	2½	2	0	8	2½
15	17	5	6	8	4	1	4	10	2	5	5	2	3	6	8
16	20	6	0	10	10		19	1½	2	1	8½	1	7½	8	0½
17	23	6	4	10	10	1	4	7	2	7	3	1	8½	7	4
18	20	4	6	9	0	1	6	7½	2	7	1½	2	1	5	3
19	23	4	6	10	4	1	5	8½	2	4	2½	1	7	7	6
20	23	6	4	9	6	1	4	4	2	6	0½	1	8	6	11
21	22	6	3	10	10	1	11	2½	2	12	8	2	0½	7	4
22	24	6	6	11	0	1	12	8	2	13	8½	1	10	8	1
23	25	6	6	9	10	1	17	7	2	19	1½	1	10½	11	2
24	25	5	5	9	10	1	18	8½	2	17	8	1	11	9	7
25	22	5	0	10	0	1	11	8	2	10	4	1	11	7	10

26	26	5 8	10 0	1 18 11	2 18 3	2 0	9 11½
27	20	6 0	9 6	1 16 6	2 15 8	2 2	10 3
28	19	5 4	9 6	1 14 6	2 13 4½	2 6	5 10
29	17	5 10	10 0	1 14 8	2 14 6½	2 0	11 2
30	23	7 9	12 0	1 6 0½	2 9 5½	1 6	13 7½
31	22	6 9	11 0	1 10 9	2 12 4½	1 8½	12 8½
32	18	4 8	10 0	1 8 6	2 6 10	1 11	10 9
33	22	5 8	10 0	1 15 1½	2 14 5½	1 11	11 4
34	21	5 6	11 0	1 10 1½	2 10 7½	1 10½	11 2
35	17	5 0	9 0	1 13 7½	2 11 3½	2 6½	7 9½
36	18	5 0	10 0	1 6 7½	2 5 3½	2 0	8 8
37	20	5 6	8 10	1 2 9	2 0 9	1 8	7 0
38	19	5 0	9 6	1 2 9½	2 0 11½	1 9	6 4½
39	20	5 0	11 0	1 7 8½	2 7 7½	1 10½	8 11½
40	19	5 0	10 6	1 3 11	2 3 1	1 10½	7 9
41	18	5 6	8 0	1 4 5	2 1 7	1 10½	8 1
42	18	4 8	9 0	1 3 4	2 0 4	1 10	6 1½
43	18	5 10	8 4	1 3 8½	2 1 6½	1 10½	8 3½
44	16	5 0	7 4	1 0 3½	1 10 3½	1 10	6 8
45	16	4 0	9 0	1 1 1	1 17 9	1 10½	7 8½
46	15	4 0	8 0	1 0 4½	1 15 4½	1 10	7 0½
47	16	3 6	6 6	19 7	1 13 3	1 8½	6 0½
48	16	4 6	8 6	19 0½	1 14 2½	1 9½	5 0½
49	20	5 0	8 0	19 11	1 16 3½	1 5½	7 0
50	21	5 0	7 3	1 5 2	2 1 1	1 6	7 9½
51	19	4 8	8 6	1 2 10	1 19 11½	1 7½	8 0
52	17	4 6	8 0	1 2 11	1 19 1	1 9	8 5
Totals (supplied)	1,079	£14 8 11	£25 7 3	£69 18 2½	£118 10 8½	£4 14 6	£21 5 3
Weekly averages	22	5 6¾	9 9	£1 6 10¾	£2 5 7	1 9¾	8 2

Annual college expenditure on stores and fuel for fellows' commons = (£118 10*s* 8½*d* – £109 14*s* 4½*d*)
= £8 16*s* 4*d*

∴ average weekly expenditure on stores and fuel = 3*s*. 4¾*d*

Account for weekly commons of 9 Henry VI, i.e. 1430–1 (*King's Hall Accts.* VIII, fos. 2–4v)

COMMUNES SOCIORUM

(1) *In septimana*	(2) *Presentes*	(3) *In pane*	(4) *In cervisia*	(5) *In coquina*	(6) *Summa totalis*	(7) *Cões sociorum*	(8) *In repastis*
		s d	*s d*	£ *s d*	£ *s d*	*s d*	£ *s d*
1	20	10 4	14 6	1 6 2½	2 14 9½	1 10	18 3
2	20	9 11½	15 0	1 5 10	2 14 6	1 9	18 11
3	21	11 8	15 0	1 3 0	2 13 11	1 9	16 4
4	24	11 7	16 10	1 12 10	3 4 11	1 10	1 3 4½
5	21	11 0	15 8	1 18 8	3 3 5½	2 0	1 4 4
6	23	14 0	15 0	1 9 7½	3 2 3½	1 8	1 3 7
7	23	8 5	15 0	1 13 5¼	3 0 5½	1 8½	19 11
8	24	10 10	15 0	1 4 10	2 14 4	1 10	9 9
9	24	8 0	15 0	1 7 7½	2 14 3½	1 10½	9 0½
10	24	7 10	15 0	1 7 0½	2 13 6½	1 8½	11 2
11	21	7 10½	15 6	1 3 6	2 10 6	1 10	11 9
12	23	5 10	14 6	1 5 2	2 10 0	1 9½	8 6½
13	22	7 9	11 6	1 14 4	2 9 3	2 4	6 5½
14	23	1 8	13 8	1 9 1	2 8 8	2 0	3 5½
15	20	7 4½	10 4	1 4 7	2 7 0½	2 0½	5 0
16	22	8 3	12 6	1 2 8	2 8 0	1 10	7½
17	23	6 7½	10 10	1 5 6½	2 1 0	1 11	8 0
18	23	8 7	13 6	1 13 4	3 0 5½	2 0½	12 10
19	23	8 1½	12 6	1 9 1	2 13 10	1 11	8 8
20	25	6 9	9 2	1 12 5	2 13 1	1 11	4 11
21	22	7 11	11 10	1 3 4	2 7 3½	1 9½	7 2
22	22	8 10	13 6	2 8 3	2 3 7	1 11	11 2
23	23	7 8	9 6	1 16 9	2 18 2½	2 1	10 11½
24	22	8 7	14 6	1 12 0½	2 19 3½	2 1	12 7
25	22	9 0	11 6	1 13 7	2 18 5	2 0	13 6

26	24	8 1	13 3	1 11 9½	2 17 5½	2 0½	8 7
27	21	7 0	10 6	1 6 0½	2 7 5½	2 0	3 11
28	23	8 10	12 6	1 6 0½	2 11 3	1 10	8 10½
29	24	9 4	14 6	1 8 4½	2 16 2	1 10½	10 9
30	23	7 10	14 0	1 11 10	2 17 6	1 11½	12 1½
31	23	8 4	14 6	1 11 0	2 17 10½	1 11	11 3
32	22	7 7½	13 10	1 12 11½	2 18 8½	2 1	11 11½
33	24	9 1	13 2	1 9 10	2 15 11	1 11	10 2½
34	20	8 4	10 8	1 7 10	2 10 7	2 1	6 9
35	21	6 1	12 10	1 6 10½	2 9 6½	1 10½	9 10
36	20	8 1	15 10	1 4 5½	2 10 2½	2 0½	8 5
37	21	7 7	13 6	1 1 4½	2 6 3	1 9	8 1½
38	20	7 6	14 6	1 1 6½	2 7 3½	1 11½	6 5½
39	20	8 2	11 6	1 7 1	2 0 5	2 0	9 9
40	19	6 0	14 0	1 0 5½	2 4 1½	1 11	7 5
41	18	7 4½	13 0	1 0 9	2 4 9½	2 0	7 3
42	16	2 4½	13 0	1 1 1	2 0 0½	1 11	8 6½
43	16	5 5	11 0	17 11½	1 18 1½	2 1	4 7
44	14	6 1	11 6	15 7	1 16 11½	2 1	6 6½
45	15	4 8	11 0	15 6	1 15 0	2 1	3 3
46	17	6 6½	10 6	18 2½	1 19 0	2 0	4 2
47	15	6 1½	11 0	17 5½	1 13 4	1 10	4 11½
48	13	6 0	11 0	14 4	1 15 0½	2 0	7 3
49	15	6 2	12 6	19 0½	2 1 7½	2 0½	10 10½
50	18	5 8	12 0	1 5 2	2 7 1	1 9½	14 4
51	19	5 11	12 0	1 5 8	2 7 5	1 10	11 5
52	18	5 1	10 0	1 0 5½	1 19 4½	1 8	6 9½
Totals (supplied)	1,079	£19 19 8	£33 14 5	£69 1 5¾	£129 13 8	£5 0 0½	£26 4 8
Weekly averages	22	7 8¼	12 11¾	£1 6 6¾	£2 9 10½	1 11	10 1

Annual college expenditure on stores and fuel for fellows' commons = (£129 13*s* 8*d* – £122 15*s* 6¾*d*)
= £6 18*s* 1¼*d*

∴ average weekly expenditure on stores and fuel = 2*s*. 8*d*

PLATES

PLATE

Plate 1 [1, fo. 156]: A page of entries for 1350–1 itemising the sums paid to the college by an ex-fellow pensioner, Thomas Priour, for his commons and sizings and with occasional entries for a servant. As was usual in the earlier accounts, the weeks of the harvest year are numbered: in the later accounts the numbering is discontinued. The forms used on this page to indicate commons payments are 'p coīs', 'p. ꝯīs' and 'p.ꝯ', and for sizings, 'p r'pastis'.

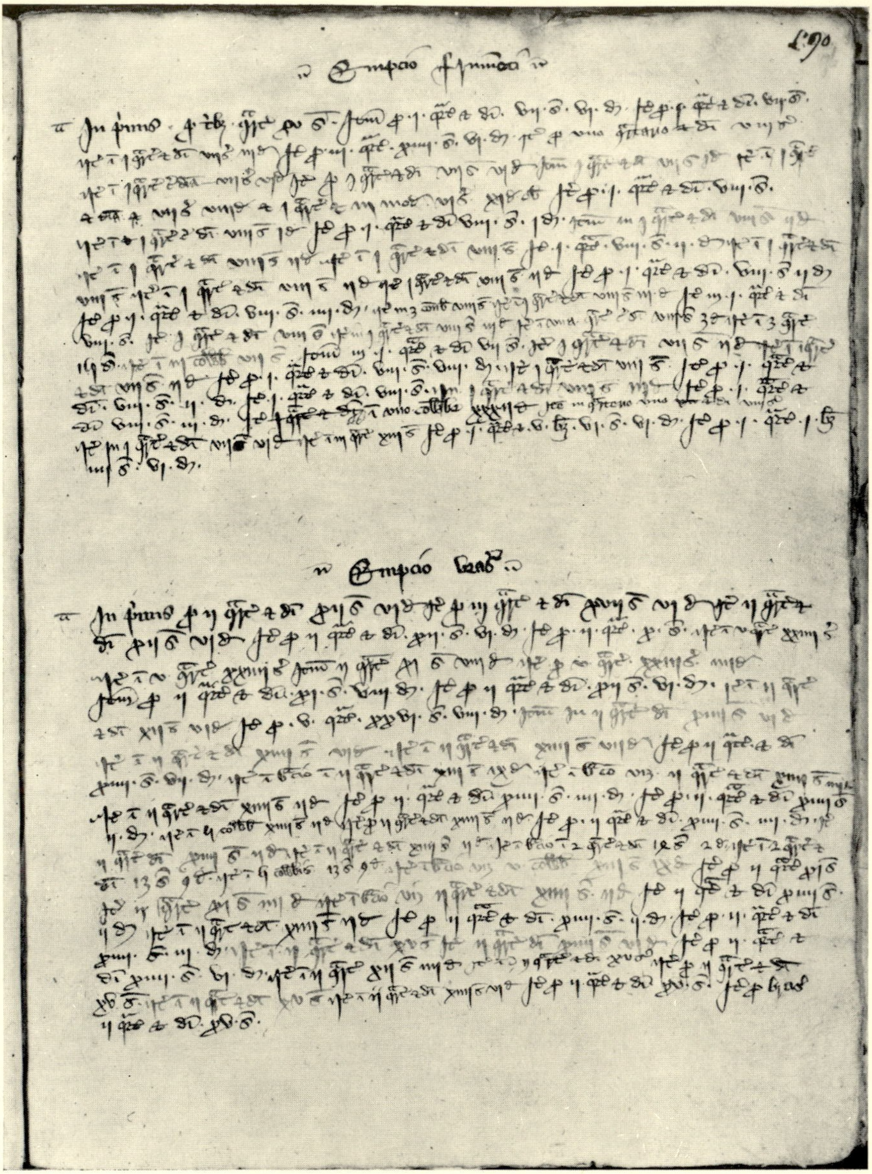

Plate 2 [III, fo. 96]: Annual entries for wheat and malt barley purchases for 1383–4.

Plate 3 [VII, fo. 136]: Three sections are shown. The first and third paragraphs record the miscellaneous expenses incurred by William Elot, the *prosecutor ad forinseca*, in 1429–30, while resident in London for the purpose of negotiating at the exchequer for the annual grant and robes due to the Society and for the purchase of cloth for the livery of the domestic servants. The second section itemises expenses arising from the maintenance of the King's Hall buildings and records the wages and commons allowances given to clayers, carpenters, daubers and a slater.

Plate 4 [IX, fo. 42]: Wages paid to the domestic staff for the quarterly terms of 1437–8. This year, the book-bearer was one Chaucy, hired at a rate of 3s 4d a quarter; but a note is added to the effect that in the fourth term he received a reduced payment because he did not work for the whole of that period.

Plate 5 [XIII, fo. 19]: The expenses incurred in 1460–1 by Richard Morgan (fellow, admitted 1454–5; vacated 1470–1) and by William Wilde (fellow, admitted 1454–5; vacated 1468–9) for the pupils in their care. As can be seen, the *pupilli* were charged at the rate of half commons (normally about 10*d* a week).

146

Plate 6 [xv, fo. 68 v]: Miscellaneous items of 'foreign' expenditure for 1476–7. The entries cover such diverse items as payments to the vicar of All Saints, expenses for *tripudiantes* for Great St Mary's, Cambridge, and for wine and spices bought for the celebration of the exequies of the founder.

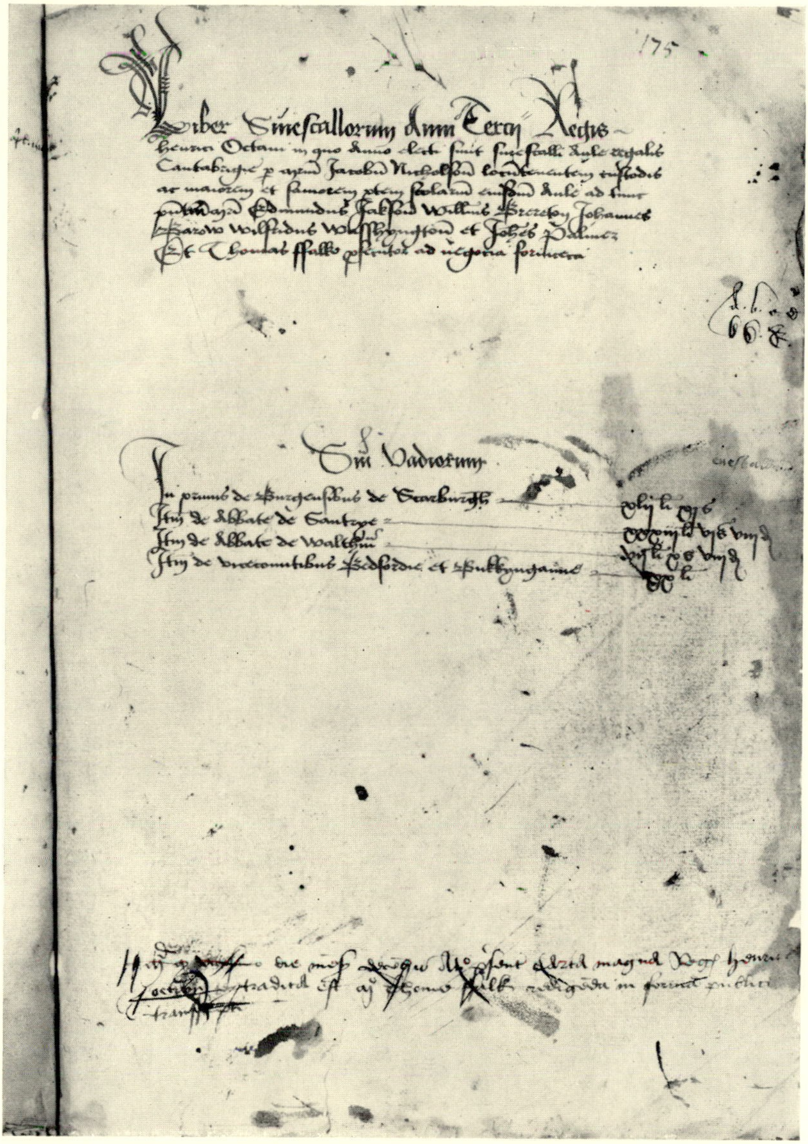

Plate 7 [XXI, fo. 88]: The title page to the account for 1511–12, giving the names of the elected seneschals for the year and the revenues received from farmed exchequer sources.

BIBLIOGRAPHY

ORIGINAL SOURCES

Trinity College, Cambridge

The King's Hall Accounts, twenty-six manuscript volumes extending from 1337 to 1544, preserved in the Muniment Room of Trinity College, O.13.1.–O.13.26. Contents of the King's Hall volumes:

Volume I	1337–8 to 1350–1	178 folios
Volume II	1356–7 to 1370–1	151 folios
Volume III	1382–3 to 1389–90	135 folios
Volume IV	1393–4 to 1398–9, 1400–1, 1401–2, 1404–5	138 folios
Volume V	1402–3 to 1413–14, 1387–8, 1399–1400	184 folios
Volume VI	1414–15 to 1421–2	153 folios
Volume VII	1422–3 to 1429–30	148 folios
Volume VIII	1430–1 to 1435–6	138 folios
Volume IX	1436–7 to 1440–1	172 folios
Volume X	1441–2 to 1446–7	175 folios
Volume XI	1447–8 to 1453–4	176 folios
Volume XII	1454–5 to 1459–60	168 folios
Volume XIII	1460–1 to 1467–8	161 folios
Volume XIV	1468–9 to 1473–4	142 folios
Volume XV	1474–5 to 1478–9	158 folios
Volume XVI	1479–80 to 1483–4	123 folios
Volume XVII	1483–4 to 1485–6, 1493–4, 1515–16	126 folios
Volume XVIII	1486–7 to 1492–3	180 folios
Volume XIX	1494–5 to 1500–1	207 folios
Volume XX	1501–2 to 1508–9	212 folios
Volume XXI	1509–10 to 1514–15	183 folios
Volume XXII	1517–18 to 1520–1	134 folios
Volume XXIII	1521–2 to 1526–7	202 folios
Volume XXIV	1527–8 to 1532–3	184 folios
Volume XXV	1534–5 to 1537–8	152 folios
Volume XXVI	1539–40 to 1543–4, 1516–17	197 folios

King's Hall Cabinet, Trinity College Muniment Room, nos. 8, 25, 27, 28, 30, 40, 41, 42, 44(1), 44(6), 44(7), 99, 102, 104, 105, 106, 109, 111, 112, 119, 120, 121, 122, 123, 124, 130, 135, 138, 139, 140, 144, 147 and 149.

The paper statutes of Trinity College of 8 November 1552, Trinity College Library, O.6.7.

James Duport, 'Rules to be Observed by Young Pupils and Schollers in the University', Trinity College Library, MS. O.10A.33.

Public Record Office

P.R.O. Charter Roll (26 March 1337): C53/124.

P.R.O. Exchequer Accounts, King's Remembrancer (E101 class): 1340–63, 1364–70, 1373–7, 1385–1408, 1417–21, 1424–34 (E101/342/2–348/33).

Bibliography

P.R.O. Exchequer Accounts, King's Remembrancer (E101 class): E101/382/8, 384/2, 385/4, 386/6, 386/18, 395/2(A), (B), (D), (E), 401/10, 409/6 and 409/12.
P.R.O. Exchequer Accounts, King's Remembrancer, Foreign Rolls (E364 class): 1370–3, 1377–85, 1408–17, 1421–4, 1434–42.
P.R.O. Patent Rolls: *Pat. R.* 38 Ed. III, p. 2, m. 10; 49 Ed. III, p. 2, m. 12; 1 Ric. II, p. 1, m. 16; 8 Ric. II, p. 2, m. 14.

Cambridge University Archives

Spurious bulls of Honorius I of 7 February 624 and Sergius I of 3 May 699, *Cabinet*, no. 115 (2 copies).
Charter of Edward II of February 1317 confirming and augmenting the privileges of Cambridge University, *Cabinet*, no. 19.
Confirmation bull of Eugenius IV of 18 September 1433, *Cabinet*, no. 114.
Parchment document, 'Processus Barnwellensis ex mandato Martini Papae V cum bullis Johannis XXII et Bonifacii IX', dated 10 October 1430, *Cabinet*, no. 108.
Registrum Magistri Thome Markaunt.

Cambridge University Library

Cambridge University Library, MS. Dd.7.17 (*Codex* of Justinian, containing the *glossa ordinaria*).
Registers of Thomas de l'Isle, bishop of Ely, 1345–61, and Thomas Arundel, bishop of Ely, 1374–88 (now deposited in Cambridge University Library).

Miscellaneous

Apostolic Letter of 9 June 1318 addressed to the University of Cambridge, Vatican Register of John XXII, LXVIII, fo. 66, no. 1230.
Merton College Bursars' Rolls, especially those for 1400, 1411 and 1429 (MR 3727, 3737, 3750) in Merton College Library.
New College Bursars' Rolls, especially those for 1383, 1393, 1394 and 1415–16 in New College Library.
Polydore Vergil, *Anglica Historia* (1st ed. Basle, 1534; 2nd ed. Basle, 1546).

PRINTED SOURCES

Cambridge University

Bradshaw, H. 'Two lists of books in the University Library', *C.A.S. Communications*, II (1864), no. xxii, 239 ff.
Cambridge borough documents, I (ed. W. M. Palmer, Cambridge, 1931).
(*A*) *Collection of letters, statutes and other documents from the manuscript library of Corpus Christi College illustrative of the history of the University of Cambridge* (ed. J. Lamb, London, 1838).
Collection of statutes for the University and the colleges of Cambridge (ed. J. Heywood, London, 1840).
Corrie, G. E. 'A catalogue of the books...given...to St Catharine's Hall...by... the founder', *C.A.S.* (quarto publications), I (1840), I ff.
'A list of books presented to Pembroke College, Cambridge, by different donors, during the fourteenth and fifteenth centuries', *C.A.S. Communications*, II (1860–4), no. iii, 11 ff.

Bibliography

'A catalogue of the books given to Trinity Hall, Cambridge, by the founder', *C.A.S. Communications*, II (1864), no. vi, 73 ff.

Documents relating to St Catharine's College in the University of Cambridge (ed. H. Philpott, Cambridge, 1861).

Documents relating to the University and colleges of Cambridge (3 vols., ed. by the Queen's Commissioners, London, 1852).

Dyer, G. (ed.). *The privileges of the University of Cambridge*, I (London, 1824).

Early Cambridge University and college statutes in the English language (ed. J. Heywood, London, 1855).

Early statutes of Christ's College, Cambridge with the statutes of the prior foundation of God's House (ed. with introduction, translation and notes by H. Rackham, privately printed, Cambridge, 1927).

Grace Book A (ed. S. M. Leathes, Luard Memorial Series, Cambridge, 1897).

Grace Book B, pt. II (ed. M. Bateson, Luard Memorial Series, Cambridge, 1905).

Hall, C. P. 'William Rysley's catalogue of the Cambridge University muniments, compiled in 1420', *Transactions of the Cambridge Bibliographical Society*, IV (1965), 85 ff.

Hardwick, C. (ed.). 'Articuli Universitatis Cantabrigiae', *C.A.S. Communications*, I (1850–9), no. xix, 85 ff.

James, M. R. 'The sources of Archbishop Parker's collection of MSS. at Corpus Christi College, Cambridge' and 'Catalogue of Thomas Markaunt's library from MS. C.C.C. 232', *C.A.S.* (octavo series), no. xxxii (1899), I ff. and 76 ff.

Minns, E. H. 'A Cambridge vintner's accounts, *c.* 1511', *C.A.S. Communications*, XXXIV (1934), 50 ff.

Moore Smith, G. C. (ed.). 'The academic drama at Cambridge: extracts from college records', *Malone Society Collections*, II, pt. ii (Oxford, 1923), 150 ff.

Searle, W. G. 'Catalogue of the library of Queens' College in 1472', *C.A.S. Communications*, II (1864), no. xv, 165 ff.

Sinker, R. *A catalogue of the fifteenth-century printed books in the library of Trinity College, Cambridge* (Cambridge and London, 1876).

Thomae Sprotti Chronica (ed. T. Hearne, Oxford, 1719) with the appended *Historiola de Antiquitate et Origine Universitatis Cantabrigiensis* of the Carmelite friar, Nicholas Cantelupe.

Warren's Book (ed. A. W. W. Dale, Cambridge, 1911).

Oxford University

Alton, R. E. (ed.). 'The academic drama in Oxford: extracts from the records of four colleges', *Malone Society Collections*, v (Oxford, 1960), 29 ff.

Canterbury College Oxford (3 vols., ed. W. A. Pantin, Oxf. Hist. Soc., new series, 1946–50).

(The) Dean's Register of Oriel, 1446–1661 (ed. G. C. Richards and H. E. Salter, Oxf. Hist. Soc., LXXXIV, 1926).

(The) early rolls of Merton College, Oxford (ed. J. R. L. Highfield, Oxf. Hist. Soc., new series, XVIII, 1964).

Jacob, E. F. 'An early book list of All Souls College' printed as an appendix to 'The two lives of Archbishop Chichele', *B.J.R.L.* XVI (1932), 469–81.

Leach, A. F. 'Wykeham's books at New College', *Collectanea* (ed. M. Burrows, Oxf. Hist. Soc., 1896), III, 213 ff.

Oriel College Records (ed. C. L. Shadwell and H. E. Salter, Oxf. Hist. Soc., LXXXV, 1926).

Bibliography

Oxford Balliol Deeds (ed. H. E. Salter, Oxf. Hist. Soc., LXIV, 1913).
Registrum Annalium Collegii Mertonensis, 1483–1521 (ed. H. E. Salter, Oxf. Hist. Soc., LXXVI, 1923).
Shadwell, C. L. 'The catalogue of the library of Oriel College in the fourteenth century', *Collectanea* (ed. C. R. L. Fletcher, Oxf. Hist. Soc., 1885), I, 59 ff.
Statuta Antiqua Universitatis Oxoniensis (ed. S. Gibson, Oxford, 1931).
(*The*) *Statutes of Exeter College, Oxford* (ed. by the Queen's Commissioners, London, 1855).
Statutes of the Colleges of Oxford (3 vols., ed. by the Queen's Commissioners, Oxford and London, 1853).

Miscellaneous

Annales Londonienses in *Chronicles of the reign of Edward I and Edward II* (R. S., ed. W. Stubbs, 1882).
(*The*) *black book of the household of Edward IV* (ed. A. R. Myers in *The household of Edward IV* (Manchester, 1959)).
(*The*) *book of fees (Liber Feodorum)*, pt. III (H.M.S.O., London, 1931).
Bulaeus, C. E. *Historia Universitatis Parisiensis* (6 vols., Paris, 1665–73).
Calendar of Inquisitions Miscellaneous (Chancery), IV (1337–88) (H.M.S.O., London, 1957).
Calendars of Papal Letters, I (ed. W. H. Bliss, London, 1893), IX (ed. J. A. Twemlow, London, 1912).
Calendars of Patent, Close and Charter Rolls (H.M.S.O., relevant vols. for fourteenth and fifteenth centuries).
Canterbury administration (2 vols., ed. I. J. Churchill, 1933).
Denifle, H. and A. Chatelain (eds.). *Chartularium Universitatis Parisiensis* (4 vols., Paris, 1889–97), II (1891).
Denifle, H. and E. Ehrle (eds.). *Archiv für Literatur- und Kirchengeschichte*, V (1889).
Devon, F. (ed.). *Issues of the exchequer* (London, 1837).
Dittrich and Spirk (eds.). *Monumenta Historica Universitatis Praguensis* (3 vols., Prague, 1830–(?)), II (1834).
Durham Account Rolls (Surtees Society), III (1901).
Erasmi Epistolae (ed. P. S. Allen, 12 vols., Oxford, 1906–58), I (1906).
Fortescue, Sir John. *De Laudibus Legum Anglie* (ed. S. B. Chrimes, Cambridge, 1942).
Fournier, M. (ed.). *Les Statuts et Privilèges des Universités Françaises depuis leur fondation jusqu'en 1789* (3 vols., Paris, 1890–2), II (1891).
Gage, J. 'Extracts from the household book of Edward Stafford, Duke of Buckingham', *Archaeologia*, XXV (1884), 311 ff.
Giuseppi, M. S. 'The wardrobe and household accounts of Bogo de Clare, 1284–6', *Archaeologia*, LXX (1920), 1 ff.
Harrison, F. Ll. (ed.). 'The Eton Choirbook: I', *Musica Britannica*, X (1956).
Leland, J. *Collectanea*, V (Oxford, 1715).
Liber regie capelle (ed. by W. Ullmann for the Henry Bradshaw Society, XCII, Cambridge, 1959).
Parker, M. *De Antiquitate Britannicae Ecclesiae* (ed. S. Drake, London, 1729).
(*The*) *Paston letters, 1422–1509* (6 vols., ed. J. Gairdner, London and Exeter, 1904).
Register of Gregory IX (ed. L. Auvray, Paris, 1896).
Register of Henry Chichele (4 vols., ed. E. F. Jacob, Oxford, 1938–47).
Riccobonus, A. (ed.). *De Gymnasio Patavino* (Padua, 1722).

Bibliography

Rous, J. *Historia Regum Angliae* (2nd ed. by T. Hearne, Oxford, 1745).

Rymer, T. *Foedera*, II, pts. i, ii (ed. A. Clarke, London, 1818).

Sarti, M. (ed.). *De Claris Archigymnasii Bononiensis Professoribus a saeculo xi usque ad saeculum xiv* (2 pts., Bologna, 1769–72).

(*The*) *Stonor letters and papers, 1290–1483* (2 vols., ed. C. L. Kingsford for the Camden Society, 3rd series, London, 1919).

Testamenta Eboracensia (Surtees Society), IV (1869).

Vita Edwardi II monachi cujusdam Malmesberiensis in *Chronicles of the reign of Edward I and Edward II* (R. S., ed. W. Stubbs, 1882), especially II, 178 ff.; also the second ed. with translation by N. Denholm-Young (Nelson's medieval texts, 1957).

Wickham Legg, L. G. (ed.). *English coronation records* (Westminster, 1901).

Wood-Legh, K. L. (ed.). *A small household of the fifteenth century* (Manchester, 1956).

SECONDARY WORKS

Attwater, A. *Pembroke College, Cambridge* (ed. with an introduction and postscript by S. C. Roberts, Cambridge, 1931).

Baskervill, C. R. 'Dramatic aspects of medieval folk festivals in England', *Studies in Philology*, XVII (1920), 19 ff.

Bean, J. M. W. 'Plague, population and economic decline in England in the later middle ages', *Econ. Hist. Rev.* 2nd series, XV (1962–3), 423 ff.

Bentham, J. *The history and antiquities of the conventual and cathedral church of Ely* (2nd ed. Norwich, 1812).

Beveridge, W. (*et alii*). *Prices and wages in England from the twelfth to the nineteenth century* (London, New York and Toronto, 1939).

Boas, F. S. *University drama in the Tudor age* (Oxford, 1914).

Brand, J. *Observations on popular antiquities* (2 vols., revised by H. Ellis, London, 1813).

Burnet, G. *The history of the reformation of the Church of England* (Oxford, 1816), I, pt. i.

Butterfield, H. 'Peterhouse', *V.C.H.* (Cambridge), III (ed. J. P. C. Roach, London, 1959).

Caröe, W. D. 'King's hostel', *C.A.S.* (quarto publications), new series, no. 11, 1909.

Carr, W. *University College* (College Histories Series, London, 1902).

Carter, E. *The history of the University of Cambridge* (London, 1753).

Chambers, E. K. *The mediaeval stage* (2 vols., Oxford, 1903).

Chibnall, A. C. *Richard de Badew and the University of Cambridge 1315–1340* (Cambridge, 1963).

Clarke, S. *A collection of the lives of thirty-two English divines*... (3rd ed. London, 1677).

Cobban, A. B. 'Edward II, Pope John XXII and the University of Cambridge', *B.J.R.L.* XLVII (1964), 49 ff.

Cook, G. H. *Mediaeval chantries and chantry chapels* (2nd ed. London, 1963).

Cooper, C. H. *Annals of Cambridge* (4 vols., Cambridge, 1842–53).

Memorials of Cambridge (3 vols., Cambridge, 1861–6).

Creighton, C. *A history of epidemics in Britain*, I (Cambridge, 1891).

Curtis, M. H. *Oxford and Cambridge in transition 1558–1642* (Oxford, 1959).

Davies, J. C. *The baronial opposition to Edward II, its character and policy* (Cambridge, 1918).

Davis, H. W. C. *A history of Balliol College* (2nd ed. by R. H. C. Davis and R. Hunt, Oxford, 1963).

Denholm-Young, N. 'Magdalen College', *V.C.H.* (Oxford), III (ed. H. E. Salter and M. D. Lobel, London, 1954).

Bibliography

Denifle, H. *Die Entstehung der Universitäten des Mittelalters bis 1400* (Berlin, 1885), I, especially pp. 352–3, 375–6.

Denne, S. 'Memoir on Hokeday', *Archaeologia*, VII (1785), 244 ff.

Dugdale, W. *The antiquities of Warwickshire* (London, 1656).

Monasticon Anglicanum (6 vols., ed. J. Caley, H. Ellis, B. Bandinel, London, 1817–30).

Dyer, G. *The history of the university and colleges of Cambridge* (2 vols., London, 1814).

Edwards, K. 'Bishops and learning in the reign of Edward II', *Church Quarterly Review*, CXXXVIII (1944), 57 ff.

The English secular cathedrals in the middle ages (Manchester, 1949).

'The Cathedral of Salisbury' and 'College of de Vaux Salisbury', *V.C.H.* (Wiltshire), III (Oxford, 1956).

'The social origins and provenance of the English bishops during the reign of Edward II', *T.R.H.S.*, 5th series, IX (1959), 51 ff.

Ekwall, E. *The concise Oxford dictionary of English place-names* (4th ed. Oxford, 1960).

Emden, A. B. *An Oxford hall in medieval times* (Oxford, 1927).

A biographical register of the University of Oxford to A.D. 1500 (3 vols., Oxford, 1957–9).

'Learning and education', in *Medieval England* (2nd ed. by A. L. Poole, 2 vols., Oxford, 1958), II, 515 ff.

A biographical register of the University of Cambridge to 1500 (Cambridge, 1963).

English Place-Name Society publications (41 vols., Cambridge, 1924–65).

Ermini, G. 'Concetto di "Studium Generale"', *Archivio Giuridico*, CXXVII (1942), 3 ff.

Fox(e), J. *Acts and Monuments* (otherwise known as the Book of Martyrs) (9th ed. 3 vols., London, 1684), III, 648.

Fuller, T. *The history of the worthies of England* (London, 1662).

The history of the University of Cambridge (ed. M. Prickett and T. Wright, London and Cambridge, 1840).

Gabriel, A. L. *Student life in Ave Maria College, mediaeval Paris* (Publications in mediaeval studies, XIV, Indiana, 1955).

Skara House at the mediaeval University of Paris (Texts and studies in the history of mediaeval education, no. IX, Indiana, 1960).

The college system in the fourteenth-century universities (Baltimore, 1962).

Galbraith, V. H. 'The literacy of the medieval English kings', *Proceedings of the British Academy*, XXI (1935), 201 ff.

Gibson, S. 'The University of Oxford', *V.C.H.* (Oxford), III (ed. H. E. Salter and M. D. Lobel, London, 1954).

Gray, J. M. *Biographical notes on the mayors of Cambridge* (reprinted from *Cambridge Chronicle*) (1921).

Hargreaves–Mawdsley, W. N. *A history of academical dress in Europe* (Oxford, 1963).

Harrison, F. Ll. 'The Eton Choirbook', *Annales Musicologiques*, I (1953), 151 ff.

Music in medieval Britain (London, 1958).

Hartshorne, C. H. *The itinerary of King Edward the Second* (privately printed, 1861).

Harvey, P. D. A. *A medieval Oxfordshire village, Cuxham 1240 to 1400* (Oxford, 1965).

Haskins, C. H. *Studies in mediaeval culture* (Oxford, 1929).

Haskins, G. L. 'The University of Oxford and the "ius ubique docendi"', *E.H.R.* LVI (1941), 281 ff.

Hay, D. *The Anglica Historia of Polydore Vergil* (Camden Series, 1950), LXXIV.

Polydore Vergil (Oxford, 1952).

Bibliography

Hill, J. W. F. *Medieval Lincoln* (Cambridge, 1948).

Hodgkin, R. H. *Six centuries of an Oxford college* (Oxford, 1949).

Hunt, R. W. 'Medieval inventories of Clare College Library', *Transactions of the Cambridge Bibliographical Society*, I (1950), 105 ff.

'Balliol College', *V.C.H.* (Oxford), III (ed. H. E. Salter and M. D. Lobel, London, 1954).

Jacob, E. F. 'Petitions for benefices from English universities during the Great Schism', *T.R.H.S.*, 4th series, XXVII (1945), 41 ff.

'English university clerks in the later middle ages: the problem of maintenance', *B.J.R.L.* XXIX (1946), 304 ff.

'On the promotion of English university clerks during the later middle ages', *J. Eccles. Hist.* I (1950), 172 ff.

'Founders and foundations in the later middle ages', *B.I.H.R.* XXXV (1962), 29 ff.

Jenkinson, H. 'The use of arabic and roman numerals in English archives', *The Antiquaries' Journal*, VI (1926), 263 ff.

Jones, W. H. S. *A history of St Catharine's College* (Cambridge, 1936).

Ker, N. R. *Medieval libraries of Great Britain* (2nd ed. London, 1964).

Knowles, M. D. *The religious Orders in England*, II (Cambridge, 1955).

Knowles, M. D. and R. N. Hadcock. *Medieval religious houses* (London, 1953).

Kuhl, E. P. 'Chaucer's "My Maistre Bukton"', *Publications of the Modern Language Association of America*, XXXVIII (1923), 115 ff.

Labarge, M. W. *A baronial household of the thirteenth century* (London, 1965).

Leach, A. F. *A history of Winchester College* (London, 1899).

The schools of medieval England (London, 1915).

Littleton, A. C. and B. S. Yamey (eds.). *Studies in the history of accounting* (London, 1956).

Lloyd, A. H. *The early history of Christ's College* (Cambridge, 1934).

Luard, H. R. 'A list of the documents in the University Registry, from the year 1266 to the year 1544', *C.A.S. Communications*, III (1864–76), no. xxxviii, 385 ff.

Lunt, W. E. (ed.). *The valuation of Norwich* (Oxford, 1926).

McConica, J. K. *English humanists and Reformation politics* (Oxford, 1965).

McKisack, M. *The fourteenth century, 1307–1399* (Oxford, 1959).

McMahon, C. P. *Education in fifteenth century England* (reprinted from *The Johns Hopkins University Studies in Education*, no. 35, Baltimore, 1947).

Madox, T. *The history and antiquities of the exchequer of England* (1st ed. London, 1711).

Magoun, F. P. 'Chaucer's Great Britain', *Mediaeval Studies*, XVI (1954), 131 ff.

Magrath, J. R. *The Queen's College* (2 vols., Oxford, 1921).

Maxwell Lyte, H. C. *A history of Eton College 1440–1910* (4th ed. London, 1911).

Miller, E. *Portrait of a college* (Cambridge, 1961).

Morgan, M. M. 'The abbey of Bec-Hellouin and its English priories', *Journal of the British Archaeological Association*, 3rd series, V (1940), 33 ff.

Mullinger, J. B. *The University of Cambridge* (3 vols., Cambridge, 1873–1911).

Munby, A. N. L. 'Notes on King's College library in the fifteenth century', *Transactions of the Cambridge Bibliographical Society*, I (1951), 280 ff.

Myers, A. R. 'The captivity of a royal witch', *B.J.R.L.* XXIV (1940), 263 ff.

The household of Edward IV (Manchester, 1959).

Neill Wright, G. G. *The writing of arabic numerals* (London, 1952).

Niermeyer, J. F. *Mediae Latinitatis Lexicon Minus* (Leiden, 1954–).

Bibliography

Otway-Ruthven, J. *The king's secretary and the signet office in the fifteenth century* (Cambridge, 1939).

Owen, D. M. 'Ely diocesan records', *Studies in Church History*, I (ed. C. W. Dugmore and C. Duggan, 1964), 176 ff.

Pantin, W. A. 'College muniments: a preliminary note', *Oxoniensia*, I (1936), 140 ff. 'The halls and schools of medieval Oxford: an attempt at reconstruction', *Oxford Studies presented to Daniel Callus* (Oxf. Hist. Soc., new series, XVI (1964)), 31 ff.

Parker, R. *The history and antiquities of the University of Cambridge* (London, 1721(?)).

Parry, A. W. *Education in England in the middle ages* (London, 1920).

Peacock, G. *Observations on the statutes of the University of Cambridge* (London, 1841).

Peek, H. and C. Hall. *The archives of the University of Cambridge* (Cambridge, 1962).

Pegues, F. 'Royal support of students in the thirteenth century', *Speculum*, XXXI (1956), 454 ff.

Perroy, E. *The Hundred Years War* (English ed. translated by W. B. Wells, London, 1951).

Phillimore, R. *The ecclesiastical law of the Church of England* (2nd ed. by W. G. F. Phillimore and C. F. Jemmett, 2 vols., London, 1895).

Pollard, G. 'Mediaeval loan chests of Cambridge', *B.I.H.R.* XVII (1939–40), 113 ff.

Potter, G. R. 'Education in the fourteenth and fifteenth centuries', *Cambridge Medieval History*, VIII (ed. by C. W. Previté-Orton and Z. N. Brooke, 1936).

Powicke, F. M. *The medieval books of Merton College* (Oxford, 1931).

Powicke, F. M. and E. B. Fryde. *Handbook of British chronology* (2nd ed. London, 1961).

Raby, F. J. E. *A history of secular Latin poetry in the middle ages* (2 vols., Oxford, 1934).

Rait, R. S. *Life in the medieval university* (Cambridge, 1912).

Rashdall, H. *The universities of Europe in the middle ages* (3 vols., ed. by F. M. Powicke and A. B. Emden, Oxford, 1936).

Rashdall, H. and R. S. Rait. *New College* (London, 1901).

Reaney, P. H. *A dictionary of British surnames* (London, 1958).

Richardson, H. G. 'The schools of Northampton in the twelfth century', *E.H.R.* LXI (1941), 595 ff.

Roach, J. P. C. 'The University of Cambridge', *V.C.H.* (Cambridge), III (ed. J. P. C. Roach, London, 1959). 'The Victoria County History of Cambridge', *C.A.S. Proceedings*, LIV (1961), 112 ff.

Robinson, F. N. (ed.). *The works of Geoffrey Chaucer* (2nd ed. Boston, 1957).

Rogers, J. E. T. *A history of agriculture and prices in England* (7 vols., Oxford, 1866–1902).

Rouse Ball, W. W. *The King's Scholars and King's Hall* (privately printed, Cambridge, 1917). *Cambridge papers* (London, 1918). *Cambridge notes* (Cambridge, 1921).

Royal Commission on Historical Monuments (England), City of Cambridge (H.M.S.O. 1959), II.

Ryan, L. V. *Roger Ascham* (Stanford, 1963).

Salter, H. E. 'An Oxford hall in 1424', *Essays in history presented to R. L. Poole* (ed. by H. W. C. Davis, Oxford, 1927), pp. 421 ff. 'The medieval University of Oxford', *History*, XIV (1929), 57 ff. *Medieval Oxford* (Oxf. Hist. Soc., 1936).

Saltmarsh, J. 'King's College', *V.C.H.* (Cambridge), III (ed. J. P. C. Roach, London, 1959).

Salzman, L. F. *Building in England down to 1540* (Oxford, 1952).

English trade in the middle ages (Oxford, 1931).

Sayle, C. E. 'King's Hall Library', *C.A.S. Proceedings*, XXIV, old series, no. lxxii (1921–2), 54 ff.

Simon, J. *Education and society in Tudor England* (Cambridge, 1966).

Skånland, V. 'The earliest statutes of the University of Cambridge', *Symbolae Osloenses*, fasc. XL (1965), 83 ff.

Smith, A. H. *New College, Oxford and its buildings* (Oxford, 1952).

Smith, W. J. *Five centuries of Cambridge musicians* (Cambridge, 1964).

Stamp, A. E. *Admissions to Trinity College, Cambridge* (ed. W. W. Rouse Ball and J. A. Venn, London, 1916), I, 79–140.

Michaelhouse (privately printed, Cambridge, 1924).

Stanier, R. S. *Magdalen School* (2nd ed. Oxford, 1958).

Steel, A. *Richard II* (reprinted Cambridge, 1962).

Stenton, F. M. 'The road system of medieval England', *Econ. Hist. Rev.* VII (1936), 1 ff.

Sterry, W. *The Eton College register 1441–1698* (Eton, 1943).

Stokes, H. P. 'The mediaeval hostels of the University of Cambridge', *C.A.S.* (octavo publications), XLIX (1924).

Stow, J. *The Annales of England* (London, 1605).

Streeter, B. H. *The chained library* (London, 1931).

Thompson, A. H. 'Cathedral Church of St Peter York', *V.C.H.* (Yorkshire), III (ed. W. Page, London, 1913), 375 ff.

Visitations of religious houses in the diocese of Lincoln (Lincoln Record Society, 7), I (1914).

'The medieval chapter', *York Minster historical tracts 627–1927* (London, 1927), no. 13.

The register of William Greenfield, archbishop of York (1306–1315), I (Surtees Society, CXLV, 1931).

Thompson, C. J. S. *The witchery of Jane Shore* (London, 1933).

Thomson, D. F. S. and H. C. Porter. *Erasmus and Cambridge* (Toronto, 1963).

Tilley, A. 'Greek studies in England in the early sixteenth century', *E.H.R.* LIII (1938), 221 ff., 438 ff.

Tout, T. F. 'The English civil service in the fourteenth century', *Collected Papers of T. F. Tout*, III (Manchester, 1934), 191 ff.

The place of the reign of Edward II in English history (2nd ed. by H. Johnstone, Manchester, 1936).

Trevelyan, G. M. *Trinity College: an historical sketch* (Cambridge, 1943).

Ullmann, W. 'Thomas Becket's miraculous oil', *J.T.S.* VIII (1957), 129 ff.

'The decline of the chancellor's authority in medieval Cambridge: a rediscovered statute', *Historical Journal*, I (1958), 176 ff.

'The University of Cambridge and the Great Schism', *J.T.S.* IX (1958), 53 ff.

Principles of government and politics in the middle ages (2nd ed. London, 1966).

Venn, J. *Biographical history of Gonville and Caius College*, III (Cambridge, 1901).

Gonville and Caius College (College Histories Series, London, 1910).

Early collegiate life (Cambridge, 1913).

Venn, J. and J. A. Venn. *Alumni Cantabrigienses*, pt. I, vols. I–IV (Cambridge, 1922–7).

Bibliography

Victoria County History of Oxford, III (ed. H. E. Salter and M. D. Lobel, London, 1954).

Victoria History of the County of Cambridge and the Isle of Ely, III (ed. J. P. C. Roach, London, 1959).

Wakeling, G. H. *Brasenose monographs*, II, pt. i (Oxf. Hist. Soc., LIII, 1909), xi.

Walford, C. *Fairs, past and present* (London, 1883).

Walker, T. A. *Peterhouse* (College Histories Series, London, 1906).

Warner, G. F. and J. P. Gilson. *Catalogue of western manuscripts in the old Royal and King's collections* (London, 1921).

Warton, T. *The history of English poetry* (3 vols., ed. R. Price, 1840).

Watt, D. E. R. 'University clerks and rolls of petitions for benefices', *Speculum*, XXXIV (1959), 213 ff.

Weiss, R. 'Henry VI and the library of All Souls College', *E.H.R.* LVII (1942), 102 ff.

Humanism in England during the fifteenth century (2nd ed. Oxford, 1957).

White, R. J. *Dr Bentley* (London, 1965).

Wickham, G. *Early English stages 1300 to 1660* (2 vols., London and New York, 1963).

Willis, R. and J. W. Clark. *The architectural history of the University of Cambridge and of the colleges of Cambridge and Eton* (4 vols., Cambridge, 1886).

Winstanley, D. A. *Unreformed Cambridge* (Cambridge, 1935).

INDEX

abacus, at King's Hall, 114

Abyndon, Henry, master of children, chapel royal, 62

accounting, method of, King's Hall, 114, 116–17, 118–21, table 3(119), table 4 (120)

accounts, medieval, as source material, 5

accounts, weekly commons, King's Hall, 114, 126 ff.; data from, table 5 (opposite 126), table 7 (133), table 8 (136–7); description of, 121–5

Adam, William, King's Hall fellow, 69

admission charges
English and French colleges, 137 n. 1
King's Hall, 137–8; diverted for 'studies', 220

Albon, John, King's Hall ex-fellow pensioner, 265, 293 n. 8

Alcock, John, bp. of Ely: commons rate for Peterhouse, 140

ale, 84 n. 5; commons, King's Hall, 123, 124, 125, 126, 127, 128, table 5 (opposite 126), 207, 237

Alexander IV, pope: bull for Salamanca University, 36 n. 1, 37

All Saints in Jewry, Cambridge
church of: *tripudia* in, 224; vicar of, 242
parish of, 224, 230, 240, 241

All Souls College, Oxford, 237 n. 11, 295; book-bearer, 232 n. 7; civil law, works on, 254 n. 4; devotional duties, 227 n. 4; library, 250, 257 n. 2

almonds, 124, 134, 212, 259 n. 3

almoner, king's, 95, 282, 287, 288

almonry, clerks of, 61

Alnewyk, William, King's Hall commoner, 273 n. 1

Amory, William: King's Hall contracts, 215 n. 5

Anglica Historia (Polydore Vergil): criticisms of King's Hall, 154–5, 156 *see also* Vergil, Polydore

Appilton, King's Hall commoner, 278

arabic characters, King's Hall accounts, 114, 117

Aragon, king of, mission to, 284

Ardern, Thomas, King's Hall fellow, 143 n. 5

Arundel, John, logic notebook of, 69 n. 1

Arundel, Thomas: as archbp. of Canterbury, 103; as bp. of Ely, 101; visitation of King's Hall, 102, 103, 171, 172, 173, 187, 248

Ascham, Roger, 290, 296

Ashman, Thomas, King's Hall fellow, 68

Aspilyon, Thomas, King's Hall fellow, 75

Asteley, Geoffrey, King's Hall fellow and ex-semi-commoner, 264

Aston, Thomas, King's Hall fellow, admitted from chapel royal, 187 n. 1

Attilbrigge, Robert, King's Hall fellow, 213 n. 3

Auberinus, Caius, Italian *poeta*: as Cambridge lecturer, 228

auditor, papal, 295

Ave Maria College, Paris, 59 n. 2, 75 n. 2; admission charges, 137 n. 1; commons expenses, 139 n. 2; patronage arrangements, 149 n. 2

Avignon: Edward II's mission to, 25, 33; university of, 108

Ayscogh, Robert, King's Hall commoner, 273 n. 1, 277

Ayscogh, Robert, warden of King's Hall, 196, 280 n. 1; career of, 285, 293 n. 2; as chancellor of Cambridge, 285, 295

Ayscogh, William, bp. of Sarum, 285

Badlesmere, Lord: mission to Avignon, 33

Baggeshote, John de, warden of King's Scholars, 9 and n. 2

Bainbridge, Reginald, King's Hall fellow: as Cambridge proctor, 296 n. 1; as master of St Catharine's College, 296

331

Index

Blythe, John, warden of King's Hall, 280 n. 1; career of, 289, 291 n. 4, 293 nn. 1, 2; as chancellor of Cambridge, 289

Blythe, Thomas, King's Hall fellow: as Cambridge proctor, 296 n. 1

Bochrer, John: King's Hall contracts, 216 n. 2

Bologna, university of, 107; as *studium generale ex consuetudine*, 40, 300

Boncour, college of, Paris, 13 n. 4; bed furnishings, 137 n. 1

Boniface VIII, pope: bull for Avignon University, 108

Boniface IX, pope: and Cambridge University, 35, 109 n. 5, 111

Bonworth, King's Hall commoner, 269

Bordeaux, 27

Bost, Henry, warden of King's Hall: career of, 288

Bothe, King's Hall fellow, 68, 70 n. 3

Bothe, Edmund, King's Hall fellow, 293 n. 2

Boynton, King's Hall fellow and ex-commoner, 264

Brasenose College, Oxford: college lecturers, 81 n. 2; library, 250; term *pupillus*, 74 n. 1

Braunden, the kyngs jogular, at King's Hall, 225; *see also* minstrels

Brayne (Braine), John, King's Hall fellow, admitted from Eton, 185 n. 5

bread, 84 n. 5; commons, King's Hall, 123, 124, 125, 126, 127, 128, table 5 (opposite 126), 207, 237

Bretoner, Joachim, King's Hall fellow, 293 n. 2

Brittany, 288

Brocok, William de, King's Scholar, 198 n. 1

Brome, Adam de: chancery clerk; founder of Oriel College, 12 n. 1

Bromyard, John: at Cambridge University, 28 n. 2

Browne, Alan, King's Hall fellow, 68, 70 nn. 1, 3

Broyke, Elizabeth, King's Hall tenant, 78

Brynkley, Reginald *or* Richard, King's Hall fellow, admitted from Eton, 185 n. 5

buccinator, 223, 225 n. 1; *see also* minstrels

Buckby, Northamptonshire, 9 n. 1; King's Scholars at, 9 n. 2

Buckmaster, William, King's Hall fellow, 209 n. 6; as vice-chancellor of Cambridge, 295

budge (white fur), for King's Scholars, 199

Bugby, John, grammar master, chapel royal, 62

Bukden, Galfridus, King's Hall servant, 237

Burgundy, mission to, 284

Burnell, Robert, chancellor of Edward I, 159 n. 1

Bury, Richard de, 14

Bury, Simon de, warden of King's Scholars, 199 n. 2, 247

Butler, David: King's Hall contracts, 215 n. 5

butler's department (*promtuarium*), *see* domestic departments

Byneau, Stephen de, King's Hall fellow, 295

Byngham, William, founder of Godshouse, Cambridge, 80

Cacheroo, John, King's Hall fellow, 152, 153 n. 5

Caius College, Cambridge, 46 n. 1, 73; chapel of, 3; tutorial system, 71; *see also* Gonville Hall

Calais, 247

Cambrai, Treaty of, 292

Cambridge, borough of, 124, 140, 202, 212 n. 1, 215, 216, 235, 241, 263, 268, 294; burgesses of, 32; castle, 78, 217 n. 15; charters confirmed, 32; Hagable Rolls, 78 n. 5; justice of the peace, 283, 285, 286, 288; mayor of, 32, 187, 225, 297–8; minstrels, 224 and n. 10; plague at, 220–2, 240; tradesmen, 241 n. 3, 242

Cambridge, colleges of, 3, 17, 30, 72, 73, 85, 88, 89, 162, 262; building materials, 217 n. 13; civil law, works on, 252–3, 254; civil lawyers, 256; college liveries, 199; dovecots, 244 n. 5; and external authority,

333

Index

Index

Grimesby, John de, King's Hall fellow and ex-semi-commoner, 264

Gros, John, King's Scholar and King's Hall fellow, 199 n. 2, 200

Grym, John, King's Hall ex-fellow pensioner, 266

Gryndon, Laurence de, King's Hall fellow, 153 n. 3

Gunthorpe, John, warden of King's Hall: career of, 287

Gybson, King's Hall tenant, 78

Gylmyn, John, King's Hall tenant, 241

Hadlee, John, alderman of London, 206 n. 3

Hales, Richard(de), King's Scholar and King's Hall fellow, 199 n. 2, 200, 220 n. 5

hall(*aula*), *see* domestic departments

Hall, John, King's Hall fellow, 75 n. 3, 209 n. 6

halls, Oxford University, 43 and n. 5, 49, 219; commons rate, 141 n. 2; system of fining, 176; tutorial organisation, 68–9

Hamecotes, Richard, King's Hall fellow, 206 n. 3

hard fish (*piscis durus*), 212

Harlaston, Roger de, King's Scholar and King's Hall fellow, 176 n. 4, 293 n. 4

hay, 212, 215

Hebrew
Cambridge University: public lecture on, 84
King's Hall: public lecture on, 85; regius professorships of: Oxford and Cambridge, 81–2

Henry III, king of England: episcopate under, 23 n. 2; support of university clerks, 11

Henry IV, king of England, 62, 203 n. 4, 283, 284

Henry V, king of England, 62, 186 n. 2, 188, 198 n. 5, 284, 285

Henry VI, king of England, 19, 21, 26, 63, 104, 196, 200, 218 n. 8, 257, 272, 284, 285, 286, 294; and subjection of King's Hall, 188–93

Henry VII, king of England, 193, 196, 287, 288, 292

Henry VIII, king of England, 1, 61, 156, 196, 290; as founder of Trinity College, Cambridge, xi, 20 n. 1, 112, 290, 294; regius professorships of, 81–2

Hereford, Nicholas of: as commoner at Queen's College, 261 n. 8, 269

Herford, Walter de, King's Hall fellow, 64, 247

herrings, barrels of red and white, 212

Hesill, Thomas, King's Hall fellow, 207 n. 2

Hetersete, Thomas, warden of King's Hall, 174, 195 n. 6; as chancellor of Cambridge, 282 n. 4

Hethe, Nicholas, King's Hall fellow, 153 n. 5, 290 n. 6

Hildersham, Ely diocese, rectorship of, 143 n. 5

Hintlesham, Suffolk: church of, appropriated to King's Hall, 101, 115 n. 3, 166, 206, 218 n. 1; farmers of, 206 n. 3

histrio, 223, 225; *see also* minstrels

histriones ville, 224; *see also* minstrels

hock-tide, 229; 'hocking', 229–30; King's Hall payment to Hock 'wyfs', 229–30

Holbroke, John: as chancellor of Cambridge, 110 n. 2

Holcot, Robert: at Cambridge University, 28 n. 2

Hole (Hoole), John, King's Hall ex-fellow pensioner, 265, 293 n. 2; livings held by, 266

Holme, Richard, warden of King's Hall, 195 n. 6; career of, 284

Holmes, Richard, King's Hall servant, 246 n. 3

honey, 124, 134, 246

Honorius I, pope: spurious bull for Cambridge University, 107 n. 4, 109, 110, 111

hoods
Cambridge University, 199
King's Hall, 199 n. 1; miniver as lining for, 198

Index

St Just, Thomas, warden of King's Hall, 10 n. 2, 62 n. 5; career of, 286–7
St Katherine, hospital of, London, 93
St Neots, alien priory of, Huntingdonshire, 163, 203; prior of, 203
St Peter, Northampton, church of, 10 n. 2, 92, 93, 203
St Rhadegund, Cambridge, nuns of, 241
Salamanca, university of: bull of Alexander IV, 36 n. 1, 37, 38, 107
Salisbury, earl of: minstrels of, 225
Salisbury, nascent university of, 18 n. 2, 50 n. 1; *see also* De Vaux College
Salle, John, King's Hall fellow, 121 n. 2
salmon, 84 n. 5, 212
Salmon, John, bp. of Norwich: benefactor of University Hall, 29; royal mission to Avignon, 33
salt, 124, 134, 212; salt-cat, 244 and n. 7
salt-fish, 212
Salter, H. E., 49 n. 1, 51 n. 4, 69, 269
Salzman, L. F., 8
Sarum, bp. of: William Ayscogh as, 285; John Blythe as, 289; Richard de Medford as, 291
Saunford, Alexander de, King's Hall fellow, 294 n. 2
Sautre (Saltrey, Sautrey), abbey of, Huntingdonshire, 163, 167; abbot of, 203, 204
Sautre, John, King's Hall fellow, 165
Sawser, John, King's Hall fellow, 213 n. 3
Say, William, dean of chapel royal, 19
Say, William, King's Hall swanherd, 245
Scarborough, town of, 167; burgesses of, 204
Schropham, John de, warden of King's Hall, 169, 170, 174, 195 n. 6, 280 n. 1
scolaris (*scholaris*)
　Exeter College, Oxford: = undergraduate commoner, 69 n. 3
　King's Hall: = fellow (*socius*), 11 n. 1, 184; = private pupil, 69 n. 3; special meanings, 184–6, 197

Magdalen College: = *demies*, 185
Oxford College statutes, 73
Trinity Hall, 185
Scotland (Scots), 33; missions to, 282, 284, 291, 292; universities of, 301
Screne, King's Hall fellow, 264
Scrope, Richard, warden of King's Hall: career of, 286; as chancellor of Cambridge, 286
seal, King's Hall, 218, 219
seasonings, 116, 124, 126, 208
Sechevill, John, King's Scholar and King's Hall fellow, 165, 220 n. 5
secret seal, reign of Edward II, 22
secretary, king's, 282, 284, 285, 291
sedge (*segg'*), 116, 212, 215; commons, King's Hall fellows, 124
Selby, Ralph, warden of King's Hall, 282, 284; career of, 283
semi-commoners, King's Hall, xiii n. (*d*), 131 n. 1, 259, 265, 273; analysis of, 273–9, table 18(275); chapel royal recruits as, 186; promotion to fellowships, 264; tutoring of, 75; = undergraduate private pupils, 70, 71; *see* commoners
seneschals (*senescalli*), King's Hall, 57 n. 2, 67, 68, 70, 75 n. 3, 115, 125, 131, 163, 167, 168, 170, 187, 194, 205 n. 4, 206, 207, 209, 211, 233, 238 n. 9, 240, 246 n. 11, 280, 297; analysis of committees of, xiii n. (*g*), 148, 161, 177–82; and contracts, 212–14; degrees of, 177–80, table 12 (178), table 13 (179); division of function, 166 n. 5, 181 n. 3, 207–8; salaries of, 177 n. 1, 208–9
senility: as exemption from academic duties, 89–90
Sergius I, pope: spurious bull for Cambridge University, 107 n. 4, 109, 110, 111
servants, private, King's Hall fellows, 218, 242–4, table 15 (243), 273
Shalston (Shalleston, Challeston), Henry, King's Hall fellow, admitted from Eton, 185 n. 5
Sharp, Andrew: King's Hall contracts, 217 n. 15

351